HAVING THEIR CAKE...

ADVANCE PRAISE FOR *HAVING THEIR CAKE*...

"Disturbing and deeply thought-provoking, this book challenges the relevance of much in the current 'governance' debate. While we bicker over rearranging the deckchairs, is our industrial Titanic already slipping beneath the waves?"

Marcus Alexander, Adjunct Professor of Strategy, London Business School and Director, Ashridge Strategic Management Centre

"Written with sharp insight, wit and wisdom, this is a splendid and disturbing book. It urges us, with passion and carefully researched precision, to debate those issues which are crucial for the health of our society, in economic, political and human terms. It is both prophetic and practical."

Professor Jim Hughes, Strathclyde University Business School

"This very readable book demonstrates the obscene self rewarding, symbiotic, relationship between much of the top management of British business and 'the city'. A relationship based on extreme short-termism that is systematically destroying value in large swathes of British business. Be prepared to be angry and to demand change."

George Phillipson, ex-Director, Redland PLC

"Having Their Cake offers a rich picture of where we are today and how we got here. Remarkably, this picture has never been assembled in such a multi-faceted way before. Anyone concerned to strengthen the wealth-creating potential of UK companies will want to absorb and act on its messages."

Simon Court, Chief Executive, Value Partnership Ltd

"I agree with the book's basic analysis. I think the book develops arguments which need discussion and debate."

Sir Geoff Mulcahy, CEO, Kingfisher plc, 1983 – 2003

"Whilst many may find the book controversial, nevertheless there is, I believe, a good case for a wide debate about investment and management and such a debate would be of great interest to pension fund members, employees and smaller investors."

Ian Hamilton, former Chairman, Lafarge Redland Pension Scheme Trustees Ltd

"This is a most timely book. It spotlights what is wrong with the management/markets 'system'. It is perceptive in its diagnosis and witty in its presentation. To many it will be very provocative in its views about what needs to be changed. Many in the 'system' will resist its proposals, but at the very least the book will raise the level of debate about how wealth can be created in future and not needlessly destroyed as now."

Max Burgess, independent consultant in business strategy and organization

"This book makes a lot of points that are long overdue. The challenge is – how to make real changes effectively."

Sir Austin Pearce CBE, former Chairman of Esso and British Aerospace

"Congratulations. Well targeted, highly topical and lively to read."

John Monks, former General Secretary, Trades Union Congress

"Addresses a highly significant and topical issue and does so in a readable style drawing on the authors' long experience in industry at executive director level."

Philip Sadler CBE, Vice President, the Ashridge Business School

HAVING THEIR CAKE...

How the City and Big Bosses are Consuming UK Business

Don Young
& Pat Scott

KOGAN PAGE

First published in Great Britain and the United States in 2004 by Kogan Page Limited
Paperback edition 2005

120 Pentonville Road
London N1 9JN
United Kingdom
www.kogan-page.co.uk

British Library Cataloguing-in-Publication Data

A CIP record for this book is available from the British Library

ISBN 0 7494 4461 4

Typeset by Saxon Graphics Ltd, Derby
Printed and bound in Great Britain by Creative Print and Design (Wales), Ebbw Vale

Contents

Preface

THE WORLD MOVES ON

The world does not stand still. Time passes and things happen. Since we stopped writing this book in the late spring of 2003 events have continued to unfold. The corporate governance debate raging on as a backdrop to other company dramas has made for a lively summer.

For this brief review, we will focus on some major trends and developments that appear in the main body of the book.

Shareholder activism

The summer started with unprecedented shareholder votes against pay proposals, most notably at GlaxoSmithKlein. Warren Buffet added his voice to the chorus in his annual statement to the shareholders of Berkshire Hathaway, urging shareholders to rebel against excessive executive pay.

Activism hasn't stopped there. September saw the resignation of Richard Grasso, chairman and chief executive of the New York Stock Exchange, in response to investor outrage at his compensation package. In October we saw shareholders in News Corporation force a withdrawal of a controversial share option package. In the UK the Association of British Insurers has written to Barclays demanding an explanation for the promotion of Matt Barrett to chairman contrary to a key Higgs recommendation, and shareholders have forced Michael Green to stand down as chairman designate of the to be merged Granada and Carlton.

This latter event has caught the headlines, with some commentators speculating on whether the very public actions of Mr Anthony Bolton of Fidelity mark the beginning of a new era. What is new is the very overt manner of Green's ousting. The fact is that events such as this have been commonplace, but handled discreetly behind the scenes. Perhaps the public airing of such disagreements will help to raise public awareness of what transpires between investors and managers, and the massive influence of investors over managers.

It still remains to be seen whether this little storm will have any impact on the intricate and difficult tasks of knitting together two previously rivalrous organizations.

Fears are raised by an article in The Observer Business section of October 26, 2003. Having ousted Michael Green of Carlton, investors, led by Fidelity, are threatening, according to 'inside sources', to remove Charles Allen of Granada, if he does not 'deliver the goods, and fast'. In particular, they are quoted as wanting cost savings of £100 million from the merger, rather than the £55 million of 'synergy' benefits promised.

It would seem that despite a more muscular stance, investors have learned nothing about what it takes to run or merge businesses.

Fund management

In April, the *Financial Times* supplement for fund managers (FTfm), Barry Riley called for a reprofessionalisation of fund management on the back of a return to private or mutual ownership, stating that 'Banks and insurance companies... have a generally poor record in the stewardship of fund management businesses.' One restructure of the industry that does now look likely is an end to soft commissions.

Turning the tables on investment funds, Unilever called upon its shareholders to account for their failure to vote at its last general meeting.

On the downside, in July we were warned in the *Financial Times* that investors and pension funds are plunging deeper into illiquid and riskier assets as the search for yield hots up against a background of low inflation and low interest rates.

Banks in the dock

The summer has seen a flurry of fines and settlements, ranging from a US$1.4billion settlement agreed by 10 Wall Street banks in respect of their bull market research. In addition, these banks have agreed to separate their investment banking and research activities.

In the UK, Lloyds TSB has been fined £1.9million and has agreed to settle compensation of a further £98million, in respect of mis-selling precipice bonds.

Corporate governance

The Higgs report has entered the realm of official UK Corporate Governance codes, albeit with two key provisions watered down. These were the proposal that the chairperson should not sit on the nominations committee (aimed at curtailing the appointment of 'chums' to the board) and the recommendation that a senior non-executive director should have a direct line to shareholders.

Executive pay

The CBI and trade unions were in agreement on the need to end 'rewards for failure' and we are told that both the Association of British Insurers and the National Association of Pension Funds will issue revised guidelines.

On the broader issue of pay levels, the Association of Chartered Certified Accountants has called for disclosure of the chief executive's pay as a multiple of the average worker in the company, forecasting that the comparison would put pressure on the differentials.

Education

It appears that our call for more education in financial understanding for ordinary savers and investors will not fall on deaf ears. The Financial Services Authority, with a duty to promote financial awareness, has set up an advisory group to establish, by 31 March 2004, 'a clear view of what the industry, the government, and other parties should best do.'

CBI caught out?

As we have observed in the main body of the book, the CBI and others have made a special thing of complaining about excessive regulation, punitive taxation and bureaucracy generally as being the fundamental causes of low productivity and underperformance by British companies. Whilst we have strong sympathy with the need to control the rush of regulation, it would seem to us that the root causes of poor performance lie with poor management and a lack of investment in the 'tools' to do the job.

Of late, the CBI's cries about the murderously high burden of tax on business have become particularly strident. The employers' body has claimed that New Labour has added £54 billion to company tax bills since coming into power.

However, a report in the *Financial Times* of October 14, 2003 exposes the CBI's position, 'According to independent tax analysis, the government has reason to feel aggrieved by the CBI's analysis'. Research by the Institute for Fiscal Studies suggests that the tax burden on business is only marginally higher than when Labour came into power. Several of the CBI's bold claims in its press release are not supported by more detailed research, or even by its (own) more balanced report. The CBI argued that, 'between 1995 and 2000, the main business tax bill rose as a share of gross domestic product from 9.5 per cent to 9.9 per cent but the Treasury had a ready response'. It pointed out that that the CBI's own report showed the share of main business taxes in GDP had fallen to 8.9 per cent, lower than when labour had come to power.

The CBI could make a far bigger contribution to industry by focusing on the real issues.

Companies and jobs

In recent weeks, Amersham International, a major biotechnology company, has been acquired by General Electric of the US. Several newspapers seemed to think that it was some kind of accolade that the CEO of Amersham had been appointed to a senior position in GE. Time will tell what will happen to the R&D activities and strategies of Amersham.

BAe Systems, Britain's last really large high technology engineering company, continues to look for a US partner, having apparently failed to consummate a 'marriage of equals' with General Dynamics. In the long run, the merger of BAe with an American partner looks more and more likely to turn out as an American takeover.

At the lower technology, lower skill end of the market, call centres, a locomotive of employment growth, seem destined to migrate to India and other countries at an ever-accelerating rate. Led by HSBC, an increasing number of banks, insurance companies and others, such as BT are exporting call centre jobs in what is predicted to be hundreds of thousands. Hoseasons, a smallish holiday company, commented that it had no intention of exporting customer service jobs, as 'people are our only source of distinctiveness'. Is there something that they know that HSBC and the rest do not?

The Chancellor of the Exchequer, Gordon Brown, responded to strong protests by trades unions about the massive loss of manufacturing jobs, by indicating that things will improve as a result of a better exchange rate. He managed to avoid any mention of the behaviour of managers or investors.

There is little news of new jobs being created as a result of research, innovation or long-term investment.

So there has been a lot of activity, but what about progress?

Well, yes and no. It is good to see some of the more contentious points moving forward. However, we are still applying sticking plaster to the symptoms of the disease, rather than addressing the disease itself.

We are still not seeing any real debate on the issues of separation, both of the CEO from the company and of the fund manager from the risk taking investor. We are still not seeing any real acknowledgement of the unintentional damage that this separation, and the resultant behaviour of the two pools of key players, is doing to industry and society.

These will not be rectified by the sticking plaster approach. Speaking of society, Krishnamurti once said 'It becomes obvious that there must be a total revolution. A different kind of culture must come into being. Unless there is a deep, psychological revolution, mere reformation on the periphery will have little effect.' What applies to society also applies to our industrial and financial compact – we need fundamental change at system level.

Our propositions stand.

Acknowledgements

Any book is a complex creation. Sometimes books are the product of the original genius of one individual, but mostly they are shaped and stimulated by many ideas and influences, many of them at a subconscious level. Most authors are therefore the products of their experiences shaped by contacts and relationships going back often many years.

So it is with us. This book is underpinned by strong values, the products of long experience and a fair deal of thought. We have both seen a lot of the 'what not to dos' of business life, and have sometimes been inspired by the rewards of successful efforts. We would say that all success in large organizations is the creation of the collective and aligned efforts of many people.

Occasionally, there comes a *moment juste*, when one outstanding individual has personally shaped the destiny of a company. But even then, success is generated by many people working together, stimulated, led or driven by an inspirational leader. We have learnt that the rarest quality in such powerful people is knowing when to go and leave lesser mortals to get on with their business. So, this book is the creation of years of often hard experience, shaped by the views and experiences of a myriad of people with whom we have worked over the years.

When we decided to research that which eventually became the tangible product before you, we set up a programme of interviews and discussions with many people. We also spent many days in libraries, such as those in the London Business School and the Institute of Fiscal Studies, read the business press and many periodicals assiduously, and ploughed our ways through many a business book. But the greatest stimulation came from the many discussions and conversations that we had with colleagues and those in management, consultancy and the financial markets who were kind enough to give us their time, experience and viewpoints. These people, especially, helped to shape this book and we would like to give them our sincere thanks, first pointing out that the responsibility for the conclusions reached in the book is ours!

First and foremost, we owe a great debt of gratitude to Charlotte Young, who has challenged our ideas, encouraged us and carried out a comprehensive edit. Her inspiration and way with ideas and words have been invaluable.

Then, we owe much to the following people, who willingly gave us their time. They are:

Managers

Sir Colin Southgate, Sir Austin Pearce CBE, George Phillipson, Robert Napier, Sir Geoff Mulcahy, Dick Olver, Juggy Pandit, Pat Scannell, Paul Hewitt, Peter Mills, Ian Reid, Bob Nellist, David Sheppard, David Creed, Robert Gibber, Charles Ashcroft, Rupert Perry, Gerald Corbett, Ian Hamilton, Debbie Howard, Bob Andrews.

Consultants and business academics

Marcus Alexander, Simon Court, Sean O'Hare, Lord Vernon, Gurnek Bains, John Dunn, Paula Alexander, Philip Sadler.

Search consultants

Nigel Smith, Philip Vivien, Stephen Bamfylde, Andrew Lowenthal.

Financial markets

Bob Pringle, Nick Fitzgerald, Nigel Turner, Charles Packshaw, Mark Astare, Peter Newman, Liz Hewitt, Peter Cazalet.

Senior secretaries

Cathie Hill, Ann Shaxon, Jenny Assem.

Others

Mark Goyder, John Monks, Terry Leahy.

We are equally grateful to those dozen or so people who preferred to be acknowledged in spirit only. You know who you are!

Part I

About the book and the values behind it

Introduction to Part I

In the comedy programme *The Fast Show*, two characters were talking together. Said one, 'I went down the pub the other night. The place was full of blokes, they were drinking, chatting, telling jokes and laughing... *What the bloody hell was all that about?*'

One afternoon in late 1997 we found ourselves having a similar conversation. We were in the middle of a takeover battle, on the defending side. Lafarge, a large French building materials company, had bid for Redland, our employer.

We are from very different professional backgrounds: Don from marketing, operations and human resources, and Pat finance. We had worked together for many years and in more than one company, and had observed the same events from different perspectives.

As a main board director responsible for the whole Redland group, Don was wondering at the focus of the defence. Two large businesses doing real things in the real world through real people were being treated like commodities. The two 'principal' directors, the chief executive and the finance director, had been whisked away to a place known by some as the 'War Room' and others as 'The Bunker', where they and their advisers plotted ways to extract value for these commodities. In the space of a few weeks any links between directors and business seemed to have been severed. What was going on?

As a veteran of more than 300 'deals' (although never before on the receiving end), Pat had a very different slant. In her experience there comes a point in every transaction when the 'deal' becomes more important than the subject. The process becomes transaction driven, and the removal of key decision-makers into a new environment was an important part of achieving this mind shift. The break with 'normal reality' was quite deliberate.

OK, perhaps this is simplistic. Perhaps it was unreasonable to expect the defence team to be focused on anything other than getting value for the shareholders. After all, the outcome would be in their hands. Perhaps Pat was being overly cynical.

Yet still there was a dislocation from reality. The priorities were askew. The real drivers of business value seemed to count for little in this process. Most stakeholders in the business were bystanders, spectators of the drama playing centre stage. On top of it all, some organizations seemed to be making disproportionately vast amounts of money out of Redland's distress.

And it wasn't just Redland. This was happening all over the place.

We're not naïve idealists. Through long careers in private-sector enterprises we had both risen to roles at the apex of large publicly quoted companies. We had worked in many industries and in many companies, some huge, some relatively small. We had also separately set up small companies from scratch and participated intimately in growing them to be successful.

We had worked with a vast array of people in a varied assortment of organizations, ranging from some that were stable and successful to others that were in the depths of crisis. And we had experience of working with colleagues from many cultures, so could compare our perspectives with those of other countries.

So we'd been around and seen it all, or a lot of it at least! If we felt there was something amiss with the situation, then it was worth further investigation.

But of course, at the time we were busy. We had a corporate battle to fight; we had parts to play in Redland's great life and death drama. Saving the world would have to wait until later.

After the takeover of Redland we both separately decided that the time had come to 'go plural'. One of the advantages of being away from the constant time and travel demands of a senior executive role is the opportunity to explore topics that are deeply interesting. For us, one of these is 'What drives the behaviours of top management and their counterparts in the financial markets?'

This is particularly interesting because, while it will be evident to any observer that top managements and the various players in the markets have a deep influence on each other, and that they are interdependent in many, many ways, not much has been written on how the complex of their interrelationships works.

So, our '*Fast Show*' conversation might go something like this:

'There's all these companies, some are doing well, some are doing badly, sometimes one buys another and sometimes one disappears.

'Then, there's all these people, called bankers and investors, stockbrokers and analysts and journalists, who spend a lot of time thinking and talking about the companies.

'Then there's another bunch of people, called chairmen, non-executive directors and chief executives and finance directors.

'They all use funny language, such as P/E ratios, shareholder value and beta factors. And these chairmen and chief executives and such also spend a lot of time wondering what the investors and others are up to and how they might help or threaten them.

'One thing, though. They all seem to earn a ton of money.'

'What the bloody hell's all that about?'

A LOOK AT THE SYSTEM

So how do the many players in the financial markets and their supporting casts interact with the top managements of larger quoted companies? What are the effects of these interactions on companies, employees, industry and the wider economy?

We talked with over 60 individuals at the heart and round the periphery of the financial markets, from chairmen and chief executives to brokers, analysts and investors. We explored research into the impact of 'deals' and considered what other commentators had said on the subject. We discovered a complex array of interactions, some of them quite direct and obvious, others much more diffuse and subtle.

Our investigations, and therefore the book, started with us holding a reasonably open-minded position. We knew from experience and direct observation that the financial markets had a very significant influence on the attitudes, confidence and frequently the actions of top managers. But we did not formulate definite hypotheses about the broader nature and significance of the interfaces between the markets and management until we had interviewed many people and listened to their perspectives. Thus the three major 'propositions' that you will find in Chapters 9–11 developed out of our investigations, rather than driving them in the first place.

For a number of reasons, not the least of which is the fear of becoming an 'insider', the communications between companies and the markets are often very indirect, based on hints, circumlocution and sometimes deliberate leaks. At the centre of it all is a genuine market complete with a full cast of characters, and rumour and gossip abound.

Through many conversations with many different people we have built up a picture of what happens between the 'City' and companies, who does what, what interests drive their behaviours and what we believe are the effects of a *'system' of interactions.* We have deliberately introduced the word 'system' to describe the ways in which top managements and the markets interact. We think it is reasonably accurate to believe that there is a system at work that connects the interests of the key players in the financial markets and in companies.

Two definitions of a 'system' seem, between them, to capture what we mean:

a complex whole, a set of connected things or parts; an organized body of material or immaterial things

and

a group of bodies moving under mutual gravitation.

Perhaps the second definition most accurately describes how this particular system works!

We are not alone in thinking of the management–City nexus as a system. So do the many regulators and governmental bodies that try to act as referees.

As with all systems, there is an inside and an outside. We try to identify who is included in this system, who is not; whose interests are served by the system and whose are not.

We did not discover a great plot to defraud society, deliberately disadvantage others or to enrich insiders by corrupt means. If we had, we would have exposed it and become rich! Or dead!

The system is not like that. It is much more a diffuse but well understood set of arrangements that are used, often successfully and occasionally not, to serve the interests of the participants.

The surface lubricants that keep the wheels turning are relatively harmless: meals, shooting parties and entertainment at cricket matches, rugby games, regattas, opera and concerts. Underneath is thicker glue: contacts, wealth, appointments, careers, reputations and honours – all within the reach of system participants.

There is a considerable diversity of views about the markets and the ways in which they operate. However, everyone we spoke with believed that having competition for capital to finance industry is the best way of encouraging efficiency, necessary change and adaptation. We strongly agree with this view.

But behind what many people said was an often unspoken assumption that markets can be perfect. By 'perfect', people seemed to mean that equity markets can be relied upon to make rational decisions about the allocation of capital among competing companies, based on objective information and rational analysis. In a perfect world, efficient, growing companies would attract the most capital, and managements that misused assets would be replaced, or the assets redistributed.

Much of the language of the financial markets is based on rational, mainly numerate, analysis. Investors often judge top management on how adept they are with 'the numbers'. Readers may be relieved to hear that we do not plan to dwell on financial analysis, numbers, or how to create perfect markets. Our main concern is human behaviour. It is about companies as human communities, not just as bundles of assets. It is about the interests of people and how they make the market work. In this sense, it could be described as an investigation into human nature and how it will always subvert and distort theories such as that of a perfect market. (Thank the Lord!)

Thus many of the analyses of how things work are based on verbal descriptions, not on 'hard' numerical facts. This must inevitably be so, because we are describing a system of human interactions. We have been as stringent as we possibly can in cross-checking what we were told, but we are inevitably dependent to a degree on the views of others.

To reduce the risks of developing a distorted view of what goes on and of reaching unbalanced conclusions about causes and effects, we invited a 'panel' of experienced people from business, the City and business schools to critique our research and conclusions. We would like to thank all of you who helped us in this way. Your views were invaluable.

We would encourage readers to use the book to develop their own views about how companies and markets operate, and whether the current 'system' needs to be challenged. Because of this, it is appropriate to spell out our own views and prejudices at the beginning. So here goes!

SOME UNDERLYING VALUES: WHERE WE ARE COMING FROM

- There is such a thing as society.
- The economy is an integral part of a society.
- The main goal of a society should be to strive to ensure the greatest well-being of all its members.

The performance of a society as a whole and each of its constituent parts, including its economic component, should therefore be judged by the degree to which it contributes to the overall well-being of its members. If any element – political, military, economic – is manifestly serving only the interests of a small part of society, with the effect of damaging its overall interests, then action should be taken to modify or regulate what it does so that its contribution to the whole can be positive.

The same applies to the so-called global economy. If the functioning of the global financial system is manifestly damaging the interests of 'global society' (and it may well be – think about the possible relationships between regional wealth and poverty, instability of governments, violence and international terrorism), then its activities need to be realigned with those interests. That is a major purpose of international co-operation.

To allow the self-interest of a nation or individuals to be separated from the interests of society will more likely than not create corruption and distortions in the effective use of resources for the benefit of society as a whole. Equally, to argue that the interests of individuals are more important than those of the society of which they are a member is likely to result in significant distortions in the effective use of resources and also behaviours by some individuals that will seriously damage the overall interest.

Eric Hobsbawm, the distinguished historian, made these points brilliantly:

> Government, the economy, schools, everything in society, is not for the benefit of the privileged minorities. We can look after ourselves. It is for the benefit of the ordinary run of people, who are not particularly clever or interesting (unless, of course, we fall in love with one of them), not highly educated, not successful or destined for success – in fact, are nothing very special. It is for these people, who, throughout history, have entered history outside their neighbourhoods as individuals only in the records of their births, marriages and deaths. Any society worth living in is one designed for them, not for the rich, the clever, the exceptional, although any society worth living in must provide room and scope for such minorities. But the world is not made for our personal benefit, nor are we in the world for our personal benefit. A world that claims that this is its purpose is not a good, and ought not to be a lasting, world. (Hobsbawm, 1998)

It also seems to us that the above propositions are not at all incompatible with a strong belief in capitalism. However, they do mean that, no matter how difficult, the formation of policy needs to be underpinned by the capacity to make balanced and sometimes complex judgements.

For example, encouraging free competition in the provision of consumer goods is almost certainly the best way of making sure that consumers get choice and the best deal. In some other spheres of activity, however, where there are a number of overriding societal interests at stake, it has become manifestly clear that allowing market forces to determine outcomes has severe limitations. More complex arrangements need to be made. The provision of an effective national transport infrastructure in Britain has been clearly demonstrated as one of these spheres.

In another dimension, it would seem that highly rewarding individuals with special talents who make an exceptional contribution would make it easier to retain those talents. But allowing a complete 'free-for-all' has been demonstrated as causing damaging distortions: for example, vast wealth contrasted with miserable poverty, or very high reward for moderate or poor performance.

Therefore, it is appropriate for a society to take an interest in the complex matter of deciding what means will be used to determine the distribution of wealth and what should be done about abuses.

All of this means that individuals, organizations and governments cannot avoid having to cope with considerable complexity and, often, having to face up to issues that have no one clear solution. This fact is clearly regarded as irksome by some, who prefer simple, overriding rules to guide action.

An example is the assertion that top managements of large enterprises are likely to become confused if they have to cope with a multiplicity of possibly conflicting goals. A single overriding objective of maximizing shareholder value will serve to focus their efforts. Furthermore, the argument goes, if shareholder value is maximized, the interests of all other stakeholders will also be fully served. So far, this has not been demonstrated to be true. There is, however, a body of evidence that seems to indicate that good managers are perfectly comfortable with balancing the demands of many different constituencies when they make strategic decisions. Perhaps this is what being good at strategic management is all about!

So, it would appear that the desire of bright, fact-dedicated people to find analytical and even mathematical models that will solve all our problems has usually been thwarted by human nature and, more particularly, human behaviour. This is unlikely to stop them trying, nor will it stop others (who do understand human behaviour) from using the arguments produced by the proponents of pure logic to further their own ends.

We would remind readers of John Maynard Keynes's remark, 'Capitalism represents the most astounding belief that the most wickedest of men, doing the most wickedest of things, will be for the good of everyone'! Doubtless many of Enron's shareholders really did believe that that company had found a new business paradigm, one that would benefit the world!

Why, you might ask, have we spent so much space talking about the good of society? Well, we think that the field of investigation of the book – the functioning of the financial markets and how they interact with management – has great importance for our society.

We are after all, talking about the apex of our economy. Large, publicly quoted companies represent a huge amount of value. Their performance and behaviour has profound effects on the well-being of millions of people who work for them, or whose pensions depend crucially on their long-term performance.

Also, it is an inescapable fact that certain kinds of industries that require very heavy investment in R&D or expensive plant, or need the application of complex bodies of knowledge, or extensive international marketing and distribution networks need large organizations to attract the capital and support the business. The performance of large companies is likely to determine whether many key industrial sectors are represented in any developed economy.

It is therefore worth asking, echoing management guru Charles Handy – what are the underlying purposes of such companies? Is it simply that they are there to make as much money as possible for 'shareholders', whoever they may be? Or should large companies that produce goods and services for billions of people globally, and employ millions of those people, doing things that can often enhance or destroy the social and physical life of communities, have purposes that are deeper than simply making money?

On another level, we see the public's disillusion with leaders in general. It is bound to be damaging if the public view leaders of major industrial companies as a venal and self-centred bunch, interested only in enriching themselves, no matter what the consequences to others. In the end, societies are likely to be healthier if leaders have a concern for, and are bonded with, the people they lead.

We aim to present a picture of what goes on between companies and the markets that is as untainted by our own views and prejudices as possible.

Towards the end of the book we offer you the chance to act as 'jurors' and decide what you believe and what might be done about the things that need changing.

We hope that you find the book stimulating and thought-provoking.

1

Something's happening! Changes in the industrial landscape

The past 30 years have seen a lot of change.

One morning in October 1960, 12 young men dressed in their best suits gathered at a conference table in Unilever House in London. One of them was Don Young, then a third-year undergraduate at the London School of Economics. Looking around, he wondered if the other 11 applicants for a graduate management traineeship felt as nervous as he did.

A rather imposing, well-dressed man entered the room. He began to brief the applicants. All, with the exception of Young, were undergraduates at the universities of Oxford and Cambridge. He gave a thorough history of the company, its products and international spread, and a description of the three-day selection board.

Then he said, 'Should you be successful and join Unilever, we would expect you to have a full career with us. Entrants through the Unilever Companies Management Development Scheme can reasonably look forward to reaching senior management after 10 to 15 years, and some of you could reach the very top of the company before you retire.' This message was intended to motivate, and indeed it did. In 1960, young men considering a management career knew that a life inside an international blue chip company, together with the opportunity to rise through the organization to senior management, was as good as it could get.

Managers were groomed in the culture, organization and products of their company. They had pride in the organization and pride that they were part of something important.

This is not to say that everybody stayed with the same company. Some trainees found that management work was not for them. Some became frustrated by a three-year traineeship with little responsibility. In those days, however, attrition tended to be mainly at the early stages of careers. People who persisted in moving from one organization to another were suspected of lacking in loyalty. Redundancy in managerial jobs was almost unknown.

Many would pose the challenge that this allowed complacency and inefficiency to flourish, and undoubtedly they are right. Some things were bound to change, but have the changes been for the better?

CHANGES IN MANAGERS' CAREERS

The 1970s saw the beginning of mass redundancies for executives. As companies failed, downsized and merged, carnage struck the ranks of middle and senior management. A whole class of people learnt that loyalty and reliability did not guarantee security.

Today, a few companies still offer the possibility of full careers. But the concept of careers as the property of individuals and not organizations has firmly taken root. Today's generation of aspiring managers, once they have gained a little experience, are likely to make their own judgements about whether the organization suits them and, if it does not, to have no hesitation in moving.

We have seen the rise of the professional manager who, it is believed, can manage anything. Management is seen as a process that can be applied to all situations. An affinity with what is being managed is no longer deemed necessary.

SUCCESSION PLANNING

Succession planning and grooming for key positions was once regarded as crucial to a company's survival. For many years it was the preserve of the Personnel Department, which kept organization charts that included details of all senior managers and identified the immediate and longer-term successors for each job. Any enterprise with a significant number of jobs for which there were no short-term replacements was considered to be at serious risk.

Today we tend to encounter a more informal approach to succession planning, with more emphasis on personal contact. Individuals are encouraged to take the initiative to explore development possibilities and future jobs, with the emphasis on processes for matching talent to organizational change.

Why is this? Mainly because the future shape and nature of jobs and organizations are not very predictable. Also, many individuals are unlikely to stick around long enough for the company to move them up the career ladder in an orderly fashion.

Thus in the space of 30 years we have seen massive changes in the nature of management careers and in the expectations of individuals.

CHANGES IN MANAGERIAL ROLES

All of this has been accompanied by seismic shifts in the status and roles of managers. Once upon a time, management was defined as a set of roles in an organization, which itself was a collection of hierarchical positions. Managerial rank and status were demonstrated by important 'markers', such as the size and location of offices, dining room entitlements and the size of the company car for very senior people. Senior managers often strolled back to their offices after lunch at 2.30 pm, smelling subtly of gin and tonic and good wine.

In some cases the status differences led to even more bizarre practices. A brewery, which shall remain nameless, had a directors' dining room from which females (even executives) were banned. Each lunchtime witnessed the Victorian spectacle of the managing director standing at the top of the table, carving the joint for his male colleagues!

This comfortable and ordered middle-class life, with its predictable symbols of superior status, has disappeared, to be replaced by a different set of relationships.

THE RISE OF THE TRANSIENT 'SUPERSTAR' EXECUTIVE

In the past few years, the public profile of top managers has increased markedly. In the past, a few industrialists and entrepreneurs hit the headlines, often as much for their private as for their corporate activities. Some readers may remember that Sir Bernard and Lady Docker used to drink pink champagne, Hanson and White used to make acquisitions and own racehorses, Slater speculated, Goldsmith accumulated and 'Tiny' Rowland was the 'unacceptable face of capitalism'.

As one top compensation consultant put it, we are now beginning to see the emergence of the CEO as a 'star' in his or her own right. The press and financial markets like to personalize large enterprises by associating them and their fortunes with a few high-profile names. So, for example, the British Petroleum Company becomes 'Lord Browne', Lord Marshall and Rod Eddington were reported to be fighting over the future of British Airways, and the 'villain', Lord Simpson of Dunkeld, is spending some of his Marconi severance pay on the golf course.

Behind all this publicity and froth, other things are happening. Top executive pay has burgeoned and so far the rises show little sign of moderating. Disclosure of director's pay in accordance with Greenbury's recommendations has led to higher rather than more moderate pay levels as executives play 'catch up'. Truly, 'stars' seem to merit Hollywood-style pay packets.

Accompanying the meteoric rise in pay differentials between top managers and ordinary toilers has come another kind of change. In a study by Cranfield University, *The Life and Times of the CEO* (Harrington and Steele, 1999), it is revealed that the average tenure of a FTSE 100 CEO is now four years one month, as opposed to nine years nine months for the CEOs of the top 100 unquoted companies.

At the very least, this can be described as a marked change from the old days of career managers who tended to stay loyal to one company.

ORGANIZATIONAL TURBULENCE

Once upon a time, organizations were regarded as solid and permanent edifices. In the 1960s the Ford Motor Company employed a draughtsman whose sole task was to draw, and occasionally modify, the organization charts of the company. Another manifestation of the turbulent change of the past 30 years has been the demise of the solid, permanent and reassuringly constant organization.

Driven by core process engineering, culture change programmes and, above all, by a remorseless drive to reduce cost, organizations have been downsized, de-layered and hollowed out. Whole swathes of middle management roles have been eliminated and it has become a mark of pride for many a red-blooded CEO to boast to his or her peers and approving investors about the diminutive size of the corporate office.

Today's organizations are flat and lean. They are pared down, in theory able to react to sudden and rapid change. Many functions have been outsourced to specialists. The provision of general business services has flourished as one of the most rapidly growing industries in recent years. Organizations have changed dramatically, from structures that saw themselves as proud and permanent to temporary and even disposable commodities.

It would be good to think that changes in organizations had been led by thought, knowledge and deep insight. After all, there is much excellent thinking and advice on organization available from such experts as Henry Mintzberg and Gareth Morgan. Alas, there seems to be little systematic evidence that most top managers are anything but woefully ignorant on the subject of developing an appropriate and effective organization. So what has driven change? We will explore this in later chapters.

COMPANY SURVIVAL

On 1 July 1935, a new index, known as the FT 30, appeared in the *London Financial News*. An article in the *Financial Times* of 11 January 2000 pointed out that only five companies from the original index – Blue Circle Industries, GEC, GKN, ICI and Tate & Lyle – had survived to 2000.

Less than a year later, yet another had fallen, Blue Circle having been acquired by the French cement company Lafarge. Furthermore, Marconi, GEC's successor, has plunged violently from the FTSE 100, and ICI is under City pressure concerning its borrowing levels.

Other great names, part of the index in 1950, have disappeared or changed out of all recognition. Electrical and Musical Industries, Hawker Siddeley, Dunlop Rubber Company, Leyland Motors, Morris Motors, Swan Hunter, Turner & Newall, United Steel and Vickers are just a few examples.

Dramatic as it may appear, this rate of change is positively sluggish compared with what happened to the FT 30's successor companies in the 14 years between 1987 and 2001. Of the top 115 companies since 1987, 30 (26 per cent) have remained independent and pretty well in the same shape, in terms of industry scope. Of the rest, 47 have been acquired, 16 have been demoted or gone private, 14 have merged as the dominant partner, and 8 have de-merged, still leaving one or more parts trading and in the top 115.

If we move forward a few years, of the 1991 FTSE 100, 35 were still there in pretty well their original form by 2001, but 65 had been acquired, merged, gone private, exited the top 100 or simply disappeared.

The life spans of companies are decreasing rapidly. Any particular reasons? We shall try to find out later.

SIZE RELATIVITIES OF LARGE COMPANIES

The relative sizes of companies in the FTSE have changed rather markedly in very few years:

- In 1994, the top five companies by market capitalization were 12.5 times bigger than the bottom five.
- In 2000, the top five companies were 31 times larger than the bottom five.

- By February 2003, the top five companies were over 67 times larger than the bottom five.

To put it another way, the FTSE 100 is becoming heavily weighted towards a relatively small number of monster companies. By the end of 2001, 52 per cent of the market value of the FTSE 100 lay in the top 10 companies. Given the emergence of tracker funds and index-related benchmarking, the actions of relatively few organizations now have a massively disproportionate effect on many shareholders' hopes of wealth.

DISAPPEARING INDUSTRY SECTORS

The spread of industry sectors represented in the FTSE 100 has changed over the years. In 2001 only six of the top 100 were in the engineering and manufacturing sectors, once the United Kingdom's pride, with a further four in the knowledge-intensive pharmaceuticals sector. There are no large UK-owned companies that major in investment banking.

The representation of retailing, retail banking, media and support services companies has grown rapidly, in both absolute and relative terms. The manufacturing sector, which encompasses many of the world's advanced technologies, is the largest one in France and Germany (over 60 per cent), Japan (52 per cent) and the United States (30 per cent), but second (23 per cent and rapidly declining) in the United Kingdom to financial services and banking, which has become the dominant sector.

THE RISE OF FOREIGN OWNERSHIP

Foreign ownership of British enterprises has burgeoned in recent years and this trend looks set to continue. A few examples will illustrate:

- There are no significant British players left in investment banking, automotive manufacturing, IT and telecommunications manufacturing or computer manufacturing.
- Invensys, a company showing all the signs of severe post-merger malaise, leading towards possible extinction, is the last large British company in the electronic and electrical equipment sector.
- About 50 per cent of Britain's manufactured exports come from foreign-owned companies.

BURGEONING MERGERS AND ACQUISITIONS

UK companies are acquiring abroad at an even greater rate than most of their foreign competitors. In 2000, UK acquisitions abroad cost £181 billion compared to investments by foreign companies in the United Kingdom of £65 billion. In 2001 the levels fell to £40 billion and £22 billion respectively.

Is all this change a symptom of something significant?

One of the major drivers of the changes has been mergers and acquisitions (M&A). The total volume of M&A activity has burgeoned in the past 30 years, both in financial value and in total number of transactions. The same period has seen a dramatic rise in hostile takeovers and cross-border acquisitions.

During the 1990s, acquisitions of UK companies (by both UK and foreign investors) climbed from around £20 billion in 1990 to a peak of £170 billion in 2000. Although 2001 saw a fall-off to £50 billion (due to a market slowdown, which accelerated after 11 September), activity is forecast to rise whenever market conditions improve (*Financial Times*, February 2002).

LEVELS OF INVESTMENT

Foreign companies in the physics-based technologies (engineering, electronics, telecommunications manufacturing, computing, IT hardware and software) generally invest in R&D and capital expenditure at a far higher rate than their British counterparts. This is true abroad, but foreign companies also spend more on capital investment than British counterparts *in Britain*.

The bright spots in British manufacturing industry are pharmaceuticals and aerospace/defence equipment, where large British-owned companies are investing at a rate at least comparable to their international competitors. But, as of early 2003, it looks as though the long-term future of BAE Systems as an independent British quoted company may be in serious jeopardy, as a toxic mixture of government and stock market pressures may cause it to look for a US partner. As with Lucas Industries, this is likely to result in strategic decision making moving across the Atlantic.

Apart from these sectors, only food manufacturing and retail keep up with the investment levels of foreign companies.

ACCOUNTING BECOMES A CREATIVE ART

Alongside the increase in 'deal' activity came increasing sophistication in both financing mechanisms and accounting treatments. In theory, a company's accounts are supposed to show a true and fair view of its financial condition – profit or loss for the year and assets and liabilities at balance sheet date. For many reasons it can be difficult to show an absolute picture – valuation issues and grey areas of accounting treatment are two reasons – but one could be forgiven for thinking that some of the mechanisms used were a deliberate attempt to mislead.

'Off balance sheet' financing is a way of borrowing money without appearing to do so. In the 1980s and early 1990s a number of 'financially engineered' products were developed which enabled users to understate borrowings on the face of the balance sheet and which were designed specifically to enable companies to sidestep borrowing restrictions in conventional bank loan agreements.

It was argued that the true position was clear from a reading of the small print (notes to the accounts), but accounting regulators were sufficiently concerned to tighten up the rules. Still companies sought ways around them. One of us was asked to speak on the subject at the 1994 annual conference of the Association of Corporate Treasurers. An audience keen to learn the latest 'wheeze' was not impressed by a speaker asking whether we should even be considering a practice that misled equity investors and lenders alike! Almost a decade later we read of the collapse of Enron – as a result of 'off balance sheet' liabilities.

The second area was the accounting treatment of mergers, acquisitions and other reorganizations. In essence, many finance directors sought to keep the full impact of major structural activity outside the main 'headline' figures of the profit and loss account, burying reorganization provisions and costs either as part of goodwill on acquisitions, adjusted in the balance sheet, or 'below the line'. So seriously was this practice pursued that one FTSE 100 finance director took counsel's opinion to force the auditors to allow him to book a disputed reorganization as an 'extraordinary' item!

Very full provisions were often made, serving to flatter future earnings. Some of these techniques were highlighted in Terry Smith's well-known book *Accounting for Growth* (1996), and accounting rules have been tightened up to prevent some of these practices. Yet new ones are ever developing, as we have seen with the revelations over the way some dot.com companies calculated turnover, for example.

Are the increasing levels of acquisition activity implicated in some of the above practices becoming more commonplace? Acquisitions require chunks of finance, which can increase the attractiveness of 'off balance sheet' arrangements if the alternative is high leverage. And the large adjustments required to book acquisitions are tempting places to bury tidying up provisions!

FINANCIAL MARKETS HAVE ALSO SEEN DRAMATIC CHANGE

In parallel to the revolution that has swept through management and industry, an equally intense holocaust has engulfed the institutions and management of the financial markets. Once upon a time, the City's traditions and long-established precedents ruled the day. Gentlemen were gentlemen and recognized each other as such, and outsiders and women knew their place. The pace of work was relatively gentle and the quality of relationships with clients tended to be based on mutual loyalty and regard.

There was little pressure for short-term performances at the expense of the long term. A fund manager described meetings with pension fund trustees in the 'old' days. An amiable ramble around the previous six months' fund performance, provided there were no real disasters, was followed by a good lunch. Over the years, fund managers and trustees became quite closely bonded by feelings of mutual commitment and loyalty.

He contrasted this with today's meetings, where performance against an index has replaced relationships. Fund managers are in no doubt that if they do not perform in the short term they will be replaced. A pension fund financial adviser commented that today trustees seldom show any concern for developing a long-term relationship with their fund manager suppliers.

Philip Augar, in his excellent book *The Death of Gentlemanly Capitalism* (2001), describes the City pre-'Big Bang' as akin to a London club. Its institutions and values reflected three pillars of conservative England: the public school, the gentleman's club and the country house. Entrants from outside this privileged circle rapidly assumed the accents and habits of the prevailing class.

The suddenness of 'Big Bang' and the deregulation of the London financial markets found most of the old institutions and people completely unprepared for the onslaught of foreign, initially US, competition. Much of the old City fell to the American and latterly, European, invaders.

Small, intimate, almost family businesses have been replaced by large, increasingly integrated international banks, in which 'school' refers to where a person's

MBA was earned. And as with management, the nature of careers and employment in the City has dramatically changed. Driving ambition, sharpness, pace and stamina have become the prevailing requirements for success. Relationships with clients have become more transactional and less personal.

One experienced chief executive commented that in his time as a CEO, loyalty in relationships with advisers had almost entirely evaporated. Both managers and their advisers had little enduring regard for each other.

Nature abhors a vacuum, so what has replaced clubbability and relationships in the financial markets? Money? Power? We will explore this in future chapters.

MANAGERS' ATTITUDES AND VALUES TRANSFORMED

Managers in the 1970s

In 1984, Professor Jay Lorsch of Harvard Business School was invited to work with the top managers of Thorn EMI in a one-day workshop. The then top management group of that company were a pretty disparate group, as the 1979 merger between Thorn Electrical Industries and EMI had brought together two very different companies.

Thorn's interests ranged from electrical retailing and TV rental, through TV manufacturing and lighting to domestic appliances and mechanical engineering. Thorn was also into hydraulics, gas metering and flow measurement, and had a joint venture with LM Ericsson, the Swedish telecommunications giant, to manufacture telecommunications equipment for the British market.

EMI, on the other hand, was in medical scanners, advanced radar systems, audio and video tape manufacturing, modems, film and video production, recorded music and music publishing, music retailing, thermal imaging equipment, command and control systems for warships, electrical degaussing equipment, machine tools, bingo halls, cinemas and restaurants. And it had run out of cash.

To add spice to the merger, Thorn's business was concentrated in the United Kingdom, or in the old English-speaking Commonwealth countries, such as Australia and New Zealand. The Thorn senior management came mainly from manufacturing, production engineering and selling backgrounds. They viewed themselves as practical, no-frills, down-to-earth people.

EMI, by contrast, was a very international company, with widespread activities through North America, the Far East and continental Europe. EMI had been an artistic and clever company, with many famous inventions to its name. Indeed, it was the cost of trying to market the company's latest invention, the CAT scanner, that had brought the company down.

EMI's top management were mainly well-educated Englishmen, many from the great English public schools and the universities of Oxford and Cambridge. The one Indian director had attended the Doon School in India and Oxford University. One Thorn director, shortly after the merger, was heard to describe his new EMI counterparts as 'the Exotica'.

A major public justification given for the merger of the two companies was 'synergy'.

The top management team attending the Lorsch seminar were a varied bunch. Some had come from the Thorn camp and a few from EMI, but a lot were new recruits to the company. Most of the recruits were reeling from the sheer complexity of the merged company, and from a terrible feeling that the enterprise was bleeding to death.

The newly appointed chairman did not share this gloom. He had a truly daring vision for the new company. Against a background of converging of audio and visual techniques and with massive changes in broadcasting technologies, he proposed to exploit merger synergies by creating a company that would be a world leader in entertainment and broadcasting, defence electronics and aerospace manufacturing, and in electrical retailing and home electronics equipment rental. The company's position in aerospace would be secured by a merger with British Aerospace, and all the rest would be sold off.

The chairman's colleagues were staggered by the sheer scale and audacity of the vision. Such mega-transformations were still very rare in those faraway days. They were also, in the main, totally confounded by what they saw as the monstrous impracticality of it all. Some maintained that the gap between the capabilities of the current management of the company and what was needed to save the firm from ruin was so wide that nemesis was not far distant. Others, while impressed by the scale of the vision, wondered where the money was going to come from, as the company seemed to be close to breaching its banking covenants. A few were concerned for the future of their own business groups, which did not feature prominently in the vision. Most were not at all convinced that any real synergistic opportunities could be created from two such disparate organizations as Thorn and EMI, still less from the entity envisioned by the chairman!

This, then, was the context in which Professor Lorsch was to explain the strategies chosen by the leaders of very successful companies, which turned out to be a million miles away from the proposals on the table. Professor Lorsch and his co-author Gordon Donaldson had published their research findings a year or so before in a book entitled *Decision Making at the Top* (Donaldson and Lorsch, 1983). Both authors were senior professors at Harvard Business School and two of the most eminent business academics of their time.

From the Fortune 500 they selected 12 enterprises that had led their industrial sectors by all significant external measures for over 30 years. Then they systematically interviewed the top managers of the companies to discover what drove them as managers, how they took key decisions, what their values were and what they believed had made their companies so successful. Here are some of the key findings:

- The CEOs were very similar in three ways. First, they were all in their fifties or sixties. Second, all bar one had spent at least 20 years with their companies. Eight of the 12 had served for more than 25 years and six for more than 30 years. Third, they were relatively wealthy, with their wealth coming from high base pay and considerable stock holdings.
- All were very performance orientated. Invariably, they drove for strong competitive market performance, industry leadership and superior financial performance. They believed very firmly that financial performance was an outcome of having the best products, technology, products or services and the strongest people and organization.

- The vast majority were also financially conservative. They were strongly orientated towards minimizing their company's dependence on the capital markets. Acquisitions were mainly regarded as a strategy to be adopted only when other methods of growing the company had been exhausted. A fairly typical view is demonstrated by the following quotation: 'The guys who are always thinking of taking over think dollars, not people, product or jobs.'

The top managers of the best-performing companies in 1979 believed that their overriding goal was to hand the company on in good shape to the next generation. They were concerned to generate and sustain a superior financial performance in order to have the resources to invest in the company, to attract and motivate good people and give a fair return to shareholders. They believed that good performance was generated from within the organization, by innovation, by being superior to competitors at 'doing the business', by providing better products and services than their competitors and above all by having a superior organization, management and workforce.

Last, they were very careful to minimize their dependence on capital markets, as already mentioned, because they believed that too much alignment with the markets would force them to make decisions that might not be in line with the best long-term interests of the company.

In a passage that seems a little incredible in today's climate, Lorsch and Donaldson comment that one of the most important and challenging tasks of top management is to 'create an organization which is capable of large, complex and interdependent tasks… Such organizations take decades to create.' Even more interesting, they commented that from a US national standpoint, such organizations are a vital and scarce resource. So, here are two of the greatest contributors to management thinking of their time contending that the main value of a business lies in the quality of its organization!

Cut to the managers of today…

Twenty years later, much seems to have changed in the values and alignment of top managers. Today, in many quoted companies the main focus is on the capital markets and keeping investors happy.

It was possible to detect subtle changes happening in the attitudes of top managers even in the 1980s. For example, take the chairman's statement of Redland plc, 1983: 'On behalf of the shareholders, of whose loyalty we are always mindful, I wish to express to my board colleagues and to my fellow employees, great appreciation for the way in which we work happily and productively together in building a fine and progressive enterprise.' This chairman seems to be identifying himself closely with the shareholders.

In the 1990s, many companies sought to align their causes with those of 'the shareholders' through the introduction of a plethora of shareholder value-related financial measures and incentive plans. Much of this was also accompanied by rhetoric that followed a line that the governing, or overriding, objective of the enterprise is to 'maximize the wealth of shareholders'.

A 1993 quotation from William Smithburg, CEO of the Quaker Company, describes the changes as follows: 'EVA [economic value added] makes managers act like shareholders. It's the true corporate faith for the 1990s.'

Coca-Cola, an enthusiastic proponent of EVA, described its mission simply: 'Ours is a mission with one simple goal: to create greater value for our share owners. That is the main purpose of the Coca-Cola Company.' In its magazine *Journey* the company featured an article entitled 'Is share-owner value a threat to your job? Or will it sustain your career?' In it the then chairman, Roberto C. Goizueta, explained why the company had chosen 'share-owner value' as its mission rather than others such as customer service or job creation and security. He wrote, 'Society demands that creating share-owner value is the job of the company.' In a society based on democratic capitalism, people create specific institutions to meet specific needs. For example, governments are created to help meet civil needs, churches are created to meet spiritual needs, and so on. Businesses, according to Goizueta, are created to meet economic needs. Trouble starts, he argues, when institutions try to broaden their scope beyond their 'natural realms'. As a clinching argument he cites the fall of the former Soviet Union and asserts that, 'The collapse was driven by that government's insistence on running businesses and other functions of society that should have remained outside the domain of government.'

It is not our intention to debate the propositions made by Mr Goizueta, but to contrast them with the positions of his colleagues of 20 years before. The main difference seems to be a reversal of the definitions of ends and means. Goizueta seems to define the end as being the creation of shareholder wealth and the means as the production of a 'universally appealing product that meets a fundamental human need', a strong organization, and so on.

By contrast, in the 1970s, managers seemed to value the life and enduring success of the enterprise as the fundamental end. Satisfactory shareholder returns *resulted* from pursuing the prime goal. Even more fundamental, the 1970s managers do not seem to question the fact that they must balance the needs and wants of multiple stakeholders in order to meet their ends, whereas Mr Goizueta seems to be saying that a company can have only one prime objective, that of creating share-owner value. What if the most shareholder value could be created by sacrificing the organization, and the interests of the other stakeholders? Coca-Cola is an excellent and highly responsible company, which we are sure would never indulge in such activities as 'gouging' customers (to quote Goizueta) and partners to create share-owner value overnight. But it might be a temptation to some…

So, how did these rather fundamental changes come about in such a short time? One insight is provided by Allan Kennedy in his book *The End of Shareholder Value* (2000). Kennedy argues that a new and very aggressive breed of investment banker grew up in the 1970s and early 1980s. These bankers realized that if companies were not maximizing future cash flows from the assets invested in the business, then their stock market values would be depressed by comparison with their underlying value. Thus by buying the assets cheaply and by selling them off or by working them harder, they could release huge streams of value and enrich themselves and investors. The actions of these corporate raiders, argues Kennedy, caused businesspeople across the board to become aware of the idea of shareholder value. Armed with this new understanding of value and anxious that they might end up as a target for raiders, managers in the United States started to realign executive compensation schemes to place an increasing emphasis on stock options, tying managers' future pay directly to their success in raising companies' stock prices.

Of course, this was not simply a US phenomenon; companies such as Slater-Walker, Hanson Trust, Williams Group and individuals such as James Goldsmith were early British players in the game.

In the 1980s, argues Kennedy, managers began to mimic the corporate raiders by selling or closing underperforming parts of their operations; slashing costs to improve across-the-board performance; closing older plants, moving production to new, lower- cost venues in developing countries and outsourcing any activities that outside vendors could apparently accomplish at a lower cost. The results of these actions, especially in the latter half of the 1990s, were significant increases in corporate performance and profitability, an unprecedented rise in stock market values and booming executive pay levels as managers cashed in on what had become extremely valuable options in a bull market.

Executive attention shifted from the business to the share price. By the late 1990s, argues Kennedy, spurring the share price to the highest level possible had become an end in itself for many, many top executives, who would go to great lengths to achieve it.

As the share price became the main source of reward or sanction for executives, almost a surrogate for career success, so did more and more executives begin to consider what actions would please the financial markets. The implication of Kennedy's assertions is that many managers these days regard a high share price as the end, and anything that might boost it as the means.

So we have seen a significant shift in management emphasis and motivation. The 1979 Lorsch and Donaldson research was into the best rather than the typical company. However, it is almost certainly valid to say that the vast bulk of top 1970s managers had a different framework of values to those of today. These people were reported to be very concerned with issues to do with status, position and power. 'Making it' was parodied as having the keys to the directors' washroom (they really did exist, as did individual facilities for the most senior people).

A top manager in the 1960s and / or 1970s tended to identify with a company, liked power and influence, enjoyed the trappings of status, was ambitious in a career sense and was comfortably off financially. Money tended to be viewed comparatively, as a measure of success relative to a peer group, rather than an end in itself. Order and discipline were much valued. The organization was valued as the setting in which status and power could be exercised. Top managers had an implied duty to be good role models for those they led.

By contrast, all the contemporary CEOs whom we interviewed believed that satisfying the 'shareholders' (which in larger quoted companies means investment fund managers and to a lesser degree the press and sell-side analysts (see Chapter 2)) was the overriding objective. This finding is strongly reinforced by the Cranfield University survey mentioned earlier, *The Life and Times of the CEO* (Harrington and Steele, 1999). Respondents from large quoted companies believed that the key challenges they faced and the factors most affecting their tenure in the job were 'constant pressure from financial institutions to meet performance expectations' and 'increased pressure from all aspects of the media'.

They also believed that the pressures were becoming more severe and would continue to do so: 'Life will be harder – the markets will always want more.

They are increasingly unforgiving. A company could not now get away with even one set of disappointing results. It is a very visible stage.'

Other changes can be seen through the language used by managers. These days, no top manager worth his or her salt would miss an opportunity to declare undying commitment to the cause of shareholder returns. At a more subtle level, there is a tendency to describe enterprises in terms of 'activities' and 'assets', or 'units'. For example: 'During this past year, our management has undertaken a comprehensive reappraisal of those parts of the group that are earning inadequate returns on capital employed. Some business units have been disposed of, others are being re-engineered to enhance customer service and to raise individual and collective performance standards…' Or, 'More generally, we recognized that the group had in place a broad spread of assets and good market shares around the world.'

The meteoric rise and subsequent crash of Marconi (formerly GEC) must be one of the major corporate dramas of recent years. John Mayo, the ex-deputy chief executive, wrote a series of articles for the *Financial Times* a few months after he left the company. His story demonstrates the degree to which the priorities of both investors and management have shifted away from the underlying business. Said Mayo, shareholders wanted three things from the new management at the then GEC company. First, they wanted 'the unwinding of the poison pill joint ventures, one effect of which was to protect management from unwanted takeovers'. Second, they wanted 'focus, so they could allocate their funds according to sectors'. Third, the business had to invest its pile of cash, 'as cash cannot earn the cost of capital'.

With the shareholders' focus on portfolio rationalization rather than the underlying business, it comes as no surprise to hear that:

> We then set out to maximise shareholder value through 'Project Superbowl'. After a complex form of auction, we transferred the defence business to British Aerospace who gave our shareholders more than 36% of their enlarged group. Marconi shareholders received, directly and tax free, more than £6.5 bn of new BAE Systems shares and loan notes, worth well over £2 per Marconi share. Marconi received nothing; this was a spin-off, not a sale.

And later:

> I therefore recommended a 'Superbowl Two' transaction. I wanted us to negotiate with prospective partners simultaneously, and indicated that we could get significantly higher value from seeking a merger partner who was prepared to pay a premium and offer a cash or cash and bond alternative. I obviously needed board approval to do this.

A number of points emerge from these quotations:

- First, Mayo seems to be primarily addressing a financial-sector audience, as, it might be argued, would any top executive in today's environment. These days, jobs are believed to be in the gift of the market!
- Marconi management seemed highly focused on maximizing shareholder value by transaction.
- The old GEC was disposed of through the sale of assets and activities. The new Marconi was created by the purchase of other assets. Having

> completed this, the company still did not have critical mass in its new markets. At this point, Mayo proposed an immediate merger with another company in an attempt to leverage a premium for Marconi's shareholders.

This line of thinking would not disgrace a top investment banker.

However, some non-executives spoke out strongly against this proposal, one arguing, 'We didn't give up on the beaches of Dunkirk, and we are not going to give up now.' Mayo's non-executive director sounds much more like someone close to the business!

So, it would appear that today's managers are speaking, thinking and possibly acting more like their counterparts in the financial markets. In the 'old days', the best managers were closer to the business and seem to have regarded their companies almost as living organisms, possessing valuable skills, able to learn, adapt, grow and endure just like any other organism. The organization could be seen as a special-purpose community. The roles of the leaders were to give it guidance and direction, to help it to succeed and avoid danger, so that it would survive and prosper down the generations.

Today's top managers, on the other hand, whatever their private proclivities, seem to feel compelled to think of their enterprises as bundles of assets or activities that can be shuffled, bought and sold. And in the view of the 'owners' of the enterprise, the investment fund managers, anything that might stand in the way of the easy liquidation of assets is to be avoided.

Some argue that there is a division of responsibility in the modern-day company. The 'operational' management (of the various divisions or subsidiaries) are there to 'run the businesses'. Top management (at 'group' level) are there to manage the portfolio.

If this were so, then the balance might be all right. However, to quote one interviewee, a subsidiary finance director:

> The trouble is, we're not left alone to deliver our promises. You go through the business planning round, agree investment levels and performance targets. You manage the business even better than target. Things are going well. Then, halfway through the year, you get a message to cut capital expenditure or costs. Someone else isn't performing, so we all have to take short-term, and damaging, action to shore up the year's results for the City. It turns off management and damages the business.

Associated with all the above are the facts that director tenure has become very much shorter, and total pay, driven by share-related remuneration, has dramatically increased. We have a vastly different scenario as compared with that of the 1970s. Now, the trend seems to be towards top managers who will seek to bring about restructuring and change in order to influence the share price of their companies and realize wealth for themselves. Is this a valid conclusion?

Yes, according to Tony Golding in *The City* (2001). Golding asserts that the relationships between top managers and the financial markets changed in a quite fundamental way in the 1980s. He calls the changed relationship 'the new industrial compact'. Once upon a time, many managers kept a prudent distance from investors and from time to time complained publicly about 'short-termism' on the part of the markets. Now, Golding says, 'Industrialists no longer make speeches about short-termism because the rules of the game have changed. Today's CEOs and FDs accept the process of regular dialogue, the mantra of shareholder value, target-setting and performance appraisal as a fact of life.'

He goes on to say that many industrial managers now have very similar time horizons to those of fund managers. 'Inevitably, the evidence points to the conclusion that managers have adjusted to institutional timescales rather than vice versa.'

Golding's conclusions are that managers are prepared to accept a job in which they may not last very long and in which an undue amount of time must be devoted to responding to the constant demands of investors, sell-side analysts and the media for two important reasons: ambition and money. Chief executives thrive on challenges, are personally resilient and enjoy the public exercise of power. They also have the opportunity to earn a great deal of money. In the financial arrangements implicit in 'the new industrial compact', the rewards for success are extremely high, primarily in the form of share options and bonuses. Success, in the form of a high share price, will generate considerable wealth.

And should things not work out entirely as planned, there is a second possibility. They can always receive or engineer a bid for or break up the business, benefit from the share options (which will vest on a change of control of the company) and still be an institutional hero, earning the chance to do it all over again! In the worst case, if none of the good things above work out and top managers are forced by institutional pressure or board machinations to leave the company, there is still the consolation of a terminal pay-off!

In order to meet their side of the 'compact', managers must be prepared to demonstrate complete commitment to the interests of shareholders (in reality, investment institutions), be prepared to confide in them, warn them of impending moves, or sound out their attitude towards any proposed corporate development. They must also be prepared to put up with a considerable amount of apparently unreasonable behaviour and conflicting or inconsistent demands.

However, says Golding, prudent managers tend to keep their views about investor behaviours to themselves, because, 'The upside is financial security, and quite possibly substantial wealth, while the downside would be the inability to get another job in a quoted company, anywhere!'

WHAT IS DRIVING ALL THIS CHANGE?

We hope that you will agree that the very nature of industry in the United Kingdom has undergone tremendous change in the past three or four decades. We have also sought to demonstrate that the ways in which managers think and act seem also to have undergone a quite radical transformation.

It is quite obvious that many of the changes that have been experienced in the United Kingdom are simply the effect of the radical shifts that have happened in the global economy, and of the vulnerability of an established manufacturing and industrial economy, such as the United Kingdom's, to changing international competition. So, are all of the manifestations covered in this chapter simply an inevitable consequence of natural, uncontrollable events, in which the industrial economy and the financial markets are helpless pawns in a chaotic universe?

We would strongly contend not. Different mature economies have developed in different ways, despite being generally subjected to the same pressures. One salient difference between developed economies is the way in which industry is financed and the pressures that are brought to bear on organizations as a result.

The perspectives on what makes for good companies and a good economy differ significantly between Germany, France, the Netherlands and Sweden, on the one hand, and the United States and United Kingdom, on the other. One of the salient differences in Germany, France, the Netherlands and Sweden is the view that the interests of multiple stakeholders and society as a whole must be taken into account when large corporations and those who provide them with capital make important decisions. These convictions have a marked effect on the behaviour of top management and investors.

There are also many large differences in the structure of financial markets, behaviour of investors and means of financing industry between the United States and the United Kingdom. For instance, bond financing has been far more prevalent in the United States, the relative sizes of the industrial and financial sectors are markedly different, and it is reported that there is a wider variety of specialist investors in the United States.

It is therefore not valid to argue that the 'arrangements' we have for financing industry in Britain are simply the result of vast forces beyond society's control. The bulk of the book is, in effect, an examination of these 'arrangements', how they work and what effects all of this has on companies and the industrial economy.

In Part II we examine some of the most important 'arrangements' that affect the performance, success and very nature of industry in the United Kingdom: the roles and inter-relationships of top managers and the financial markets.

Part II

The financial markets and top managers

Introduction to Part II

In Chapter 1 we saw that the worlds of investing in and managing large companies have undergone seismic changes in the past few decades. We have also seen that the relationships between top managers and the financial markets have changed over the same time: witness Tony Golding's idea of 'the new industrial compact'. We now seek to examine the parties to this 'compact' and how they relate to each other.

The financial press devotes a large slice of its coverage of business to reporting the thoughts and actions of a large number of different players in the financial markets and their counterparts in companies, normally those top managers who have a 'public' profile. Often, this coverage gives the impression that the markets and management are at war with each other. 'Shareholders' are quoted as being outraged at yet another rich pay-off by the CEO of a troubled company. Analysts, investors and City sources are quoted as baying for the blood of the leaders of companies that have failed to live up to their expectations.

On the more positive side, some top managers have a period of stardom, during which their profiles are burnished and they can do no wrong. Press and investors alike sing the praises of these heroes of industry – for a while, because it is just as possible for a star to become dim and plunge from the stellar firmament as it is for others to rise and replace that star.

All this publicity and reportage is very interesting, but does it get behind what really happens at the interfaces between management and markets? The next three chapters attempt to look at the 'actors' involved in the great industrial drama, and how they get on together.

2

Who are the actors in the business–City nexus?

It is commonly (and accurately) accepted that the pressures on larger enterprises and their managements have grown inexorably over the past few decades. The barriers to the global movement of capital and both industrial and consumer products (despite some protectionist 'glitches') have reduced dramatically. So have barriers to the movement of production. Driven by huge pressures on costs and improvements in communications and transport, many industries have located production in the cheapest regions of the world. This syndrome does not just affect manufacturing of standard products. There has, for example, been a strong movement of software development to the Indian sub-continent, where there is an educated and relatively cheap workforce. Call centres, an engine of UK employment growth, are now following.

Alongside these changes has come an 'internationalization' of financing. The 'US' style of raising equity and debt from capital markets rather than relationship institutions is creeping across the globe. This trend is apparent in countries such as Germany and France, where public equity was historically a small component in company financing. In practice, this has meant the increased presence of US and, to a lesser degree, UK investors as holders in the equity of larger companies in those countries, with all the pressures that come from such investors. This was brought home with a shock to many Germans when Vodafone, a British raider, acquired Mannesmann, Germany's third largest company. However, this process works both ways, as many British and US quoted companies are being acquired by continental European rivals.

The explosion in information and communications has put pressure on enterprises to be more responsive to external events and fashions. This has fuelled the rise of management fads. A plethora of new techniques and movements, from core process re-engineering, corporate renewal and culture change to value-based management, have been pushed by large consultancies. The instant nature of information tends to support an increase in the number of 'crazes' that come and go, usually with few enduring effects. Moreover, the growth in the number of information workers, people with portable skills who can make their own choices about where to work, is predicted by many pundits to be about to change the relationships between employers and their staff in quite fundamental ways.

If we link all of this together with the fact that 'events', such as oil shocks, wars and terrorism, seem to happen in an ever more interconnected world, it is quite clear that being a top manager is no picnic these days. The job of steering a large enterprise through the minefields and shoals of markets and competition, of leading increasingly independent employees, and all in an environment of close scrutiny by a critical press and public waiting for the next 'Fat Cat' scandal, would seem to need people with special talents.

THE MAIN SOURCE OF PRESSURE

However, these factors did not seem to concern very much the managers with whom we spoke. They accepted such pressures as being normal. The pressure that all of them feel the most comes from the financial markets, and in particular from investors and the press. All the many managers we interviewed maintained that the factors that mattered most in determining whether they were a success or failure originated in the financial markets.

They expressed their views in quite consistent ways. Most mentioned their company's share price and comments in the press or by stockbrokers' analysts as being a proxy vote on their performance. All felt that their boards were powerless to resist strong pressure from investment institutions and were sure that their career prospects were in the hands of the financial markets.

Our findings are strongly supported by the survey briefly referred to in Chapter 1 conducted by Cranfield University School of Management in conjunction with Sanders & Sidney plc and 3i venture capital investors (Harrington and Steele, 1999). In this survey, primary pressures mentioned by CEOs of larger quoted companies were, first, constant pressure from financial institutions to meet performance expectations; and second, increased pressure from all aspects of the media. As a typical CEO said, 'Performance is the main factor affecting tenure – those who deliver tend to stay. It is driven by shareholders; it is OK when the results are as expected but a poor year's performance can nullify five previous good years. Even the tabloid newspapers will not tolerate poor performance.'

Obviously, these managers, like our interviewees, believed that the financial markets are the most important influences on their success. We will examine how these influences are brought to bear. While we will mainly concentrate on the key players in the markets, we will also look at some of the large cast of supporting actors around the fringes of the main action.

INVESTORS AND INTERMEDIARIES

We should start with a clarification. A quick reading of the financial press would leave the impression that the investment institutions are the real shareholders.

True, they buy, hold and sell shares and other instruments, but they do this as intermediaries on behalf of the real, risk-taking shareholders.

There are two large categories of 'real' shareholders. The first is private investors; the second, holders of personal pension plans and members of pension schemes, or the holders of insurance policies, endowments, unit trusts and other similar investments. These are the people taking the real financial risk. However, in most cases there are brokers and fund managers, working for the investment institutions, acting as intermediaries between the shareholders and the enterprises in which their money is invested.

If the true risk-takers are pension fund members and corporate pension providers, the health of their investments will be taken care of by a board of trustees, representatives of the members, who are usually advised by a pension fund manager and an external financial adviser. Investors in personal pension plans, unit trusts or insurance-based products will from time to time receive a report detailing the performance of their investments, often in rather general terms. Typically, these reports will contain a description of what has affected the performance of the particular investment and, if performance has been less than sparkling, comforting words of commitment to making things better in the future. Many private investors accept the performance of their investments as a *fait accompli*, a tendency exacerbated by an air of mystique, probably encouraged by the professionals, that confuses the layperson.

Unfortunately, the history of the past 20 years of shareholder and private pension plan 'democracy' has been deeply marred by scams and rip-offs perpetrated on the consumer by the financial services industry.

The net effect of this system is to place considerable power in the hands of the investment professionals, who manage other people's money with the declared intention of maximizing returns consistent with a specified (but somewhat general) risk profile. The means by which they do this is generally left to the professionals.

To complete the background for those readers who are not completely familiar with the workings of the financial system, large public companies can raise money in three ways. The first, and in the United Kingdom historically the most important, is through equity: issuing shares in the stock market. Investors are open to buy and sell the shares. If more people want to buy them than sell them, the value of the shares will go up. Conversely, if investors think that the company's future performance will be worse than that of alternative opportunities, they will sell, and the price of the shares will go down. The alternatives are borrowing, either from the same investment institutions by issuing bonds, or from the banks.

Our main concern in this book is with the relationships between companies and the equity market, still the main source of public company finance in the United Kingdom, the source of approximately half of public company financing in the United States, and an increasingly important source in continental Europe. British companies are therefore more dependent on equity finance than their US or European counterparts.

The aim of this chapter and the next is simply to identify who are the main and supporting actors in the financial markets and companies. We will also seek to clarify what is important to each.

THE CAST OF ACTORS

Investment institutions

An investment institution is an organization that invests in the financial markets on behalf of the owners of capital. There are many such institutions (also referred to as fund managers), with many different approaches to investing. Institutions and their senior staff are reckoned by top managers to be the most powerful force in the markets, because they make most of the buying and selling decisions that determine the share prices of companies.

Many London fund managers are part of large investment banks these days. These banks are, in the main, US, Swiss, Dutch or German owned.

Managers

In the eyes of the financial markets, 'managers' tend to be only those people who are visible to them. Generally, this category will include chairpersons, senior non-executive directors, chief executives and finance directors. In very large companies, some very senior general managers may also be presented to the markets.

Stockbrokers

Stockbrokers are the agents who handle the buying and selling of shares. They often provide managers with personal advice and guidance on dealing with the markets, and carry the company's message to investors. All brokers employ salesmen and many also employ 'sell-side' analysts.

Sell-side analysts

Sell-side analysts produce in-depth analysis of companies and their prospects, and issue 'buy, hold or sell' recommendations for their shares. Most analysts are employed by stockbroking companies, many of which are in turn owned by the large integrated investment banks. There are now a very limited number of independent analysts.

Investment bankers

Investment bankers (also known as merchant bankers) advise managers on buying or selling significant assets and on raising capital. They make their money from transactions, including acquisitions and disposals.

Commercial banks

Commercial banks (sometimes known as 'clearing banks') lend money to companies. Most of the commercial banks are involved in the full spectrum of activities from fund management to commercial lending.

Financial PR companies

Financial PR companies advise managers on the full spectrum of press, investor and public relations activities. Some will also act as coaches and guides to individuals anxious to maximize their City profiles.

Financial advisers to pension funds

Financial advisers to pension funds are often powerful but generally shadowy figures. Their power comes from their knowledge of the cast of investment actors and the fact that they advise pension funds on choosing fund managers. It is thus good for a fund manager to be on an adviser's list.

Large executive search companies

Large executive search companies are not central actors in the relationships between companies and the financial markets. However, some of the more powerful figures in 'headhunting' are important to managers as promoters of their reputations and as informants on the job market. Search consultants are also important communicators and networkers, as it is their job to know what is going on in the job market.

Accountants, auditors and consultants

The big accountants perform audits of the accounts of companies and report to shareholders on whether their published accounts show a 'true and fair' picture of the company's financial performance. An accountants' report is also often required as part of the shareholder reporting processes in large transactions. In addition, they also offer a wide range of specialist financial services, including tax advice.

Lawyers

Lawyers offer a wide range of advice on commercial law in many jurisdictions, from the preparation of legal agreements, to support in making acquisitions and disposals and advice on employment issues. The United Kingdom has not yet reached the point where, as in the United States, senior individuals are invariably represented by an aggressive attorney at hiring and firing times. But we are getting there!

Big strategy consultants

Although companies such as McKinsey and Bain are not formally involved in the financial markets, they have strong informal relationships with many of the main players. One of the more lucrative offerings from such consultants is advice and help in managing mergers and acquisitions. Their support in developing corporate strategies is also of interest to the markets.

Compensation and benefits consultants

The larger consultants conduct worldwide research into executive pay and benefits, and advise companies on what they need to provide their top managers to be 'competitive' in the global market for talent. Often such companies also provide actuarial support and benefits advice to pension funds. The advice of these consultants is often quoted (sometimes inaccurately) to justify levels of top executive compensation.

The financial press

Last, but not least by any means, is the Fourth Estate. Every newspaper has a financial section; some papers, such as the *Financial Times* and the *Wall Street Journal*, are mainly dedicated to financial and economic issues. Then there is a vast array of specialist periodicals, such as the *Investors Chronicle* and *The Economist* that are serious and influential sources of information and viewpoints on financial, economic and political issues.

Many elements of the financial press are closely networked with analysts, investors and financial PR agencies. They can therefore be a formidable source of 'scuttlebutt' about managers and companies.

This, then, is the main cast of actors in the continuously evolving drama played out between companies and the financial markets. Some important influences have not been mentioned, in particular the regulators and government, but we will touch on their roles later.

It might be noticeable to some that there are many interests not represented on the stage. In particular, we might mention the real risk-taking investors, employees, customers, suppliers and the community or 'society'. That is because, although serious reference may be made to them from time to time, there is not a shred of evidence that they have any real influence on what goes on between top managers and the markets. At best, they are distant spectators, excluded from the stage. At worst, they do not even hold a ticket to get into the theatre!

Having introduced the cast, we will now endeavour to identify what drives those who occupy the centre of the stage, examining the most important influencers in some detail. Before we do this, it is important to touch briefly on one significant trend that has had a profound effect on the organization and behaviour of the UK financial market: the concentration of power in the hands of a relatively small number of integrated investment banks. Philip Augar, in *The Death of Gentlemanly Capitalism* (2001), describes how the functions of stockbroking, investment banking, research and analysis, and investment management have increasingly come under the control of huge banking organizations. He contrasts the values and behaviour of these organizations with that of their predecessors in the London market, describing a shift from what were essentially upper-middle-class English partnerships, concerned to give a service to their customers and make a good living without breaking sweat, to integrated, aggressive, ambitious money-making machines. It is these organizations that now drive the business agenda. Today, most of the big integrated banks are either US, Swiss or German owned – there are only a handful of British ones left.

Remember therefore, as we consider the cast, that many of them are likely to be closely related!

THE KEY ACTORS IN THE FINANCIAL MARKETS AND WHAT DRIVES THEM

Investment institutions

At the centre of the City–company nexus are the investment fund managers.

Investment institutions are many and varied, but their functions tend to be similar. They take other people's money and invest it, according to published or agreed criteria, in theory to make the highest returns they can for their clients. As clients have a multitude of objectives – for example, capital appreciation versus cash income, low versus higher risk, short versus longer timescales – so the strategies of investment institutions' various funds will tend to cover a wide spread.

Pension funds still occupy the centre of the investment stage, and it is worth examining pensions investment to generate some understanding of a cycle that ends up by placing huge pressures on companies to deliver continuous above-average performance.

Despite the much-publicized withdrawal by many companies from final-pay pension schemes, company and individual pension schemes will for the foreseeable future generate massive flows of cash to be invested in the capital markets. A typical larger company pension fund will have a board of trustees. Their role is to protect the rights of employees who are members of the pension fund. One function is to ensure that the members' funds are prudently invested, so that future pensions can be paid.

In reality, over the past decade or so, this has come to mean that pension fund trustees judge their investment managers by whether or not they are able to beat an average or index. The pressure tends to be increased when top managers are a significant influence in trustee boards, because they will also want to maximize returns so that the cost of the pension fund to the company will be kept as low as possible. It is our experience that many top managers also enjoy second-guessing fund managers – after all, it gives them a chance to display their skills and also put their tormentors in another domain, the fund managers, under a little pressure!

Fund managers whose investment performance falls below that of the chosen comparators tend to be replaced. The few old-timers left in fund management contrast today with a past environment when indices were less important and they were given much more time to rectify a performance lapse. As fund managers typically report four times a year on their performance, two bad quarters will place extreme pressure on them to 'do something'. They also know full well that the financial adviser to the pension fund will have a list of alternative fund managers readily available.

So what in times gone by tended to be an alliance between fund manager and company based on relationship and performance has become one based on short-term performance alone. This is one start point of a cycle of pressure that has totally transformed the relationship between large companies and their investors.

What drives the investment institutions?

Investment management is a competitive business. It is also a business in which the 'stars' can make very big money and wield great power. Messages from fund managers to CEOs are not easily ignored.

As has been indicated, the investment industry abounds with indices, league tables and other devices that purport to measure the comparative performance of funds in relation to their rivals. Relative performance is crucial, because it will strongly influence the success of an institution in attracting funds from investors. The size of the funds under management will determine the fees earned by an institution and in turn by its managers.

One side effect of this measurement against an index or average is herd behaviour on the part of institutions. So great is the fear of mistakes in investment policy that the behaviour of the large institutions tends to converge, with everybody seeking to stay with the crowd and gain small advantages at the margins. This means that London lacks the variety of investment strategies found in the much larger US markets.

Some investment managers will look for investments they calculate to be undervalued in relation to their long-term prospects and then hold the investments for the long term. However, such is the pressure generated by pension funds and by the prevailing culture, it is not surprising that institutional investors in the main tend to take a short-term view and be very active in changing their holdings. This is, after all, the way in which they themselves tend to be measured. Thus companies that diverge from expectations tend to feel the heat from investors quickly and intensely.

What are fund managers good at?

One of the stockbrokers whom we interviewed was quite sure that the City, in its various manifestations, knew everything that mattered about business. He said that increasing specialization within fund management meant that investment management decisions for individual companies are being devolved within institutions. This in turn means that CEOs are being increasingly exposed to younger fund managers and are often upset by being grilled by 27-year-olds. 'What the CEOs don't realize', he said, 'is how good these youngsters are.'

Fund managers' intelligence on companies comes from a variety of sources. Prime among them are presentations made to investors by the top managers of companies. Large companies will typically present twice a year.

Much store is placed on these presentations. In addition to the information presented on strategy and performance expectations, managers get rated on substance and style. Such issues as whether they are telling a good 'story', how well they appear to know the business, how good they are with 'the numbers', how confident they appear to be, how committed they are to producing what investors want, are believed by investors and analysts to help them develop informed judgements about companies and their management.

As a direct result of these and other private and public encounters, CEOs, finance directors and, sometimes, company chairpersons are informally rated by investors. Thus is a considerable circulation of gossip created about senior managers. This gossip is couched in very familiar terms, with the subjects often being referred to by their first names or nicknames, rather in the style of *Hello* magazine! Perceived confidence, presentation skills and reputation management assume great importance.

Second, a huge amount of financial and anecdotal information is generated by 'sell-side' analysts, who generally work for stockbrokers and produce publicly available research on companies, in addition to specially commissioned studies. However, owing to developing suspicions that 'sell-side' analysts were becoming biased in their analysis by the pressures to sell the services of the banking company and stockbrokers that employed them, institutions have developed analytical skills of their own. Institutional investors' analysts, commonly known as 'buy-side' analysts, tend not to publish their research. Many believe that this makes it more impartial.

Then, institutional investors have access to the enormous information machine – created by banks, researchers, specialist institutes and agencies, and PR companies – that supports the financial markets and press. To this must be added the already mentioned rumour and tittle-tattle that inevitably gets generated in a complex, competitive market, where getting in first with a juicy piece of information may generate a veritable fortune.

So, what skills do institutional investors deploy to make sense of the huge pool of available information and understand the companies in which they might invest?

Managers and people in the financial markets tended to diverge sharply at this point. Managers felt that investors are excellent at all forms of financial analysis and have a good understanding of industry economics and competitor analysis. In addition, they have a great deal of specialist knowledge about the economics and structures of particular industries. However, many managers were also strongly of the view that there is a lack of understanding of the processes of managing and developing effective organizations. It would not be putting it too strongly to say that they generally believe that they are dealing with very bright people with a good theoretical business education and with an accounting or banking bias. However, they also feel that these individuals understand little, and care less, about the more intimate and complex matters of leading and managing a large organization.

One very senior manager declared that he was leading a process of quite radical organization change that, when complete, would significantly enhance the performance of the business. Because the process of change was long and complex, he had no intention of even mentioning it to investors until it was beginning to generate tangible results. They would not understand it, he said. Another of our interviewees, a very experienced and successful CEO, declared that 'they don't understand how a business works'.

Some managers commented that institutional investors tend to categorize companies by 'a headline, three bullet points and a profile of the chief executive'. Managers thus tend to communicate with the markets in these terms. For example, one manager expressed his strategic objectives in 'City' terms as follows:

Year 1: Consolidate

- Bring order to mess left by predecessors.
- Reduce stocks.
- Manage cash.
- Fill holes in management.

Year 2: Profit recovery

- Use new systems to focus ordering and branch stocking.
- Consolidate product lines.
- Close unprofitable branches.

Year 3: Return to growth

- Exploit strong brand and customer loyalty to open new branches.
- Develop new product lines.
- Leverage franchise opportunities.

The same manager also commented that the other ingredients for success with investors include 'telling it like it is'; keeping it short and simple; confidence; quick wit; being good with numbers; and making it clear that the interests of investors are paramount. He expressed the latter point as 'making it clear that I will do anything to meet their agendas'.

City interviewees agree with managers about the primacy of industry, market and financial analysis, but feel that they understand a great deal about managers, organizations and management. However, their focus seems to be on a few individuals; they describe organizations as 'the structure' and think of management as consisting of decisive actions by the leadership figures with whom they are familiar.

What do the institutions want of companies?

First and foremost, they want managers to think and act as though their interests and the interests of investors are synonymous. Then, they want complete openness in reporting, so that they can avoid being unpleasantly surprised.

Fund managers' ideal companies will produce above-average growth, year in, year out. Sir Clive Thompson, the CEO of Rentokil Initial plc, was for many years known as 'Mr Twenty Per Cent' and much lauded for continually delivering an annual growth rate at or above this magic figure. There is a preference for companies that produce the desired rate of growth by 'active' means. Institutional managers, along with investment bankers and stockbrokers, tend to feel that 'active' managers – those who make acquisitions, do deals, cut costs, and so on – are more decisive and able than their colleagues who keep their heads down and stick to their knitting.

However, double-digit organic growth will do as second best. One of the managers whom we interviewed made the point that investors are not necessarily short term in outlook. He said that, provided it was supported by a good 'story', a long-term investment strategy could attract investor support. He slightly spoilt the effect by then saying that even one slip from the promised programme and results could lead to a rapid withdrawal of support, as investors hate uncertain long-term payback more than anything.

Companies with modest and cyclical growth are labelled 'dull' and tend to lack support. One person we interviewed described Rolls-Royce plc as a 'boring Midlands engineering company'.

Investor support is rather fickle. Companies that falter or, even worse, promise a particular rate of growth and 'fail to deliver' will be severely punished.

It might be interesting to compare a list of factors reported to be liked and disliked by institutional investors with some of the investment philosophies attributed to Warren Buffett, one of the most successful investors of all time. Here are some of the factors that institutional investors like, according to our interviewees and writers such as Tony Golding:

- Focus and commitment to a core business. Therefore, 'non-core' activities should be de-merged, spun off or carved out. Not so long ago, a degree of diversification was approved of. Fashions change.
- Managers who manage their business portfolios like they manage an equity portfolio. In effect, this means a high degree of corporate activity and, particularly, regarding the enterprise that they lead as a group of 'assets' that can be shuffled, bought and sold.
- 'Biddable' companies. They intensely dislike anything that might prevent a company from being acquired, and like to feel that there could always be a bid for their holding in a company.
- A clear 'strategy'. This means an understandable way of keeping future earnings moving ahead. We have previously mentioned a distinct liking for a high level of M&A activity as part of a good strategy. Strictly speaking, large acquisitions ought to be regarded with suspicion by institutional investors, not only because of their value-destructive history, but also

because if new shares are issued, there is a risk that future earnings per share may be 'diluted' (bad word). However, it is at this stage that 'synergy' (good word) can come to the rescue.

Companies planning a big acquisition will invariably issue a list of expected merger synergies, and investors will usually vote in favour. Acceptance will be made easier in large integrated investment banks, because the investment banking and stockbroking arms will benefit from acquisition-generated fees.

- Moving on and forgetting yesterday. This factor means that investors tend to have very short memories and are always looking for the next opportunity. It also means a very distinct preference for dealing with problems by transactional means. It is regarded as better to divest or close a troublesome business than to enter a lengthy process of improvement.

The contrast of these values with the investment philosophies of Warren Buffet, the durable guru of Berkshire Hathaway, could not be more stark. Here are some of Buffet's investment tenets:

- Always invest for the long term.
- Buy companies with strong histories of profitability and with a dominant business franchise.
- Risk can be greatly reduced by concentrating on a few well-understood holdings.
- Much success can be attributed to inactivity. Most investors cannot resist the temptation to constantly buy and sell.
- Lethargy, bordering on sloth, should remain the cornerstone of an investment style.
- Wild swings in share prices have more to do with the 'lemming-like' behaviour of institutional investors than with the aggregate returns of the companies they own.
- Do not take yearly results too seriously. Instead, focus on four- or five-year averages.
- Buy a business, don't rent stocks ('shares', in the United Kingdom).
- Look for the business with a consistent operating history.
- Remember that the stock market is manic-depressive.

Why the differences? Maybe the main one is that Mr Buffet and his partner have been leading investors since the early 1970s and have quite different life and investment philosophies from those of 30-year-olds who want to be rich quickly and believe that they are only as good as their last two quarters' results!

Readers might like to reflect on the likely differences top managers would experience if a major stakeholder in their company was Berkshire Hathaway or an 'active' institutional investor.

Before we close on institutional investors, it is worth mentioning the growing trend towards 'passive' equity investors. Driven by cost and performance concerns, many pension funds and individuals have decided to place a significant part of their moneys into 'tracker' funds. These funds invest in the stock market, tailoring their holdings to match the profile of a chosen index, say the FTSE 100. Performance of these funds should closely follow that of the chosen index. Theoretically, in the long run, tracker funds will perform as well as active ones, because no active fund will beat the average for ever. In practice, one effect of such funds is to increase the volatility of share prices, as they are forced to buy and sell to match the profile of the market. Therefore, for example, when Vodafone made its massive £110 billion acquisition of Mannesmann, thus vastly increasing that company's market capitalization, tracker funds had to sell other stocks in order to purchase Vodafone. Up went Vodafone, down went the others, for reasons totally unconnected with underlying performance!

One small final point. The government and others hope that 'shareholders' will be able to curb the perceived excesses in top management pay, and improve corporate governance generally. Maybe Arthur Burgess, the retired group treasurer of BG plc, should have a last word on investors. He wrote on the subject in the October 2001 issue of the *Treasurer* magazine:

> But, in the modern world of finance, shareholders, especially shareholders of big companies, are not disparate – the pension funds and the insurance companies – a clique with about as much independence as a flock of sheep or a herd (is it a herd?) of lemmings. Very large sheep, huge lemmings. Creatures capable of moving funds the size of a medium-sized modern state, managing portfolios representing a substantial percentage of the total value of the stock market.
>
> Driven by the twin sheepdogs of the equity analyst and the media pundit (neither of which has ever managed a whelk stall) big shareholders move as a group to lionise or despise management teams of a particular company or sector. Managers of industrial companies consequently attempting to be loved by essentially faithless shareholders fruitlessly chase objectives quite inimical to the long-term well-being of their businesses.
>
> The result is wild fluctuations in share prices, often bearing little relationship to their true worth. Indeed, it would be little exaggeration to liken share valuation to decisions by the clothing industry as to which fashions are 'in' and which are 'out': should skirts be short or long, should men's jackets have three or four buttons?

Are these the people we are looking to for improvements in corporate governance? We will return to this subject later.

Investment bankers

Investment banks are often referred to as 'advisers'. Their main functions are to assist corporate managements in preparing strategies for financing their businesses, to value deals that managers may wish to make and to support companies in planning and executing transactions, such as acquisitions or de-mergers.

Investment bankers make most of their earnings from corporate finance transactions, including mergers and acquisitions. In good years, when there is a high level of corporate 'activity', top bankers can earn massive fees.

Rule 3 of the City Code on Takeovers and Mergers requires boards of directors to obtain competent independent advice when mounting bid defences. An investment bank will invariably be retained for this service. Given that the bidding side will also be 'advised', it is no wonder that these banks thrive on 'active' management.

Table 2.1 illustrates this. It is the scale of advisors' fees for a £1.8 billion bid defence. The acquirer's bid price was 320 pence per share. The investment banking advisers in this case were J P Morgan and Lazard's. It should be remembered that the bidding company also incurred fees of at least this level.

Table 2.1 Advisers' fees

	@ 320p		**@ 350p**		**@375p**		**@400p**	
	£m	%	**£m**	%	**£m**	%	**£m**	%
J P Morgan	3.00	0.18	3.00	0.16	4.87	0.25	6.75	0.32
Lazard's	5.00	0.30	5.75	0.31	8.36	0.43	10.97	0.53
Cazenove	3.17	0.19	3.47	0.19	4.69	0.24	5.92	0.28
Hoare Govett	1.17	0.07	1.28	0.07	1.67	0.09	2.06	0.10
Brunswick	0.80	0.05	1.00	0.05	1.50	0.08	2.00	0.10
Lawyers	1.00	0.06	1.00	0.05	1.00	0.05	1.00	0.05
Accountants	0.25	0.02	0.25	0.02	0.25	0.02	0.25	0.02
Other	1.00	0.06	1.00	0.05	1.00	0.05	1.00	0.05
Total	**15.39**	**0.93**	**16.75**	**0.90**	**23.34**	**1.21**	**29.95**	**1.45**

Further evidence comes from Blue Circle, which reported spending £35.7 million on advisers, also in defending against a bid from Lafarge. A year or so later, the Blue Circle board recommended an increased offer to its shareholders, incurring more fees along the way. Given these levels of reward, it should be no surprise that investment bankers are highly supportive of deal-driven activity, expressing high levels of conviction that mergers and acquisitions create shareholder value.

In addition to the lure of big money, deal-making brings additional benefits to the players involved. For some people, the buzz bestowed by working intensely with top managers on deals that will change many people's lives is irresistible.

Bankers are very active in promoting deals, usually by creating 'ideas' and 'strategies' for acquisitions, mergers and de-mergers that will be actively sold to potential 'customers', including top managers, investment institutions, the press and any others who might have influence. An experienced City lawyer estimated that investment bankers initiate 50 per cent of all acquisition proposals. The bankers' cause is likely to have received a considerable boost as a result of the development of the large integrated US investment banks.

Investment bankers had a mixed reputation with the managers we interviewed. Some older, more senior individuals are well rated and trusted by managers. Their advice is respected and listened to, and it is felt that they can put the interests of companies and managers before their own. Such individuals are also felt to have considerable influence when it comes to managers' career and employment prospects.

But managers mainly felt that the majority of bankers were aggressive, ambitious and money-driven people, albeit very intellectually able. A business school professor we interviewed, asked to develop and run business strategy programmes for younger bankers, commented that while very bright, most were almost totally analytical and convergent in their thinking. He said that if they were presented with ambiguity or what they saw to be excessive complexity, they became aggressive and sought to find quick and clear solutions. He described them as bright 'puzzle-solvers', who tended to become frustrated if faced by long-term, ambiguous problems.

There is also a somewhat sinister side to the promotion of 'deals' by investment bankers. We have already seen how much psychology is tied up in deal-making: greed, fear and ego. One leading investment banker described some of his colleagues as 'good at capturing the wishes and views of the chief executive, then leading him where they [the bankers] want him to go'. Inevitably this will be in the direction of deals, and consequently fees.

Unlike shareholders, the investment bankers seem to be in a 'no lose' situation. Whether the deal is a good one or not, they get their fees. If it's a good one, then they are in a position to recommend the next deal. If it's a bad one, then there may well be a disposal to handle. In fact, as John Plender, writing in the *Financial Times*, put it, 'What a business – fees for putting Humpty on the wall, fees for pushing him off, fees for putting him back together again.'

Stockbrokers

The prime function of stockbrokers, as their name implies, is to buy and sell shares on behalf of private, institutional and corporate customers. They make their money from the volume of share transactions that goes through their company.

Most of the 'sell-side' stock market analysts are employed by broking companies. The higher the reputation of the analysts, the more business it is felt will be attracted to the broking company. Brokers also employ specialist salespeople to push shares to investors.

Most listed companies retain a broking company as the 'house brokers'. This means that the broking company will be at the forefront of all new issues. More important, the house broker is likely to provide private advice and guidance to top management on how to handle relationships with investment institutions and the financial markets generally.

The ability to develop good and trusting relationships with managers and all other players in and around the financial markets is of crucial importance to brokers. Senior stockbrokers, who are well known to anybody who understands the markets, are important sounding boards of City opinion on top management appointments and thus wield considerable informal influence.

'Sell-side' analysts

Analysts have been the subject of much adverse publicity in recent times.

The function of researching companies has been established as a serious professional activity only for 20 or so years. The main focus of analysis and company research has been to provide investors with good insights on companies' performance prospects through analysing their strengths and weaknesses with reference to competitors and markets. A good analyst, through personal contacts with top management, could go some way to ensuring that fund managers saw trouble coming in time to do something about their shareholdings. This ability was of great value to investors and rewarding to analysts. Conversely, if analysts got it wrong, as we will see in the Redland case study in Chapter 7, it could be seriously damaging to their income and reputation.

Analysts' reports go into considerable detail about many facets of a company's activities, and usually result in a recommendation on what attitude investors might assume towards owning shares. Increasing professionalism brought analysts power and influence, to the extent that good analysts became a source of competitive advantage to the broking houses that employed them. Top analysts became stars in their own right and commanded star rewards. In the early 1990s, through their influence on investment institutions and their contacts with top managers and special relationships with the press, top analysts were felt by managers to wield considerable power. The support of a top industry analyst was decidedly career-enhancing, even for well-established managers.

Trouble for analysts as a breed really seemed to begin with the development of integrated investment banks. It did not take long to see that a good analyst could attract business to the broking side of the business, but, more important, their reputations and knowledge could also attract more deals to the investment banking arm. Thus analysts started to be rewarded for the volumes of business they attracted to the bank. In other words, they became regarded as promoters of the overall business. This led to questions about the objectivity of their analyses, and to the gradual build-up of the capability to do independent analysis by investment institutions.

More recent events have tarnished the reputations of 'sell-side' analysts still further. They have been accused, in the United States in particular, of pushing the sale of shares in dubious Internet companies to private investors, making billions of dollars for their employers and leading many investors to lose their shirts.

The publication of a number of explosive e-mails from one Merrill Lynch analyst expressing negative opinions about shares he was recommending has confirmed the long-held fears of many about analysts' objectivity. This episode and others similar have dealt yet another blow to the already tarnished ethical reputation of the financial services industry. It is not yet evident whether the same practices are prevalent in the London market, but the same organizational arrangements tend to prevail, and the industry is considering whether to restructure in order to restore confidence.

The financial press

There are many excellent financial and management journalists. At random, we would pick out Anthony Hilton, financial editor of the London *Evening Standard*, and most of the financial editors of the British broadsheets, together with management journalists such as Simon Caulkin of the *Observer*, as offering informed and thoughtful perspectives on the world of business.

However, the average standard of financial journalism is, in our view, trivial, sensation-seeking and of deplorably low quality. The press in general has a very strong tendency to represent business as a sort of soap opera dominated by heroes and villains. The fact that many elements of the press are closely networked with other players in the financial markets and management makes their influence on managers very strong, as many a top manager who has got on the wrong side of investors, stock market analysts and influential journalists can attest!

We would pick out two strong proclivities manifested by the press, as well as by the financial markets, that have a generally negative effect on the business environment.

The first is a marked tendency to reduce the world of large businesses and the inevitably complex organizations that support them to a few larger-than-life individuals.

Here is an example. It concerns Sir Graham Wilkins, an individual known to both the authors, who died on 2 July 2003. Sir Graham was chairman of Thorn EMI plc at a time when we were both working for that then troubled company.

Sir Graham was a splendid individual, well regarded personally by all who came into contact with him.

He was projected into the role of chairman from non-executive director following the sudden dismissal of Peter Laister as chairman and chief executive, following a period of hyperactivity in which Thorn EMI (itself the result of a 1979 merger) attempted to create a merger with British Aerospace and did make the acquisition of Inmos, a semiconductor manufacturer, which proved to be a financial disaster.

However, the writer of Sir Graham's obituary says, 'While his predecessor at Thorn EMI had gained an unfortunate reputation for prevarication, Wilkins was focused and decisive.' How trying to engineer the biggest merger in British industrial history could be construed as 'prevarication' beggars the imagination!

The writer goes on to say, 'Recognising that there was excess capacity in the television manufacturing industry, *he* restructured Ferguson and cut a thousand jobs. *He* made management changes at Inmos, Thorn EMI's struggling semiconductor business, and *supervised* an overhaul of the roster of artists signed by EMI, which had become unbalanced' [emphasis added]. The reality of the matter was that the board appointed Colin Southgate as Managing Director at the same time as Sir Graham became part-time chairman. Southgate, with a growing group of new appointees whom he and his colleagues brought into the company at corporate and business group levels, instituted an extensive and detailed review over several years of the whole range of Thorn EMI's many businesses. The key to the success of the turnaround of Thorn EMI's fortunes was very detailed operational knowledge and focused improvement and restructuring programmes, together with extensive disposals, conducted by a large cast of corporate and operating managers, led by Southgate.

Sir Graham was a million miles away from this operational and detailed knowledge. He did, however, provide valuable overall support to the work of the management and, in particular, added weight to a relatively inexperienced corporate team in communicating with the financial markets.

The damaging aspect of the journalists' spin is to mislead readers into believing that company chairs and boards can do any more than support or challenge those who do understand and know the business at a level of detail to make sensible decisions. But above all, such journalism lends weight to the extremely damaging assumption that industry is run by superhero individuals and not by large groups of people managing large and complex organizations.

From this misconception can flow many other evils, such as an assumption that complex problems can be 'fixed' to ridiculous timetables. This latter tendency has come to pervade the whole of our society. We will touch on this topic later in the book.

The second tendency can be exemplified by a fictional headline: 'Gripfast Industries has another good year, and continues to be well managed.' Readers may protest that they have not often seen such a headline in the financial press, and they will be right. Such good news is not news at all and certainly will not be felt by journalists to sell newspapers. Most journalists need stronger meat than that. High-profile hirings and firings, corporate scandals and disasters, big moves and deals – these are the daily meat of many sections of the financial press. And because yesterday's news is not news at all, there is a strong tendency to characterize the world of business as a series of high-profile actions, big decisions and bold moves, rather than the warp and weft of managing a business from the basis of detailed involvement in operations, which research shows to be the basis for good management at both strategic and operational levels. Thus large sections of the financial community, supported by the press, have developed a 'move on and don't look back' mentality, which may, among other things, inhibit learning. Again, we will touch on this issue as the book unfolds.

Other actors

We have identified a number of other actors who have roles in the drama that plays between the financial markets and top managers. We will try to identify what roles these more peripheral players assume when we come to examine how the markets and top management interact. At this stage, it is probably sufficient to have identified the roles and interests of the central players in the financial markets.

As might have been demonstrated, it appears that all is not well with the current arrangements. What seems to be emerging is a strong sense that the intermediaries in the markets have been turning the game to their own advantage, at the expense of the 'real' shareholders, not to mention employees, customers, etc.

We will now move on to the main missing actor in the drama: top management.

3

Management

A man who had just been hired as the new CEO of a large corporation met with the outgoing CEO, who gave him three numbered envelopes. 'Open these if you run up against a problem you can't solve,' he said.

Six months later, sales took a downturn and the new CEO was really catching a lot of heat. Uncertain about how to proceed, he remembered the envelopes. He went to his drawer and took out the first envelope. The paper inside simply said, 'Blame your predecessor.' The new CEO called a press conference and tactfully laid the blame at the feet of the previous CEO. Satisfied with his comments, the press – and the City – responded positively, the share price began to pick up and the problem was soon behind him.

About a year later, the company was again experiencing a slight dip in sales, combined with serious product problems. Having learnt from his previous experience, the CEO quickly opened the second envelope. The message read, 'Reorganize.' He did, and the company quickly rebounded.

After several consecutive profitable quarters, the company once again fell on difficult times. The CEO headed straight for the third envelope. The message said, 'Prepare three envelopes.'

In this chapter, we will take a look at another major group of actors in the City/business drama: the top management of large quoted companies.

You might like to envisage the dynamics that influence what happens in industry as a system of concentric circles. The nearer an actor is to the centre of this system, the more influence they will have on outcomes. Using this model, top managers and investment institutions occupy the centre spot, with other players, such as investment banks and all the others that we identified in the previous chapter, occupying more peripheral positions of influence. Right at the outside, some would argue, acting as spectators and sometimes cannon fodder, are employees, customers, suppliers and all the other supposed stakeholders.

So, let us consider the roles of top management, how these have evolved in the past few decades, and what effects any changes may have had on management behaviour. We will do this under four headings:

- A short, coarse history of British management.
- How top management tends to be structured and organized in larger British-owned companies.
- Corporate governance: what it is and what it is not.
- Who are the top managers? How are they selected and appointed? How are they paid? What sort of values and skills do they have?

FIRST, A FEW POINTS OF CLARIFICATION

We have defined top management in the same way as the financial markets and press do, namely, as being those managers who are visible to the external world. Generally, this will be the chairperson, CEO, finance director, senior non-executive director and some other non-executive directors. These are the roles that receive the attention of the markets and press. Other managers, no matter how important their roles or influence on the performance of the enterprise, tend to be cast in the role of 'Her Indoors' – doubtless worthy people, but not important players in the drama.

Sometimes analysts or investors will rate a company as having 'strong management'. By this they mean a good CEO and finance director, supported, it is vaguely assumed, by other able, but usually invisible, people. By and large, employees in general do not get much of a look-in, except as costs to be reduced.

Contrast this to the view taken by the Ministry of Defence in the early 1970s when evaluating the key staff of a large high-technology defence communications project. Senior managers leading the project were very upset when the MoD key staff list failed to mention any of them, but contained the names of middle-ranking technical managers and technicians. When challenged, Ministry staff retorted that the people they had identified were, in their view, the only ones who were absolutely crucial to the success of a very high-technology project.

We will start by conducting a brief review of the main trends shaping British management over the past 250 years. We do not make any claims to historical accuracy, but hope that some of the influences that we identify may ring a few bells with readers.

A SHORT, COARSE HISTORY OF MANAGEMENT IN BRITAIN

The Industrial Revolution began in Britain. Actually, it was preceded by the Agricultural Revolution, which, among other things drove people off the land and into nascent industrial cities, and stimulated demand for agricultural machines. By the late 18th century, Britain possessed a considerable empire, a source of raw materials and a captive market for manufactured goods.

The drivers of the Industrial Revolution were the emerging demand for machinery and manufactured goods, the growth of a breed of entrepreneurs, technological invention, and the increasing availability of finance through the nascent money markets, mainly in London. These markets, even in their early days, could be volatile. The 'South Sea Bubble' episode, caused by 18th-century speculators stampeding to put money into some very dubious opportunities, has an eerie resonance with the recent Internet madness. *Plus ça change*, when it comes to greed!

The combination of cheap raw materials, emerging markets, technological innovation, entrepreneurship and available finance was a potent source of energy for industry. A class of entrepreneurs, many of them engineers, invented machines and standardized ways of mass-producing goods and equipment in larger and larger factories, powered by water and then steam. With the enrichment of this entrepreneurial class came the exploitation of the labouring masses, increasingly driven into burgeoning industrial cities from the countryside by enclosure and the lingering death of peasant farming.

Early attempts to develop collective representation for unskilled workers were dealt with briskly, usually by expulsion to the colonies! Nevertheless, the backlash from the exploited masses did eventually come a century or so later.

Meanwhile, the English social class system began to exercise its influence. Royalty and the English aristocracy were appalled by the idea of soiling themselves with 'trade', but they were very interested in the financial fruits of industry. Industrialists, for their part, having made a financial pile, rapidly moved into another kind of pile, building country houses and castles across England, Scotland, Wales and Ireland. In this and other ways they sought to emulate the aristocracy, and, in the process of so doing, to cut themselves off from their own workforces.

Because it was not really socially acceptable for well-bred people to go into manufacturing or trade, the growing middle classes tended to ensure that their children found respectable occupations in the professions, armed services or Church.

As the founding entrepreneurial class began to pass into history, or country estates, there was no professional industrial managerial class to follow them. Professional people, as we have seen, went into 'clean' professions, such as the law or, later, accounting or banking. Thus unlike the United States and Germany, Britain did not capitalize on its early lead by building a solid professional managerial and engineering class. Instead, managers used the class system to ensure that there was a sort of quasi-militaristic gradation of status roles in industrial organizations. This internal class divide was supported by a panoply of status symbols in and outside the workplace. Doubtless, similar systems of status existed in the United States and Germany, but in those countries they were moderated by professionalism. In Britain, for quite a long period, senior management was a position in a class pecking order and much less a role defined by performance and output requirements.

There were, of course, many exceptions to this generalization. People like William Lever, the Rowntrees and the Cadburys built great companies on the principles of product innovation, creative marketing and, above all, respect for the education and well-being of their workforces. But these enlightened people were the exception, rather than the rule.

The British Empire declined before and between the two world wars, and, given the lack of a class of professional managers, so did the dominance of British industry. It fell increasingly behind the developing industrial might of the United States, Germany and, later, Japan, all less hamstrung by the class system, worship of amateurism and social distaste for 'trade and industry'.

The Second World War marked the end of empire. Britain emerged in debt to the United States, and without the benefits of a fresh start bestowed on the Germans and Japanese by the destruction of their old industrial infrastructure. After the war, organized labour got its own back on a generally lacklustre managerial class, assisted by government and the socio-economic experiments of nationalization and centralized planning of the 1950s.

In the 1960s there was a false dawn. A new class of entrepreneurial 'heroes' rose up, and, claiming to have superior ways of extracting value from badly managed industrial assets, began to make rapid inroads into some of the old heartland areas of industry. It took some years to expose the fact that these new entrepreneurs were simply exploiters of badly managed assets, with no intention of investing for a new future.

Meanwhile, bright, well-educated young chaps continued to avoid industry and choose careers in the civil service, the City and the professions or armed services. A few famous companies, such as BP, Shell and Unilever, recruited good-quality graduates and developed high-class management cadres. But in the 1950s and 1960s, even going into one of these companies felt a little like being recruited into the administrative class of the civil service.

The development of management as a profession, backed by specialist higher education in the form of the MBA, was left to the Americans. The idea of professional education in management was a late starter in the United Kingdom. Here, the nearest thing to a management education was (and to some degree, still is) training in accountancy. The British higher education elite was initially horrified at the prospect of contaminating its academic purity by close contact with industry, as readers of *Warwick University Ltd* might remember (Thompson, 1970).

The net impact of all these forces meant the spectacular decline of industry in the United Kingdom. However, despite the destruction of huge swathes of manufacturing by the Thatcher/Howe fiscal reforms of the early 1980s, with the opening up of a more flexible economy as a result of the demise of the 'old' trade unions, industry and commerce in Britain is experiencing something of a revival. The 1980s and 1990s have seen the rise of the concept of 'shareholder value' and an apparent accord reached by investors and managers that maximizing shareholder value is a good common goal.

Have we at last broken down the 'two sides of industry' schism? Is it a new, emergent class of professional managers that is leading an industrial renaissance? Have we at last broken the shackles of the class system and encouraged the very brightest and best of our qualified youth to make common cause with industry and commerce? Let us see.

TOP MANAGEMENT: STRUCTURES AND ROLES

Let us consider a 'typical' board of directors of a large company quoted on the London Stock Exchange.

First, the board will be divided between executive and non-executive directors. In these days of the Combined Code of Corporate Governance, very few listed companies have no non-executive directors. They are also seen as important by investors, who believe that the detached and essentially shareholder-oriented perspective of non-executive directors is vitally important.

Executive directors will usually consist of the Chief Executive, who is responsible for managing the company; the Finance Director; and a number of other executive directors with either functional roles, like the Human Resources Director, or executive management roles, like the Divisional Chief Executive.

The non-executive directors will usually include the Chairperson, Deputy Chairperson or senior non-executive director, and other non-executive board members. Sometimes the roles of Chairperson and Chief Executive are combined and performed by one individual. This is a very unpopular configuration with investors, who generally do not like too much power to be concentrated in the hands of one person. Many also believe that the pressures of performing the combined roles effectively have become too great.

Sometimes the board of a large company will contain, as a non-executive director, an executive director from another company 'on the way up'. Some believe that experience gained round the boardroom table is a vital part of the grooming of the up-and-coming senior executive.

The Chairperson

The role of Chairperson can vary considerably from company to company, depending on individual predilections, personality and company needs or history. Some chairpersons' roles are restricted to managing the board, and their influence will not stretch far into the company. In other cases, a more executive chairperson may be quite actively involved in the internal affairs of the organization. But, as a minimum, all chairpersons will have certain basic roles.

The first, as the name implies, is to manage the board and its meetings, and to make sure that the governance functions of the board are properly performed. In doing this, most chairpersons are closely supported by the Company Secretary.

The Chairperson will take the lead in the appointment and removal of other directors – in particular, the Chief Executive. An understanding and skilful chairperson can be of very great assistance to a chief executive who is open to having an experienced mentor.

Chairpersons are also an important point of contact for investors who have messages that they wish to pass to management. It is usual for investors who have a problem with the performance or management of a company to approach the chief executive first, and if they feel that this contact has not achieved the desired effect, to go to the chairperson.

A last port of call, if neither Chairperson nor Chief Executive is sympathetic, is the Deputy Chairperson, or senior non-executive director. If this happens, matters will have reached a pretty serious pass, and heads are likely to roll.

Executive and non-executive directors

In most companies, the Chief Executive and Finance Director will conduct normal communication and contacts with the financial markets. They will routinely present to investment institutions once or twice a year. This means quite a lot of presentations for CEOs of larger companies, some of whom estimate that they spend up to 40 per cent of their time on matters connected with the financial markets and press.

Finance directors are important supporters for chief executives in presenting to investors, as their intimate grasp of the 'numbers' lets the CEO deal with broader aspects of strategy. Finance directors also tend to deal with the extensive communication that routinely passes between City analysts, the financial press and companies.

Although all directors are in theory equal in law, it is not at all unusual for executive directors to feel that they are less equal than their non-executive 'peers'. For example, it would not be all that normal for each director to have an equal say on the appointment of a deputy chairperson or even a new non-executive director. That decision is likely to be made by the Chairperson and the other non-executives, in consultation with the Chief Executive.

In many companies there is quite a sharp divide between non-executive and executive directors. It is quite usual for executive directors to meet before board meetings to make sure that all are 'singing off the same hymn sheet' in the way they handle issues in front of the non-executives, and, in turn, for non-executive directors to meet informally with the Chairperson.

Many companies have some kind of executive committee that has formal powers delegated to it by the board. Such committees are usually chaired by the Chief Executive and contain executive directors and other senior executives with significant corporate responsibilities. It is often this kind of committee that deals with the real business of directing the company, leaving the full board with the role of responding to propositions put to it by the executive through carefully prepared presentations.

The non-executive role has undoubtedly moved on from that said by Lord Boothby in the 1960s to be 'like a permanent hot bath'. He described his duties as follows: 'No effort of any kind is called for. You go to a meeting once a month in a car supplied by the company. You look both grave and sage.'

Changed it may be, but there is still an issue about how well a non-executive can really know the organization, and in particular the financial detail. Often, therefore, non-executive directors are very dependent on the information fed to them by the executive. This means that the relationship between the Chairperson and Chief Executive is particularly important in ensuring that non-executive directors get a 'full and fair' view of what is really going on inside the company.

This problem is exacerbated by the amount of time that non-executive directors spend on the role. Many of them are very busy people with a heavy executive workload elsewhere or multiple non-executive and other responsibilities. According to the Independent Director Survey published in 2003 by IRS (Independent Remuneration Solutions) in association with 3i, on average, independent directors of companies with turnover in excess of £1 billion spend an average of 26 days each year on their duties. This breaks down as 16 formal meeting days, 7 days preparing and travelling, and 3 days on plant visits and other non-formal occasions. These estimates are, in the authors' experience, on the high side. It is not unusual for non-executive directors to miss at least one of the average of 12 board meetings. Also, the busier non-executive directors (those who are highly 'plural', having multiple appointments), or non-executive directors with full-time executive roles, may attend only for a part of some board meetings. If we add in the difficulties of interpreting what is happening through the medium of board papers and presentations, then it is not difficult to understand that by the time non-executive directors come to exercise their powers to check the executive, matters may have reached crisis point.

Non-executive 'failure to act' on deteriorating performance before it hits financial crisis has also been a repeated feature of corporate life, from Sears through Equitable Life, to Marconi and Enron in more recent times.

On 25 April 2002, Lord Young of Graffham, in his departing speech as president of the Institute of Directors, questioned whether it can ever be possible for non-executives working on a part-time basis to know enough about what is going on in an organization to blow the whistle on bad practice and decision taking. Why bother with non-executives at all? he asked. We will consider this and other points later in the book.

Meetings and committees

Continuing with our look at boards, it would be accurate to say that they function mainly through formal meetings, either of the whole board or of special-purpose sub-committees. Obviously, there will be informal contacts, particularly between Chairperson and Chief Executive, and sometimes non-executive directors may be informally consulted on particular matters. Such 'soundings' may be about business decisions or matters of procedure. In this case, they may be initiated by the Chief Executive after consultation with the Chairman, or conducted by the Company Secretary by agreement with the Chief Executive.

Regular board meetings

Formal meetings of a board will usually consist of regular board meetings. The maximum annual number is generally 12, and often in practice some boards may make do with as few as 8. Board meetings preceding the company annual general meeting and reporting of results to the City are usually 'three-line whip' affairs.

Although board meetings always have formal agendas and minutes, they can occasionally be dramatic and interesting, such as the one where a newly appointed Chief Executive sat outside while the board wrangled over a bid by one of its non-executive members to be appointed to the role. The unfortunate new appointee was notified after lunch that the job he had been offered was no longer available! However, this scale of drama is very rare.

Most board meetings tend to centre around presentations of results by the chief executive and finance directors, with further presentations on issues or proposals requiring board approval. Directors are at liberty to raise any issue under the 'any other business' item at the end of the meeting, but in practice seldom do. There is a strong tendency for many board meetings to be rather formal affairs, with little spontaneity, exploration of ideas or learning.

Boards will usually have sub-committees, two of which have an important role to play in ensuring good corporate governance.

The remuneration committee

As its name implies, this body is mandated to determine the level and make-up of the remuneration of directors, and often to agree policy guidelines for senior executive pay more generally. The committee will usually employ an independent firm of compensation consultants to give them advice rich with research data on the executive pay market and on significant trends in pay and benefits. Some people have tended to lay blame for burgeoning top executive pay at the door of such consultants, but this is rather unfair, as they usually simply report their research and comments, but do not make any decisions.

These are supposed to be made by the committee, which is normally made up of the Chairperson and all or most of the non-executive directors.

The group of people who, if they so decided, could have a dramatic impact on top executive compensation are members of FTSE 100 remuneration committees. Readers can find who they are by reference to company annual reports.

Criticisms of remuneration committees are well publicized and not invalid. Certainly, as we shall see, there is a certain 'brotherhood' of top managers with a shared perception that generosity given may mean generosity received. One of the authors was called many years ago by a remuneration consultant who was advising his company on top executive pay. 'You will have no problems in getting through a big rise for X [the CEO],' he said. On being asked why, he said that he happened to know that the chairman of the remuneration committee had himself received a very generous increase in his role of chairman/CEO of another company!

The audit committee

The second body of importance is the audit committee, formalized as one of the Cadbury recommendations (now part of the Combined Code on Corporate Governance). Generally, the purpose of this committee is to make sure that the company is managing its financial affairs in an effective, honest way and that proper standards of probity and accuracy are reflected through the financial planning, reporting and control procedures. In practice, the audit committee, comprising solely non-executive directors although advised by executives and outside experts, is heavily dependent on the Finance Director and, in particular, on the company's auditors.

The law requires auditors to give an opinion on whether the financial statements presented in the company's annual report and accounts 'give a true and fair view' of the state of the company's affairs and its profit and cash flow statements at a particular date. In addition, the auditors will report to the audit committee on any shortfalls in the standards or practice of accounting.

If the auditors feel that they have reason, they can 'qualify' a company's accounts, which means that they are not satisfied that the accounts, for whatever reason, do give an accurate picture of the state of the company. Needless to say, finance directors pay great attention if the reasons for qualification appear to be serious.

Auditors and the audit committee therefore have great potential power. So why is there so much concern at present?

In recent years, firms of auditors have been exposed to great pressure to reduce the cost of the audits of large companies. Auditing fees have declined. For many of the big accounting companies, a neat way out of this bind was to build a consulting business that hopefully could leverage on the relationships already established through the audit. In time, the growth of consulting meant that the audit took second place in generating revenues, with the inevitable conflicts of interest that, for example, seem to have characterized the relationships between Andersen and Enron.

But far more important is the increase in sophistication and complexity of the ways in which large companies use financial, tax, funding and accounting 'innovations' to improve apparent and actual performance. This all makes the work of auditors more complex and difficult, and the financial affairs of some companies are so full of 'smoke and mirrors' that it is not at all easy to judge what a 'true and fair view' might actually be. To exacerbate matters, the really smart brains tend to gravitate to the more creative end of finance and not so much to auditing.

Other meetings

Boards will have gatherings other than the strictly formal meetings. These will be different from company to company, but it is not unusual for a day or more to be spent each year at an off-site strategy discussion between management and non-executive directors. Sometimes companies will rotate board meetings around their various locations to give non-executive directors a feel for what the company actually does, but these events can be rather superficial.

Finally, non-executive directors may be invited to management conferences, where, over a few drinks, they might have some chance of getting a real sense of what is going on inside the company!

Many people are beginning to feel that large company boards, as currently constituted, are not capable of regulating the affairs of complex international enterprises, or of making a quality contribution to their direction. Given the somewhat incestuous nature of the relationships between the 'great and good' of management, and the increasing influence of investors and others in the financial markets over careers and reputations in management, we may be getting a glimpse of a closed system of mutual interest that is not necessarily there to further the interests of society at large. We will review these issues later in the book.

DIRECTORS' DUTIES AND CORPORATE GOVERNANCE

Corporate governance has received a lot of attention in recent years. The laws and rules that affect governance derive from a wide variety of sources.

The duties and restrictions that will limit what directors of companies can do or direct what they should do derive from statute law, common law and case law. The main statute is the Companies Act 1985. The directors of a company listed in the United Kingdom also have to abide by the Listing Rules published by the Financial Services Authority regulating the freedom to act without shareholder consent and communications between listed companies and their shareholders and potential investors. The Listing Rules include the Combined Code as an appendix, and listed companies are expected to comply with its provisions.

In addition, there are a huge array of guidelines issued by such institutions as the Investor Protection Committee, made up of representatives of such bodies as the Association of British Insurers and the National Association of Pension Funds.

On top of this, numerous committees, usually chaired and manned by members of the great and good of the business world, have deliberated and reported on such matters as the duties of directors, open reporting and executive compensation.

Nowadays, the annual reports of quoted companies contain compendious sections on corporate governance containing statements of company provisions in relation to codes of best practice in an array of different fields ranging from health and safety and compensation policy to accounting and financial disclosure and environmental protection. So, there is no lack of guidance for companies on standards and best practice when it comes to directing a quoted company in an honest, ethical, safe and environmentally friendly manner.

In Europe, for example, there are 39 codes governing the behaviour and actions of directors of companies. As is often the case, the United Kingdom leads the way, having adopted 11 codes and having many guidelines published by investor bodies such as the Association of British Insurers (ABI). The ABI guidelines cover such matters as executive compensation, share capital management, duties of directors and shareholders, disclosure, social responsibility, share incentive schemes, and many others.

Here is a 'potted' version of the legal position regarding the duties, responsibilities and liabilities of directors. These are not combined under one authority, but arise under the Companies Act, common law, court judgments and other statutes, rules and regulations:

- Shareholders, the owners of the company, delegate their power of authority over the company to a board of directors who share responsibility for the governance of its affairs.
- The directors may determine how they exercise the power, provided that they stay within the provisions of the Memorandum and Articles of Association of the company. These rather turgid legal documents describe such things as the name, aims and objects of the company and how directors shall be appointed and removed, how general meetings shall be conducted and how the issue, purchase and sale of shares will be handled.
- Directors additionally have a variety of legally defined responsibilities, determined by a very large number of authorities. Responsibilities to employees, for example, are defined by Health and Safety and Employment legislation.

But if we come to the crucial question, which is, 'On whose behalf are directors exercising their powers?', the answer seems pretty unequivocal. *Directors are acting on behalf of the owners of the company, and the owners are the shareholders.* Shareholders own the company, and directors must act in good faith in the best interests of the company. Where there is a conflict between a director's personal interests and those of the company, the director must always favour the company. A director owes his or her duties to the company only, but directors need to have regard to the interests of the company's stakeholders (shareholders, employees, the general public, creditors and other business partners).

In practice, this means that the bulk of directors' obligations are to further the interests of shareholders. As investment is mainly carried out on behalf of shareholders by fund management institutions, they tend to exercise massive proxy influence over directors, although this may not be the strict legal position.

When asked what obligations directors had when a company was bid for by a potential acquirer, an experienced City lawyer said, 'For practical purposes, directors would be sensible to regard their duties as being 99 per cent towards maximizing the value of the company for shareholders.'

An observer of the whole corporate governance scene is left with the strong sense that whatever the words may say, the thing that really matters in the end is whether investors are happy with management's performance.

TOP MANAGERS IN PROFILE

There have been many analyses of the leaders of large companies, in both the United States and the United Kingdom. There has been even more published on what top managers ought to be like and what they ought to do. We have drawn on many published sources in preparing these profiles and have supplemented these with our own research and impressions drawn from many meetings and discussions, plus many years' experience of working with corporate leaders.

Who are they?

The chairpersons and senior non-executive directors

Let's start with the chairpersons and senior non-executive directors of FTSE 100 companies. Poring through lists (as we did) compiled from a painstaking reading of company annual reports, a reader would take away the immediate impression that there is a limited field of choice when it comes to selecting people for these roles. While there is no stereotype, chairpersons and senior non-executives tend to be ex-chief executives of large companies, supplemented by ex-civil servants and politicians, plus some senior City luminaries. To add a little variety, there is a smattering of women who have been successful in business, civil service or politics and a number of foreign businessmen and retired US ambassadors to the Court of St James.

That's it, really. There is no sense that companies have brainstormed creative ways of introducing fresh thinking into their boards. Nor is there much evidence that there has been a huge concern to tap into research or creative thinking about different forms of organization or better ways of unleashing employee creativity.

It is hard to shake off the feeling that there is a series of lists of safe, suitable and visible candidates held by the relatively small number of executive search consultants who perform the delicate and sensitive task of fingering the great and good for roles that have, up to now, not been very demanding. This feeling is reinforced by the true story of the new chairman who, at a pre-board meeting board dinner, asked, jokingly of course, whether any of his colleagues read the *Guardian* or *Independent* newspapers. There was a long silence. 'Good,' he said. All this becomes understandable when you remember that the chairperson's and senior non-executive's main job is to keep the 'shareholders' feeling comfortable that their interests are properly represented in the board. It is very unlikely that people who have radical or unconventional views about the purposes of industry or the powers of investors would be very popular!

Statistically, of 86 chairmen (and we mean men) of FTSE 100 companies, 34 have been awarded knighthoods and 7 are members of the peerage. Pretty well all of them come from business or financial backgrounds. Nearly all of them have multiple directorships; the 86 people that we analysed possessed at least 240 company directorships between them, in addition to a number of trusteeships of artistic or charitable enterprises.

Non-executive chairmen and directors tend to have greater longevity than CEOs. Many chairmen have survived through multiple changes of executives, although evidence is emerging that investors may press the chairmen of great disasters to resign alongside the executive incumbent.

Other non-executives

For senior non-executives (or deputy chairpersons/chairmen, as they are sometimes known), the profile remains the same. In fact, in many cases the people are also the same! Quite a number of people are chairperson of one company and a non-executive director of others. We analysed the incumbents of 85 of the FTSE 100 deputy chairperson roles. This time, there were two women in their ranks!

Among this group of 85 people, 24 possess knighthoods and 9 peerages, so once again, the great and good are well represented. This group is even more 'plural' than the chairmen, holding at least 270 directorships between them.

A third group of non-executive directors have past or current City backgrounds. These may be in banking, broking, investment management, accountancy and, very occasionally, consulting. Nearly all FTSE 100 companies have at least one director who would be able to supplement the experience of the other directors by a financial markets perspective.

Nearly all boards have between 5 and 10 non-executive directors with multiple interests. An exception at this time is Morrisons, the supermarket operator, where Sir Ken Morrison presides over a board that mainly consists of people who run the business. This is emphatically not popular with investors, who like a large degree of 'independence and objectivity' in their directors.

In the United States it is likely that non-executive directors will feel increasing heat, as Lord Wakeham, holder of multiple directorships and the unfortunate chairman of the Enron audit committee, may be able to testify. However, it is maybe a little bizarre that non-executive directors, who, according to Lord Young (and certainly our observations), are unlikely to know much about the business, are the people with tenure, while chief executives move in and out through the revolving doors with increasing rapidity.

A systematic analysis of the educational or social backgrounds of non-executive directors shows some noticeable features. First, a large proportion have financial or banking backgrounds. Among those with a university education, there is heavy representation from Oxford and Cambridge, followed somewhat distantly by London and then Durham and Bristol universities. Scottish-based enterprises, mainly but not exclusively in the financial services industries, have a very heavy representation from Scottish universities, particularly Edinburgh.

Chief executive officers

The other role that features large in the eyes of the City, press and public is of course that of Chief Executive Officer. Chief executives of large quoted companies carry more pressure than any other managers and are the most transient of all senior executives, with an average tenure of just over four years in FTSE 100 companies (Harrington and Steele, 1999), although this average obviously covers quite a range of different lengths of tenure.

A study by Booz Allen & Hamilton published in June 2002 pointed to an average tenure of European chief executives as six and a half years, compared to the US figure of nine and a half years. (Considerably less in Fortune 500 companies: just on five years, in fact.) In all cases tenure is shortening, dramatically so since 1995, with the incumbent more likely to be forced out than die in office or leave of his or her own accord. The report states that, 'Today's Chief Executives are like professional athletes – young people with short, well compensated careers that continue only as long as they perform at exceptional levels.'

A large number of CEOs of FTSE 100 companies come from outside the company that they lead. In 2001, 12 CEOs had spent the whole of their working lives with one company and a further 10 had spent their careers within one industry sector.

In terms of educational and specialist backgrounds, 28 FTSE 100 CEOs had accounting or banking backgrounds, with a further 5 having actuarial qualifications. Nine were engineers, and 10 chief executives had MBAs. These days, most CEOs have higher educational attainments. Of those who went to a university, Oxford and Cambridge still supply the most top talent. (Sources: company annual reports and *Who's Who in Business and the City*).

Women are no better represented in the ranks of top 100 company CEOs. We counted one, Marjorie Sciardino of Pearson plc.

As might be expected, the average age of CEOs, at 49, is considerably lower than that of their non-executive colleagues.

What are they like? What do they value?

Of course, the question of what CEOs are like or what they value is impossible to answer objectively or completely accurately. Top executives are human beings and therefore each one is unique and different.

What we can do, however, is to identify a number of factors from comments made by people who are used to observing and assessing top managers – in particular, comments by executive search consultants and business psychologists. We can then draw attention to a number of behavioural factors that can be observed from top executives' actions in recent times, add in our own observations and experience and let you, the reader, make your mind up about the kinds of people we have described. In doing this, our main focus is on the holders of chairperson, chief executive and finance director positions, as these people are the most visible to external observers.

At this stage, it is worth mentioning that there is no such thing as a 'man [or woman] for all seasons'. A company in crisis and facing immediate ruin will require quite different leadership from one that is well founded and plans to spend the next 10 years building solid organic growth. It is our experience that most top managers who love the drama and immediate challenges of a crisis become a dangerous liability if put into situations requiring patient attention to detail and relentless consistency.

Successful top managers

Successful top managers have an unusual amount of energy and stamina. They can absorb, and frequently dish out, amounts of pressure and stress that would make many people give up, and they often enjoy it!

Most people who have reached the top job in a large quoted company did not do so by accident. At some stage they decided that they were going to get to the top and devoted sufficient energy and attention to making sure that they did. They are therefore quite capable of taking tough action against others if the situation needs it. Of course, they will all have different styles of being tough, from downright confrontational to positively subtle, but be certain, they are capable of taking care of their own interests.

Nearly every successful top manager will have well-developed political antennae. Life at the top is very political, not necessarily in the sense that we might expect from professional politicians, but because at the top of large organizations there are even more senior people to set the rules of behaviour. Because most of a top manager's colleagues are also strong-minded, when it comes to making decisions and taking action it is often less a matter of what is rational or 'right' and more a matter of 'who is for and against what'.

Top managers are also likely to be confident and able to be 'out there on their own', with a desire to challenge the status quo and keep the organization moving ahead.

Top characteristics

Research conducted by YSC Ltd, a leading London-based business psychology consultancy, indicates a number of characteristics and conditions that will determine success in CEO roles. Successful CEOs tend to have good networking and communicative skills and to use them to promote themselves and their agendas, inside and outside the organization. They can balance opportunistic deal-doing with developing the strengths of their organizations and teams. Some very successful top managers have made it up the ladder because they have had an influential patron.

Prospects of success are markedly increased if they are internally grown and know the industry and the organization that they lead. Then they will be able to understand where the levers of power are and how to use them. They will be able to understand the competitive structure and cyclical dynamics of their industries and make informed judgements about the timing of strategic actions. They will have come to the top job via a variety of functional and middle management roles and not have missed out on experience in the middle of organizations.

The evidence is that transplanting managers at the top executive level from one organization to another is quite risky, but there are ways of reducing the risks. An organization that has become run-down or degenerate will almost invariably benefit from a fresh perspective and new blood at the top. When managers are transplanted, it is often helpful to appoint a duo with complementary skills. The case of Archie Norman and Allen Leighton in Asda is often cited as one such successful example. The consultants also commented that a good grounding in business analysis, combined with open-minded curiosity, is likely to be a positive feature in 'transplants', as these characteristics reduced the risks of individuals seeking to exactly replicate experience that has worked elsewhere.

Difficulties experienced by transplants are exacerbated by not understanding how to work the organizational levers in the new company, or not really understanding the industry or the specific roots of underperformance. Newcomers, especially those in a hurry, tend to initiate changes that do not percolate down the organization, and go for 'solutions' that have quick impact but may not be sustainable.

Changing profile

So, while the profile of a top manager is rather complex and contingent, it is almost certainly valid to say that certain characteristics have become more marked in recent years. Some of these are:

- The inclination to use transactional methods to develop their companies. So, skills in cutting deals and making bold 'moves' have become more

commonplace and more valued. There also seems to be a greater trend towards serial transactions, with new deals often following well before previous ones have been assimilated.
- The tendency to act quickly and decisively when problems occur or opportunities arise. For example, the speed of announcing and implementing lay-offs has increased markedly over the past few years.
- More emotional detachment from the organizations that they lead. It was noticeable that many of those we interviewed described CEOs they knew in such terms as 'charming but cool underneath' or 'apparently friendly but ruthlessly determined' or 'affable, but impossible to get close to'.

An experienced business psychologist, who specializes in assessing top managers, summarized contemporary trends succinctly. He commented that management was becoming more like politics in the senses that timescales were compressing, that image was becoming as important as substance and that many top management careers were likely to end with 'failure', increasing the pressure to cash in on the good times quickly.

At the end of 2001, tenure in top management roles was still decreasing, supporting a tendency on the part of managers to try to make a quick impact through deals and transactions. There was also some evidence, he said, of a convergence between the personal characteristics of people in the financial markets and those in management, especially in roles such as finance director. Thus it is possible that top managers are becoming more individualistic and self-seeking, with a decreasing concern for the long-term well-being of a wider community.

There is some evidence that more young people from the 'elite' universities are interested in entering management. The majority of those who do are coming in after qualifying as accountants or obtaining an MBA. There is a marked tendency still for such people to try to avoid the grind of working up through the organization by taking a functional fast track and entering general management via such roles as finance or strategy director. However, the vast majority of graduates from business schools such as Insead and London Business School still tend to go directly into jobs in the financial markets or consultancy, where it is possible to attain high earnings at an early age.

These analyses are supported by several very experienced top managers. One said, 'There is no longer support for people who want to build a business over the long term', while another thought that, 'There are "growers" and there are buyers and sellers. The "growers" don't get a look in any more.' A more cynical ex-colleague said that many contemporary top executives are driven by 'ego, power, career and money'. It is to the last of these topics that we move next.

How and what are managers paid?

> It is vital for this group to employ people of the high calibre essential to the successful leadership and efficient management of a global business at the leading edge of the telecommunications industry. The scale and complexity of the group continues to grow, with operations in 29 countries in five continents.
>
> The executive talent needed to maximise returns for shareholders in this industry is very scarce and the future success of the group will depend upon its ability to provide remuneration packages which are competitive in actual and

> prospective value when measured against the best in the industry. (Vodafone Annual Report 2001 – the year for which Vodafone reported a £13.5 billion loss)

The tone and content of these statements are very familiar. They represent some of the drivers of the explosion in top executive remuneration in the United Kingdom and the United States in the past 20 years or so. For British managers, the driving forces for pay have often been comparisons with the United States.

The main arguments behind emulating US practice have been those so eloquently expressed in the Vodafone report. These arguments are: 'We are highly international, we need the best people, the market is very competitive, we are totally committed to creating shareholder value, we need to pay in line with the best in the industry.' As the best managers have often been assumed by Brits to be American (they must be, look how much they are paid!), the result has been for large British quoted enterprises to follow US habits and practices.

This trend first became apparent in the 1970s, as British companies began to make more acquisitions in the United States and top UK managers found that US divisional managers were earning more than they were. Pressures were increased when Americans began to be imported to lead British companies with their HQs in the United Kingdom. For ambitious British top managers, it was bad enough if they were paid more 'over there', but for them to be paid so much more and be 'over here' was difficult to stomach!

A trailblazer, both in terms of coming 'over here' and in importing US-style remuneration to the United Kingdom, was Richard (now Sir Richard) Giordano, who was appointed Chief Executive of BOC following the takeover of Airco, a US gases company, by BOC. Mr Giordano was appointed CEO of this prominent British company, moved to London and became one of the first chief executives in Britain to be paid over £1 million. Since then, he has sporadically appeared in the press, sometimes connected with a pay controversy, as in the case of the increase granted to Cedric Brown, CEO of British Gas under Mr Giordano's chairmanship.

Naturally, British top managers, more than their European colleagues, who were less exposed to US habits, did not simply accept the US–UK differentials lying down. It was probably in the 1970s that the profession of compensation and benefits management, long since established in the United States, began to emerge, and with it the increasing use of bonus plans and the newly available grant of share options. Also of that era was the interestingly shadowy 'Chairman's Group', a sort of pay club for the great and good, which enabled the chairpersons of selected large companies to meet and discreetly compare detailed notes on each other's compensation arrangements. To the authors' knowledge, this group was still in being in the mid-1990s.

Today it is certainly the case that most chairpersons and CEOs will know about the large consultancies such as Watson Wyatt, Towers Perrin, Mercer and Monks Partnership, all of which will support HR directors and compensation committees with copious data and tailored comparisons of their pay arrangements.

Two other noticeable influences have put strong upward pressure on pay. The first is the emergence of the 'star' system. As sections of the general public have an insatiable need to create icons and celebrities, so do the financial markets and the press. So, as we have seen, BP becomes 'Lord Browne' or Vodafone becomes 'Chris Gent' and Bob Wilkins reshapes EMI's artist rosters. For the duration of their stardom, such top managers can, and do, command very high remuneration, without much complaint from the investment community. As a result of the reduction of large and complex organizations to a few high-profile individuals, the perceived need for such individuals has burgeoned, and with it their pay.

A second pressure is more subtle. The argument behind it is based on the premise that a company wishes to be an above-average performer, and 'upper-quartile performance deserves upper-quartile pay'. It is an easy step from there to a position of being compelled to pay upper-quartile remuneration to attract and retain the talent that will deliver (at some time in the future) the upper-quartile performance. In no time at all, the whole world is seeking to pay at the upper-quartile level, with the effect of ratcheting top executive compensation ever upwards.

Remuneration committees making judgements on the pay of their peers have manifestly not been able or willing to put a brake on the soaring rewards of top managers. Shareholders, in the form of investment institutions and their associations, such as the Association of British Insurers, have from time to time intervened when a particularly noticeable event has occurred. An example of such an event was the decision to award Sir Christopher Gent, the CEO of Vodafone, a £10 million success bonus for achieving the takeover of Mannesmann. It has to be repeated, not for creating shareholder value over a respectable period of time as a result of the successful assimilation of Mannesmann, but simply for making the acquisition. Vodafone was forced by investors to convert half the bonus to shares and delay payment contingent upon the achievement of some (unpublished) targets.

More recently, shareholders have objected strongly to proposals by GlaxoSmithKline for a package for its chief executive, Jean-Pierre Garnier, which included a large amount of 'severance benefits' were he to leave the company, no matter what the reason. In April 2003, 49 per cent of shareholders rejected or abstained on a resolution over directors' pay at BAE Systems, and a month later Royal & SunAlliance's proposals for pay for its new management attracted a 35 per cent revolt.

Investors have, however, been relatively reluctant to act, and they have often not supported small shareholders when they have tried to exercise restraint. We are reminded of the comment made by a City figure, that good corporate governance will not improve this quarter's investment returns. Some might speculate that the earnings enjoyed in good times by senior City operators considerably exceed even those of most top managers and that this also might serve to reduce any sense of outrage at executive excesses!

Pay structure

So, how are senior managers rewarded? Many years ago, senior managers received a salary, were members of a pension scheme that would pay two-thirds of salary on retirement and had a company car and driver provided. Bonuses were rare, salary increments were given according to performance and from time to time a general cost-of-living allowance was awarded. Aspiring top managers, lunching in their middle-ranking dining rooms, would amuse themselves speculating on whether it was possible to attain a salary of £2,000 per year before the age of 30!

If we advance from those sepia-coloured days to the present, we find that things have changed out of all recognition. The information that follows is from a survey conducted by executive compensation specialists Monks Partnership (2001). Their data sources were the annual reports of FTSE 100 companies. What they found was as follows:

- The increase in annual cash earnings, which is defined as annual basic pay plus annual bonus, for 2001 compared with 2000 was over 16 per cent for CEOs of industrial and service companies and over 18 per cent for financial and property companies.
- The average annual increase enjoyed by the same group of CEOs for the previous eight years was 8.75 per cent for industrial and service companies, and 13.25 per cent for financial and property companies. This means that the CEOs of industrial and service companies received increases over 10 years of 86 per cent and those of financial and property companies (including investment institutions) 106 per cent.

  These data are backed by later research by the shareholder activist body PIRC. PIRC's research indicates that the cumulative salaries for all directors of FTSE companies increased by 92 per cent to £579,000 between 1993 and 2002. PIRC commented, 'Companies are prone to act in a herd-like way on pay, justifying changes [increases] in salary, bonus or incentives as necessary to compete for talent. This is another way of saying that they need to keep up with the "plc Joneses".'

  The wider workforce received much less than half this level of increases.
- In addition to base annual pay and annual bonus, 35 per cent of companies provided their CEOs with a long-term bonus scheme and also with share options. Then, a further 33 per cent of companies allowed their top executives to defer the payment of their annual bonus, and, if they volunteered to do this, would usually 'match' – that is, double – the bonus at the end of the deferral period. This is one means of trying to hang on to the 'best of the best'.
- The biggest bonanza in the 1990s has come in the form of share options. The topic of share option and other share-related plans is rather complex, but the basic dynamics are simple. A company grants an individual 'options' to purchase shares at a date in the future at a price fixed today. The delay period before the individual can 'exercise' – that is, buy the shares – is often three years. At the end of the option period, individuals may buy the shares. If the price at the end of the period is higher than at the beginning, they will benefit to the value of the difference. Individuals may simply buy the shares and simultaneously dispose of them, realizing the profit and avoiding any risks involved in holding the shares.
- A neat twist on share options is the fact that they will normally 'vest' upon a change of control of the company. This means that individuals will be able to have the difference between the share price of their options at the time of grant and at the time the company is acquired. As acquirers always have to pay a premium, this means that some individuals can enjoy a bonanza, often running into millions of pounds, if their company is sold. Some might argue that there is temptation to become transactional lurking behind this provision!
- In addition to the remuneration arrangements mentioned above, top managers have very generous pension plans. Government restrictions put in place in the late 1980s placed a cap on the earnings that qualified for pension. In the late 1990s this stood at about £85,000. Most companies

simply ignored this cap, and the tax penalties incurred, and simply topped up the pension provisions of senior managers to the level of their actual pay. Further restrictions are to be introduced shortly.

While companies are abandoning final salary-based pension plans for employees at large, claiming that they can no longer afford them, it will be interesting to see what happens to the provisions for top managers.

- In addition to cash, shares and pension-related benefits, many top managers enjoy a range of less visible, but nevertheless useful, perks. Most top managers will have the use of a company car and driver. Many will have quite generous expenses, and a significant number of companies will have accommodation available to top managers – for business use but, in practice, for private use as well. One company known to both the authors kept apartments in London and New York, which were available to top managers, with precedence being granted to the CEO. Fewer UK companies than US ones provide exotic benefits such as the use of private jets, but a significant minority do.

To conclude, it is worth placing the topic of pay in some perspective. Top managers hold extremely powerful and influential roles. In times of difficulty, crisis or tremendous opportunity, powerful leaders can make a huge difference and create enormous value. These are the times when leaders need to stand above their organizations and initiate changes that the wider organization could not have envisaged.

But most of the time, life is not like that. When the strategy is to build a business, or grow by organic means, leaders need their organizations at least as much as the organizations need their leaders. So, to behave as though there is a need for exceptional individual vision, crisis leadership or single-handed heroics from the top all the time is just plain silly, or self-serving. Most of the time, as we shall see later in the book, such behaviours from the top will create damage and destroy value.

IN A WORLD OF THEIR OWN?

Here is a last thought on the topic of remuneration. What do you, the reader, believe the differential should be between the pay of top managers and the average pay of employees in their organizations?

Well, in 2001 their pay – that is, all cash payments received in the year, ignoring perks, benefits and shares – was 68 times the average for all employees, and still increasing. The range among the FTSE 100 companies that we analysed was from 17 times to 110 times. The median annual pay (excluding any share-related rewards, long-term bonus plans, pension contributions or other benefits) of CEOs and executive chairpersons in 2001 was £1,037,000. The differences between sectors were marked, with CEOs of utility companies earning a median sum of £610,000, and those of banks, insurance and other financial services companies (the guardians of the shareholders' interests) earning a median of £1,439,000.

At the conclusion of our research, it was hard to avoid the feeling that top managers increasingly live in a world that is more and more cut off from their own organizations and from the world of the average citizen or consumer. Let us explain this startling notion.

To start with non-executive directors. The majority of these people are very busy, with multiple responsibilities, so their contact with the organizations of which they are directors is mainly by attending board meetings, reading board papers and listening to presentations from the executive. Typically, non-executives will arrive and leave such meetings by chauffeur-driven car, and have no real chance to get to know very many staff. Non-executive directors are almost totally dependent on synthesized financial information prepared by the executive. Their ability to qualitatively check the validity of such information is limited by time and access to the organization. In this regard, many non-executive directors are in a very similar position to investors. Things may not be much different for executive directors, and in particular CEOs.

A trusted subordinate once said to his boss, who had been making trenchant statements about what the consumers of the diverse group's products wanted: 'What do you know about consumers? Each morning, at about 7.30 am, your large car, with tinted windows, driven by your chauffeur arrives at your large house, which is separated from the equally large houses of your rich neighbours by several acres of land. For the next hour or so, you sit comfortably in the back of the car and read the newspapers, look at some work memos or make telephone calls, until your car arrives at the office. Then the chauffeur leaps out, opens the door and you sweep into the lobby of the office, greeting the receptionist as you walk to the lift. (One of your predecessors used always to travel by himself in the lift, because Security kept it clear for him.) You go up in the lift until you reach the 12th floor, and then you get out and walk past your two personal assistants, who are there to make sure that you are not bothered by others unless you choose to be, and sit behind your large desk in your huge office. There you receive people on your terms, dictating the agendas of your many meetings, often eating a sandwich at lunchtime by yourself.

'In the corner of your office is a large screen, which gives you access to full data on the financial markets, and, in particular, to the company's share price. If you really want it to, the executive data system will give you almost instant access to the up-to-date financial results of all the company's major businesses at the touch of a button.

'When you travel, itineraries will be arranged with scrupulous efficiency by your senior personal assistant, with a schedule arranged according to your wishes. You will be driven to the airport by your chauffeur and picked up and taken everywhere at the far end by company employees. In between, you will have travelled first class on the aircraft, in a special seat that enables you to avoid contact with others if that is what you want. The company maintains rather splendid apartments in at least two capital cities, which you and members of your family use as a matter of course.

'When you go on vacation, your holiday arrangements will most likely have been made by your personal assistant and you will stay in places generally frequented by people like you.

'At Christmas, your personal assistant will give you a series of greeting cards with lists of recipients. All you have to do is to scribble your name, and put a personal message in the ones that she has put aside specially.

'Because you are very powerful and can easily intimidate people more junior than you, there is a tendency on the part of many people to tell you what they think you want to hear.

'The only times you meet people on their terms is when you present to investors, press and analysts and occasionally get subjected to questions by particularly important journalists. Oh, I was forgetting board meetings, when the non-executives can be a little difficult. But that is not very often.

'Finally, to cap it all, you are paid at a level that exceeds that of your senior PA by a factor of 85.

'And', said the brave subordinate, 'you have the gall to speak to me of consumers [or employees, for that matter]!'

There may be an element of exaggeration to what the subordinate claimed, but not much.

Remember too, many CEOs come from outside the companies that they lead. Their average length of tenure is four years. It is possible to see that they can be as cut off from their own organizations as the CEO in the above example was from his consumers. Add to this the fact that the real judgements on their performance and skills come from outside the company, from the non-executive directors, investors and the press, and it does not take too much imagination to see that not only can CEOs become cut off, they can very easily align themselves psychologically with the financial markets rather than their enterprises.

POSTSCRIPT

We nearly forgot to mention what it is that turns top managers on and off, what their careers, wealth and tenure are based upon. It is something that some CEOs will go to amazing lengths for. It is watched by millions and by a small number of CEOs with rapt attention. It is seen as so important that some CEOs, when out of their offices, are said by their secretaries to call in to check on it at least three times a day. What is this all-important factor?

It is the level of the company's share price. The share price, the factor that drives so much management behaviour and so many actions, is in turn driven by a number of underlying forces. It is investors acting in the stock market that determine what happens to a company's share price. They will be interested in the future prospects of the company, essentially as measured by their estimations of its future cash flows. Many other factors, such as their views on industry sectors and such things as the competence and 'market-friendliness' of the CEO, will also determine whether investors buy, sell or hold their shares in the company.

Therefore, the mechanism of the share price is the key link between the financial markets and top management. In the next chapter we will examine this and the many other linkages that connect management and markets.

4

Dancing partners: the relationships between managers and markets

Back in the old days, when every town of any note had a ballroom, which in those more decorous times fulfilled the functions of a night club and singles' bar, Saturday nights would witness the scene of hundreds, maybe thousands, of couples on the dance floor, performing the elaborate steps of the waltz, foxtrot, quickstep or, more exotically, the tango.

A prominent investment banker, a product of those times, used to liken the relationships between managers and the financial markets to a large ballroom. 'Everybody has a pretty shrewd idea of why they are there and what they would like out of it,' he would say, 'and everybody knows what to do to the music, despite the fact that there are no written rules. Therefore you can have a whole ballroom floor with thousands of people doing the same thing because all of them know what to do. If you don't know, you will pretty soon have to get off the dance floor, without consummating your desires!'

This metaphor appealed to us, because it is a good way of illustrating how the relationships between the various players and the financial markets work. Everybody knows what they want, everybody has a shrewd idea of what the other dancers want, and although there are rules governing the conduct of the dance, much of the action and interaction is influenced by unwritten norms and conventions.

We fell so strongly for the metaphor that we began to stretch it a little. Back in the 1950s, young men would feel themselves obliged to go to dancing classes, usually run by ladies of indeterminate age with dyed hair, always called 'Mrs' something, although their marital status could frequently be open to doubt. There, blushing adolescent clods with two left feet were taught the basics of the quickstep and waltz, the minimum entry qualification for joining the mating game.

In the same way, there are guides and instructors for managers who wish to have discreet lessons in how to comport themselves on the great dance floor of the financial markets. Stockbrokers are always ready and willing to help in this regard. One of our respondents outlined a quite extensive range of advice that he would from time to time offer to clients, including how to handle awkward, rude or unreasonable questions from fund managers. Financial PR consultants offer similar services: it was recently reported that Nigel Whittaker, who was once responsible for public affairs with Kingfisher plc, has set up a consultancy with the explicit purpose of grooming CEOs and others to look good and present themselves professionally.

As our investigations for this book progressed, we were regaled with much fact and opinion about the motives and actions of the various parties involved in the City and in management. What emerged was a very complex system comprising many actors, with different but frequently intertwined interests. We were also treated to a rich diet of beliefs and perceptions about the habits and motives of the many actors and what each could do to or for the others.

Let us start with a description of the interests of each of the salient 'dancers' on the floor, and how they often intertwine with those of others. We will begin with top managers. The two roles to focus on are those of CEO and Finance Director, as these are assumed by the City to be the most important.

DANCERS ON THE FLOOR

Managers

We have known a great many CEOs and finance directors, and while it is not possible to stereotype them, we can generalize a little about their interests from our interviews and from personal observation. Despite all their differences, top managers generally seek the following:

- A good reputation. Public reputations for CEOs and finance directors are mainly moulded by the financial markets and press. Many managers go to considerable lengths and use considerable resources to build their images. Some CEOs will also aspire to an honour, and there are known (to insiders) patterns of behaviour that will help this cause. Finance directors will be aware that building a good reputation with the markets will increase their chances of attaining a CEO position.
- Accumulation of wealth. Despite the publicity, not all top managers are greedy individuals. A fascination with reward is more a systemic infection that affects top managers as a class. For many, reward has an important value not only in its own right, but also as an index of comparative prestige and approbation. Thus the upward spiralling of top manager pay has been boosted by everybody striving to keep up with his or her peers.

  The greatest explosion in managerial rewards of recent years has come from tying rewards to performance and actions that will please the markets. Thus the key to very high rewards is a high share price, and much thought and effort go into managing expectations to achieve this.
- A successful career. This aspiration has tended to degenerate of late to 'being around for long enough to accumulate some wealth', as top management becomes increasingly like politics.

- Doing a good job. We have not met many top managers who were not strongly motivated to do their best. The trouble is, that the ultimate judge and jury these days are the investors, press, analysts and other external observers, so no matter how well regarded a manager may be by customers or staff, he or she knows that this regard will count for little unless the press and markets are satisfied.

Investment institutions or fund managers

Tony Golding, in *The City* (2001), says, 'The institutional investor's Valhalla is a world where every stock in the portfolio outperforms by, say, 10 per cent every quarter ad infinitum.' As this is an impossible goal, investors tend to seek a range of qualities from their portfolio that they assume will enable them to outperform whatever norm or index that they are measured against. Readers will remember that fund managers who cannot claim out-performance will pretty soon find themselves losing funds under management, or getting fired by pension fund trustees.

All this pressure is then transferred to the companies in an institutional investor's portfolio. Investors will seek to buy cheap and sell dear, thus they are always on the lookout for undervalued shares. Once they hold shares, they will look for very high performance from their holdings. Ideally this means that companies outperform the market, or act in ways that will increase their share price. Frequently, this means creating a degree of excitement through activism of one sort or another. And if a share is in the doldrums, fund managers will be very pleased if they can realize a premium through the sale or acquisition of the company concerned.

Fund managers, analysts and the press alike tend to identify companies with their leaders, thus further increasing the pressures on those executives.

Brokers

Brokers occupy an important position in the web of interactions between managers and markets. Although their basic role is to buy and sell shares, they can also act as guide, adviser and 'go-between' for managers and investors. The success of brokers is, in the end, measured by the volumes of shares that they buy and sell on behalf of clients, but this business will be attracted by the reputation of the broker's senior staff. As we saw in Chapter 2, successful brokers in London will be appointed as 'house brokers' to companies and will tend to capture all transactions related to those clients.

If a chairperson or CEO is contemplating a major move – for example, an acquisition, disposal or change of management – he or she will often wish to take soundings to gauge likely investor reaction. This can be done through their house brokers, or with the advice of the broker, directly to chosen investors.

On the other hand, investors may wish to send messages to companies about what they would like them to do. Such wishes may represent the investment manager's views about the composition of the company's business portfolio, or ideas about creating additional value by de-mergers or disposal programmes.

As well as sending signals directly and via their shareholdings, investors can, and do, send messages via brokers. Such messages can be amplified by quietly briefing the press via analysts or directly. If the message is one that may create good transactional business, the chorus of signals about the need to act can become quite deafening!

Broking companies employ market-makers, who used to be called 'jobbers', and specialist salespeople who sell shares, predominantly to investment institutions. Market-makers will buy, hold and sell shares on behalf of their broking house, thus taking the risk of being caught 'long' or 'short' holding shares that move in price. They can also cause movements in the share prices of particular companies if they buy or sell in sufficient volumes.

Salespeople are responsible for selling shares to institutions. They are constantly in touch with investors, trying to create interest in shares. They mainly do this by producing and pushing 'ideas' – some piece of information or angle that will move shares. These ideas may originate from the salespeople themselves, from analysts or, significantly, from investment bankers who are trying to set up deal opportunities. Salespeople and market-makers are thus one of the prime wellsprings of the vast amount of market rumour and speculation that swirls around managers and their companies and can create short-term share price instability. As can be seen, most of this is not rooted in anything more substantial than the need to sell shares.

One of our management respondents told us that if an investment institution agreed to buy a particular share if it was 10 per cent cheaper, then the salespeople would work hard to create ideas or rumours that would shift perceptions of the company's performance down.

Analysts

Stock market, or securities, analysts are generally employed by brokers, although there are still some independent companies. Analysts, as their name implies, study companies, assess their strengths and weaknesses, and issue advice to potential investors on their likely prospects. Broking houses have always realized that a reputation for good analysis would attract broking clients, especially for new share issues. As the functions of investment banking, broking and investing became grouped under the same umbrella in vast integrated banks, it became apparent that a good reputation for analysis would also attract clients for the vastly lucrative investment banking advice.

Thus the profile and rewards of analysts began to rise and rise. Rather than simply being rewarded for the quality of their analysis, they began to be awarded bonuses on the deal flow for broking and banking. This incestuous and damaging practice is now under attack, but analysts still depend on their reputations for their income. Reputation means perception: expertise in an industry sector, being at the centre of things, being in the know and getting it right in their analysis of companies' actions and performance.

Analysts are a vital link in the two-way flow of information and opinion that flows between companies and the markets. Reports that Jack Grubman, the telecommunications analyst with Salomon Smith Barney, attended board meetings of WorldCom to provide 'market colour' to mergers and acquisitions discussions indicate how seriously analysts' opinions are taken.

They are also a key link between professionals in the financial markets and the press. They both have a similar interest in finding angles and stories about people and companies. Journalists will use analysts to give them advice, stories and views about companies, as well as quotes about the views of investors.

As analysts are also closely in touch with fund managers, they can be a very communicative line between institutions and the press. Woe betide the unfortunate executive who has incurred the displeasure of investors and the analysts, for he or she will be briefed against without mercy!

Investment bankers

Investment banks tend to have a relatively low public profile. But seen from inside the financial markets, bankers occupy a central position.

The reason for this is simple: they generate huge revenues for the integrated companies that employ them – more, for example, than the brokerage arm. In this sense, bankers will tend to drive the priorities of the big international investment banks.

It should be no secret by now that investment bankers feed off deals and corporate transactions. These will include advising companies on acquisitions, bid defences, selling sizeable assets, de-mergers and large transactions involving financing. Bankers will also advise management on financial strategy and on the best ways of financing growth. But fundamentally, bankers are there for the centrepiece of the industrial drama, the large deal. We have already seen the bankers' and other advisers' fees for a relatively small transaction, the defence of Redland against the cash bid by Lafarge.

Readers do not have to use too much imagination to see that the fees earned on really big deals can be very substantial indeed. This being the case, it should not be surprising that investment bankers will go to considerable lengths to encourage deals. They have a ready audience in British top managers, who are among the world leaders when it comes to taking the transactional route to corporate development.

Bankers, driven by their hunger for fees, are extremely active in ensuring that managers do not miss any opportunities. To do this, they will produce 'ideas' for creative and attractive deals. These ideas will be 'sold' to anybody who might influence the initiation of deals, but investment institutions, managers and the press are certainly three typical groups of recipients.

There cannot be a single company that has not been the subject of a banker's 'idea' at some time or other. These ideas may cover opportunities for synergistic mergers, great opportunities for creating value by de-mergers, 'split-offs', 'carve-outs', 'spin-offs', buy-outs or buy-ins. Any transaction that may create an interesting angle on how value may be created will be considered and sold with great enthusiasm, whether the subject is interested or not.

The financial press

We cannot complete a section on the sinews of communication and interaction that bind managers and markets without touching on the financial press. Nearly all newspapers have a financial section, but it is the broadsheets that carry the most weight with managers. In fact, many managers will be avid scanners of a wide variety of the media, certainly including the *Financial Times* and the *Investors Chronicle*. For a modest fee, the company's financial PR adviser will scan all the media and provide a complete press cuttings service – international if required. Backing the press is a variety of other media, of which radio and TV are probably the most important.

These days, top managers will almost invariably be trained in how to project themselves to the media, and financial PR and other communications companies provide in-depth coaching, with copious feedback and advice on how they 'come across'.

The quality of business journalism, as we have seen, varies vastly. Senior financial journalists can be extremely weighty and influential figures, often with perspectives and opinions that seem to indicate a greater degree of balance and maturity than is sometimes seen from the markets. Most managers feel that it is important to stay on side with broadsheet City editors and some journalists. Behind the senior quality figures lies a large 'tail' of financial hacks and headline writers, many of whom echo what is fed to them by analysts and seem to have little judgement, memory or sense of process.

But be they good or bad at their work, all journalists will be on the lookout for a story or an unusual angle on events affecting managers and companies. Having a copious supply of insider sources and contacts is crucial to a top financial journalist, who will go to considerable lengths to cultivate them. Returning favours from contacts will include acting as a conduit for 'leaks' and angled stories from the financial markets. Sometimes, when the markets are working full-time to press managers to do something, the noise in the media can become deafening. One manager described it as akin to being attacked by a 'poisonous swarm' of noisy insects.

Smart managers will therefore use the press for their own purposes, but also be extremely wary about which journalists they talk to and not view all publicity as good publicity. The backing of a good internal public affairs manager and / or a financial PR adviser is therefore seen as extremely important in these image-conscious times.

Other 'dancers'

There are many other 'dancers', and we have not mentioned such important actors as regulators, the Takeover Panel, the Bank of England and the Treasury, as the scope of this book is focused on the relationships between managers and markets. We will, however, pick out three other influences that have distinctive interests and some clout. They are:

- *Search consultants* have an interest in the maintenance of a significant turnover of top managers and in external, rather than internal, appointments to top jobs. Thus 'headhunters', as they are known, will willingly subscribe to the story that managers will become stale if they stay in post too long and that external appointees are often better than internal ones, as they will be fresher and more objective. Search consultants, by virtue of their work, are ardent networkers and can carry 'the word' about managers' strengths and weaknesses between companies and the markets.
- *Compensation consultants* are sometimes blamed for causing the explosion in top managers' compensation and benefits. They have certainly been very creative in helping companies to design elaborate and creative compensation and share plans. Furthermore, they are mines of information about what the 'market' (meaning other companies) is doing, thus enhancing the pressures to ratchet compensation up to the levels of the 'leaders', who, it is assumed, may steal the cream of available talent. But they have also been

used by compensation committees as authorities to justify their actions. Witness the following, taken from the annual report for 2000 of a FTSE 100 company, Powergen.

It states in the report that it is the policy of the board, 'supported by its independent consultants', to keep the compensation package of executive directors and senior executives under constant review. The aims of doing this were to ensure competitiveness and to align the interests of executives with those of shareholders. Following the most recent review, it was demonstrated that 'certain non-cash benefits were out of line with best practice'. The compensation committee decided therefore to make an enhanced grant of share options to several directors – in some cases, more than doubling them. Not long after this, the company was bid for, with the effect of vesting the options at the completion of the deal.

- *Management consultants* are not directly involved in the dance, but some have become cheerleaders for the kinds of strategies that will be approved of by the markets. In the past, consultants were avid promoters of core process re-engineering, overhead value analysis, outsourcing and other 'active' measures that were strongly applauded by the markets as contributing to value creation. Latterly, many consultants have climbed on to the M&A bandwagon. So, while warning, rightly, of the risks of destroying shareholder value, they offer a remedy, which is to use their services to avoid the many pitfalls that follow an acquisition or merger. This is music to investment bankers' ears, and, we assume, lucrative for the consultants!

So, these are some of the 'dancers' on the great ballroom floor. We hope that we have been able to show that, while each has separate interests, they are, to a very great extent, mutually interdependent. The financial markets need industry to provide investment opportunities and for their vast fee income. Managers of large quoted companies are, in turn, dependent on the markets for capital and, to a large extent, for their careers, reputations and wealth. As a result of this mutual interdependence and the stakes that all play for, it should be evident that many of the 'dancers' watch each other like hawks, so that even their smallest and most nuanced acts are noted and analysed for significance.

FOUR BELIEFS AND PERCEPTIONS ABOUT MANAGERS AND MARKETS

As we amassed information and opinions through our investigations for this book, we unearthed a fund of beliefs, perceptions and stories about managers and markets. Some of the strongest perceptions were held by managers about the markets and began to fall into clusters and form patterns. We believe that several of these patterns of perception are worth exploring, because they are strong enough to drive the actions and reactions of those who hold them. So, here are some of the most significant of these beliefs that can have the effect of shaping management behaviour.

1. The markets are powerful, very fickle and will be quick to punish. One of our respondents told the following story, which he said was from his personal experience. He was the CEO of a large company and also the deputy chairman of another company. One morning, he received an urgent telephone call from a prominent fund manager 'star' whom we will call X.

X sounded very brisk. 'I would like to see you urgently. Is five o'clock today OK?' Our friend made rather vague noises, signifying acquiescence. 'Good,' said X, 'I'll see you at five.'

At the appointed hour, in walked X, accompanied by two junior colleagues. Without any preliminaries, X expressed sorrow and concern about the state of health of the CEO of the company of which our respondent was deputy chairman. 'His ill health is obviously affecting his performance, I think he has completely lost the plot,' X observed.

There followed a very long silence, and then, knowing that he could not avoid a response, our friend enquired what X wanted done. An even longer silence ensued. In the end, in desperation, he said, 'I suppose that you want us to have him resign?'

After another significant silence, X rose, expressed satisfaction at a successful meeting and left. A month later, the CEO resigned.

A second story comes from a senior search consultant. He told us that he conducted a difficult assignment to find a finance director for a large FTSE 100 company. At the end of an exhaustive search process, the field of candidates was narrowed down to one person, who was interviewed by most of his potential executive colleagues, several non-executive directors and the chairman. All felt very positive and the search consultant began to feel that his quest had been successful.

The last hurdle was the board appointments committee and an urgent meeting was fixed, to which the search consultant was invited. The chairman opened the meeting by summarizing the background and credentials of the candidate and reporting that all who had met him felt that he was an excellent fit, both for the job requirements and with his potential colleagues. A rustling of acquiescence among the directors was broken by one non-executive director who had not met the candidate, a senior investment banker.

The senior banking figure cleared his throat and said he felt duty bound to say that his soundings among contacts in the markets had unearthed some rather negative feelings – not universally, but one or two quite significant people seemed to have reservations... The search consultant said that his prime candidate moved from a strong number one position to the bottom of the list in just a few seconds!

Both these stories were told to us as personal experience and 'gospel' by the respondents and it should be evident that it does not take too many such tales of this kind to convince managers that it is best to stay on the right side of the markets. That impression was strengthened when one of the authors asked two of his board colleagues why they (and the non-executive directors) had agreed to what seemed like obscene advisers' fees for the Redland bid defence. His close colleagues said that they had also wanted to negotiate harder, but had received no support from the non-executives. 'Remember also', said the colleague, 'that I will want to get another job after this is all over.'

Here are some mechanisms by which the markets can communicate views, pleasure or displeasure to or about managers:

- Rising or falling share price.
- Briefings and rumours through the press, PR departments and consultants.
- Direct communications from investment institutions to directors.

- Sending the message through the house broker.
- Analysts' reports, which can often contain very personal comments about individuals.
- 'Ideas' and proposals for deals, M&A opportunities or restructuring from investment bankers. There is also great conviction that bankers will use many media, including the press and brokers' salespeople, to put pressure on managements to be active.
- Recommendations, references and positive or negative responses to 'soundings' about candidates for top jobs.

2. *Big Brother is watching you – constantly and minutely.* This set of beliefs is held most strongly by the top managers of the largest 100 companies. It is apparent that the intensity of the scrutiny from the markets decreases the further a company is below the FTSE 100, as institutions do not have the resources to thoroughly analyse companies below the FTSE 250. Whether being 'thoroughly analysed' is a blessing or a curse will, we hope, emerge as the book unfolds. (One certain fact is that top manager tenure increases the smaller a company becomes, to the point that the tenure of bosses of the top 100 non-quoted companies is more than double that of companies in the FTSE 100.)

One stockbroker respondent told us that the finance director of a large company was surprised to see reports in the press and to receive calls from analysts demanding to hear the truth about the impending disaster in the company's South-East Asian operations. He made non-committal noises to the analysts, who were preparing downgrading messages, and set about finding out what it was all about. Eventually he found that a report had appeared in a Malaysian regional newspaper, quoting an area manager as saying that the market for the company's products was weakening! This article had been picked up by the financial markets' information machine, had fuelled suspicions already held in some City quarters and was given high prominence.

Managers know that they are being scrutinized – how could they miss the fact?

- The CEO and finance director will present to institutional investors once or twice a year, more if there are problems or moves afoot. They know that their presentations will be carefully watched for issues of both form and substance.
- Companies will report to shareholders, usually twice a year, through the annual general meeting and reporting of half-year results.

  The annual general meeting provides a once-a-year opportunity for smaller investors to gain exposure to the directors and to question them. Unless there is special drama in the air, these meetings are rather sparsely attended by institutional investors. They will have had their chance to scrutinize managers through the special presentations mentioned above. If there are particular resolutions to be voted upon at the meeting, institutional investors will vote by proxy.

  Annual general meetings can be noisy and sometimes turbulent affairs. They are an opportunity for pressure groups, such as equal opportunities and environmental campaigners, to have their say, sometimes to the embarrassment of directors.

  Occasionally they can throw up funny or poignant moments, such as the time that a very small and very old lady stood up at the back of a meeting and asked the chairman to repeat what he had just said about the profit recovery programme. The chairman, shouting and enunciating his words very clearly, said, 'Madam, I said that it could take us several years to get performance back on track.' 'Could you do it a little more quickly?' asked the little old lady. 'You see, I am 90 years old and haven't got all that much time!'

In theory, annual general meetings represent the democratic right of shareholders to call management to account. In reality, however, the will of the generally absent institutional shareholders is all that matters.

- Analysts tend to specialize in particular industrial sectors and watch companies and managers in their sector like hawks. They strive to ensure that no fact, rumour or snippet of information about the companies that they follow goes unnoticed.

  They are also very active in their questioning of the finance director and possibly the CEO – and the fruits of this scrutiny will be published for all to see. As the analysts' stock-in-trade is data, information and gossip, they are also very important in the reputation-forming or reputation-destroying game. Many managers feel that analysts function on more than one level. Much of their work is based on financial and numerate data, but many feel that there is also a strong emotional basis to their opinions.

  So, managers believe that it helps to be liked by analysts. Conversely, those who have incurred the displeasure of analysts can find that their actions receive a negative spin. As these same analysts are a prime source of information for financial journalists, this spin can become magnified into a campaign. Sometimes analysts will develop a line about a company. This can be negative or positive, but once analysts have declared a view and recommendation, they can stick to them stubbornly, despite contrary evidence.
- With the reduction in faith in the independence of 'sell-side' analysts has come the growth of another class of analyst, the so-called buy-side analyst, whose work is for the investment institutions and is not usually published. But it was reported to us by a broker that many sell- and buy-side analysts communicate closely and frequently, thus increasing the intensity of scrutiny and analysis of companies.
- Finally, managers know that the financial press is always vigilant. Most top managers with whom we have worked tend to scan the *Financial Times* daily, looking for news that may impact on them or people that they know. As we have said, the press tend to be very tightly 'plugged in' to the financial markets through journalists' close contacts with analysts and investors.

Lest readers may come away with the view that all this scrutiny is one-way, let it be said that managers deploy considerable resources to unearth intelligence that will help them to anticipate what is going on in the markets. So, in-house and external advisers will prepare daily press comment analyses, brokers will provide updates on investor sentiment, and investor relations and financial PR houses will track share movements and immediately report if there is any unusual buying or selling activity. All this has meant a burgeoning in the size and cost of the information and advisory services available to managers to help them be sensitive to, and to manipulate information for, the financial markets.

We thus have a situation in which there are vast amounts of data, information, stories, rumours, gossip and tittle-tattle flowing through the financial markets, with all players, including managers, straining themselves to pick up anything that might help or hinder their causes. In addition, there is a considerable volume of 'spin' and deliberate leaking of 'information' that is angled to do down an adversary or make something happen that is beneficial to the leaker.

3. The financial markets are hungry – and demanding. Tony Golding portrays a new CEO as being greeted by the proposition that he or she has a limited time to convince the watching financial markets and press that he or she is making an impact. One of our search consultant respondents observed that the perceived 'time to impact' had reduced to six months in the minds of many candidates. So, says Golding, 'Our new CEO is surrounded by cheerleaders – investment bankers and securities analysts – waving banners with 'MORE CORPORATE ACTIVITY PLEASE' written on them.'

We have seen that investment bankers present companies with a continual stream of unsolicited M&A propositions, sometimes reinforced by 'ideas' to investors and leaks to the press. Certainly, Redland, both in its acquisitive phase and when it was struggling to recover from the effects of all its acquisitions and 'moves', received a plethora of ideas – only they were different ideas: for the next acquisition in the bullish growth phase, and on how to break the company up and create more value when it was suffering. Of course, most of these ideas were from the same bankers!

Readers will see elsewhere in the book the assertion by a senior lawyer that more than 50 per cent of all M&A activity is originated not by management but by bankers, analysts or investors looking to generate fees, sell shares or realize quick 'value' by having the company sold or broken up. Occasionally managers acknowledge the active role of investment bankers in bringing about deals.

Here is an excerpt from the Redland annual report of 1982 by the then chairman, Sir Colin Corness. 'By good fortune of timing and following entirely independent evaluation by each company of the other as a desirable merger partner, we found ourselves brought together with Cawoods Holdings Limited upon the initiative of Baring Brothers and Co. Limited, who for many years have advised both companies.' He finishes his statement by saying that he would like to 'add a special word of thanks to our professional advisers for their most competent handling of the complex Cawoods merger transaction. I am confident that it will prove to be a most important milestone in the progress of our company.' Most of the assets acquired were sold not many years later.

The lifeblood of the financial markets is action. Bankers live off deals and corporate transactions. These will include advising companies on acquisitions, bid defences, selling sizeable assets, de-mergers and large transactions involving financing. Bankers will also advise management on financial strategy and the best ways of financing growth. But, fundamentally, bankers are there for the centrepiece of the industrial drama, the large deal.

Investment institutions, paradoxically, tend to be convinced that activism is best for them, despite Warren Buffett's proposition that he makes 'more money when snoring than when active'. Many investors like the idea that their holdings are tradeable and may throw up gains from the sale of the company. They are also likely to be influenced by the prevalent belief that good management is active management and the fact that securities houses (brokers) make their money from the movement of shares and bankers from deals – and this influence will be strongest if they are owned by a large integrated bank.

It is not hard to see that many a manager will be strongly influenced by the chorus of approval that is generated (for a while, anyhow) by action, and needs to be very strong-minded to risk being labelled 'boring', especially if a major slice of his or her wealth is tied to investor approval.

4. The markets like managers to be big, bold, reliable, decisive, charismatic, communicative and dedicated to their interests. By now there should be no need to labour this point. But there may be serious contradictions in the requirements of the markets from managers. Ideally, managers should 'deliver' exactly what they 'promise'. Any form of commitment to a definitive level of performance tends to be taken by investors and analysts as a personal 'promise' to them. Managers are required to 'deliver' to these promises or be punished by a downgrading of the share price of their company, and of their reputations. Witness some of the reactions of the investors to the downgrading of BP's growth forecasts, or the near-hysteria that greeted Redland's reduction in dividend (featured in a subsequent chapter). In both cases, and many more, the attentions of the financial markets and press turned rapidly on the top figure in the company. So, Lord Browne moved rapidly from having a godlike status to being a man whose appetite for the fight was suspect, a possible candidate for retirement, and Robert Napier of Redland became a target for the 'chop'.

Sir Clive Thompson, CEO of Rentokil, has recounted to business school students the chastening experience of going from having the heroic status of 'Mr Twenty Percent' to a less than positive position when the performance of the company he led slipped from that magic and 'promised' rate of growth.

So, managers are supposed to be totally reliable. But not 'boring'. They are also expected to be bold and exciting, and will be much appreciated if they deliver the rock-solidly reliable performance through a series of bold deals or strategic 'moves'. The fact that there may be a contradiction in the longer run between bold deals and reliable performance simply means that the heroes will at some stage develop feet of clay, and had better cash in on their popularity while it lasts!

Next, a top manager should ideally exude charisma, and possess superb communication and presentation skills. It is expected that a good deal of the charisma and polished communication will be devoted to assuring the financial community that the manager in question is totally dedicated to the investors' cause – as one of our respondents said, 'convinced that I will do anything to serve their interests'. A solid grasp of numbers and an ability to keep the message simple and easily digestible by very busy people (fund managers) is also much appreciated.

It will be evident that not all managers will easily match up to the ideal profile – we will also examine later in the book whether there is any connection between the markets' views and what really makes for good management – but for now we can report that many managers do try quite hard to match these perceived requirements. Thus much emphasis is placed on 'grooming' them to be able to present an acceptable public face. The burgeoning industry of advisers and consultants will, for a consideration, provide close support for managers to help them develop their images. Also, much attention is now placed on the quality of presentation, maybe even at the risk of downgrading the substance. Managers who do not match up to public requirements are publicly advised to improve, as in the case of Sir Philip Watts, the chairman of Shell, who was advised to view some of Lord Browne's presentations!

More seriously, it may be the case that many more managers are also *acting* in ways that will please the markets, and are actually being decisive, making deals and being totally responsive to investors' needs – but we will see about this in later chapters.

We started this chapter with a dance floor metaphor to describe how the relationships between managers and the financial markets work. We will finish with another notion – that these relationships are truly symbiotic…

> SYMBIOSIS – An interaction between two different organisms living in close physical association, usually to the advantage of both, or, a mutually advantageous association or relationship between persons. (*Concise Oxford Dictionary*)

Large companies need very substantial amounts of capital and borrowings to fund their businesses. The financial markets provide this at competitive rates, but would like the highest returns for the risks that they are taking. Out of this simple relationship has grown a huge, hungry industry, as the investment markets have found more and more profitable ways of serving the recipients of capital, and managers have found that they have become high-profile public figures, capable, with a few strings attached, of amassing considerable fortunes. Thus has a rather simple symbiotic relationship become over time a very involved, intricate and extensive one.

A FINAL STORY

With such a strong dependency on City popularity to keep the opportunities coming, it is perhaps not surprising that corporate bosses are sometimes tempted to 'repay favours with favours'. We were told that at a board meeting of a company that was subject to a takeover bid, the chairman proposed that a particular investment banking house should join the defence team. As the company had not worked with these particular advisers before, several directors questioned what value they might add. The chairman insisted, and an argument developed. The argument was abruptly terminated when the chairman announced that if the advisers were not appointed, he would have to 'consider his position'. As the resignation of the chairman at the beginning of a bid defence was felt to be very bad news, the directors agreed to the addition to the team.

Later, another non-executive director revealed that the investment bank in question was a lavish supporter of shooting, a sport both he and the chairman were avidly interested in. 'It is well known by some', said the director, 'that the bank has provided our chairman with sport for many years.'

Part III

Why do some companies get into difficulties?

Introduction to Part III

In the previous chapters we have examined some of the 'happenings' that seem to have beset the British industrial economy and looked briefly at some of the most influential actors on the industrial stage, and how they interact with each other. We are aware that we have not considered the role of a third key actor, government, but that is beyond the scope of this book.

We are now going to seek out the behaviours of the management and financial market 'actors' and to try to describe their impact on the large enterprises that they lead and influence. We start this process by casting an eye on the kinds of strategies and actions that seem to increase the risks of companies underperforming and, at the extremes, failing completely.

British managers are frequently accused of causing a wide range of problems, including the decline of high-technology industries and manufacturing, lack of investment in R&D and productivity-enhancing capital expenditure, and all-too-frequent 'cock-ups' due to a lack of attention to the fundamentals of good management. These manifestations, if true, are likely to be the symptoms of something deeper. The 'something' can be thought of at two levels. First, what do managers actually do or not do that causes the problems? And second, what deeper values and beliefs drive what they do?

We are not going to attempt to delve deep into the underlying values and beliefs that drive the 'system', although it could be fun to do so in the future. For now, we would simply comment that if we were investigating this topic, we would be inclined to start by asking why 'ownership' is always described in a financial and legal sense and not in terms of psychological commitment and level of skilled contribution. We suspect that lurking in the deeper psyche of those who direct our affairs is the conviction that property and money are the most important things, far outstripping human ingenuity, commitment and loyalty in terms of inherent value.

In these chapters, leaving the deeper values of our leaders unexplored, we are going to consider a number of different ways in which managers, often supported by the financial markets, can act to weaken the long-term prospects of the companies they lead. The general descriptive material is, we hope, enriched and deepened by the real case of Redland plc, a company that derived enthusiastic support from investors to grow through ever-larger acquisitions, and then plunged suddenly to the status of a pariah, leading to its eventual takeover by a French company.

Today's corporate environment is challenging and unforgiving. Companies face pressure from demanding financial markets, international competition, environmental shocks and almost instant information availability. When companies and their leaders get into trouble, they do so very publicly.

Hardly a day seems to go by without a report of some company or other in trouble. Is there more difficulty and failure than usual?

After a period of sustained economic growth and optimism it might seem reasonable to expect the rate of failures to increase. Added to that, we are still seeing the aftershocks of the dot.com, telecommunications and other 'bubbles' – orgies of over-optimistic investment. The stock markets plummet, billions of pounds worth of shareholder value is being written off as lost and destroyed, and pension funds (and their sponsor companies) are reporting billions of pounds worth of lost value and underfunding.

Is all this simply inevitable, or do managers behave in ways that make the incidence of failure more likely? And is the incidence of these behaviours increasing?

We assume that top managers intend their companies to be successful. This usually means satisfying the needs of customers and investors, and most leaders would publicly agree that a skilled and committed workforce is an important ingredient for success. Management would not intentionally set out on courses that result in difficulty or disaster. However, discussions with many people in industry and the financial markets, together with available research, indicates that there are certain kinds of behaviours and actions that, singly, but more often in combination, increase the likelihood of 'unintended outcomes'.

When an enterprise hits the rocks, it is unlikely that there is one single cause of trouble, or that the problems have occurred suddenly. The reasons for failure are often extremely complex, and problems may take years to show themselves. Our own and other people's experiences have been extremely important in identifying some root causes of problems that are more easily recognized from inside the organization.

Many external commentators are not able to identify the deep roots of problems as they see only the more obvious and often final symptoms. But as we examined and thought about more and more cases, some patterns began to emerge. It seems that some factors are more instrumental in causing failure than others. In these chapters we will explore six.

In Chapter 5 we look at the consequences of inappropriate mergers and acquisitions (and disposals). This topic is worth a chapter on its own.

In Chapter 6 we consider some destructive behavioural traits:

- managerial insularity and complacency;
- following strategies that are not 'natural' to the organization;
- neglecting and abusing the organization;
- placing excessive reliance on charismatic, 'superhero' leaders;
- giving unbalanced attention to stakeholder needs.

We fully accept that this list is not exhaustive, and that some problems have multiple and intertwined roots. However, we believe these six to be significant causal factors in many major corporate disasters.

Chapter 7, a case study of how Redland plc rose to dizzy heights then crashed to earth as a takeover victim, shows how some of these traits can arise, and how they can lead to unintended and disastrous consequences.

Then, just to give consideration to the opposite side, and because we are not obsessed with failure, Chapter 8 will consider the management behaviours that are more likely to result in business success.

5

Factors causing failure: mergers and acquisitions (and disposals)

The prospect of a big takeover causes more excitement in the financial community than any other kind of event. A whole industry swings into action to support the deal. Investment banks, financial PR companies, stockbrokers, corporate lawyers and accountants are all there to support or, in some cases, initiate deals. All earn huge fees from a big transaction. Coming along behind are the consultants, who can also make big money helping clients to manage post-deal mergers.

For those on the inside, deal-making offers a special buzz. Conceiving of and negotiating deals is one of the few actions that top managers can execute almost by themselves. No need to influence, cajole or network with myriads of people to achieve results that will be ascribed to the efforts of the many! A big deal can be consummated by a very small team: the CEO, the finance director and a few corporate staff, supported by external advisers.

With the thrill of negotiating the deal – planning the conquest, as it were – big acquisitions can take on a life of their own, rather like military campaigns. Advisers often help to sustain the drama by setting up places, called 'war rooms' or something similar, from which the general and his or her troops can plan and execute their campaign.

The rewards for a successful general can be enormous. As we saw in Chapter 3, Sir Christopher Gent, the CEO of Vodafone, was awarded a bonus of £10 million for simply completing the takeover of Mannesmann, one of the biggest corporate deals of its time, although subsequent investor pressure resulted in half being in shares, and contingent upon performance. In addition to the financial rewards, great reputations stand to be gained or lost. Being labelled a great deal-maker carries a huge and very seductive cachet.

British companies lead the way in the international M&A league. In the period January to June 2000 they completed deals costing more than twice those of the nearest contender, France, and two and a half times as much as those of the United States. Over a longer time span, British companies have been international leaders in selecting the transactional route to corporate growth.

So, with all the expensive expertise dedicated to delivering the deals, and all the excitement surrounding them, surely M&A activity is one of the best ways of creating value. Or is it…?

THE RESEARCH EVIDENCE

The research would seem to imply otherwise! In his book *Why Acquisitions Fail* (2001), Denzil Rankine lists 11 studies of acquisitions ranging from the early 1970s up to 1998. Testing for value added against a range of measures, these showed failure rates ranging between 44 per cent and 79 per cent.

In KPMG's 1999 study of acquisitions and mergers made by large quoted companies, over 80 per cent of the acquiring company senior executives interviewed believed that their deal had resulted in enhanced value for shareholders. 'Yet the analysis showed that 83 per cent of mergers had failed to produce any benefits for shareholders, and, even more alarmingly, over half actually destroyed value. Not only that, but less than half of the interviewed directors had conducted a formal post-deal review', said KPMG's head of M&A integration, John Kelly.

By 2001 the picture had improved, but only marginally. About 30 per cent of M&A deals created value, while 31 per cent destroyed value and the rest made no discernible difference. Once again, managers seemed remarkably incurious about the impact of their deals, as 75 per cent did not intend to conduct a post-project review or measure shareholder value when evaluating the success of a transaction.

Equally worryingly, according to this survey, over a third of acquisitions made in the boom period of 2000–01 are already being unscrambled, and approximately a third of the CEOs who made them have left their jobs! Furthermore, over half the acquisitions made in the period 1996–98 have not yet been fully integrated.

So what about the external, or shareholder, perspective? Surely acquisitions are good for the share price, aren't they? According to the David Hume Institute (Peacock and Bannock, 1988), it is the shareholders in the target company that benefit! The Institute conducted exhaustive research into the immediate and wider effects of mergers and acquisitions. It found that in the four months before and up to an acquisition, there was an average increase of 30 per cent in the share price of the vast majority of the sample of target companies, but an increase of less than 1 per cent in the share prices of only half of the bidders. The rest suffered share price decreases. The researchers concluded that, 'All the gain in share price goes to the shareholders of the acquired company.'

Furthermore, performance of the acquiring companies tended to deteriorate relative to that of competitors and their own previous performance for at least two years following the acquisition. The researchers concluded that:

> The net effect of mergers on shareholder wealth is uncertain and probably small. There is a balance of evidence that abnormal gains are positive in the very short run, although this is far from conclusive. It is fairly certain that the net gains decline over time, and, in the long run, may actually be negative.

But surely M&A activity keeps management on their toes? Some would argue that the purposes of the stock market are to pool society's savings and to allocate them to the most profitable use. The dynamics of the market help to ensure that the assets are most profitably employed. Two mechanisms make sure that this happens: the threat of takeover and the actuality of mergers and acquisitions.

Proponents of this theory maintain that even if two managements are maximizing the returns from their companies, putting the two together may well yield a better result because of efficiencies of scale. When bidders pay a premium for the companies they acquire, this represents the 'unrealized efficiency gains' that will be unlocked by the merger.

In 1990 the Institute for Public Policy Research published the results of a study into this theory, querying whether it works quite as postulated. The report states, rather baldly, that the purity of the efficient market theory is distorted by several factors:

- Investing institutions tend to base their decisions on short-term market situations rather than long-term value expectations.
- Fund managers will nearly always accept immediate gain rather than long-term possible gain, therefore making takeovers easier than the balanced value argument might indicate.
- It is just not true that share prices always reflect true long-term expected earnings, as 'Myopia, herd behaviour, fads, fashions and short term-ism all get in the way.'

The researchers conclude, '*If takeover bids were always a success and led to an improvement in the productivity of the companies involved in the business combination, then British industry should be significantly outperforming foreign competitors*' (our italics). Instead, often the outcome of seemingly compelling mergers and acquisitions is loss of value. Before we examine the difficulties that arise in making good returns from acquisitions, let's look at a specific case and see what can happen.

INVENSYS: AN ACQUISITION CASE STUDY

Invensys is the product of the merger of Siebe, a very successful engineering company, and BTR, also an engineering business, renowned under Sir Owen Green for its financial disciplines and skill at making acquisitions. After Green retired, the company seemed to go off the boil, and by October 1998, when it merged with Siebe, it was a middle-sized engineering conglomerate that had been through several bouts of restructuring.

At the time of the merger, BTR was ranked number 73 out of the FTSE 100 and had a market capitalization of £3.6 billion. Siebe, the initiator of the merger, was ranked number 64 and had a market capitalization of just under £4 billion. The pre-merger combined value of the companies was therefore £7.6 billion.

In October 1999, a year later, the market valued the combined entity at £10.5 billion, ranking number 29 in the FTSE 100. So there was such a thing as synergy after all!

Alas, not for long! By November 2000 the profits of the combined entity had plunged from £295 million to £66 million. Just before the merger, Siebe by itself made profits of £486 million. By January 2001, market value of the new company, Invensys, was £4.4 billion.

For those with tender sensibilities, it gets more extreme. The year 2001 saw an outburst of ferocious corporate activism with two major disposals, three acquisitions, one major external appointment (a Mr Bob Hitt!), three business restructurings, one significant business initiative, 5,600 employee lay-offs and a series of profit warnings to the City. It might be said that the average employee was entitled to wonder, 'What on earth was all that about?'

Shortly after this, Mr Yurko, the once well-rated chief executive of Siebe, left the company and was replaced as CEO by Mr Heythornthwaite, previously of Blue Circle (bought by Lafarge). He rapidly announced 'a major strategic review', focusing on big disposals, to a mildly pleased City. Describing 'last-chance' restructuring plans aimed, among other things, at reducing crippling debt levels, he told investors that the company had previously 'pathologically over-promised' since its creation, and identified the problems as being rooted in the 'marketing and management approach'.

On 17 March 2002 the market capitalization of Invensys was £4.2 billion and its ranking in the FTSE 100 was 62. Full circle, in just three and a half years, and at what cost to shareholders?

On 23 March 2002, under the heading 'Invensys Starts Assets Sell-off', the *Guardian* announced the sale of the group's valves business to a US rival and the handover of the management of its entire IT operations in more than a dozen countries to IBM (for a consideration of £70 million per year). The battery division was sold to Emersys of the United States a few days later. By September 2002, Invensys ranked at number 76 and had a market capitalization of £2.58 million.

Even the authors could not predict what a disaster this Frankenstein creation of deal-hungry managers would become. By February 2003 Invensys had plunged to number 99 in the FTSE 100, with a market value of £700 million.

As the book must now go to press, we should finish this sorry tale with an article from the *Observer* of 16 February 2003. Under the heading 'Invensys Mergers Turn to Dross', the correspondent says:

> Two out of three mergers fail to create value. And if anyone doubts this they should ask shareholders in Invensys, the company with the crazy name and crazy strategy. The engineering and controls firm has spent years building up its empire only to offload vast chunks of it along the way when hindsight invariably struck... On Friday Invensys's shares slumped by 53% after warning its second half figures would be 25% below those of the previous six months. They are now worth just 19p, a sixth of what they were valued at a year ago. In Invensys's sorry case, the whole is really less than the sum of its parts.

It is our strong impression that in the middle of all this mayhem, there can have been almost no time to consider managing the business. Speak of creative destruction!

Later the same month the shares fell further to 14.5p on fears that the group would breach its banking agreements within a year.

Perhaps the abbreviation M&A should be changed to M,A&D: mergers, acquisitions and disposals!

REASONS FOR FAILURE OF MERGERS AND ACQUISITIONS

If we stand back from the wreckage and try to put the whole issue of mergers and acquisitions into perspective, it would seem that there are several kinds of reason for making acquisitions and several different ways of going about mergers. As a result, M&A activity can result in the destruction of value for three reasons:

- inappropriate strategy or reason for acquisition;
- paying too much;
- failure to integrate and deliver the benefits.

Inappropriate strategy or reason for making an acquisition

There are many reasons for making acquisitions, some excellent, some inappropriate. Management can feel under pressure to grow faster than the existing business makes possible. Fund managers need a high proportion of stocks in their portfolios that will grow faster than the average, otherwise they will not beat the index and will stand the risk of being fired. In their turn, they can put great pressure on companies to grow, preferably perpetually.

So growth is a highly valued state, and ambitious managers will labour greatly to achieve it. For those in a hurry, the route of acquisitions has a tremendous charm and there are many friends in the City who will be fertile with ideas on how to make them. One experienced finance director likened introducing a new and ambitious CEO to an investment banker as being akin to exposing a 15-year-old son to the madam of a particularly attractive bordello!

Other factors can also come into play. The idea of being the biggest, of being an industry leader or of being a celebrity, with power over a vast empire, appeals powerfully to many a captain of industry. We have known people who were driven to acquire by sheer competitiveness, or a desire to do better than a rival. Of course, such childish motives could never be aired in public, hence the charm of 'synergy' or 'unlocking hidden value'. One driver of construction materials company Redland's acquisitions through the 1980s and early 1990s (see Chapter 7) was the desire to be bigger, as was probably the case with Grand Metropolitan in the 1980s, and many of the privatized utilities later.

It is hard to find a sensible reason for the takeover by Thorn Electrical Industries of EMI in 1979, other than the fact that the two companies had been bitter rivals in the past and the chairman of Thorn was keen to crown his career with something really big. Among the synergies claimed to be available from this merger were the benefits of combining the manufacture of TV and video equipment ('the hardware') with the production of films, home videos and recorded music ('the software'). Further synergies were claimed to be possible from combining EMI's engineering expertise with Thorn's strong positions in home domestic appliances.

It subsequently proved almost impossible to combine EMI's undoubted expertise in advanced military electronics with the design and manufacture of appliances such as microwave ovens. Even more fanciful was the idea that the folk who ran film and music companies had anything in common with those who manufactured TV and video equipment. The shambles caused by this merger took many years to unscramble.

Not deterred by the awfulness of the Thorn EMI experience, Sony acquired CBS Music in the mid-1980s to gain captive music repertoire to play through its sound equipment. The consequences of the coming together of Japanese engineers and Californian music men were ludicrous, and after a short while, Sony exited very expensively from recorded music and returned to its hardware 'knitting'.

So, sometimes management can get carried away by the idea of generating value from perceived 'synergies' that prove elusive. Lex Service Group (now RAC plc) is another example. In the 1970s, Lex was thought to have discovered the philosopher's stone, the notion that there was deep synergy between all service businesses. Lex, a motor vehicle distribution, sales and service company (which also believed that university graduates should run all its garages), set out to pioneer this discovery and made extensive acquisitions in recruitment agencies, travel agencies, international luxury hotels, semiconductor and auto parts distribution and several other kinds of business.

A vivid moment in this quest for greatness happened at an internal conference in 1972, when some of the assembled managers speculated that Lex was shortly destined to grow to the size of ICI, then the bellwether of British industry. It was noticeable that this excitement was not shared by some of the old sweats from the motor distribution divisions, who saw their hard-earned cash being spent on the wonderful new strategy.

For a number of reasons, synergy proved hard to unlock (lack of understanding of the acquired businesses, acquisitions too expensive, lack of cash, organization not capable of coping with such diversity), and the great edifice crashed to earth, accompanied by the discordant sounds of huge value destruction. Lex survived by the skin of its teeth and sensibly returned to serving the needs of motorists, which it does to this day.

A more recent example has been the alliance of Boots, the high street chemist, with Halfords, retailer of bikes and car spares. Purchased as part of a £900 million acquisition including Payless DIY (also subsequently sold at a loss), Halfords sat uncomfortably under Boots for more than a decade. In June 2002 the chief executive said, 'We wouldn't buy Halfords now.' In April 2002 the company confirmed that it would be happy to sell it.

The disaster to end all disasters has been the much-trumpeted merger of AOL and Time Warner. The trumpeting was done at the time of the merger, by the banking and investment community, but also by Ted Turner, the media tycoon, who compared his feelings about the merger to his first experience of sex!

This dream partnership turned nightmare announced losses in January 2003 of more than $99 billion. At the time of the merger, the stock market value of the combined entities was $318 billion. In January 2003 that value had declined to $62 billion. This was a marriage made in hell of two companies with totally different cultures, with businesses that were synergistic only in the heated minds of top managers and bankers.

Why do they continue to do it? Why does the world let them?

There are yet more inappropriate reasons for making acquisitions that contain the seeds of disruption and value destruction. Often, management can't face the alternative: growing the business. As one now retired senior executive from a major UK plc put it, 'For a chief executive not to be "doing something" is a failure, and there is enormous pressure from the merchant banks to do deals.' A retired ex-head of corporate finance in one of the leading banks put it another way: 'There is an argument that size facilitates the next stage in the strategy. This is valid if the strategy is well constructed, but many aren't. There is also an underlying assumption that the only acceptable strategy is to get bigger.' Another head of corporate finance at yet another bank described the motivation for deals as being driven by the chief executive's desire to make a 'dramatic statement about his relative strengths'. (Sounds a little like male deer at rutting time!)

Yet another reason emerges: the short time frame in which a chief executive is expected to make things happen. A newly appointed chief executive has some two years to make an impact on the business. A senior in-house lawyer described the process in the following terms: 'Internal change is slow. An acquisition is a default position. The rewards are praise and being written about.' And if the underlying business still isn't delivering a year or so later, the CEO can always make another one! In fact, faced with these pressures for speed and growth, and with personal fortunes depending on stock options, it can be little wonder that managers are easily persuaded to the lure of a 'transforming takeover'.

Furthermore, managers can feel under enormous pressure from the markets to solve problems by acquisition. Ian Robertson is deputy chief executive of Wilson Bowden, a house-building business, and in 2001 one of Britain's top-performing companies. In early 2002 he is reported by the *Sunday Times* to have said, 'Don't take this as sour grapes, but sometimes corporate activity begets attention and pays off in share price terms. We were pushed hard about why we didn't go down the route of making acquisitions. We thought we could deliver the margins and returns without acquisitions. But some of the companies now in the top 200 have been given credit for their corporate activity.' The *Sunday Times* describes this insight as 'intriguing'.

His experience was confirmed by Sir Ralph Robins. Retiring after nearly 50 years with aero-engine manufacturer Rolls-Royce, during which time he helped to raise the company's share of the global aero-engine industry from 7 per cent to 30 per-cent, said at his last results meeting that the City did not seem to understand the long term nature of the business: 'People are impatient and won't wait long for their returns.'

So, good acquisitions happen for the good of the company but, as we have seen, there are many other reasons for spending huge amounts of money, many of them poor and with the potential of catastrophic outcomes. One theory propounded by a commentator was novel: executive directors should be forced to work only three days a week. That way they would have time to run the business but no time to spend thinking up ways to waste the shareholders' money! The problem is, many of them would spend three days a week dreaming up ever more creative deals and no time running the business!

Even when the reasons for making acquisitions are good, however, the deal can still fall at one of the other two hurdles, which we now examine.

Paying too much

The second reason that mergers and acquisitions result in destruction of value in the acquiring company is quite simple: the acquirer pays more than the acquisition is worth.

It all starts at the valuation stage. Valuing a company is a tricky subject at the best of times. Valuing for acquisition is even trickier.

The first step is to look at what the company is worth. Then you need to look at what it's worth to you by valuing the improvements to business or cost savings that will be achieved by combining the two entities. Almost inevitably you will need to pay a premium to acquire a company. If you bid for a quoted company, you will need to pay over the current share price to persuade investors to vote in your favour. Thus synergies, the benefits of bringing two entities together, are needed to finance the premium.

As soon as you start to calculate value, you need to make assumptions. These assumptions drive the numbers in the financial model.

One retired senior financial executive from a FTSE 100 company expressed concerns about the valuation process: 'There is a real danger implicit in the valuation models used to justify the prices paid for acquisitions. Firstly, they depend upon the assumptions, which can be flexed to favour the deal. Secondly, they tend to consider one model only rather than a range of probable outcomes. Thirdly, they are heavily dependent on the least scientifically calculated number, the terminal value. Many acquisitions are justified on the basis of the terminal value, which is essentially a guess about what the business will be worth after ten years.'

One reason for over-valuation of synergies and future business is an over-optimistic vision of new market opportunities. Take the example of Marconi, heavily investing in telecommunications on a market model that has so far failed to materialize. Vodafone, which made many big acquisitions, and invested heavily in third-generation mobile phone licences, and ICI are other companies that hoped to solve strategic issues through big acquisitions. Telewest is another example of a company investing heavily in its vision of a new market.

John Plender, writing in the *Financial Times* in February 2002, pointed out how these over-optimistic visions can spread from one company to another as the same individuals sit on several boards. Considering the cases of Marconi and ICI, he commented that 'Boardroom incest led in this instance to a duplication of similar errors on a very grand scale.'

Even the experts find it hard to agree. Thames Water agreed to acquire E'town, a US water supply and waste treatment group, in November 1999. In May 2000, following a worse than expected set of results from E'town, one investor, Value Management and Research, described the price as 'an excellent display of destruction of shareholder value', whereas an analyst from Merrill Lynch disagreed. 'The E'town purchase does look expensive, but on balance I am more positive than negative about the deal.'

Even if you can get the valuation right, that may not be the end of it. Someone else may come along and offer more. The hopeful acquirer finds him- or herself in a bidding situation. Then things really start to hot up.

When the acquirer is faced with a fight, adrenaline starts to flow at board level. The glare of publicity can start to distort thinking. A 'got to get the deal' mentality can emerge, pushing aside financial prudence. 'Groupthink' (Janus, 1982) can kick in, enabling otherwise sane directors to believe ever more optimistic twists in the valuation assumptions, allowing them to contemplate an ever-escalating price.

Three facets of groupthink can seriously distort acquisition thinking. The first is suppression of personal doubts. In a group context, doubters tend to self-impose censorship on their misgivings, sometimes out of fear of appearing soft or lacking courage in front of the other group members. Thus invalid assumptions are permitted to continue unchallenged.

A second, and more sinister, aspect of groupthink can happen at the same time, when 'mindguards' start preventing dissent. A mindguard is someone who takes it upon him- or herself to protect information reaching the group consciousness by placing social pressure on a dissenting member, sometimes quite blatantly.

Sometimes investment banks, with compensation riding on success of the bid, play this role to keep up pressure at the very top. A partner in a leading law firm with many years' personal experience of working on acquisitions described the process: 'A culture of fear develops once the deal is under way. The investment banks are running the show and will not allow anyone to stand in the way of successful completion.'

The third facet is rationalization, where the group pools a story line to justify the predetermined course of action. This builds confidence and reassures the group members, while at the same time turning attention away from facts that may challenge the assumptions. And so a previously cautious and competent board can persuade itself to pay away more value than the acquisition can ever deliver.

It is also possible to pay too much because you are lacking in critical information. This can particularly be the case in hostile bids for quoted companies, as the bidder has no rights to inside information or fails to conduct 'due diligence', the process of examining a company's internal affairs to ensure that the valuation assumptions are realistic.

Even with an agreed deal there is some dissent as to the value of due diligence. One retired industrialist quoted Arnold Weinstock as holding the opinion that due diligence is almost a waste of time without some inside knowledge. However, the KPMG research (KPMG, 1999) identified due diligence one of the key determinants of value in an acquisition.

So, you get the acquisition strategy right, and you ensure that you pay the right price for the deal. What more can go wrong?

Unfortunately, there is one more pitfall.

Failure to integrate and deliver the benefits

As we have seen, the price paid for almost all acquisitions can be justified only by the realization of 'synergy' benefits: the business improvements and cost reductions that will flow from combining two operations. These benefits are realized by a process known as integration: the bringing together of the old and new organizations to create the new entity with a different new culture, market approach and cost base.

In its 1999 report *Unlocking Shareholder Value: The keys to success in M&A*, KPMG identified selecting the management team, resolving cultural issues and integration project planning as three of the six critical keys to successful mergers and acquisitions. Yet a 2002 survey by the same company found that two-thirds of the companies bought between 1996 and 1998 still needed to be properly integrated.

It is worth considering the two types of mergers and their integration implications. First, there are those that require the merger of the acquirer's business with that of the acquired company. We will call these Type 1 mergers. Second, there are those that leave the acquired organization as a free-standing entity, or which require collaboration at the senior levels only. We will call these Type 2 mergers.

Type 1 mergers

The Type 1 form of merger, requiring detailed and intimate integration of different organizations, is by far the more difficult to achieve successfully. This is because of the sheer complexity involved and also because most of the knitting together that will create synergy is way below the line of sight of those who conceived of and led the acquisition. As for the investors who provided the funding, all this value-creating activity could just as well be happening on the planet Mars. That may be why making acquisitions is easy and making them work successfully is so hard.

Here are two examples. One is of success and one of failure to achieve the desired 'knitting' and synergy.

Once upon a time, Bird's Eye Foods conceived of a clever way of ensuring supplies of raw material for fish fingers, one of its most valuable products. The company bought a fish processing company in Newfoundland, Canada. Its plants were close to the then rich fishing grounds of Newfoundland and Labrador and, because it was on Canadian soil, it would be inside the 200-mile (320-kilometre) fishing limit that Canada was predicted to be about to throw around its waters.

Many, many problems followed the acquisition, and we will not go into most of them, but one particular niggle was that the quality and cost of the processed fish coming from Newfoundland were a long way short of satisfactory. The local production manager, a Bird's Eye expatriate, reported that the methods used by fish filleters in Newfoundland were pretty crude by comparison with those of Bird's Eye in the United Kingdom.

Attempts to tell this to the Newfoundlanders fell on deaf ears. Eventually it was decided to ask for six fish filleters to come out from the Bird's Eye factory in Grimsby to Harbour Grace, Newfoundland, to teach the locals how to fillet fish efficiently, fast and without leaving unnecessary bones in the fillets.

The person who made the request was dismayed when he saw who emerged into the arrivals hall at Gander Airport. He knew that at least three of the arrivals were regarded as 'difficult to manage' in Grimsby.

However, after some initial skirmishes, the filleters went to work on the line in Harbour Grace. They were cold-shouldered by the locals for the first month, but gradually the barriers came down and the Grimsby men began to be accepted as ordinary working people just like their Canadian counterparts.

After a couple of months, Newfoundlanders were asking for tips on how to fillet, and after six months, the Grimsby men had been able to 'teach' their colleagues most of what they knew. Several of the Grimsby men went on to manage satellite fish plants, and at the end of a year, Newfoundland filleting performance had improved out of all recognition.

When the Grimsby men went back home, they did so with some sadness, as they had made many close friends, even with the British managers who were also working in Newfoundland. After they got back to Grimsby, three of the six became supervisors, one went into the quality control department and the other two were reported as being much less 'difficult'.

Both sides had gained something, so two plus two really did equal five in this case.

The reason for telling this tale is to make the point that most synergy benefits are like this: small mutual gains, many, many of which are needed if a large acquisition is to pay its way.

The second story comes from Lex Service Group in the early 1970s. That company, pursuing its dream of synergistic development, had acquired several luxury hotels in Britain. Searching for some way of adding value to the hotel business, a top manager in the Lex corporate office declared that what the hotel group needed was a really 'hot' car sales manager. These guys could really show the hotel people how to do it.

So, without much consultation, he ordained that a highly regarded performer should be dispatched from selling Volvo cars to a senior UK hotel sales position. The new sales manager took to hotels like a duck to water. Unfortunately, the aspects of the business he found most attractive were those connected with providing entertainment and fun for guests. After several drunken incidents, it was eventually discovered that the 'star' had selected a mistress from among the hospitality staff in one of the hotels and had taken her on a round-the-world sales trip, all expenses paid. He was summarily dismissed. Lex Hotels learnt little about selling; the car division lost a good sales manager.

In this case, the 'synergy' was imposed from a great distance and two plus two ended up as zero. The furious top manager accused the hotel group management of having corrupted his protégé.

The disruption factor in Type 1 mergers

It should not take too much imagination to sense what typically goes on inside two organizations that are to merge. No matter how good the planning by integration teams, there will still be a huge amount of disruption, usually for reasons that are rather basic, even primitive.

There will be competitiveness and defensiveness, there will be tribal behaviour and there will be a sense of winners and losers. There will be uncertainty on the part of the staff from both sides. People will spend an unusual amount of time on their own concerns. The two organizations will have different ways of doing the same things and there will be contradictory views about which ways are best. Systems, procedures and habits of behaviour will be different and people will not know what is really expected of them. There will almost certainly be a lack of trust, so many people will be trying to 'second-guess' what others are saying. Nobody will take risks or unnecessary initiatives.

There will often be a need for the losers to mourn what they have lost and come to terms with the fact that things will be different in the future. To cap it all, many people are likely to be losing their jobs, or facing job changes, with all the inevitable disruption that this causes.

Frequently, in the rush to make quick 'synergistic' cost savings, people with valuable skills and knowledge will be laid off and some of the company's future lifeblood of talented young people will leave because they see no opportunities for promotion.

Even the threat of takeover can cause disruption and stasis. A director of a large company whose top management were willing participants in merger discussions reported that when the merger intention became known to the staff at large, 'everything just stopped'. When the merger was reported to the competition authorities, which then spent 15 months in a protracted investigation, 'The whole organization froze for that period. Nothing was done beyond simply keeping the business ticking over. We lost a lot of ground to our competitors.'

All this quite basic human and emotional stuff, usually invisible to the distant figures who make and support the deals, is the main reason why the performance of many enterprises suffers. The disruption and uncertainty caused by a big merger can go on for many years, so the world, which has a short memory, will have forgotten the original events if the merger fails to deliver the promised results.

BMW is an example of where unfolding events proved it would have been better to 'stick to the knitting' rather than try to leverage synergy benefits from a market it was not familiar with. On 12 March 2002 there was a small item in the *Guardian* financial section. It was headed 'Record Profits for BMW'. 'The year 2001 was by far the most successful in the corporate history of the BMW group,' the Bavarian-based carmaker said. In this year, the carmaker increased its capital spending to record levels, while also increasing profits by about 9 per cent. The CEO remarked that his greatest achievement was to get out of the Rover Cars entanglement.

BMW got itself involved in a large acquisition with the much-publicized purchase of Rover and found that it was out of its depth in a new market, with a turnaround on its hands. When it sold Rover, acquired for about £800 million, for £1.00 and returned to its long-term core strength – making fast, superbly engineered quality cars for the upper half of the market – the company blossomed again.

Incidentally, BMW bought Rover from British Aerospace, which had acquired Rover some years before, on the (completely barmy, but nevertheless seriously considered by some analysts and press commentators) grounds that there was 'synergy' between aircraft and car technologies. BAE sold Rover as it returned to its own core businesses of aerospace and defence.

Research on post-merger growth

Before we leave the matter of merger synergies, it is worth considering the findings of a joint study by McKinsey and Southern Methodist University, called 'Mastering revenue growth in M&A' (*McKinsey Quarterly*, Summer 2000). This study examined 193 acquisitions made between 1997 and 1999. All were worth more than $100 million. A further study was made of 160 acquisitions by 157 quoted companies.

The researchers examined the importance of maintaining growth through and after an acquisition. They found that achieving growth synergies is much more important than cost reduction, and maintain that:

- To counteract a 1 per cent shortfall in growth after an acquisition, the acquirer must achieve additional cost savings of 25 per cent.
- Revenue growth of 2–3 per cent can offset a shortfall of 50 per cent in cost savings.

These facts have very serious implications, as the two studies found that growth is seldom maintained. In the first, only 9 per cent of companies were showing any growth at all nine months after the acquisition. The other study reached a similar conclusion: only 12 per cent of companies had managed to accelerate growth after the acquisition and the rest trailed the industry average growth rates by an average of 4 per cent.

Two very big and relatively recent mergers have been the coming together of Glaxo and SmithKlineBeecham and the Vodafone–Mannesmann merger.

Leaving aside the topical question of goodwill write-offs, it will be interesting to follow the fortunes of these companies, watching out for signs of the benefits, including value creation, promised by management at the time of the merger.

Chris Gent has now retired and will not be there to see the final fruits of his labours. In December 2002, Alex Brummer, in his *Daily Mail* City column, had the following advice for his successor: 'It would also be sensible for the new leader finally to take a scythe to Vodafone's accounts and to eliminate all the goodwill and other accounting devices which flatter its performance.'

Typical events following a Type 1 merger

The sequence of events that can be sparked off by a big merger goes as follows:

- Acquisition is made, driven by top management visions of future markets, assumptions of synergy or expectations of other benefits.
- The first drive after merger is for cost savings. This usually means closures and lay-offs, possibly in both companies.
- Defensive behaviour caused by cost reductions increases the difficulty of putting together the different parts of the merger.
- Expected real (not cost-saving) synergy benefits either do not materialize or take far longer to capture than expected.
- The management of the acquiring company, driven by the need to demonstrate benefits, look aggressively for more cost reductions, reduce investment and generally tighten up.
- Competitors have a field day, owing to disruption and a host of other factors. Market share is lost.
- Performance of the combined enterprise starts to slip markedly and more drastic actions are needed to keep investors happy.
- Results slip further and drastic action is taken, such as disposals at great value loss.

It should not take too much imagination to visualize several terminal scenarios from this sequence. However, the process described above may take five years or more to play out, by which time most of the world will have completely forgotten the root causes of the problems.

Type 2 mergers

The second type of acquisition, that of an entity that is not merged with the new owner's organization, also raises some difficult issues, particularly the question of how the acquirer will add value in order to cover the acquisition premium. It is usually not sensible simply to leave the purchase alone.

A common way of 'adding value' to a non-merged purchase is to impose very strict financial controls, to strip out cost and to restrict all kinds of expenditure. This process can produce quite spectacular performance improvements, as costs are slashed and margins increased. The effects of this are likely to stay positive for quite some time, particularly if the acquirer is good at acquisition accounting.

Trouble, when it eventually comes, can be sudden and spectacular. Witness the fall from grace of Tyco, the huge US conglomerate, and the de-merger of Hanson Trust.

Typical events following a Type 2 merger

Here is what tends to happen:

- The company makes an acquisition.
- It rapidly strips out costs and restricts capital and revenue spending, as well as using as many acquisition accounting devices as it can. Fortunately, owing to a tightening up of accounting standards, the scope here is nothing like it was in the 1980s and early 1990s.
- Performance of the acquired company increases, cash is released, and investor support is attracted.
- Time for another acquisition. Repeat the post-acquisition process. Performance continues to show spectacular progress. Support for further deals is very high; the reputation of the company and its leadership soars.
- By this stage, it is possible that the performance of earlier acquisitions is beginning to decline, owing to a lack of investment, demotivation and departures of key staff.
- Now make bigger or more acquisitions, in order to maintain momentum and keep the growth line positive.
- As more of the previous acquisitions begin to fade, there is a need to increase the size of new acquisitions, to keep the 'top line' moving.
- Eventually there are no more good deals left, or the size of the next target makes it a difficult contest.
- With no more assets to strip, the performance of the 'old' businesses becomes more apparent. Support declines.
- Now is the time to do one of two things. Either declare that some of your existing businesses are 'core' and can be managed for organic growth, or break the whole group up (Hanson and Tyco ended by doing this).

When companies behave like this, in addition to the slow strangulation caused by lack of investment and an excess of control, employee motivation and creativity tend to suffer. One company that was well known for its acquisitive habits used to send its financial analysis teams to the acquired company's premises in a cavalcade of large black BMW cars. Said a manager in one acquisition, 'These people caused quite palpable fear; many of us decided at the moment they arrived that we were going to leave as soon as possible.'

Besides the previously quoted Tyco and Hanson Trust, companies that have made the acquisition of squeezing of 'soft' assets their primary corporate strategy have included Williams Holdings and Tomkins plc. All fell from grace in one form or the other.

So, delivering all the integration benefits is a tough hurdle, and one that, research shows, many managers fall at. The merger of Hewlett Packard and Compaq has been sold on the back of $2.5 billion synergy benefits that the market sees as deliverable. Watch this space!

SUMMING UP ON MERGERS AND ACQUISITIONS

So, where does that leave us on acquisitions? As we shall see later, the destruction of shareholder value caused by the M&A boom of 1995–2000 reached staggering levels, to the point that a lay observer might doubt the sanity of those who proposed and funded many of the disastrous deals.

Given that there are so many ways in which they can lead to massive value destruction, and given that it is reported that more than a third of the biggest international takeovers agreed at the height of the bull market were, in the summer of 2002, being unwound, is it time to call a halt to merger activity?

Some would say yes, and several newspaper articles have called for a significant slowing down. However, according to Stephen Murphy in *KPMG Perspectives* (March 2002), 'If deals often fail to create value it might be tempting to think that part of the solution might be to do fewer deals. Unfortunately for many leading companies that simply isn't an option; industry convergence, deregulation, technological change and a host of other factors can create conditions in which consolidation or realignment becomes an absolute strategic necessity.' (*Hmmm, many companies?? – authors.)*

Perhaps the last word (for now) should go to the head of corporate broking at one of the largest banks: 'Some managements are simply not good enough to execute the strategy. Well-executed mergers, tied into the success of the business, will create enormous amounts of wealth and value for other people. Management should be encouraged and rewarded for this, not for mediocre performance.

'The issue is, how do you make sure that the value destroyers are shown the door? There is far too much reward for failure and mediocrity, including additional positions on other boards for failures!'

Both the comments quoted above are made by people who could be argued to have a systematic bias towards transactional strategies.

What is absolutely clear is that far too much M&A activity is initiated for the wrong reasons, consummated at inflated prices and then very badly managed. As a conclusion, we feel confident in suggesting that great benefits would accrue to the economy in general if the volume of M&A activity were drastically reduced, and skilful managers concentrated on developing their businesses by more 'organic' means, as we will see in later chapters.

Iceland Foods

Watch for the 'big strategic move' and the major acquisition.

Iceland Foods was one of the success stories of the 1980s and 1990s. A commitment to good value and quality enabled this frozen foods retailer to grow rapidly and achieve national status.

The guiding light of Iceland was Malcolm Walker. In his chairman's statement of 21 March 2000, he said that he was 'delighted to report a third successive year of double digit earnings growth. This has been driven by a continuation of our strong sales performance.' Commenting on the outlook for 2000, he said, 'Our core business is in excellent shape. Like-for-like food sales in the first 11 weeks of the year are up 6 per cent. Our home shopping service is growing strongly. We believe that Iceland's responsible approach to food retailing combined with the expansion of home shopping and new concepts will extend our customer appeal still further. This will enable us to fulfil our commitment to delivering continued growth in shareholder value.'

This sounds very much like the language of a manager who knows and is committed to his business. There is maybe just a hint of a visionary strategy to come.

Cut to July 2000. This time, the half-year statement is a joint one by Malcolm Walker, Chairman, and Stuart Rose, the new Chief Executive. In the report, they say:

> The core Iceland business maintained a robust performance in the first six months of 2000, with like-for-like food sales up six per cent and group pre-tax profit up 10 per cent. We continue to differentiate Iceland from its competitors through an emphasis on Food You can Trust, *announcing in June that we would convert our complete frozen vegetable range to organic at everyday supermarket prices in October this year. The merger with Booker has created a unique new business serving retail and trade customers through both traditional and new economy formats. Our integration teams are up and running, and our experience to date underpins our confidence in the delivery of our forecast cost savings, and in our ability to seize the expected opportunities to drive top line growth* [our italics].

Now on to the chairman's statement of March 2001:

> In June 2000 Booker plc was acquired. This more than doubled our turnover and created a unique organization providing food and household consumables to UK markets through retailing, wholesaling, foodservice and household consumables. *The combination of the two companies was expected to yield substantial synergies. It became evident in January that trading had been poor, expected synergies were not going to be achieved and other costs, particularly the cost of reversing Iceland's conversion to organic vegetables, were likely to be higher than expected* [our italics].
>
> We issued a trading statement on 22 January 2001 and on 31 January, your board made a Stock Exchange announcement that revised profit to £62 million. This was accompanied by the resignation of Malcolm Walker as chairman and I took his place. This announcement was followed by a further statement on 15 March 2000 revising expectations down still further to approximately £40 million. The reasons for these shortfalls were in part due to difficult trading conditions, but also to *poor execution of the merger of Iceland and Booker and a flawed move into organic vegetables…* [our italics]. Pre-tax exceptional items of £145 million have been charged to cover a number of items, particularly a £72 million write-off of the Booker pension scheme surplus and £30 million as a result of the review of accounting policies.
>
> This performance was totally unacceptable to your [completely new] board and has resulted in the group requiring a recovery plan to restore value.

The chairman went on to announce that Stuart Rose, CEO, who had joined the board from the acquired Booker on 26 June 2000, had resigned to join Arcadia plc in November 2000.

In the 2001 report the new CEO, Bill Grimsey, said:

> Iceland started the year strongly with first half like-for-like sales, growing by 6 per cent gross of promotions, *but in the nine months following the Booker acquisition it increasingly lost touch with the real needs of its core customer base.*
>
> … The problems of uncompetitive pricing *were exacerbated by the flawed move into organic vegetables. To achieve this, a significant part of the world's supply of organic vegetables was secured under contract for three years…*
>
> *Unfortunately, whilst the move generated considerable media coverage, it was largely irrelevant to the concerns of the typical Iceland customer, and was not readily accepted by them* [our italics].

By early March 2002, Iceland had changed its name to Big Food. At this time, the chief executive, Bill Grimsey, confessed that the latest sales figures were 'disappointing'. The *Guardian* business section describes the company as having debts of £430 million, suffering falling sales and losing customers. The share price was 116p, the lowest since October 1997. At the end of 2000, the share price was 346p. Some financial information concerning the company is given in Table 5.1.

Table 5.1 Iceland's financial position (£000s)

	2001	**2000**	**1999**	**1996**
Turnover	5,279	1,918	1,742	1,429
Pre-tax profit	(121)	58	55	56

On to a report in the *Guardian* of 14 September 2002: 'With demotion to the FTSE Small Cap index looming this month, the Big Food Group's name is looking increasingly inappropriate. So, too – if the gossips are to be believed – is its status as a publicly quoted company.' The report goes on to say that there is a very strong feeling that the company would 'find it easier to complete its restructuring programme away from the glare of the City'.

This is a rather sad, but not unusual, story. It appears that from what management say, the company was reduced to a shadow of its former self by a combination of a large acquisition in parallel with the introduction of the grandiose and inappropriate new organic food strategy. Either of the two events could have been extremely damaging; both in combination seem to have been nearly fatal.

Saddest of all is the comment by new CEO Grimsey that, 'In the 9 months following the Booker acquisition it [Iceland] increasingly lost touch with the real needs of the core customer base.' We are not acquainted with the perspectives of Iceland's employees, but wonder what they must feel.

But now we want to touch on other ways to get into trouble in Chapter 6...

6

Other 'failure' factors

As we have seen from the previous chapter, the path of mergers and acquisitions can more easily lead into the quicksands of decline and failure than to the sunlit uplands of seamless growth. But there are many other routes that lead to trouble…

MANAGERIAL INSULARITY AND COMPLACENCY

Insularity can arise from two quite different ways of behaving. Top management may be focused on the organization and away from the 'outside', or may be focused towards the 'outside', and in particular the City, and away from the needs of the organization. Complacency, or self-satisfaction, comes into the equation when the appropriateness or efficacy of the focus is not questioned.

Inward focus

Inward focus is not necessarily a wholly bad thing. Some companies criticized for being conservative or 'boring' have well-defined characteristics:

- They focus on one set of core skills in one or a small number of industry groups.
- They show a tendency towards continuous adaptation and improvement as opposed to bold or quantum changes.
- They regard change as incremental, building on an established base, rather than transformational or built on new 'visions'.
- Business development comes from the inside, concerned with innovation, product development and building market shares. When such companies acquire, they tend to make small, incremental purchases in their core business domains.
- They take a very conservative approach to financial risk.

- Managers are developed from inside the business and are required to spend a long time learning before being promoted to top jobs. External recruitment tends to be into middle management or into specialist roles.
- The whole orientation of the enterprise is towards sustaining the business and long-term success.

On the whole, research suggests that this approach tends to be adopted by successful businesses. Nevertheless, there is a large body of evidence showing that management can become insular and stuck, even arrogant, if they are lulled into a sense of invulnerability by success or simply through ignorance and complacency.

Marks & Spencer is thought by many to be an example of such insularity. Highly successful, and regarded as the 'blueprint' for all other retailers during the early 1990s, the famous retailer had created a very strong, inward-looking and rather change-resistant culture. The result of this was that the company lost touch with changes in clothes retailing and came to be regarded as old-fashioned by many consumers. Sales, profits and the share price plunged. A fresh, outward-focused management team at the top shook the whole edifice up, disposed of the disappointing acquisition of US clothes retailer Brooks Brothers, and is delivering improved results.

In the same way, IBM, described some years ago as 'managed by its culture rather than its managers', also became transfixed by its success and failed to recognize or respond to crucial changes in market dynamics and customer attitudes. Again, new leadership, who concentrated rigorously on the fundamentals of the business and refused to be drawn into deals and transactional antics, was needed to rebuild the company through rather drastic change measures.

In neither case was the failure catastrophic. New management seems to have succeeded in keeping the businesses intact.

Problems do seem to arise when top managers become insular and cut off from both their customers and their staff. Close-knit cadres of top managers, strongly bonded by long association or affiliation to strong leaders, can develop a resistance to feedback from the organization. As we saw in the previous chapter, they can develop the pattern of thinking described as 'groupthink', which can result in all manner of inappropriate behaviour ranging from wild corporate escapades to complacent inertia. In particular, the 'unanimity illusion' makes it particularly difficult to challenge beliefs and decisions previously made by the group.

Outer focus

On the other hand, some managers become cut off from their own organizations and customers by identifying too closely with the financial markets. They may never achieve real connections with staff and customers because they are not there long enough, or they may believe that the 'upward and outward' focus is best for the business or for their own reputations. Ironically, Marks & Spencer has also been included in this category by some commentators, who cite Sir Richard Greenbury's determination to deliver to the City profits in excess of £1 billion as leading to some of the decisions unpopular with customers!

The corporate management of Redland plc, our case study in the next chapter, also tended to be somewhat isolated from operations and aligned with the City, with consequential neglect of the organization and infrastructure, management development and capital expenditure.

So, an important challenge is to ensure that people appointed into top positions remain open to feedback from many sources, balancing the demands of the community of stakeholders.

CREATING STRATEGIES THAT ARE NOT 'NATURAL' TO THE ORGANIZATION

'Strategy' is one of the most overused and misused words in business. Conventionally, it is used to describe pretty well anything that top management do or wish to do. For example, whoever heard of a large 'unstrategic' acquisition?

So much has been written about business strategy by so many extremely clever people that we cannot hope to add to their brilliance. We just wish to make a few simple and, we hope, practical observations. Let us begin with two examples.

In early 2002, IBM ran a series of TV advertisements. One of these shows an obviously top manager (physically big and imposing, and speaking with a US accent). He stands, while his audience sits around him. He speaks words roughly along the following lines: 'Here is the strategy report (taps thick brochure). Two million bucks' worth of pure consulting genius. The board is hot for it, I'm hot for it. What do you think? Will it work?' There is a tense silence, and then the subordinates, one by one, say 'No!' The ad goes on to indicate that the reason for this dreadful put-down of consultants and the board is the lack of an appropriate systems infrastructure, which, for a consideration, IBM will supply.

The second example is very similar, but from real life. A real business-unit managing director commissioned a strategy study from the group planning department. At the end of the presentation, he thanked the staff of the department, very politely. There was a silence and then the head of planning said, 'Well, what do you think?' 'Oh,' said the managing director, 'it's a great report and you propose a brilliant strategy, but we have no chance of implementing it. We haven't the experience, skills or the quality of managers to do it.'

Two kinds of strategy

Crafted, or 'grounded', strategies

What these two examples show is that there are two quite different kinds of strategy, one of which mostly works and one of which mostly doesn't. The kind of strategy that mostly works may not be written up in consultant reports, strategy manuals or grand corporate 'vision statements'. Such strategies come from within organizations. They are usually the result of long experience of people in many functions and at many levels working together. They generate an almost unspoken unity of purpose between the wider workforce and top managers, who generate respect and commitment because they know the business, the people, the technology, the customers and the capabilities of the organization.

The essence of the strategy being used comes from a deep and detailed understanding of what the enterprise is good at and how it can win competitively. It is not theoretical, but based on knowledge of 'what happens now' and how this can be improved, adapted and developed to meet changing market circumstances.

In this kind of setting, information and intelligence about all kinds of things (competitor action, performance shortfalls, glitches, problems and successes) flow rather freely because of the existence of informal networks of people who regularly communicate up, down and across the organization. Top managers are in touch with what is going on in their organizations because they are 'plugged in' to these networks.

Because there is already a well-developed understanding of what is to be achieved and what is important, decisions get made quickly and problems are solved informally, often through a kind of shorthand developed over many years of understanding. Business strategy development, or strategic change, will normally happen as a result of a process of adaptation, with new imperatives and plans being communicated by leaders formally, but also, more important, by word of mouth and many, many day-to-day conversations and meetings.

If you don't believe this, read John Kotter's study *The General Managers* (1986), a real investigation of what excellent top managers actually do, rather than theories about what they ought to do. Kotter's findings are reinforced by that other great observer of and thinker about management, Henry Mintzberg. Mintzberg, from his extensive observations of what managers actually do, describes the involved, knowledgeable and practical process of strategizing as *crafting* strategy. In an article for the *Leader to Leader Institute Quarterly*, describing his observations of John Cleghorn, the CEO of the Royal Bank of Canada, Mintzberg (1999) says:

> His strategy process appeared to be one of *crafting*: to foster a flexible [organization] structure and open culture, to see the strategic implications of initiatives, and to integrate them with overall vision. *This requires detailed, nuanced knowledge of the organization* [our italics].
>
> Of course, this approach, based on rich, grounded information, does not make someone a strategist: that depends on one's capacity for creative synthesis. But I believe that such a style of managing is a prerequisite for developing strategic insights. It is the ability to move between the concrete and the conceptual – not only to understand the specifics but also to be able to generalise creatively about them – that makes a great strategist.

A few moments' thought will generate the insight that there is not much scope in this kind of strategy process for impatient, short-horizon CEOs supported by armies of external consultants. Yet all the evidence seems to show that the crafting process works.

Synthetic strategies

A different and very common kind of strategy process has many forms and names, but only one substance. It produces synthetic creations constructed by people at the top of the organization, or outside it. If external consultants prepare such strategies, they may have conducted a lot of analysis of markets and competitors, and worked with top management to put together strategies that look very convincing. Such strategies might also be described as imported, imposed or theoretical, in that they tend to rely heavily on externally generated analytical information, and little on intimate, detailed knowledge from the front line of the organization. One warning sign, however, can be that the strategy document contains a flow diagram, usually but not always linear in form, which frequently has an arrow or segment of an arrow at the end, labelled 'IMPLEMENT'.

The trouble usually starts when the strategy is revealed to the wider organization. Most people in the organization were not involved in the construction of the strategy. They may not understand it, may not agree with it, or may not comprehend what they should now do that is different. Furthermore, many may not be clear whether they will emerge as winners or losers when the new strategy is implemented. If the organization is large and complex, or if the strategy is difficult to understand or entails a lot of change, it will be enormously difficult to implement.

Sometimes, when organizations are in need of fundamental change and redirection, this is the only way to go. However, it has to be understood that this kind of strategic change will take years. In a very large organization it would be optimistic to expect a major change in strategy to be complete in less than 10 years.

All this may be difficult to accept by those who do not understand what real organizations are like, or who have been brainwashed by analysis and flow charts with a little arrow with 'IMPLEMENT' at the end, but please bear with us until later in the book.

To reinforce what we have said, we were pleased to find that Scott Adams, the creator of the Dilbert principle (Adams, 1996) in what is without a shadow of doubt one of the best business books of all time, finishes his book with two fundamental principles. They are:

- Companies with effective employees and good products usually do well, left to their own devices.
- Any activity that is more than one level removed from your people or your product will ultimately fail or have little benefit.

The trouble with most 'synthetic' strategies is that they are devised not one or even two levels removed from employees and customers, but often 10 levels or more removed. Even worse, if the strategic thinking originates from the work of external consultants, it then has to be processed through the brains of top managers before being revealed to the wider organization.

For a little light amusement, let us assume that for each level of organization the strategy has to pass through, the process of achieving understanding, commitment and action by people who serve customers increases in difficulty by a factor of 10. This means that the 'pure consulting genius' in the IBM advertisement could be 10 million (8 layers) or even 10 billion (11 layers) times more difficult to enact than going to frontline staff, explaining the problems that need to be solved and inviting them to devise a strategy, with a little help to deal with issues beyond their control! Well, why not?

In addition to the complexities of enacting a strategy through a large organization, there is also the issue of time. Top managers who are well bonded with their organizations and have extensive networks of colleagues at many levels can short-cut the usual process of 'cascading' down (consultant-speak) changes in strategic direction and are also likely to be much better informed about what is really going on in the business.

But 'active' and ambitious CEOs – who, remember, are likely to have about four years to make their mark – have no time for building elaborate networks and forging widespread contacts and alliances. This must be why so much that is deemed to be strategic tends to concern M,A&D activity, portfolio changes, restructurings, high-profile hirings and firings or grand cost-reduction exercises. These cut out the need to have deep understandings of the organization and the 'strategy in use'.

If a management is really 'active', as, for example, seems to have been the case in Invensys and Marconi, it will circumvent the organization altogether and act unilaterally from the top, creating 'strategies' and enacting them solely by transactional means. A common habit, akin to creating synthetic strategies, is that of formulating objectives that come from outside the organization, normally driven by 'City expectations'. Usually these objectives have no connection with an understanding of industry dynamics or company capabilities.

Marconi's 2000 annual report gives a vivid flavour of the kind of 'visionary' strategies that can be created by a small group of people at the top of an organization:

> Marconi is pursuing a once-in-a-lifetime opportunity to transform communications and knowledge management. The moment is unique because right now, the landscape of communications and information is being transformed beyond recognition.
>
> *The Marconi Vision*
>
> Marconi intends to drive the transformation and convergence of communications and information.
>
> We will add relevant information and knowledge management to our customers' businesses. We will meet the needs of carriers by defining the new public network.
>
> In this way, we will profit and grow, supplying the picks, shovels and maps of the new internet gold rush.

By 2001, John Mayo, deputy chief executive was celebrating a good transformational job well done. He said in the annual report of that year:

> Since 1997, we have made the transition from slow-growth conglomerate to fast-growth technology company.
>
> *Fully Integrated Company*
>
> Going forward, we will manage Marconi as a fully integrated company, not as a conglomerate...
>
> Our new divisional organization is up and running, management is in place and we are already selling solutions.

Most readers will not need to be reminded that the new and visionary company was created by selling most of GEC's 'old' businesses and buying a very expensive set of companies in industries that, by and large, Marconi's management knew little of!

It is interesting to recall that some investors happily advanced Marconi money to pursue its visionary path, in the same way that they did for Iceland Foods to help fund its revolutionary organic food strategy, or to Enron to help that company transform a whole industry.

The trouble comes when the corporate music has to stop, and top management become dependent on an organization that was in no way involved in creating the strategy.

An article in the *Financial Times* of 20 December 2002 headed 'Ebbers' undoing: how the deals ran out, doubts set in and the house of cards fell down' says it all: 'Feted on Wall Street, the telecoms tycoon had an insatiable appetite for acquisitions. But, as the second part of an FT analysis shows, when industry regulators called a halt to the 15-year spree, the company's efforts to maintain momentum grew desperate – and then blatantly fraudulent.'

NEGLECTING AND ABUSING THE ORGANIZATION

Neglect, ignorance and abuse of the organization that actually 'does the business' are some of the most common causes of long-term underperformance. The reasons for this are not too difficult to understand. Let us put ourselves in the shoes of an ambitious top executive, a man (it is usually, but not invariably, a man) with a big ego in a hurry to make big things happen. Like many of his counterparts, our man has a need to make his mark with the people who matter. These people will be the non-executive directors who hired him and an ever-attentive and judgemental audience in the City and the press. He is a somewhat impatient person, so a 10-year timescale is not what he has in mind. After all, he has been hired and given very strong incentives to show results – and fast.

So, what can he do?

First, it is important to have a few people who can be trusted. After all, there is limited time to get to know internal people well, and many of them may be part of the problem, rather than the solution. Frequently, the best thing is to bring in people who are already known, people whose loyalty is unquestioned.

Next, a coterie of trusted people having been created, consultants can be hired to give a rapid 'fix' on what is going on in the company and what needs to be done. As time is limited, the options for action are also limited. Typically, the consultants might indicate that some parts of the business are seriously under-performing, some are good performers and could be added to, but overall, costs and overheads are too high.

What to do? Well, first initiate a serious cost-reduction drive. In doing this, it is usually better not to involve too many of the longer-serving employees, who will probably create unnecessary complications. Best to create teams of highly incentivized 'Young Turks', leaven them with consultants and quickly start cutting the costs, working to very tight deadlines. The aim? To cut variable costs by at least 10 per cent within months, then make a real assault on fixed costs.

As the consultants have pointed out, 'Costs walk about on two legs', so legs must go. If possible, it is better to dress this bald fact up a little, so give the project an attractive name. We have actually experienced an overhead reduction projects that was called 'Project Rainbow' and widely communicated by external consultants to employees under that name. The 'overheads' were not fooled and renamed the project 'Price Slaughterhouse and the Cull'!

Next, to the 'no brain' actions. The poorly performing businesses must go. So, put teams of advisers and some internal financial people to work and find buyers as soon as possible.

Now for the good news. There is a solid base of good business that can be built upon. Again, the quick way to get action is to put together teams of advisers and internal people to review the acquisition possibilities and to focus on targets for purchase. The all-important share price will be considerably boosted if it is subtly leaked that there is a growing 'war chest' for acquisitions that is being swelled by the proceeds of the disposals and cost reductions.

We will leave our hero at this time. He and his colleagues are likely to be too busy to notice our departure, but not too busy to take heart from the healthy rise in their share price.

So, what is significant about this not entirely incredible story? Well, the first point to make is that the ambitious and impatient executive managed to get a lot of things to happen without involving the wider organization at all. He and his supporters did a lot of things, like making disposals and planning acquisitions, which need only a few internal people and a lot of external advisers to implement. Other actions, such as the cost-reduction drive, were done *to* the organization, rather than *with* it.

But at the end of the period of activism (and there always is an end to such episodes), what is the internal scenario likely to be? There will be, for better or worse, a different business portfolio. Some businesses will have been disposed of, and we will never know whether their problems could have been rectified by management action, given more time. There will be a number of un-integrated acquisitions and there will be a lower-cost, but neurotic, organization.

Worse still, there is likely to be quite a lot of hidden damage. The bout of activism forced on the organization by outsiders and consultants will almost certainly have developed schisms between the top leadership and the wider organization. Trust between leaders and led will almost certainly have been damaged. Good people may have left, customers may have been confused, and progress in the existing business is likely to have been 'frozen', to the benefit of competitors.

By the time the leadership has moved on, enriched by the consequences of a rise in the share price, the already damaged organization will experience yet another change at the top. If the new leaders find that things are looking much more difficult than external perceptions might have shown, then they also may indulge in a bout of remedial action, to the further detriment of the organization and business. Thus a descending spiral is set in train, which will probably end in break-up, sale or descent into the merciful anonymity of the lower ranks of quoted companies, or maybe the realms of private financing.

Within a very short time, investors, who will have moved on to the next thing, and the press, which seems to have little memory, will have forgotten the whole episode. And what is likely to have happened to the leadership? As likely as not, they will have moved on to the next challenge, acquiring a healthy tranche of share options on the way in. The really smart ones among these serial heroes will in a relatively short time have amassed enough to give it up and go 'plural' with a few non-executive directorships and the like.

There will be those who will accuse us of cynicism and others who will argue that the actions described may have been necessary to shake a torpid organization out of its lethargy. This latter point is absolutely correct. Organizations that are in the depths of crisis and have but one chance of survival will need drastic action and there may not be too much time to involve the wider organization. In these circumstances, action of the kind we described may be perfectly legitimate, to create the chance of survival. And when the crisis has been weathered, sensible crisis leaders will hand over the reins to those who have a longer-term orientation, or they will adapt their behaviour and seek to bond more closely with the organization. But it is also important to mention that the actions we described, if forced on a relatively healthy organization, *may actually bring on a crisis that did not previously exist*.

As a last word on the subject, there was a small item on the TV news in October 2001, shortly after the Twin Towers outrage. As all will remember, the airline industry had taken a big hit, and massive lay-offs were instantly announced in various companies, in one or two cases the day after the tragedy. A manager from the aircraft servicing and repair company Marshall's Aerospace was interviewed about the cancellation of contracts by British Airways, which was a serious blow to the business. The reporter asked how large the consequential lay-offs would be. 'There will be no lay-offs at this time,' said the man from Marshall's. 'We have spent many years building a highly skilled and valuable workforce that is the mainstay of our business and are not going to waste that lightly.' Marshall's is a privately owned company.

PLACING INAPPROPRIATE RELIANCE ON CHARISMATIC, 'SUPERHERO' CEOS

We have described some of the antics that managers in the heroic mould can get up to when they are parachuted into an organization with the assumption that they can transform it quickly by the simple exercise of almost magical personal genius.

Occasionally, there is a need for very high-ego, high-profile figures. An organization in an advanced state of decline, approaching a crisis, may well be one. But, where this is not the case, it is hard to see how such heroes can add value to the workings of a well-managed and capable enterprise. It is much more likely that they will create disruption and damage, as Rakesh Khurana describes in the *Harvard Business Review* (2002). Khurana asserts that the notion that business invariably needs charismatic figures in leadership positions is a relatively new phenomenon. He describes three reasons for this:

1. A new breed of investor emerged in the 1980s, and they were intolerant of what they (often justifiably) saw in the contemporary top manager as a part of an insulated, self-interested elite. They wanted CEOs who could shake things up and put an end to 'business as usual'. This change, says Khurana, coincided with two other changes.
2. An almost religious conception of business emerged, exemplified by the appearance of such words as 'mission, 'vision' and 'core values'.
3. All this was exacerbated by 'the rise of so-called populist capitalism, whereby ordinary Americans made investing the country's most popular participatory sport. To serve the public's growing appetite for business news, the mass media greatly expanded coverage of corporate doings, focusing – as always – on personalities and easily comprehensible narratives. In this environment, a new breed of corporate leader, today's charismatic CEO, began to appear.' Exactly the same seems to have happened in the United Kingdom, as we saw in Chapter 2.

This new kind of CEO was expected to provide a vision of a radically different future and to attract and motivate followers for a journey to a new promised land. Such heroes were supposed to have the gift of tongues and to be able to inspire employees, investors, analysts and the press. But, says Khurana, charisma, like its close relative romantic love, can be blinding, with severe consequences.

The first trap is what social psychologists describe as the 'fundamental attribution error'. There is little evidence that except in very exceptional circumstances, such as those we described at the beginning of this section, the CEO's impact has a fundamental effect on the performance of large organizations. Studies indicate that up to 60–65 per cent of businesses' performance is attributable to industry and economic effects, and much of the rest to the strengths or weaknesses of the wider organization and deep competencies within it. How can a single person, usually with short tenure, actually have any real effect on these fundamentals? Moreover, one effect of the 'fundamental attribution error' is to lessen the tenure of CEOs, because, if the great hero fails to save the day, he or she is likely to be quickly replaced by another.

Another effect of attribution is that of attaching great significance to extraordinarily superficial descriptions of people. Khurana describes the deliberations of a board appointments committee that attached tremendous importance to a candidate's strengths because he 'had worked for Jack Welch' (of GE). Similarly, many Americans believe that Ronald Reagan won the Cold War and that Alan Greenspan runs the US economy. On this side of the Atlantic, many people seem to believe that the prime minister 'runs the country', and newspapers occasionally fret about who will do it while he is on holiday!

The cult of the charismatic hero also leads to another effect: that of the attractiveness of the external, publicly high-profile appointee. Khurana's article quotes a director of a major US company: 'The person coming in from the outside has a clear mandate… He is not beholden to anyone. There is so much baggage. Organizational boxes, the people in boxes, probably half the businesses that were bought now should be chucked… [As an insider] you are part of the process… You turn to an outsider and then you can watch the blood spray [!]. You don't see many examples of internal candidates getting to the top of the system and then laying waste to the existing culture.' This man sounds more like a Viking marauder of AD 400 than a modern manager! Readers might like at this stage to contemplate two things:

- Organizations that have been well managed are unlikely to benefit from blood spraying on the walls.
- It is a known fact that the symptoms so vividly described by our director are most likely to have been the result of the attentions of a high-ego superhero than a good industrial manager.

Khurana goes on to describe the destructive effects of many of the erstwhile superstars such as Skilling of Enron and Nasser of Ford. He concludes:

> Faith is an invaluable, even indispensable gift in human affairs. In the realm of religion, it is said to move mountains… Yet today's extraordinary trust in the power of the charismatic CEO resembles less a mature faith than it does a belief in magic. If, however, we are willing to begin rethinking our beliefs about leadership, the age of faith can be followed by an era of faith and reason.

In conclusion, it is worth considering the sources of much of the 'superhero' propaganda. Apart from the publicity machines of the charismatic heroes themselves, the cult of personality seems to have common currency among investors, analysts, the press and many executive search consultants. The fact that these people might want to see a high turnover of top managers, simple, compelling personal stories, quick action or gossip, rather than boringly consistent attention to fundamentals, might make us pause and wonder whether the ridiculous cult of personality has really yet run its course.

CEO turnover

One last set of facts ought to make the demise of the imported 'superstar' absolutely mandatory. A direct effect of the 'star' system is frequent replacement of CEO incumbents. After all, reason investors and others with clout, the man or woman at the top is the visible leader, and when things go wrong, what is more sensible than replacing the leader with a better one? Thus the firing of CEOs has become a commonplace event in both the United States and the United Kingdom, and a growing habit elsewhere.

Margaret Wiersema reported on her research on the matter in the *Harvard Business Review* (2002). She examined all instances of CEO turnover in the largest 500 US companies in the years 1997 and 1998. In that period there were 83 CEO 'successions'. Wiersema estimates that 71 per cent of these successions were involuntary; in other words, the CEOs left as a result of pressure. The commonest source of this pressure was the investment markets, acting through the external directors of the company. This means that, for the research period, only 29 per cent of CEO successions were routine, occurring because the incumbent reached retirement age.

Overall, 36 per cent of the CEO replacements were from outside the companies, a considerable increase on previous practice. But, even more important, a massive 61 per cent of replacements for CEOs who were forced out came from outside the company.

Very good, one might say; active shareholders exercising their rights, holding CEOs accountable and acting responsibly to improve performance. What could be better than that? 'Blood spraying on the walls' is the way to squeeze the maximum performance from investments!

Well no, actually, not at all. *The facts are quite different from the opinions of investors and, it would appear, many non-executive directors. In those companies that forcibly replaced their CEOs:*

- Operating earnings were no different for the two years after the bloodletting than for the two years before.
- Exactly the same was true for operating earnings compared with the industries represented by the companies.
- Returns on assets were slightly less for the two years post-bloodletting.

Even worse for those who will only be satisfied by blood on the walls, the performances of the companies that practised routine succession were better for the two years following the CEO change than those of companies that forced out their CEOs – on all measures. Another commonly held belief blown: high-profile firings don't work! The most 'active' of all remedies exposed as a myth!

Wiersema concludes that the reasons for the failure of the 'real man's' favourite remedy are not difficult to understand:

- Investors, the main source of pressure for dismissals, do not understand the real reasons for the problems, which are invariably much more complex than investment managers would understand.
- Exactly the same applies to the instruments of the investors, who actually carry out the removals of CEOs: the non-executive directors. Wiersema contends that these worthies are generally too distant from the problems and the organizations to understand the real roots of problems, and are therefore unable to specify what attributes in the new appointee might give the best possibility of success. Furthermore, they are unable to guide the new incumbent in the crucial first months of his or her tenure because they do not know enough about the company to do so.
- Selection decisions concerning the new CEOs are driven by investors' concerns and are therefore too much driven by outside people, headhunters and investors, rather than a rich and deep internal understanding of the problems.
- The arrival of a new, frequently external, high-profile, high-ego leader, under intense pressure to produce quick results, often deepens a crisis, or causes a crisis even if there was none before.

Are these facts likely to change the beliefs of investors? We doubt it, as most people involved in the investment management game do not understand enough about how businesses run to appreciate the reality behind the facts. It is far easier to hold on firmly to a superficially attractive and emotionally satisfying set of beliefs.

UNBALANCED ATTENTION TO STAKEHOLDER NEEDS

The relatively recent dominance of the industrial agenda by the financial markets has created a whole range of noticeable impacts on the behaviour of managers and on the performance of the enterprises that they lead. We have seen from previous chapters that CEOs believe that the strongest influences on their success and well-being are the press and investors. It is thus hardly surprising that many managers react by trying to act in ways that will please these two interrelated influences. And some overreact in ways that cause serious damage to their enterprises. Here are some examples of how:

- By making risky performance promises. Investors like managers who 'deliver on tough promises'. The tendency for some managers is to make commitments to investors that will be delivered only if everything goes right. When, as frequently happens, unforeseen events cause shortfalls against the targets, managers can react by taking action that causes damage to their companies. Such action can range from dubious accounting to drastic cost-reduction exercises, or the shelving of planned investments.

  Often the initial reaction is to find ways of hiding the problems, because issuing 'profit warnings' is not taken to kindly by investors. Then, when the problems do emerge, they may have been worsening for some time and require drastic action, against a background of very critical and demanding investor reactions. In more extreme cases a cycle of destabilization may occur that will do serious damage to the company, laying it open to takeover or break-up.

- By creating a fixed performance target and flexing all other actions around it. It is not uncommon for companies to treat the commitments that they have made to the financial markets as fixed, and investment and costs as flexible elements. If this behaviour becomes endemic, it can lead to long-term underperformance and eventual catastrophic failure.
- By overreacting to the apparent needs or wants of the financial markets. All large companies and their top managers are the subject of periodic rumours and speculation by the markets and press. From time to time, bankers, journalists and investors may develop strong views about what companies should do. These views usually entail doing something 'active', such as changing management, selling or buying businesses or de-merging parts or the whole of the company.

  Sometimes the pressure is short-lived and the markets move on to something else. On other occasions the pressures are more persistent. It takes real character and confidence in their business understanding for managers to resist such pressures. Many have succumbed, with very mixed results. Accountants, bankers and journalists can be very wrong, especially when long experience and complex judgements are needed. More seriously, it may be that the immediate needs of bankers and fund managers are not in the long-term interests of companies.

  Examples of companies that have succumbed to the temptations of fashion or have been pressurized into taking action are not uncommon. The recent histories of the Internet and telecommunications industries abound with examples of companies that have invested heavily in ventures that have, in retrospect, been disastrous. Marconi, most dot.com companies, Energis, WorldCom, BT and many others, including even Vodafone, have come to some grief on the communications miracle that has not yet come to pass.

  For some time it has been apparent that the financial markets, supported by the press, believe that the retailing group Kingfisher is worth more to them in bits than together. Apparently standing in the way of consummating this belief was Sir Geoff Mulcahy, a major architect in the building of a very valuable international retailing group from the unpromising beginning of Woolworth, a basket case of the early 1980s. What looked to outsiders like a long-term orchestrated campaign to remove Mulcahy resulted in his departure in 2003. Rumours now abound of bidders from the United States and continental Europe for the parts of Kingfisher.

  At a more serious level, Enron was the creation of an ambitious management aided by bankers, accountants and, it is reported, the consultancy firm McKinsey, which is said to have helped the company to devise some of the strategies later exploited by management. Enron, in a very real sense, was the creation of the financial markets and a management that appeared to have little notion of stakeholder loyalty.
- By undervaluing the relative importance of customers and staff to the success of the business. Over-ambitious, insensitive or under-confident top managers can easily forget that the underlying influences on the performance of their businesses are not the financial markets, but the good

opinion and support of customers and employees. Neglect of either of these crucial constituencies will sooner or later have disastrous effects on corporate performance, as British Airways' top management found out in July 2003, when a misjudgement of staff sentiment about an apparently trivial matter of 'clocking on' arrangements proved to be the final straw for some members of staff. The sudden walk-out of check-in staff is estimated to have cost the airline more than £50 million in direct costs, and much more in terms of damage to its reputation among customers.

Hewlett Packard

The M&A story of 2001–02 has been the proposed merger of computer hardware manufacturer Hewlett Packard, a company that is very famous for its culture, enshrined in a creed called 'The Hewlett Packard Way'; and Compaq, a large personal computer maker. The merger proposal has brought Walter Hewlett, son of one of Hewlett Packard's founders, and Carly Fiorina, the current Hewlett Packard CEO, into head-to-head confrontation.

The issues are classical. On the one hand, Ms Fiorina, who had previously tried to merge Hewlett Packard with Price Waterhouse, claims that consolidation of the personal computer industry provides a once-in-a-lifetime opportunity to offer customers end-to-end systems solutions and that the combination will be able to offer complementary product lines in PCs, servers, storage and services support. The company backs this by offering $2.5 billion worth of synergies and 'expects these to outweigh post-merger revenue losses of about 5%'.

Ms Fiorina is reported to have a steely resolve to bring this huge merger to fruition despite much opposition. In an interview, she reported merger teams to be standing by, professed herself to be totally committed to the logic of the merger, but said that there could be some difficulties with 'the squishy bits' (the fact that the two companies have markedly different cultures). She and her opposite number in Compaq have been reported as standing to gain many millions of dollars in bonuses and other forms of remuneration when the deal goes through.

On the other side of the argument is Mr Hewlett, who opposes the merger on the grounds of over-optimism about the synergies and the fact that the vastly different cultures of the two companies will make effective integration virtually impossible. He argues that the combined company will lose 25 cents in earnings from every dollar of lost revenue. Ms Fiorina and her advisers argue for a loss of 12 cents. She also says that the merger would be substantially earnings-accretive in the first year after the merger and attacks Mr Hewlett as having a 'simplistic anti-merger bias'. Employees have weighed in with a view, mounting a demonstration demanding 'Two job losses rather than 15,000'. The 'two' are presumably the jobs of Ms Fiorina and the chairman of Compaq. The whole affair has been given a real boost by the fact that both sides have enough money to mount really lavish campaigns and use the best advisers.

Having lost the big battle, Mr Hewlett, whose family have about 18 per cent of the shares, has said that he will stay on the board to try to look after the best interests of Hewlett Packard employees and salvage something after the merger fails.

This 'spectacular' is rather special, because there has been considerable investor and press opposition to the deal on the grounds that the dream of synergy is more likely to prove a nightmare.

Readers may be interested to follow the fortunes of the merged entity to see how the share price progresses over the next few years. The authors have already placed their predictions in a sealed envelope.

7

The rise and fall of Redland plc: a case study

REDLAND'S ORIGINS AND RISE

The story of Redland is that of a company with humble origins, in an industry sector regarded by some as lacking sex appeal. It charts the rise of an enterprise to the point that the company was for a period lionized by the financial markets, press and peers alike. But its spectacular ascent proved to be unsustainable. Redland's demise contains a warning for those who hope that building relationships with the financial markets might ensure long-term support.

Redland was founded in 1919 in Reigate, Surrey. Up to and through the Second World War the company grew steadily but modestly, serving the construction materials markets in the south of England. After the war it invented an ingenious machine that made concrete roof tiles faster and better than its competitors. This invention coincided with the post-war reconstruction period in Britain and Europe. The roof tile machine attracted great interest in many parts of the world and the company entered into partnerships with foreign companies that wanted the machine and its associated technology.

By the time of our story, Redland had grown to be a large company. Its post-war growth had seen several cycles of diversification and concentration. Each period of diversification had ended in the sale of all purchases apart from those in three businesses: roof tiles, aggregates and bricks. These were effectively Redland's 'heritage' businesses.

The first and original business was the manufacture and sale of roof tiles. Traditionally, local companies had made roof tiles out of clay. With the invention of its revolutionary tile-making machine, Redland pioneered the manufacture of tiles in concrete, to a standard far superior to that of traditional clay tiles and on an industrial scale.

Next came the aggregates business. 'A very basic business,' said many financial analysts (and some Redland top managers): simply extract material from the ground and sell it. The truth is much more complex, given the variety of raw materials and end products that can be extracted; and the economic and political implications of the acquisition and holding of reserves. A full-range aggregates business is much akin to a localized version of an oil company.

Last came bricks. Surely nothing could be simpler? Again, not entirely. Bricks are produced in massive kilns, which are technically very complex and expensive. They become grossly uneconomic if not fully utilized. The industry is massively sensitive to economic cycles.

After the Second World War, reconstruction, the post-war population boom and a marked rise in the aspirations of people for a better physical environment came together to create huge market opportunities for companies in the construction and construction materials industries. Redland's superior tile machine came to the notice of Rudolph Braas, an entrepreneur whose roof tile company in Germany was also presented with massive post-war opportunities. Redland licensed it to Braas in return for a minority shareholding in his company.

Shortly afterwards, Redland persuaded the War Reparations Commission to part with its shares in Braas, thus establishing a majority holding. Not surprisingly, Herr Braas saw this as sharp practice on the part of Redland, and from then on the Germans regarded their UK shareholder with a degree of caution. It is interesting to note that despite the majority holding, Redland did not involve itself in the management of Braas.

Over time, this pattern of relationship with businesses – to take a shareholding but leave management in local hands – became the norm for Redland outside the United Kingdom. Even in the 1990s some Redland corporate managers were describing the group to their wholly owned non-UK colleagues as 'the shareholder'.

Redland grew mainly by acquisition. In 1968, Colonel Young, the chairman, reported that, owing to 23 successful bids over the previous 13 years, 'the name of Redland is constantly linked in the press with other companies which are thought to be suitable for takeover or merger'. He went on to say, 'one of the principal tasks of the new Management Board is to subject every aspect of the group's activities to a searching analysis, with a view to reconstruction or disposal if the required return on capital cannot be achieved'.

So, here we see three early patterns:

- the notion of acquisitions as the major engine of growth;
- the belief that businesses are assets that can be easily disposed of if they do not produce satisfactory returns;
- the idea that non-managed shareholdings were an easy way to international growth.

In the early 1970s a failed bid by RMC, a major industry rival, sensitized future management to the need to cultivate shareholders and stay close to City advisers.

The business became very substantial. Sales for 1982–83 broke the £1 billion mark for the first time. In the 1970s and 1980s the company went through one of its diversification phases. The range of businesses had increased dramatically. Redland was involved in aggregates, roofing, clay bricks, road marking and maintenance, reinforced plastic pipes, building claddings, fuel distribution, shipping, roof truss fabrication, traffic automation and plastic windows.

The legal and financial structure of the company had also become vastly more sophisticated. Sixteen separate holding companies in the United Kingdom, the Netherlands Antilles, the Channel Islands, the Netherlands and the United States evidenced another trend. Financial smartness, not a new thing to the company, was to be further developed under Robert Napier as Finance Director. And the management, now led by Sir Colin Corness as Chairman, were still ambitious and hungry for growth. The search for ever-larger UK and international acquisitions was intensified.

In the 1988 report to shareholders, Sir Colin announced the appointment of Robert Napier as Group Managing Director, Gerald Corbett as Financial Director, and the appointment of the heads of businesses to the board. These included George Phillipson, head of aggregates, who remained with Redland until the end.

At first glance, this was a team of all the talents. Now the chairman and all the Redland executive directors were graduates of the universities of Oxford and Cambridge, and most of them had had a distinguished academic career. However, of this group only George Phillipson, who was a long-term aggregates man, had deep industrial experience.

Also of interest was the growth in the number of advisers retained by the company. In 1984 only Barings and Barclays plc were retained as investment bankers. By 1987 the list had grown to include Barclays, Barings, Morgan Grenfell, Morgan Guaranty Trust, Morgan Stanley, National Westminster plc and S G Warburg. Redland's corporate management were clearly not averse to bankers and equally clearly had not abandoned the acquisition road to growth.

In 1991, German earnings were separated from those in the rest of Europe, showing that Braas in Germany generated profits of £85.8 million, almost half of total group earnings. Redland was becoming very dependent on the Braas partnership.

The new team was not idle. A series of smaller acquisitions and disposals allowed the group to exit from some of the more diverse businesses, refocusing on the three traditional areas. A 1988 diversification into the plasterboard industry, new to the Redland management, had turned into an embarrassing disaster. The market had turned out to be far more competitive than expected and the new venture exposed Redland's lack of operations experience. The best way was out, so the embarrassing liability was exchanged for a 20 per cent stake in Lafarge Platreurope. Later estimates calculated that value destruction from the venture amounted to £50 million.

Internal reality was not that portrayed by an admiring external world. In 1989, Redland received a very significant public accolade. It was voted the most admired company in its sector. Significantly, the write-up that accompanied the citation said:

> The building materials industry does not have obvious appeal for high flying graduates or MBA's. But Redland has found a way round that. Its job advertisements, for instance, try not to narrow down the field: the company positively welcomes candidates from outside the construction sector. The board itself includes exiles from Fisons, Schroders, Unilever and Dixons, whose diverse skills have helped shape the marketing strategy of a company which used to be highly production-oriented.

> Redland has another trick up its sleeve for luring able candidates. For the past decade or so, it has expressly used the corporate planning department as a seedbed for grooming top management talent. This gives both parties the opportunity to see whether they are suited and enables bright young hopefuls to get to know the business *without getting bored with operational routine* [our italics].
>
> Redland's clear and consistent strategy is to be a major player in relatively few sub-sectors of the construction materials industry. This explains its recent decision to enter the fast-growing plasterboard business, deemed to have many features in common with Redland's three core businesses: high entry barriers, conversion of raw materials into a finished product and a similar customer base. In view of the company's record in process innovation and financial management, it seems well placed to challenge BPB's dominance in this business.

The idea central to the paean to Redland's management was a seductive one, and peculiarly British. It was that bright people, if they put their minds to it, could do virtually anything, but could become easily bored by anything too mundane – in this case, operating a business. Still, from the outside the accolade appeared to be well merited, as did the award of the Queen's Award for Technological Achievement in 1990.

THE TAKEOVER OF STEETLEY

The way was now clear for the top team, supported by the bright young people in the corporate planning department, to prepare for the next move. The time was ripe for a really significant leap forward, one that would take Redland, in theory, to a size that would make it a difficult bid target, and, more important, establish it as a world leader in its sector.

A natural target was Steetley plc. Seemingly an almost perfect fit with Redland, Steetley was involved in aggregates, bricks and minerals. The combination of the assets of the two companies would create the largest aggregates producer in France, supplying 10 per cent of the market. This would correct Redland's long-standing weakness in an important market. The combined aggregates business would have critical mass in the United Kingdom and Spain, and important regional markets in the United States.

In bricks, the fit appeared to be almost perfect. Redland Bricks had great strength in the south-east of England, whereas Steetley was particularly strong in the North. This market synergy would be supplemented by cost savings of £10 million from the combination of the two businesses. Outside bricks, Redland estimated that at least an extra £20 million of savings could be realized from the merger synergies.

The Redland team were mainly very enthusiastic. There were some concerns about the price Redland might have to pay and whether Redland's management had the capacity and experience to deal with the complex merger of the various businesses. Some small voices in the investment community also wondered if this might not be one deal too far. Still, the balance of external opinion seemed to be positive and the banking advisers were obviously extremely enthusiastic.

In the end, Redland's hand was forced. Steetley announced that it had agreed to merge its brick-making activities with those of Tarmac. This merger would completely scupper Redland's plans. It was now or never.

Part of the fascination of acquisitions is the psychological dynamics of deals. There is the thrill of the chase and the kill, the fascination of the deal dynamics and, not least, an excitement that comes from working with enormous intensity with highly intelligent professional advisers. People working on deals often come to feel very powerful when they think of the strategic, financial and human outcomes of what they might do. History can be made quickly simply by taking risks and spending other people's money.

It is probable that the Redland management were influenced by the acquisition process and spurred on by the prospect of being thwarted. At any rate, in November 1991 Redland launched a full hostile bid for Steetley. Steetley's management rejected the offer and battle commenced.

In a message to Steetley shareholders on 19 February 1992, Sir Colin Corness was firm in his opinions: 'In our view, it cannot be in the best interests of its shareholders for Steetley to contemplate an independent future with high gearing, low interest cover and a policy of paying uncovered dividends. Steetley has paid high prices to acquire its market positions in France and Spain.' Steetley's shareholders agreed, and Redland's revised offer, valuing Steetley at £624 million, was accepted.

By 1992, Redland had come a very long way from the small but ambitious company of the 1960s. It had progressed from being a small company to a big small company and then a small big company, to its final flowering as a truly big company. In 1993 Redland entered the top half of the list of prestigious FTSE 100 companies. The future seemed pretty bright.

But there were a few small clouds of doubt on the horizon. Redland and Steetley had to be integrated. After all, at least £30 million of cost savings had been promised. If they weren't delivered, external credibility would be severely dented.

Very detailed action plans were assembled and, for a time, most people were so busy that they had no time to reflect on the wider consequences of the acquisition. These were truly significant. The cost of the acquisition was considerably higher than the £624 million quoted by the chairman in the annual report. This figure ignored Steetley debt that Redland would have to assume. As an internal rule of thumb, Robert Napier was quoting a total cost of 'about £1 billion'. To this could be added the additional £1 billion or so that had been spent during the previous three years on acquisitions, internal investments and the ill-starred plasterboard venture. There was a huge cost to recoup, and economic circumstances were hardly propitious. Cost savings and disposals were urgently needed.

An external consultant, brought in to help corporate management with the merger, produced a planning document spelling out the challenges facing Redland's management. In it he emphasized the importance of both 'hard' and 'soft' integration, pointing out that, 'Many acquisitions have failed to realize the aspirations of those making them because of failure to manage the more intangible aspects of the merger process.' The consultant felt that the Redland management did not sufficiently appreciate the growth aspects of the merger, concentrating instead almost entirely on cost reduction.

However, there are huge pressures on the top management of acquiring companies to overemphasize the tangible factors, placing little importance on the more intangible, 'softer' aspects of mergers. The critical investor audience wants the 'numbers' and tends to regard synergy and cost savings as being one and the same thing. Initiating head office management tend to be less familiar with the soft aspects of mergers. And not least, there is a perceived need to demonstrate quick wins to the investment community.

And thus it was with Redland. The immediate post-acquisition tasks were performed with expedition and great energy, to the extent that savings were realized considerably in excess of the initial £30 million target. A few months after the acquisition, Robert Napier reported, '*Now that we have integrated Steetley* [our italics], our three strong core businesses have a substantially increased presence in the United Kingdom, France and North America.'

Inside Redland, everyone realized that the end of growth fuelled by acquisitions had been reached. As one director put it, 'That's it, really. We've spent as much money as we are going to get; there is not much more to do.'

Robert Napier knew Redland needed to realize better returns from existing assets. To make things more difficult, the economy was entering a period of lower inflation. Napier had a financial and City background, but he rapidly realized that to go forward, the company needed to undergo a quantum change. His insight was to lead to a new phase in the company's story.

AFTER THE STEETLEY ACQUISITION

In August 1993 the brokers Smith New Court UK published a research paper entitled 'Redland, after Steetley: a time to take stock?'. This concluded that 'Redland is clearly quality. It is run with an attention to the concerns of shareholders that is unrivalled and, to an extent, the ability to express clear doubts on certain aspects of the group is a result of its openness. The board, furthermore, sets itself high standards and it would be wrong to assess Redland by any other.' It went on to identify problem areas as the financial structure (the strong minority shareholders in Braas and other partnerships limiting Redland's freedom of action) and in the management of some of its operations. Furthermore, 'for the longer term, unless Braas can resume its sensational growth, to justify investment Redland has to prove it can manage its extensive quarry assets to make a return substantially above the 5% we forecast for 1993. The challenge to management cannot be overestimated.'

So what were the financials at this point? Redland had issued shares to fund its continuing growth, so that the number of shares in issue at the 1992 year-end was 479 million, up from 274 million a year earlier. At the dividend level of 25p per share, Redland's dividend cover, at 0.9 times, was alarmingly akin to that of Steetley before the Redland bid! Pre-tax profits were £221 million, at the same level as in 1988 but on a substantially higher turnover. Profit margins in 1992, at 11.9 per cent, were the lowest for over five years.

In 1993, the first full year after the Steetley acquisition, sales were up 18 per cent and operating profit was 30 per cent up at £304 million. However, the Braas German roofing contribution to operating profit was still approximately half, despite all the frenetic growth of the Redland side of the business. Redland was still unhealthily dependent on the performance of Braas. To get past this dependence, the performance of the aggregates businesses needed to improve. It was unlikely that salvation would come from the brick division, where past failure to invest in modern low-cost capacity was holding back profitability.

All this would require real focus on operational management. According to the analysts at Smith New Court,

> Simplistically Redland's historic corporate culture is of a financially centralised, operationally devolved, emotionally remote style of management with the centre

> embodying the necessary corporate skills including finance. It is now Redland's prime concern to raise the standards of its operational management to provide the required counter to the skills of the centre. Although some 80% of group profits and assets are under the direct control of Redland Aggregate's George Phillipson and Braas's Erich Gerlach, both experienced operatives, we have for some time been concerned by the dominance of the group's culture by financial men. Four out of the five UK executives [directors] have only limited in-depth experience of running a business... As a board they give the dangerous impression of believing that they have experience of life at the sharp end.

The analysts concluded that Redland's corporate management needed rapidly to convert from financial wizards to seasoned operators and ended by asking whether 'middle age was likely to enhance the operational abilities of Redland's Young Turks'. Readers might like to consider this question for themselves.

As soon as the immediate pressure of the Steetley acquisition abated, Robert Napier called together the top 33 managers from the corporate centre and operations around the world. He started by explaining that Redland now had an excellent collection of assets and there was no intention of changing or adding to them. 'We don't have the money to spend, as our gearing is quite high enough and we cannot return to the equity markets in the near future.' More importantly, 'Because we have spent £2 billion over the last four years, our shareholders are looking to us to earn returns from that investment before encouraging any further spending.'

Napier asked the group of senior managers to raise its sights and consider how it might enhance performance. He said, 'Some of you may think that the line managers are not sufficiently involved in the overall direction of the group. I know that there is a view that the Group Committee is an elite operating in a rather rarefied atmosphere, and that there is too much of a gulf between the Group Committee and the rest of the organization.' The conference broke into small groups to consider such questions as 'What are the major issues facing Redland?' and 'What are the priorities for future action (strategically, organizationally and financially)?'

At feedback time, few punches were pulled. Delegates were of the opinion that there was too much separation between top and operating managers, between Braas and Redland, between the United Kingdom and the rest of the world, and between bricks and roofing. Furthermore, they thought that the company lacked any real sense of direction, strategy or vision, apart from financial goals. To crown all this, top management were sometimes patronizing and elitist and tended to concern themselves with financial matters to the exclusion of strategy, organization, culture, people and the provision of integrated and balanced leadership. However, there was a universal belief that if the directors were to involve the management more in the future, there would be a very positive response. Napier promised that the issues would be seriously addressed by the Group Committee and that, 'These issues about the Redland organization must be pursued long term and not just as the flavour of the month.'

Leaving Napier and his colleagues to ponder on how to proceed, it is worth remembering what other constraints might have impeded Redland's ability to address its problems. The twin roots from which Redland drew its success had been described by past leaders as 'partnerships and acquisitions'. Choosing good partners and managing the shareholding in the partner had become important skills for Redland executive directors. Acquisitions had been mainly initiated and managed from the top. This demanded a skill set not unlike that of investment bankers, and it was these skills that came to be valued at corporate level.

Redland's partner organizations tended to have full responsibility for running the business and competing in the marketplace. Consequently, inside Redland these aspects of management received less emphasis than they might have done in companies with a different structure. Redland managers, as the 'Most Admired Company' accolade had said, could reach the top without having had much direct involvement in 'operations'.

Redland's most important 'partner' was Braas & Co. GmbH. For reasons already explained, this relationship was wary and somewhat distrustful. Redland's ability to extract dividends and to hire or fire Braas management was restricted, such issues being formally determined through the shareholder meeting and the German supervisory board. Rudolph Braas's daughter, Helly, was the lead representative of the minority shareholders. Helly Bruhn-Braas had a fierce pride in the company her father had created and could, at the very least, be described as strong-minded and determined.

The view of Braas's executives was that the Redland top management did not have any real experience of or skill in running an operating business. Furthermore, they felt that Redland's top management were in thrall to 'the City', engendering inconsistency and short-termism. Braas's management were nervous that Redland top management would, if they could, extract excessive cash from Braas and spend it on unwise acquisitions or on dividend distributions to shareholders. In consequence, Braas was almost a 'no-go' area for Redland's top management. In addition to the trappings of the German supervisory board, the Braas management and minority shareholders had over time created restrictive legal agreements of Teutonic size and thoroughness. Redland was hugely constrained in its relationships with Braas.

There were many other examples of difficult issues in partner companies. Nippon Monier, for example, was a 60 per cent owned Japanese roof tile business. Two large Japanese firms owned the remainder. Under the partnership agreement the Japanese investors would provide many of the top managers in the joint venture. By 1993 it was becoming painfully apparent that rather than placing the cream of their talent into the joint company, the partners were more probably using it as an outlet for superannuated failures.

Along with these problems, Redland also lacked experience in integrating acquisitions. Previous deals had either been small and easily assimilated into the company's operating infrastructure, or treated as free-standing entities and not fully merged into the organization. Steetley both was wholly owned and had to be intricately merged with several Redland operations, a new experience for the Redland corporate management.

Structurally, the company had an extremely slim organization. The corporate office contained about 100 people, mostly in finance, planning and public relations. This was far fewer than in most equivalent companies in 1993. The product groups – aggregates, bricks and roofing – had one director responsible for each. These directors had no staff. The chief executive and finance director, together with the three operational directors, made up the executive board, which was called the Group Committee.

Then came the operating companies and partnerships, dozens and dozens of them, scattered all over the globe. One of these 'operating companies' was responsible for R&D and engineering, split in 1993 between concrete materials and ceramics, or clay-based materials. The two centres reported to different members of the top team.

There was no doubt that Redland could claim to have extremely low overheads. On the other hand, the Smith New Court analysts, who as good 'City' people might have been expected to laud such a slim organization, were not so certain about its effectiveness. In their August 1993 report they say:

> The image of the Redland director – whizzing round the world, dropping out of the skies – is plainly that of the flying doctor. No other company in the sector respected for managing, as opposed to directing, its operations, pursues such a way of running its business – a style which must in part lie behind the occasions of insensitivity in management's actions.

So, many organizational factors were stacked against Redland in its new phase of existence.

REDLAND'S STRENGTHS AND WEAKNESSES

Professor Lorsch of the Harvard Business School, and others like him, believe that organizations are much more rich and complex than mere structures of reporting and hierarchical authority. Organizations can be designed differently for different purposes. Many bear the hallmarks of their founders' values, and the original business 'blueprint' can last for a very long time.

Organizations are vehicles that carry the skills and experience that enable the enterprise to do its business. They embody the deep habits and values of the current and past people who worked for them – the 'culture'. The systems and processes that channel direction, communications, planning, performance management and control are an integral part of this complex animal called an organization. Leaders can have a marked impact on organizations, but can also be heavily constrained by them. Many aspiring revolutionary leaders have had their dreams of transformation frustrated because the organization did not 'go along with' their wishes. Last but not least, organizations carry deep in them the norms and standards concerning how people behave and what is reckoned to be 'a good job' or satisfactory performance in just about everything significant that people at all levels do. All this makes the challenge of engendering real and sustainable change in large organizations rather more complex and time-consuming than is understood by many of those in corporate offices or the financial markets.

Now let us consider Redland in 1993 against a few of the dimensions mentioned above.

What did the top management value? The overwhelming impression of staff was that most of Redland's top people valued speed of thought, the effective use of numbers, reaching rapid conclusions and converging rapidly on solutions. Very bright, and capable of rapid extemporization, they tended to become bored with routines, procedures, systems or processes. The results of this, combined with the company's history (remember, partnerships and acquisitions), were that there were few norms or commonly accepted rules of behaviour or standards encompassing the whole organization. One exception was the standards of personal probity and honest business dealings. Redland was an ethical company. But outside this, there was little 'glue' to bind the organization other than the travels of the 'flying doctors' and a very basic financial reporting package.

Planning is a vital business process, requiring managers to think in a structured way about what they intend to do and communicate this in an organized way to others. A managing director of one of the businesses describes Redland's pre-Steetley planning process. He received a note from head office instructing him to prepare a strategy for his business to be presented to Group Committee in a few weeks. Naturally, he was a little anxious and called his 'flying doctor' for some advice. The somewhat vague reply was that the overall objective was 'growth', and growth meant acquisitions.

Thus forewarned and prepared, the new MD made his presentation. He felt that it went fairly well. After his initial introduction, the members of the Group Committee rather ignored him and argued among themselves. He answered a few questions, left the meeting and then spent several weeks waiting for feedback, wondering whether he should start discussions with possible acquisition targets. Then, all of a sudden, word came back that growth was off the agenda. When the group's total numbers were all added up, cash was found to be short, so could he please concentrate on cash conservation instead!

From this and many other accounts, it seems that there was a dearth of standard-setting and integrating processes in the Redland of the early 1990s. Management and staff development was mainly *ad hoc*; there was little movement of people across the business internationally, or between the product areas. The inside world tended to be divided into those who were 'bright' (having been to 'good' universities and possessing strong analytical skills) and the rest. The bright ones received accelerated development without in-depth experience; the rest were substantially ignored.

R&D and Engineering, a source of Redland's heritage in roofing, were expected to sell their services to the partners and operating companies across the world. These companies had a free choice as to whether they used the expertise on offer, and many did not, as they found the services too expensive. Braas had developed its own engineering capability, which was felt by the Redland people to be a competitor. The once vital technology functions had become marginalized and noticeably neurotic.

The result of all of this was the organization that the managers at the conference had described. This company had, to quote the brokers, 'spent plentifully' on acquisitions and on internal investment. However, the fragmented nature of the organization and the varied degrees of influence that Redland had over partners meant that the results of this spending were totally inconsistent.

Programmes of plant modernization and replacement were often started and stopped according to the needs for cash to service the dividend. Braas too had certainly 'spent plentifully' on capital assets; in fact, it had significantly overspent on extremely expensive and rather inflexible plant. On the other hand, there were Redland roofing plants in Japan, the United States and such countries as Indonesia that were outdated, completely worn out and incapable of producing tiles of consistent quality.

The quality of operating management was a similar story. Redland had superb management in roofing in the Netherlands, for example, and the quality of the Braas management was claimed (by the Braas leadership, who used Redland as their comparator) to be top class. Elsewhere, standards appeared to be completely inconsistent, ranging from almost completely inept and supine to highly effective.

To make the situation worse, there appeared to be no commonly understood way of communicating about the attributes, behaviours and skills that would define what a 'good' standard of management was. Instead there was the previously mentioned tendency to define people as 'bright' (the result of a particular form of educational attainment) or 'dull' (in its absence). As in some other rather elitist cultures, there was a tendency to assume that 'bright' people were capable of being good at everything!

Now the company had come, suddenly, to the end of an era. Acquisitions were off the agenda. The Redland organization now had to focus on realizing the highest possible performance from all its businesses worldwide. This was a markedly different challenge from that of managing partnerships, planning and making acquisitions, and managing corporate finances and investor relations.

So who were the Redland top team who had spearheaded the Steetley acquisition and now had to become 'seasoned operators'? Every member of the 1992–93 top team was intellectually able. Many were quite exceptionally talented. There was a strong element that was quick-thinking, impatient and rather intolerant of those who were felt to be less bright than themselves. Some were very competitive and markedly ambitious, to the point that competition between members of the executive team for succession to the top job had almost become a way of life in the company.

Many were noticeably task oriented. According to observers, many of the top people lacked process awareness and tended to think of the 'what' and not the 'how'. Task achievement and 'ticking of checklists' was a common behaviour at the top, which all too often meant that more complex and longer-term programmes of action were not completed before being overtaken by the next 'thing'.

RETHINKING THE COMPANY

After the post-Steetley conference, the Group Committee and some senior management concluded that Redland had to become a 'management-led' company, as opposed to a financial holding. For some, such as George Phillipson of Aggregates and Erich Gerlach of Braas, this was blatantly obvious. Robert Napier and Peter Johnson felt that it was a real leadership challenge. For others, it was a less exciting proposition. The Redland's top team as a whole were going to embark on the novel journey of creating an excellent operating company; and this in the face of very tight finances.

By the end of 1993, many of the one-off cost savings had been realized or were already discounted by the financial markets. Redland's dividend payments, which were among the highest in the FTSE 100, had been necessary to attract investors to support acquisitions. Cash to sustain this level of dividend was becoming extremely tight, especially as many of the economies upon which Redland was dependent were in serious recession.

The one bright spot was the German roofing market, which had received a second-stage boost from the vast amount of reconstruction work following the opening up of the East. But, of course, this meant over-dependence on one market, and on an organization over which Redland management had little control.

Free debate had been opened with operating managers, who had been promised more involvement, together with what amounted to a sea change in corporate behaviour, but the range of options available was narrowing. In the past, the asset base had been a flexible component of the business, capable of being bought and sold to satisfy the need for cash and dividend payments. Having withdrawn from the plasterboard disaster and nailed the corporate colours to the mast of three core businesses, the company found that its scope for portfolio shuffling was drastically reduced.

Even more important, the credibility of corporate leadership depended on a commitment to managing the business portfolio that the company had so expensively bought. Manipulating the portfolio, as in times past, would be interpreted by operating management as proof that nothing had changed at the top.

The closer relationship between corporate and operating managers also brought more heat on to the head office. One of the sources of this heat was capital expenditure. Many of Redland's operations had been starved of investment, either because cash had not been available or because insecure managers had not made a strong enough case for it. Now, all that was changing, especially as experienced newcomers began to be recruited and take stock of their new responsibilities. Some of them began to make a cogent case for spending on plant, capital equipment and systems as a precondition for performance improvement. Redland was in a bind. There was not enough cash to fund high dividends and simultaneously meet the demands for replacement and improvement capital.

An opportunity for a change of face in the corporate finance function opened when finance director Gerald Corbett resigned to take on the top finance role in a very large British company. The corporate team was supplemented by the arrival of a new director responsible for organization and human resource management. The departure of Kevin Abbott, responsible for Redland's roofing operations, enabled the Redland brick and non-Braas roof tile operations to be brought under one head, Peter Johnson.

The new team set about recreating the company from the inside. Business strategies, priorities and values were debated intensely at a second conference. From these deliberations came several streams of action.

The aggregates business started a huge international programme of operational improvement and benchmarking of standards. This was led with great passion and energy by George Phillipson, who saw that his experience was at last being valued, and Bill Yearsley, a very able and operationally experienced young American who was to become his successor. Similar international benchmarking and improvement processes had already been under way in the brick businesses and these efforts were extended to roofing. The R&D and technical activities were brought together under one head and given a massive boost in support from the top.

A comprehensive programme of management improvement and development was launched. The quality and suitability of Redland's management worldwide was assessed against newly developed common standards. This inevitably meant a significant number of departures and replacements. Much effort was put into internal appointments, and pools of internal potential were identified and promoted, but many external appointments had to be made as the company had not developed enough talent. For middle and senior managers, comprehensive programmes of training and development were started, with the aim of raising skills to good international standards and improving the levels of communication and teamwork. A new group finance director, Paul Hewitt, was recruited. When candidates for the role were being considered, much emphasis was placed on performance management and operational analysis.

The quality of management systems and processes had never been a strong feature in Redland. This lack was addressed vigorously by the development of an electronic information and communication systems strategy, which would connect the corporate and operating elements of the enterprise. New business strategy, planning and performance review systems were introduced in the next planning round.

It became clear how much work was needed to bring the quality of the organization up to an acceptable international standard. Change would take many years, given the scope and complexity of the problems. Improvements were likely to be progressive and incremental rather than instantaneous. But most importantly, the changes had a unifying effect on the management of the company. At last, a common cause brought operating and corporate management together.

At the end of 1993 another international conference reviewed progress and priorities. Conference topics included culture change, guiding principles and standards, mapping business processes, processes for reducing working capital, the use of information technology by salespeople, employee involvement, new planning and performance management systems, the identification and development of core competencies and appraisal, and 360-degree employee feedback systems. A further demonstration of commitment to operating excellence was that all but one of the presenters were Redland managers.

The group results for 1993, which exceeded budget by a considerable margin, and with positive cash flow and dividend cover of 1.04 times, added to the bullishness. Managers could be excused for believing that, with some luck, Redland might have the time to reap the rewards of the massive change programmes that they had initiated.

In 1994 the good news continued. Turnover in 1994 grew by 12 per cent. The profit margin improved by one and a half percentage points to 14 per cent. Recovery of profit margins, a key objective for the year, was achieved as a result of volume increases in some markets and an improvement in underlying operating performance in others. In his 1994 CEO's statement, Robert Napier explained:

> Three key elements are critical to raise the profits earned from our market shares and our assets.
>
> First, capital expenditure will increase in order to protect and extend our leading positions in increasingly competitive markets, by developing new products and making processes more efficient, thereby improving underlying performance. The criteria for this spending will be secure paybacks by improving quality and thus value for our customers and achieving sustainable cost reductions. Total spending on capital rose from £138 million in 1993 to £174 million in 1994 and an estimated £225 million in 1995.
>
> Second, we are increasing investment directed at raising the performance of all our employees. This is reflected in the increase in training expenditure and in the

> implementation of new systems to raise standards of recruitment, appraisal and coaching. With activities in 35 countries, supported by international benchmarking, we are transferring knowledge of products and processes and increasingly also the skills of our people between our businesses...
>
> Thirdly, there was, in 1994, a significant increase in revenue and capital expenditure to improve radically the use of information technology across the group... Redland sees significant competitive advantage in being at the forefront of progress within our industry and much attention was paid in the year to raising the sights of our managers as to the opportunities provided by today's low cost flexible computer systems.

REDLAND'S FALL FROM GRACE

So why, despite all this effort and good intent, did Redland's share price crash, to a chorus of vitriolic comments from the press and financial analysts after the 1994 results presentation? The reason is that Redland did the unforgivable: it cut the dividend!

Sir Colin Corness, in his chairman's statement, said, 'I recognise that against these worthwhile improvements in performance it might seem perverse for your board to be recommending a cut in the final dividend of a third, even allowing for the fact that the yield on Redland shares was among the highest of the top 100 companies in the FTSE index.' The problem was that the 'less than perfectly timed' acquisition of Steetley, the burden of advanced corporation tax and the massive programme conducted by Braas to take advantage of the opening of markets in eastern Germany were conspiring to make cash availability very tight. Sir Colin explained that, therefore, 're-basing the dividend is in the best interests of the business and thus our shareholders... the Board recognises that it has a duty to strike a better balance between distributed and retained earnings, in line with average practice among our peer companies, so as to allow sufficient retention of cash across the group to finance replacement, improvement and growth capital investment'.

For Redland this was a major move. Previously it had set a high dividend level in order to attract shareholder support for its expansion programme. The financial community understood that the dividend was guaranteed; management would never go back on their commitment to maintain it. Accordingly, when the cut was announced, some senior analysts felt that they had been misled, and hell hath no fury like an analyst misled! Redland lost some staunch supporters, and others who had been voicing doubts about the company's prospects felt vindicated.

With one bound, Redland had moved from being a 'quality act' to something approaching leper status. From this moment on, the bias of most City analysis about the company tended towards the negative.

So why had Redland taken such a drastic step? As always, the action behind the scenes is at least as interesting as the public pronouncements.

Paul Hewitt's baptism as Finance Director came when the 1995 group budget showed that, owing to a lack of cash flow, the group would not be able to fund the capital expenditure so critical to the improvement programmes essential to move margins ahead. At another conference shortly after the announcement of the dividend cut, Robert Napier explained the alternatives explored by the board. Stopping capital expenditure would kill the efforts to improve margins, as well as undoing all the good arising from the improvement programmes. Selling something might buy 12 months, but it couldn't be right to continue financially unsound practices. Cutting the dividend could result in a share price collapse and a takeover bid, to which Napier's answer was, 'Yes, maybe, and there is a risk whatever we do… if we don't cut the dividend… we could rightly be accused of being a management which wasn't prepared to face up to issues and take action.'

The more astute among the operating managers then questioned whether the dividend cut of 33 per cent was sufficient to solve the investment/distribution problem. Napier responded, 'The argument raged between 25% and 40%. Now we have been accused of not cutting enough. I think whatever level we had cut it [to] we would have been criticised. Our advisers were very clear in their minds that more than 33% would give a clear feeling of a company in crisis and of course we are not in crisis, it was a slow death situation and it was their very strong advice that 33% was the right level.'

As the conference ended, there was still a feeling that with hard work and skill, Redland could pull through this difficult period. Few of the management delegates realized that there was much worse to come.

Paul Hewitt had a serious conviction that in capital-intensive businesses such as Redland, the best way to measure performance was to assess the cash flow returns in the business in relation to its capital value. The cost of capital to the company was easy to compute, and if a business was not generating sufficient cash to more than cover the total cost of capital, then it was destroying value and did not merit further investment. This measure of performance was unfamiliar to most of Redland's management, who were used to profit before tax or return on sales as the prime measure.

The new measure attracted considerable interest in certain quarters in Redland. However, interest turned to wary watchfulness as Hewitt demonstrated that the company had underperformed against RMC, a major UK rival, against a measure of total shareholder return. Attempts by some to prove that the underperformance was a short-term phenomenon were scuppered when Hewitt, a persistent and patient man, produced 10-year comparisons, with the same result.

Discomfort became uproar when Hewitt went on to demonstrate that the capital spent on most of Redland's acquisitions and internal investment during the 1980s and early 1990s had failed to generate cash returns at anything like the cost of capital. In effect, Hewitt was saying that Redland had taken capital from its shareholders and invested, or bought assets, at vastly inflated prices, or had failed to manage investments and acquisitions well enough to realize good returns. All in all, Hewitt calculated that Redland had destroyed some £2.4 billion worth of value over 10 years, partially offset by £0.5 billion created by Braas. The assets of Steetley were generating returns at a level less than half the cost of the capital spent. In other words, it appeared as though Redland had paid about twice what it should have for Steetley.

At the Redland board meeting in May 1995, Sir Colin Corness retired as chairman. His successor was Rudolph Agnew, a man with a high reputation in certain quarters of the investment community, a reputation earned in part by his having led a number of bid defences. The biggest and most famous was Consolidated Gold Fields' defence against a bid from Hanson. Agnew was reckoned by many investors to be a doughty fighter in contested bids and to have realized the best deals possible for them.

Agnew was handsome, could be outspoken, and possessed a powerful and at times irreverent sense of humour. He smoked large cigars, and strong French Gitanes cigarettes in between. The contrast with the sometimes austere Sir Colin Corness was remarked on by many.

On the evening of Sir Colin's last board meeting there was a magnificent gathering to mark the occasion. The invitees included the Governor of the Bank of England; his predecessor, Lord Kingsdown, now restored to the Redland board; and many, many investment bankers, stockbrokers, lawyers and sundry members of the great and good of industry and commerce, some of whom had been or were non-executive directors. Also present were many current and past executive directors of Redland, and a retired sales manager from Redland Roof Tiles, representing the staff. Some of the latter worthies spent a little time over drinks speculating on the possible changes that this particular change of chairman might bring.

Agnew regarded Redland's performance as inadequate. He reckoned that, by his rough calculations, Redland management owed the shareholders at least £1 billion and he intended to see that they received their just deserts. It was as well that he was not privy to the Hewitt analyses at this time or he might at least have doubled his demands!

Paul Hewitt was an intensely analytical and rational man. In his view, you sought the facts and when you had found them, you acted rationally in accordance with what they told you. He was thus bemused as some people simply ignored his analyses, then, when it became apparent that he was going to persist, attacked the value methodology, attempting to demolish it as superficially clever but flawed.

Another of Hewitt's characteristics was dogged persistence. Bit by bit he countered the arguments, to the point that opponents ran out of rational 'steam'. Opponents then began to suggest that the whole concept, and with it its originator, were 'too theoretical'. In some quarters Hewitt began to be labelled as clever but out of touch with operating reality. This argument seemed to be advanced most strongly by those in Redland operations where the gap between current performance and covering the cost of capital was biggest!

Hewitt persisted, and as the debate dragged on he began to attract supporters in the corporate office and in some of the operations. Gradually the size of his constituency of support increased. The 'value' argument – in Redland but not yet in Braas – was being won.

Meanwhile, head office was conducting a review of the performance and prospects of all Redland's businesses. This was driven by the strong perception that radical change was needed in the shape of Redland's business base and in its organizational arrangements. However, many were opposed to a root-and-branch approach and the review process became bogged down in disputes and politics.

At this point, Robert Napier realized that the situation had become too political to produce consensus. He took control. Supported by his corporate staff, he would formulate a clear view of how the group needed to change in order to survive. He and the corporate team concluded that:

- Redland needed to exit from the bricks business entirely. The competitive position was not tenable and value was being destroyed at a totally unacceptable rate.

- With the exception of Redland Granulats in France, the aggregates businesses were all in a position to improve and / or grow.
- The split of roofing activities in Europe was irrational and inefficient, especially as competitors were beginning to do business on both sides of the Redland–Braas divide. A logical solution would be to create an integrated European roofing business under one management led by Erich Gerlach.

For Redland, the *quid pro quo* for integration had to be more influence over Braas, reversing the trend of nearly 30 years. Could this be achieved? Informal private discussions with Gerlach and the family shareholders indicated that they too recognized the logic of the proposition, were attracted by the prospect of leading the world's largest roofing business and would be willing to cede significant control restrictions to bring the changes about. The scene was set for some very crucial decisions.

MORE RETHINKING

Now Robert Napier decided on a bold move. He decided to work all the issues and problems through with the wider management group in public forum before it was known whether agreement could be reached with the Braas minority shareholders. Furthermore, he decided to give management a real say on whether the proposed strategy would go ahead. After all, if the bulk of management were against the proposition, it would not work, no matter what the board or corporate staff believed.

Top management convened at a special meeting in Schloss Fuschl, near Salzburg in Austria. As the proceedings wore on, it became clear that there was very strong support for the propositions and great respect for what was seen as a courageous move by Napier in exposing himself to public scrutiny from his own management. As one long-serving manager observed, 'Redland has travelled far in the last few years. I just hope that we have the chance to complete the journey.'

The most fundamental decision reached was to exit the bricks business, in which Redland had a strong UK position, a difficult European joint venture and a tiny niche in the United States. The business needed very high investment in a very cyclical industry. It was concluded that Redland could not afford to sustain this business.

The chosen structure of the new business organization was as follows:

- European roofing, integrating Redland's roofing interests with those of Braas, to be called RBB;
- international aggregates;
- new or developing markets – mainly roofing businesses in Asia, South America and Africa.

There was a strong emotional undercurrent to the conference. This was the last throw of the dice for Redland. Failure to bring about the changes and make the reconfigured business the platform for significant performance improvement would not be tolerated by an already unsupportive financial community.

The agenda agreed at the conference was massively demanding. Redland management set out to negotiate a significantly different legal basis for the

Braas–Redland relationship, while setting up a totally new European roofing organization. A new group had to be created to manage the developing businesses in the rest of the world. Agreements had to be concluded between it and RBB, the European roofing business, covering technology and staff transfers. In the midst of all this, much time and attention had to be paid to Redland's European management, many of whom felt that they had been betrayed and 'sold to the Germans'.

The aggregates group had to be established, although this work had already mainly been achieved under Phillipson. The corporate office had to be significantly reorganized and reduced in size. The disposal of the bricks business had to be carried out, creating a new crop of human problems to be handled, and the raft of management and systems initiatives previously begun had to be seen through to completion. Most important of all, the performance improvement drive had to be carried forward with full energy and no loss of focus.

The biggest challenge was the renegotiation of the Redland–Braas relationship. Braas management, who had been geographically and psychologically close for decades, acted as a conduit between the negotiating parties. The Redland team perceived that its task would be difficult.

After more than six months' agonizingly slow and detailed negotiation, an agreement was struck. It gave Redland much more access to Braas cash for dividends and the ability to dismiss the top management. In return, the Redland European roofing businesses were sold to the new joint venture, of which Redland now owned an enhanced 56.5 per cent.

In negotiating terms, the Redland team had achieved as much as could be done, but it was apparent that the long-established habits of Braas's independence, unchallenged for more than 30 years, were going to be a much more difficult nut to crack. Napier and his colleagues determined to challenge strongly and immediately on any issue on which they disagreed, no matter how small. It was the only way for Redland to develop a more influential relationship.

NEW PROBLEMS

For some time, small but clear signs had been emerging that the German roofing market had reached its peak. Competition in the market was becoming tougher. Then Redland began to pick up rumours about extensive and unauthorized discounting by Braas sales staff. It rapidly became apparent that Braas top managers had little control over what was happening, either in their own sales force or in the market more generally. Furthermore, Braas management had no experience of market decline, and their financial control was loose and weak. Clouds were gathering on the horizon and they foretold disaster.

Meanwhile, other pressing problems were emerging. The French aggregates business Redland Granulats, mainly bought from Steetley and a complete mess when acquired, was proving to be a terrible headache. It appeared that whatever management might do, they could not realize satisfactory returns. Other, more drastic solutions would have to be found. Almost exactly the same problems faced the US roofing business. The competitive structure of the market and past Redland mistakes meant that nobody in the industry was making a return. Spectres from the past were closing in.

The one bright spot was in the Anglo-American aggregates businesses. Under the leadership of George Phillipson and Bill Yearsley, who had taken over North American operations, a vigorous process of operational and management improvement was beginning to bear fruit.

It was in the aggregates businesses too that Paul Hewitt's campaign to use value-based management showed its first signs of fruition. Yearsley adopted cash value added as the measure of performance for the aggregates business and started an extensive programme of change aimed at devolving more responsibility for the use of capital right down to the level of the individual quarry. Rapidly, remarkable changes in behaviour and then performance began to show.

By the summer of 1996 the future of the company seemed to be in the balance. On the positive side of the scales was the extent and speed of management action in sorting out the intractable problems, and the benefits coming from the vigorous Anglo-American business improvement process in aggregates. On the negative, the portents for the European, and especially the German, roofing businesses were becoming more and more dire, and the old habits of Braas's independence had not gone away.

Eventually it emerged that the uncontrolled discounting in Germany had almost maintained market share, but at an unbudgeted cost of probably more than £20 million! Even more frightening for Redland management was the realization that nobody in RBB knew the extent of the problem.

So marked was the decline in German performance that, after some debate, a statement was issued to the City. Although not couched in those terms, it was simply taken as a profits warning. The investment community went into negative overdrive. The share price, which had been creeping up following the formation of RBB, plunged violently. Some commentators began to call for Robert Napier's resignation. Redland was now clearly under siege.

At the beginning of 1997, it was apparent that Redland was two quite different groups, in terms of a sense of urgency and pace. Good news from US/UK aggregates, a positive joint venture in US roofing and progress on a disposal of Granulats were overshadowed by bad news from Europe. The performance of the German roofing business continued to slide, and it was becoming very clear that the skills and mindset that had worked so well in growing markets with weak competition were not going to work in competitive, shrinking markets.

Redland continued to increase the pressure for more drastic action. The RBB minority shareholders and management either resisted or agreed to act at what seemed to be a snail's pace. For example, although RBB accepted cash value added as the best measure of financial performance in early 1997, it then asserted its independence by proposing to spend several months selecting consultants to support it in a major study to consider the best means of measuring value, prior to starting an implementation study. Redland managers seethed with frustration. To them, there was sufficient experience inside the group to 'just do it'.

Confrontation was the only option. Rudolph Agnew prepared a long note for his non-executive colleagues. In it he described what he saw to be the conservative approach of the German shareholders and management, which 'denies any fast and radical action'. He went on to say:

> Robert cannot carry out his duties in the face of such blind opposition. We have a major crisis on our hands. The outcome may well dictate the survival of the company.

> The decline in the performance of RBB is becoming evident to the more astute analysts. The more sensible and intelligent fund managers may not be surprised and may not be too worried provided we – myself, Robert and Erich – can assure them that serious remedial action is in hand. This we cannot do at present.

Napier formulated Redland's demands: a 20 per cent reduction in fixed costs over two years, comprehensive review of and reduction in the number of production plants, closure or sale of historically unprofitable businesses, reduction of head office costs and much greater urgency and speed of action. This was an unprecedented confrontation!

After an initial reaction of shock and outrage, Erich Gerlach showed signs of agreement. However, the cultural differences remained. When it came to pace, Gerlach and his colleagues wanted to move in a careful, measured fashion, using extensive consultant support. Redland needed speed and urgency. The 1997 half-year results presentation was fast approaching.

The story for the investors and analysts was mixed. By comparison with 1996:

- sales were down 11 per cent;
- operating profit was down 24 per cent;
- profit after interest and tax was broadly similar;
- earnings per share were the same;
- operating cash outflow had reduced from £60 million to £18 million.

THE END OF THE STORY

Erich Gerlach was to make a presentation to the analysts and press alongside his Redland colleagues. Redland management wanted him to state a firm target for fixed-cost savings of over 100 million Deutschmarks. Gerlach would not commit himself to such a target, because he did not know the exact amount that could be achieved in advance. A small, culturally determined misunderstanding became the subject of a heated exchange.

As Robert Napier rose to his feet on the morning of 25 September 1997 to face a large audience of press and analysts, he knew that the sentiments of most of those present were against him. The audience was deeply interested only in one thing: German roofing.

Having virtually ignored Bill Yearsley, Robert Napier and Paul Hewitt, they leaned forward attentively when Gerlach rose to speak. With his usual fluent, articulate and confident style, he spoke of market conditions, plant efficiencies and capital intensity and stated that reductions in fixed costs were the greatest management priority.

Then it was question time. Most questions were directed at ascertaining a definite cost-reduction sum. Gerlach remonstrated strongly, intimating that a measured and orderly, rather than 'slash and burn', approach would be taken to cost reduction. 'We should not squeeze the lemon too hard,' he said.

The body language of the audience changed. Some closed their notebooks with an audible slap. They did not like what they had just heard.

The next day, investors reacted with a vengeance. The share price plummeted to 222.5p from a 1997 high of 455.5p. A Teather & Greenwood analysts' bulletin issued on 25 September, the day of the presentation, said it all: 'Redland's 1997 H1 results were poor, the statement discouraging and the German content of the analyst's meeting so unstructured and self indulgent as to test the patience of all present. The Chairman was sorely missed. As were his thoughts on the dividend.' The newspapers were filled with a chorus of angry analysts, and investors demanded Napier's head on a plate.

The Redland board was left with several unpalatable alternatives. Dismissal of the chief executive, known at that time as the 'Pilkington solution', might have bought some time. But what would that achieve beyond a short-term cosmetic palliative? Napier knew what needed to be done. Any replacement would face exactly the same problems.

A break-up had already been exhaustively examined, but the only likely purchasers of the 56.5 per cent stake of RBB were the minority shareholders, who were not in a position to offer a decent price, and tax problems seemed almost intractable. For the moment, the only possible course of action seemed to be to soldier on with the best speed possible.

In the meantime, the chairman, Agnew, was talking to the City. *The Times*, in an article entitled 'Dropping bricks', reported that 'The elegant Rudolph Agnew found a fittingly elegant way to bolster the shares of Redland this week. Letting slip that the state of the building materials company was so dire that it was increasingly vulnerable to a bid instantly increased the price that any bidder might have to pay.'

It did not take long to discover what price. At 8 pm on Sunday, 12 October, Robert Napier rang one of his fellow directors. He sounded calm, but a little tense. 'We've had a bid from Lafarge,' he said. 'I'm going straight to Lazard's [Redland's investment bankers] offices with Paul [Hewitt] tomorrow. Will you please take care of the corporate office and staff communications across the Group.'

Thus began the last six weeks of Redland's life. Robert Napier and Paul Hewitt moved into Lazard's office in the City, into what the advisers called the 'war room' and one Redland wag named the 'sensory deprivation chamber'. In this City office they sweated to find a way of realizing more for the company than the 320p in cash that Lafarge had offered.

As the bid was in cash, the chances of a successful fight to retain independence were slim. So, for Napier and Hewitt, future employment depended on finding a way of increasing the value of the company.

They constructed a break-up strategy of enormous cleverness and complexity, which the advisers called 'Project Starburst'. The strategy was dependent upon lining up synchronized buyers for at least six different parts of the group, guiding the German minority shareholders on how to prepare a realistic (and rapid) bid for the Redland share in RBB and solving tax problems of enormous complexity.

As the days and weeks passed, relationships between the denizens of the 'war room', especially the small army of advisers, and the Redland corporate staff became strained. Those who were running the defence 'game' became understandably immersed in the battle. One non-executive director was reported by an adviser to have instructed Redland's lawyers to sue a member of the Redland corporate staff for refusing to release personally confidential information on some of his colleagues! In this atmosphere, Don Young's suggestion that to contact Lafarge and offer to accept 350p would save much time and money was greeted by stony stares.

The whole process was felt to be deeply unsavoury by many Redland staff. The company they loved and had given their best was being reduced to a collection of assets to be sold to the highest bidder. Even the advisers' seductively attractive name for the break-up, 'Project Starburst', hid the fact that it would cause massive redundancies in many Redland operations.

Bill Yearsley sought backing to buy out the North American aggregates businesses, only to find himself unceremoniously dumped by the potential backers, who concluded that they did not need him to buy and sell a bunch of assets.

Saddest of all, many staff felt deserted by Napier and Hewitt. However unjustified this might have been, there was a feeling that the pair had 'joined the enemy'. The division between 'insiders' and 'outsiders' was dramatically illustrated by one incident. Pat Scott, as Group Treasurer, needed to organize an indebtedness statement to be included in a circular to shareholders. This is a calculation of total debt and bank balances over the whole group at a given date, and involves collecting data from every subsidiary, no matter how small or remote.

Working to tight deadlines and needing replies from all over the world, she decided to arrange translation of her request letters to speed the process for non-English-speaking recipients. Redland had its own team of translators, who set to with enthusiasm. They worked all day and into the evening and finally, at 10 o'clock, the final e-mail request was sent to a remote subsidiary. Pat hurried to thank the translators, who waved the thanks aside. 'We'd do anything needed to save this company,' one remarked, flushed with satisfaction.

Scott returned to her office subdued. She hadn't the heart to tell them that the only time the figures would be used was if shareholders were asked to vote for a corporate break-up. The 'insiders' knew; the 'outsiders' didn't.

As time passed, it became clear that 'Starburst' was just too complex to bring off in the very limited time available. Hewitt, Napier and the corporate finance staff had worked wonders to crack some apparently impossible financing and tax problems, but orchestrating so many deals simultaneously was proving to be almost impossible.

At the end of November, Lafarge increased its offer to 340p. After a very short discussion, the Redland board decided that if the offer were raised to 345p they would recommend acceptance to the shareholders. With that, the executive directors went for a drink and the rest of the board simply drifted out of the building, muttering vague farewells. Redland, an industrial company that had been founded in 1919, reached its apogee after the Steetley acquisition in 1992, then plunged to extinction in November 1997 in an investment banker's office in the City of London.

WINNERS AND LOSERS

So who were the winners and losers from this saga?

Customers and suppliers really never featured in the corporate affairs of Redland, unless the 'suppliers' were City advisers. Employees in general fared likewise. Most were never 'players' in the bigger game of strategy, acquisitions and partnerships. As events unfolded, it was to become apparent that Lafarge was not a bad new owner for the staff: it honoured all Redland's commitments in a generous spirit and was disappointed not to be able to retain more of the Redland managers.

The big losers were the ultimate shareholders. Redland had underperformed against industry leaders for many years. It raised large amounts of capital and destroyed value in spectacular fashion, mainly through acquisitions and failed ventures. An investor who bought Redland shares at over 500p in 1992 would have seen them climb to approximately 640p by mid-1993, and then steadily slide to 220p before bouncing to the final bid price of 345p in November 1997.

The winners? The biggest were undoubtedly the many advisers who supported Redland in the programme of acquisitions and disposals through the 1980s and 1990s. For example, fees for the short bid defence against Lafarge were £15.4 million at the original bid price of 320p – that is, just for being there, for achieving nothing! On the other side of the bid, Lafarge was incurring an equivalent if not greater amount of fees. Rough estimates indicate that one way or another, Redland must have spent approaching £100 million on advisers from the1970s to the 1990s.

As for those at the top of Redland, the reputations of Robert Napier and Paul Hewitt were somewhat damaged by association with Redland's demise, but, being very able men, they both found good new roles. On 27 November the City editor of *The Times* wrote, 'Rudolph Agnew relishes a takeover battle. This autumn he seemed to be almost inviting attack as he acknowledged that the sickly Redland share price made the group vulnerable. On Tuesday night, he was able to declare victory.' The lengthy article finishes, 'He must surely now feature on the very limited list of City mercenaries who can be called upon to fight in any interesting corporate battle.' The old warrior had won again!

The advisers produced an acrylic plaque of the kind invariably turned out by bankers to mark great events. It depicted the cover of Redland's defence documents. Across these was a large red stamp. It said, 'SOLD'. Underneath were the words 'Delivering greater value to shareholders'. The deal was done. Time to move on to the next.

On 1 March 2002 the Lex column in the *Financial Times* reported that 'Lafarge's much smaller [than cement] roofing and gypsum [plasterboard] operations performed badly: If they are not improved swiftly, they should be sold.'

Nothing changes!

POST-MORTEM: WHAT CAN BE LEARNT FROM THE REDLAND CASE?

First, did Redland really fail?

The company destroyed a vast amount of value in the 1980s and 1990s. As already mentioned, an internal analysis had put this at £2.4 billion. Redland, therefore, did not reward its long-term shareholders. It lagged behind industry leaders in terms of total shareholder return (appreciation in the share price, plus the value of dividends) in the 10 years before the takeover. Therefore, in this dimension Redland does not emerge as a success. And despite any 'City-speak' rhetoric about the takeover being a successful outcome, there is no evidence that the top management of Redland wished to cause the demise of the company. So, in that regard they did not succeed.

What were the specific causes of Redland's 'failure', and can any significant and more general lessons be learnt from it? We postulate that Redland failed because of a combination of the following reasons.

Problems with acquisitions

It chose the route of acquisitions as its major means of growth. It became increasingly ambitious to make larger and larger ones, and most of the larger acquisitions, as we have seen, destroyed value. It never created an organizational infrastructure that was strong enough to integrate acquisitions rapidly and effectively.

Inconsistent strategy

It did not have a clear and consistent strategy, apart from growth in financial terms. It also sought to align its tactics with the interests of the financial markets and ended up with little room for financial manoeuvre. Additionally, corporate management tended to regard City expectations as immutable, and sought to flex other items, such as capital expenditure, around them.

The company passed through several phases of diversification and concentration. In the early 1990s, even as the chairman celebrated the virtues of focus on three industries, he announced virtually in the next breath the entry into the plasterboard industry – a brand new business for the company. This venture turned into a competitive, financial and operational disaster and was rapidly offloaded.

It was not until almost the end, under Robert Napier's leadership, that it was decided to concentrate on two business areas, aggregates and roofing, where the company had real international expertise and market strength. This concentration, together with a clear focus on business and organization building, bound together by a commitment to value-based management, offered a clear way forward for the company. Unfortunately, the company was still hamstrung by the fatal legacy of its inability to control the management of Braas, whose weaknesses became evident as the German market declined and competition strengthened.

The Redland management had been strategically vulnerable in another dimension. They tended to have a rather short-term, 'event-driven' approach to decision-taking and action. This meant, for example, that they were over time outmanoeuvred by the Braas management and shareholders, who pursued a consistent strategy of gaining the maximum amount of independence. Over a period of maybe 30 years they used every opportunity that offered itself to bolster their legal and psychological independence, and as the Redland management tended to react to each 'event' as it happened, they were gradually steered into a position where their influence was rather limited.

Weak organization

Redland did not, historically, create an organization that possessed real substance and strength in depth. When the acquisition 'music' stopped, there were insufficient organizational 'levers' with which to improve operating returns rapidly and not enough time to complete the complex and lengthy task of creating them.

Thus not having a strong enough organizational infrastructure to rapidly integrate and add value from acquisitions compounded the common problem of having overpaid for them in the first place. By the time a new leadership got round to trying to build a strong operating company, it was much too late.

Lack of operating experience

Most of Redland's top management did not have deep industry and operating experience. With a few notable exceptions, they had 'fast-tracked' to the top and missed out completely on the first-line and middle-management experience that is so vital for managing for performance and integrating acquisitions.

Luck

There were economic factors beyond Redland's control that can be regarded as 'bad luck'. Many economies went into recession shortly after the acquisition of Steetley. There was a cessation of growth in the German roofing market. These would have been a difficult call for any management. However, with the glorious benefit of hindsight, it might have been prudent to have left a comfortable margin for such events, rather than adopting, consciously or otherwise, strategies that required everything to go right in order to scrape through.

ADDENDUM 1

Below is a listing of British publicly quoted companies. All these companies have been reported as having suffered significant difficulties as a result of some or all of the problems described in the Redland case. Some of the companies have become financially successful, but have at one time or another been accused of damaging the interests of customers, staff or society.

Abbey National
Amstrad
Asda MFI
Barclays Bank
BET
BICC
Boots
British & Commonwealth Group
British Aerospace
British Airways
British Gas
Britoil
BT
BTR
Bunzl
Burmah Oil
Burton Group
Canary Wharf
Courtaulds
Equitable Life
Fisons
GEC
General Accident
Glaxo (Smith Kline)
Grand Metropolitan
Guinness
Hanson Trust
ICI
Jaguar
Lloyds Bank
Lonrho
Lucas
Marconi
Marks & Spencer
Metal Box
Midland Bank
National Westminster Bank
Plessey
Powergen
Rank Hovis McDougall
Redland
Rentokil Initial
Royal Bank of Scotland
Saatchi & Saatchi
Scottish Power
Sears
Siebe
STC
Storehouse
Thorn EMI
Tomkins
Trafalgar House
TSB
United Biscuits
Vodafone
Williams Holdings

ADDENDUM 2: THE REDLAND CASE

The Redland problem is eloquently illustrated by the following three exhibits.

The first is the acrylic plaque presented, as is usual, by the Investment Bankers after Redland had fallen to Lafarge's bid. Both sides are illustrated here.

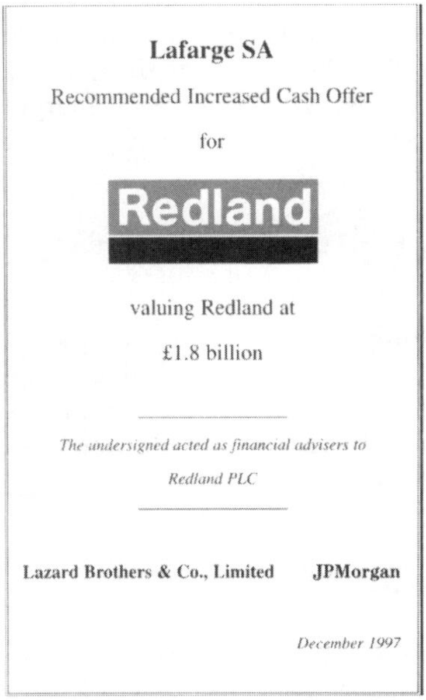

The impression left by the plaque is that great shareholder value has been created by the sale of the company. The reality is more clearly shown by the two tables below.

Table 7.1 5-Year Total Shareholder Returns (Real, yearly, above the cost of equity)

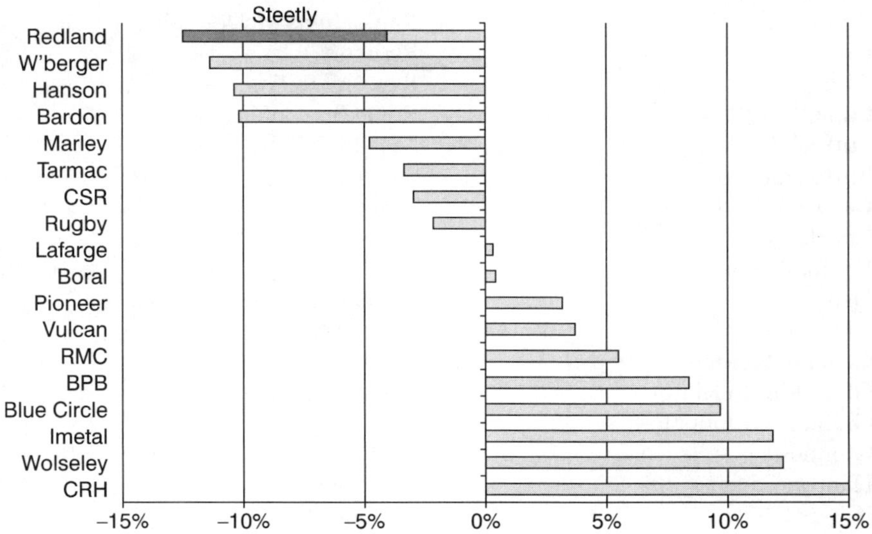

Table 7.1 shows Redland's Total Shareholder Returns (the share price, plus the value of re-invested dividends) compared with an industry comparator group. In addition to Redland's trailing position, the disastrous value-destroying effect of the Steetley acquisition is clearly demonstrated. The table is for the period 1991 to 1996.

Table 7.2 Redland's Total Shareholder Returns

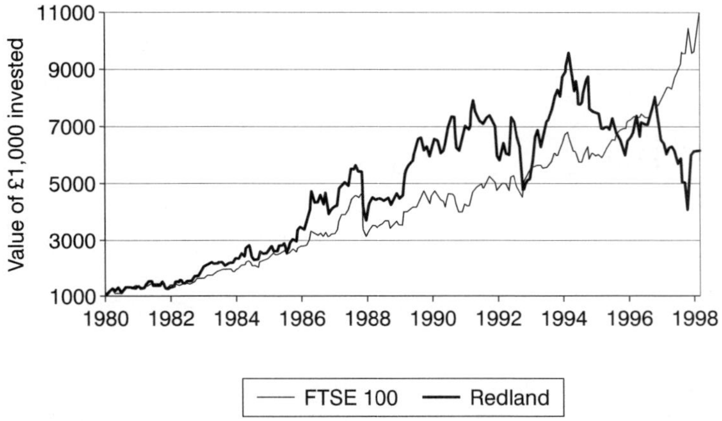

Table 7.2 is particularly interesting. It shows the company's Total Shareholder Returns in relation to the FTSE 100 from 1980 until 1997. In summary, the table demonstrates that £1,000 invested in Redland shares over the period would have generated just over £6,000, whereas £1,000 invested in the FTSE Index would have generated about £11,000.

Even more interesting, the pattern of the graph is not unrepresentative of companies that rely on 'active' means of growth, such as extensive M&A activity. Typically, such companies will generate excitement in the financial markets and attract investor support, thus raising their share prices. Then, as the damage caused by such activism is progressively recognized, market support is withdrawn, often causing a sudden collapse in the share price, as previous supporters scramble to dump the shares, or force the sale or break-up of the company in question.

The Redland graph seems to demonstrate this pattern clearly – the mid-1980s until 1992 were Redland's period of great corporate activism, with many acquisitions and new ventures, culminating in the Steetley acquisition. Also, during this period, the Redland dividend was maintained at a level that proved to be unsustainable, in order to attract investor support. The sudden collapse of the share price and therefore shareholder returns was caused by growing alarm in the previously highly supportive markets at the effects on returns of the acquisitions and the unexpected reduction in the dividend.

Thus, markets that reward companies (and their managers) for activism and creating excitement can very rapidly turn and engineer their demise when the excitement runs out.

8

So, what *is* 'good'?

We are not obsessed with failure. It is just that there are many traps and pitfalls that ambitious top managers can fall into, especially if they are in a tearing hurry. It is now time to move on and explore what managers can do to give the enterprises that they lead a better than average chance of attaining a high and sustainable level of performance. So, the question underlying this chapter is whether it is possible to define and measure actions and behaviours and outcomes that can be regarded as 'good'.

This never was going to be a simple question to answer. Maybe, once in a while, after a few drinks, we felt that it might be possible to pull out a rich haul of research on the topic of excellent corporate performance and summarize the findings, contrast them with what the markets typically want and managers typically do, and produce nice, clear solutions. This is very tempting, all the more so because there are bookshelves stacked with happy-clappy offerings with titles along the lines of 'Thirteen Steps to Great Corporate Performance'. If any authors out there have written or are planning to actually write a book with this title, our apologies, but we will not be reading it!

Certain cultures tend to encourage the belief that there are generally applicable solutions. Experts in national cultural characteristics call them 'universalist' cultures, recognizable by such characteristics as a belief that they possess 'the truth' or a superior way of life. The United States is said to have quite strong universalist tendencies, which may be why so many recipe books for managers originate from there. The United Kingdom is certainly not immune, either. If we delve back in history to the Victorian era, when the United Kingdom, like the United States today, was the dominant world power, we can find authors like Samuel Smiles who published uplifting books aimed at providing prescriptions for a Good Life, with titles like *Self Help*, *Character*, *Thrift* and *Duty*.

So, we read much literature, but with a sceptical eye born of hard experience. We read and discounted many of the 'How to Be a Great…' offerings and concentrated on those works that both seemed to have a serious research base and had been influential on contemporary thinking.

UNDERSTANDING 'GOOD' PERFORMANCE THROUGH 'OUTPUT' FACTORS

The commonest approach to measuring and judging performance is through measures of financial output, such as profit, cash generation, and so on. But let us here opine firmly that in our view there is no such thing as one universal 'good' financial performance. Strategies such as picking a single measure, like 15 per cent profit growth, year on year, have nothing at all to do with the essential dynamics of most companies.

When that measure was chosen, as it was for a period by the financial markets, it had much more to do with what investment managers wanted from their portfolios than with the performances that enterprises were capable of achieving. The fact that many companies tried ever so hard to meet or exceed such a target simply showed that their top managers were more anxious to please the markets than manage their businesses for sustainable long-term performance.

We believe that measuring a 'good' performance in the short-term (say one to five years) on simple output measures such as profit, cash flows or such measures as short-term economic value added is fraught with pitfalls. Apparently brilliant short-term performance measured by such metrics may simply mean that the company is eating its seed corn and will, at some future date, dive into steep decline. We have seen much of this in the past 30 years! Also, let us not forget the skills of some finance directors in 'dressing up' and disguising deteriorating trends so that they will not become evident for a long time.

The weakness of using short-term measures is especially marked when the aim is to compare companies' performances. The problems lie in the fact that the performance of a company, especially in the short term, is contingent on a huge range of factors, which must be understood and evaluated if an observer is to reach a fair and balanced view of current performance and future prospects.

We do not intend to dwell on these contingency factors very deeply, as they have been very well covered elsewhere, but for the record, here are a few:

- The nature of the industry – for example, whether it is capital- or people-intensive.
- The nature of industry cycles. Different industries have different cyclical rhythms. So, measuring and comparing the performance of companies in different industries must take account of this.
- The stage of development and maturity of industries. For example, companies in rapidly growing, 'young' industries are likely to need large injections of cash, and to show rapid sales growth. Companies in mature industries are likely to have the opposite characteristics.
- Changes in industry dynamics and competitor behaviour.
- The extent to which the enterprise will be affected by shifts in consumer behaviour.

The shorter the timescale, the more difficult it is to define whether an enterprise is performing well or badly, as it is almost impossible to assess the likely effects of underlying strategies, investments and improvement programmes – or, for that matter, underlying and progressive deterioration or improvement in the condition of the organization.

Those who rely primarily on output measures to understand, judge and predict company performances are likely to miss many factors that affect underlying performance. This description fits a large number of institutional investors and those who support them, as well as many non-executive directors.

The problem is made worse when the 'judges' are juggling with a large investment portfolio. Such people are likely to make quite important judgements based on rather superficial analysis of 'the numbers', a few headlines and bullet points, some gossip and impressionistic chatter about the chief executive, and analysts' reports. This is in many ways rather like 16th-century medicine, with the physician making diagnoses and prognoses based on a few visible symptoms; with relative ignorance of physiology, complete ignorance of neurology, viruses and bacteria, and nothing but the most primitive interventions available. We warmed to this analogy when it occurred to us that a very common 16th-century prognosis was bleeding the patient!

Perhaps the only satisfactory 'output' measure of performance is to rate a company's results through a complete economic cycle. That way, the relative performance can be assessed in good times and more difficult circumstances. This approach becomes more potent when the measures used indicate to what degree the company is exceeding the cost of the capital employed in the business. How many FTSE companies have managed to generate cash at a rate that exceeded their weighted average cost of capital through the boom and decline years of the past decade? Not enough, and there have been some monstrous examples of value destruction, even in the boom period. For example, *The Economist* (12 October 2002), in an article on British industrial companies, estimates that manufacturing businesses destroyed £80 billion worth of value between 1992 and 2002!

However, even using long-term output measures has considerable drawbacks. Two spring to mind:

- Output measures do not give an accurate way of understanding what is really driving underlying performance.
- They are retrospective, and may not provide a good basis for predicting future performance.

'GOOD' INVESTMENT

It is worthy of note that serious and intelligent investors endeavour by careful and lengthy study to develop an in-depth understanding of the organizations in which they invest. Having understood the business, its products, processes, people and organization very well, and having taken a careful view on its competitive strengths and weaknesses over a good period of time, they then invest with an intent to hold the shares for a long time, taking an active and involved interest in what the company is doing to maintain and improve long-term performance.

Buffett and his partner Charles Munger are examples of a relatively small number of investors with broadly similar beliefs and philosophies. Superior investors, such as Benjamin Graham, John Maynard Keynes, Philip Fisher (all major influences on Buffett) and of course Buffett and Munger themselves, have tended to possess broadly similar philosophies. The 'Golden Rules' of these 'focus' investors are quoted by Hagstrom in *The Essential Buffett* (2001) as being:

1. Concentrate your investments in outstanding companies run by strong management.
2. Limit yourself to the number of companies you can truly understand. Ten is a good number; more than 20 is asking for trouble.
3. Pick the very best of your good companies and put the bulk of your investment there.
4. Think long term – 5 to 10 years minimum.
5. Volatility happens; carry on.

There are some signs that thoughtful enlightenment may be starting to spread, the source of this encouraging statement being Deutsche Bank. It was reported in the *Sunday Times* Business Section of 27 April 2003 that:

> Karl Sternberg, chief investment officer at Deutsche Asset Management, one of the biggest investors in the British market, is one of those who want to change the relationship with the companies he invests in. 'A few years ago, companies considered questions from shareholders almost an impertinence,' he says. 'This has changed, which is excellent, but there is still some way to go. We want to take larger holdings in fewer companies and forge partnerships with the management – perhaps even take a place on their boards. We want to have greater influence on the companies we own and help them rather than be a hindrance.

On Friday 25 April 2003, Deutsche explained its new strategy to its annual client conference. Sternberg says:

> We want a debate about a better way forward for corporate governance. What is it for? In 10 years how will we test whether corporate governance has done well? The answer is that we will be looking to see if companies have been better at investing money, if profits have increased against capital they have employed to do it and if overall economic performance has improved. If we don't improve corporate performance, it has been a pointless exercise.

Sternberg's sentiments are echoed by Claude Bébéar, chairman and founder of AXA, the French insurance giant. Bébéar has written a book entitled *Ils vont tuer le capitalisme* (They Are Going to Kill Capitalism) (2003). In it he proposes that it is time to remind the average investment manager that investors have duties as well as rights and that those who take a nurturing interest in companies and hold shares rather than churn their portfolios and bet on share prices should have special voting rights.

These behaviours can be vividly contrasted with that of the average 'active' fund manager. One such manager, on interview, confessed to having 'on average less than half a day each' to evaluate information on the investments in his portfolio, let alone prospective ones. He went on to say that his prime focus was to take a gamble on what will happen to short-term share prices.

The views of the 'focus' investors about the habits and behaviour of the bulk of the investment community can be understood from a quotation by Benjamin Graham, after attending an investment conference: 'I could not comprehend how the management of money by institutions had degenerated from sound investment to this rat race of trying to get the highest possible return in the shortest period.'

Is it possible to pin down any other factors that may underlie good performance? Or is everything contingent, so that there are no processes, practices, skills or behaviours that can provide reliable guidance to those who aspire to understand what drives high and sustainable performance?

ASSESSING 'GOOD' PERFORMANCE BY WHAT MANAGERS DO: THE RESEARCH FINDINGS

Going beneath the 'numbers' and trying to understand what values and behaviours are exhibited by the leaders of high-performing companies may take us to a new dimension of understanding and foresight about judging what is 'good'. There is much research about what 'good' companies are like and how their leaders behave. We have selected two pieces of work as being quite typical of the findings of those who take the time to go and work in real time with real managers. The findings are from research, already touched on, by Jay Lorsch and Gordon Donaldson of the Harvard Business School (Donaldson and Lorsch, 1983) and Jerry Porras and James Collins, which resulted in a celebrated book, *Built to Last* (Collins and Porras, 1995).

Lorsch and Donaldson's work was completed in the late 1970s and *Built to Last* was published in the 1990s. What is quite clear is that the values and patterns of behaviour of superior business leaders did not change significantly over that time. We believe that all the available evidence, from many sources, indicates that basic 'good' management has not changed over 30 years and longer.

What has changed is *bad* managerial behaviour. In the 1970s, 'bad' managers, of whom there were many, cut themselves off from the workforce by class and status barriers; cut themselves off from their markets, customers and competitors by ignorance, complacency and inertia; and then colluded with the equally soft and amateur providers of capital in the 'old', pre-US City to keep life comfortable and unchallenging for both. In the 1990s and onwards, bad managers have aligned themselves with (by now) immeasurably more aggressive investors to get share prices up by any available means, no matter what the medium- and longer-term consequences for their enterprises. The United Kingdom's tragedy is that it has had more than its fair share of bad managers of both kinds!

Built to Last

The researchers and authors, Porras and Collins, selected a group of sustainably high-performing, 'visionary' companies and a group of 'comparison' companies not in the same performance league. They then systematically compared the differences between them and came up with a range of characteristics and behaviours that differentiated the 'visionary' set.

Included among the 'visionary' sample are such companies as American Express, Boeing, Citicorp, Ford, Hewlett Packard, Johnson & Johnson, Marriott, Motorola, Proctor & Gamble, Sony and Wal-Mart. The main criterion for choosing these obviously successful companies was exceptional long-term performance.

Their findings are very interesting. Their first observation about these highly successful companies would make most people in the financial markets frown in disagreement.

Deeper purpose

The top management and staff of these 'visionary' companies firmly believed that their enterprise had a reason for existence that went deeper than 'just making money' or 'just satisfying shareholders'. The *fundamental purpose* of these companies was not to maximize shareholder value, but to make or supply something that was significantly useful to customers. However, the researchers go on to point out that the companies were also highly committed to superior financial performance and to creating greater value for their shareholders than their competitors could. It is just that financial performance was regarded as a necessary condition and not the fundamental purpose of being in business.

A few quotations from the 'Credo' of Johnson & Johnson might illustrate this point:

> *Our credo*
>
> We believe that our first responsibility is to the doctors, nurses, hospitals, mothers and all others who use our products.
>
> Our products must always be of the highest quality. We must constantly strive to reduce the cost of these products. Our orders must be promptly and accurately filled.
>
> Our dealers must make a fair profit.
>
> Our second responsibility is to those who work with us – the men and women of our plants and offices. They must have a sense of security in their jobs. Wages must be fair and adequate, management just, hours reasonable, and working conditions clean and orderly.
>
> Employees should have an organized system for suggestions and complaints…
>
> Our third responsibility is to our management. Our executives must be people of talent, education, experience and ability. They must be persons of common sense and full understanding.
>
> Our fourth responsibility is to the communities in which we live. We must be a good citizen – support good works and charity, and bear our fair share of taxes…
>
> Our fifth and last responsibility is to our stockholders. Business must make a sound profit. Reserves must be created, research must be carried on, adventurous programs developed, and mistakes paid for. Adverse times must be provided for, adequate taxes paid, new machines purchased, new plants built, new products launched, new sales plans developed. We must experiment with new ideas.
> *When these things have been done the stockholder must receive a fair return…* [our italics].

Strong core values

The second noticeable feature of 'visionary' companies is slightly more complex. Porras and Collins observed that their sample managed to differentiate between those values and beliefs that were absolutely fundamental to the company and those behaviours and traits that were more superficial. The key behaviour of the visionary companies was that they were extremely flexible and responsive to change, *except* for changes that would undermine the core 'ideology' of the company. Porras and Collins coined an icon that resembled the yin and yang symbol, which related the mantras 'Preserve the Core' and 'Stimulate Progress'.

Stretching goals and innovation

Next, the authors of *Built to Last* observe that their visionary companies are extremely ambitious when it comes to innovation, audacious projects and risk-taking, provided that they do not challenge the core ideology or risk the whole company. The authors labelled this commitment to challenging and adventurous development as 'big, hairy, audacious goals'!

Distinctive culture

The commitment to a strong and enveloping culture also marked the superior companies, to the extent that they were described by the authors as 'great places to work *only* for those people who buy into the core ideology; those who don't fit with the ideology are ejected like a virus' (to preserve the core).

Active and experimental nature

Visionary companies are extremely active. They are described as 'trying a lot of stuff and keeping what works'. The authors observe that they indulge in 'high levels of action and experimentation – often unplanned and undirected – that produce new and unexpected paths of progress and enables visionary companies to mimic the biological evolution of species'.

Growing their own leaders

A major and significant feature is 'home-grown management'. According to Porras and Collins, the 'best of the best' promote from within, bringing to senior levels only those who have spent significant time steeped in the core ideology of the company. This important practice is seen to be a major way of preserving that distinctive core culture.

Culture of continuous improvement

Last, and obviously, given what has gone before, the great companies studied exhibited a 'relentless' pursuit of self-improvement, with the aim of doing better and better, 'forever into the future'.

It is hard to argue with the specific findings of Porras and Collins, although by focusing on a select range of factors they have given a hostage to fortune if their companies turn out to have feet of clay. But behind the 'recipes', the authors have identified two other factors that are extremely interesting and worthy of further examination.

The first is that the companies studied seemed to be quite able to espouse and practise values and strategies that some of a more purist bent might find difficult to stomach. This tendency is described as avoiding the 'Tyranny of the Or' and espousing the 'Genius of the And'. For example, it is quite practical and indeed normal for a visionary company to be absolutely committed to high internal investment in innovation and staff development *and* to creating superior shareholder value. It does not choose to do one to the exclusion of the other.

Porras and Collins give many examples of *ors* and *ands* – for example, Investment for the Long Term *and* Demand for Short-Term Performance, or Organization Aligned with a Core Ideology *and* Organization Adapting to its Environment.

Second, the authors touch on a profound idea. They call it *'clock building, not telling the time'*. The essence of this idea is that enduring, sustainable performance comes from building a company that is capable of prospering far beyond the presence of any single leader and through multiple product life cycles. The contrast would be with companies that are dependent on a single great idea or a single charismatic founder or leader.

Porras and Collins use the following analogy:

> Imagine that you met a remarkable person who could look at the sun or stars at any time of day and state the exact time and date. 'It's April 23, 1401, 2.36 AM and 12 seconds.' This person would be an amazing time teller and we'd probably revere that person for the ability to tell time. *But wouldn't it be even more amazing if, instead of telling the time, he or she built a clock that could tell the time forever, even after he or she had gone.*

If we replace 'clock building' by 'business and organization building' as the highest achievement of the managerial art, readers will get the drift.

'Good' management in the 1970s: Decision Making at the Top

Next we will move on to a slightly different piece of research, conducted by the previously featured professors Lorsch and Donaldson. Like many of the other researchers who have graced this book, Lorsch and Donaldson sought out companies that had been industry leaders for a long time. But rather than extracting the underlying principles from the results of their work, or seeking universally applicable 'rules', the two Harvard Business School professors sought to describe what they found, leaving readers a little more discretion to make up their own minds about validity and applicability to their own contexts. One of the more interesting descriptive pieces in their book *Decision Making at the Top* (Donaldson and Lorsch, 1983) is what the authors describe as the actual values of the highly successful corporate leaders, as compared with the commonly held assumptions, which they describe as popular 'myths'.

First, they state that there is a mythical assumption that the most successful top managers move between companies quite often. Not so, say the authors; the top managers of their industry leader sample had very long service, averaging well over 20 years.

Thereafter, they describe a whole series of commonly held assumptions about the top managers of highly successful companies, comparing them with the reality that their investigations revealed (Table 8.1).

Lorsch and Donaldson further enriched their presentation of the research results by quoting extensively from the successful top managers whom they interviewed. Here is what some of the most successful managers of their generation believed. Little has changed in 20 years!

About financial goals:

> We must take a long-haul view and worry about the integrity and survival of the corporation above all else.

> ROI [return on investment] is no good unless you have a strong competitive position in the market.

> Our mission is technology, market, profit.

Stay on a pay-as-you-go basis.

We want to be an all-weather company.

Be in the upper one-third of all manufacturing companies. This means having a return on equity of [X]%, steady improvement in market share, constant innovation in product and process, having the strongest management structure in the industry.'

We must grow at [X]% to survive and get the best people.

About means and strategies:

Market share comes through technically superior products.

We must be what we are: we don't want to grow by acquiring somebody and taking the acquisition route.

We must first manage well what we have right now.

We must be a leader in manufacturing methods to keep costs down and quality up.

We must compete on innovation in processes and products and not price.

We want superior performance based on products and service of excellence and quality. This will benefit shareholders, employees, customers and society in general.

Minimize acquisitions because you won't acquire good managers.

New lines of business must be comfortable to our managers, in consumer products and in the United States.

About organization and management:

We believe in a lot of participation in planning.

We get good people and keep them.

We must breed our own management.

The real problem is how to use good people efficiently. The dollars will follow the people.

We should give our employees the experience of an opportunity to grow with a stable career.

Leave initiative with the bottom. Let top management respond to what division managers want.

Don't manage like a detached investment banker.

We grow to give people a challenge.

People should make a long-term commitment to the company because we are not a hire and fire company.

We believe the CEO should have a long development period and a long term in office.

Pay constant attention to management development.

Table 8.1 Myths and realities concerning top managers

Myth	Reality
Successful top managers are driven to maximize shareholder wealth.	Successful top managers are most concerned about the long-term success and survival of the corporation.
Strategic decisions are crucially subject to capital market disciplines.	The most successful companies seek to minimize their dependence on capital markets.
The most successful top managers are mainly concerned with investor reactions and expectations.	The top managers of the most successful companies are most concerned to be highly competitive in their product markets and to meet the needs and expectations of fellow employees.
Successful top managers are mainly concerned about short-term results.	Top managers in the most successful companies are most concerned with long-term corporate survival.
Top managers of successful companies regard acquisitions as inherently bad.	The managers of the most successful companies regard acquisitions and diversification as a contingent part of their strategic armoury.
Strategic choices and decisions are rationally conceived and executed.	Successful strategic change tends to be incremental and often exploratory. It is mostly based on experience and subjective judgement, rather than rational analysis.

So, have we discovered the universal truth, a means of both describing what good companies do and predicting future performance? Not quite. There are several difficulties with using the research methodology by itself as a predictive tool.

First, further judgement has to be made as to whether particular 'virtuous' behaviours suit the business in question; in particular the relationships between chosen forms of behaviour and patterns of action and those that will create real competitive edge in a specific enterprise. For example, an ex-director of the old ICI company once described his organization as 'drowning in goodness'. He meant that the ICI leadership were too willing to try every apparently 'good' practice that was available, in the hope that if they did enough of them, performance would be exceptional. Said our ex-director, 'A little more thought about what particular behaviours, practices and skills would have made a real difference in our industry would have helped a lot.'

Second, simply describing the practices, behaviour and assumed values of a particular leadership may not tell observers enough about the quality of management and key staff in an organization.

What we can say is that understanding leadership behaviours and their impact on the quality and performance of organizations will enrich our understanding of what is likely to generate superior performance. It is certain that combining perspectives on the long-term 'numbers' and research-derived knowledge on management behaviours and actions that are likely to generate superior performance increases the likelihood of being able to understand and predict the performance of particular enterprises.

DEFINING 'GOOD' PERFORMANCE THROUGH GOOD PROCESSES

But are there other ways of enhancing our understanding of what creates 'good' performance? We think so.

Organizations that have found ways of sustaining superior long-term performance seem to give appropriate and balanced attention to the key facets of their business and to the interests of stakeholders. A good example of this is represented by the 'Creed' of Johnson & Johnson. When they get the balance right, such companies create a virtuous cycle of actions that will reinforce and deepen the competitiveness and performance of the business. Such a cycle is described in Figure 8.1.

This model seeks to identify the elements of a virtuous cycle that will result in an enterprise being able to achieve a sustainably good performance. At the centre are the enterprise's core objectives, to 'serve the needs of its customers' and to 'satisfy the needs of its stakeholders'. If these objectives are to be achieved, the enterprise must first do whatever is needed to develop and maintain competitive advantage in its chosen customer markets. To do this, it must devote permanent attention to internal processes that will enable:

- Its organization to be the 'engine' of high performance and growth. Different industries and different challenges will mean that the design and functioning of the organization will be always adapting and changing. Integral to all this is the development of staff and management to be able to learn and adapt at least as fast as change in its industry.
- The most efficient use of capital assets to support efficiency and low costs.
- The development of customer offerings and customer-serving processes that are at least as good as those of the best competitors and that are capable of differentiation from competitors in terms of quality, performance or cost. This will entail dedicated investment in innovation, product/service development and customer research.

Developing competitive advantages will mean that the enterprise will be capable of creating wealth at a level equal or superior to that of quality competitors. This is crucial to the maintenance of sustainable high performance, as it enables the enterprise to have the wherewithal to fulfil two critical needs:

- To enhance shareholder value at a level at least equal over the long term to that of its competitors for capital. Satisfying responsible investors will enable the enterprise to realize the capital that it needs to sustain and grow the business at the lowest cost.

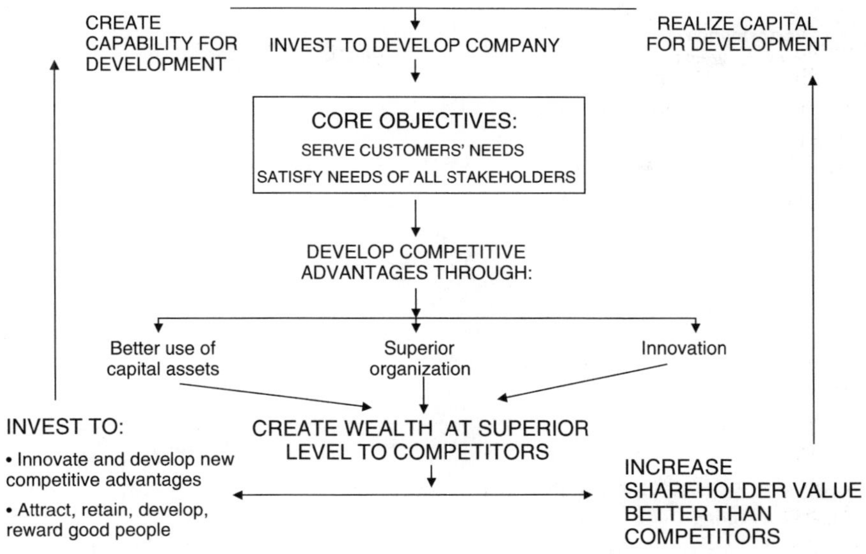

Figure 8.1 Virtuous cycle of actions: creating a sustainable business
Source: Don Young

- To enable the enterprise to maintain positive internal investment that will enable it to:
  - innovate and create new or improved forms of competitive advantage;
  - enhance the quality and performance of the organization, systems and processes, and, above all, people.

Satisfying shareholder requirements will give access to the capital *needed for investment and growth.*

Investing in innovation and organization-building will create the capability *to compete and grow successfully.*

Looking at the issue of good performance and the underlying requirements needed to sustain it in this way removes the requirement to regard the needs of any one stakeholder as paramount. Successful enterprises and their top managements will need to reconcile the demands of a range of important stakeholders and satisfy their needs. Failure to achieve a virtuous balance will almost certainly result in eventual underperformance and failure.

Figure 8.2 seeks to demonstrate that every organization can be driven too hard or not hard enough.

The important features to take from this representation are the following:

- Each enterprise will have limitations on the performance that it can achieve. 'Driving' an enterprise too hard will result in stress, underinvestment or system failure. Readers should remember that all enterprises are human institutions and are really capable of fatigue, stress and becoming 'run down'!

  Setting performance expectations too low will, on the other hand, result in complacency, excess 'fat' in the organization, low standards and

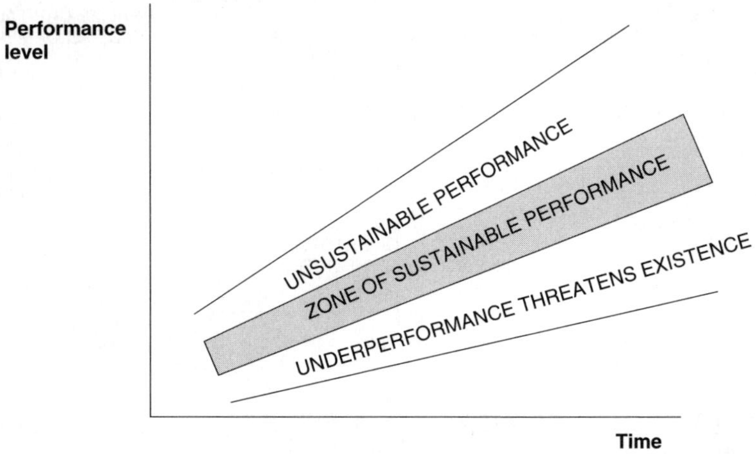

Figure 8.2 Zone of sustainable performance
Source: Don Young

expectations, all leading to competitive failure and eventually to threats to the enterprise's existence.

- The 'Zone of Sustainable Performance' represents the range of performances that will enable the needs and expectations of all key stakeholders to be met, key investment requirements to be satisfied and the organization to be 'run' at an optimal and healthy level.
- The 'Zone of Sustainable Performance' is not necessarily a straight line. It is inevitable that any successful business will experience a range of different pressures and opportunities over time. Sometimes opportunities for growth will accelerate and the enterprise will need to invest heavily in internal initiatives or in acquisitions to take advantage. At other times, the dynamics of markets and industries will mean that the most sensible options are to focus on improving efficiency and not on growth.

Sensible long-term investors will recognize that successful, high-performing enterprises will go through many different phases of growth and consolidation, giving rise to many different levels of financial performance. Equally, top managers will need to tailor their objectives and strategies to the dynamics of their own organizations and competitor markets.

We have explored three perspectives on understanding company performance and analysing whether or not particular enterprises have created the conditions that will enable them to sustain a superior performance. We now feel capable of crystallizing a lot of perspectives, research evidence and experience about what sustains high performance in companies. We feel that there is enough reliable evidence to make a well-founded and robust case. For those with the curiosity and open-mindedness to seek the truth, the data are there to be readily accessed.

BUILDING ROBUST HIGH-PERFORMANCE COMPANIES

External measures

High-performing companies will generate sufficient cash to cover their weighted average cost of capital over a full industry economic cycle, having first invested at sufficient levels to improve their sources of competitive advantage. They will generate returns for shareholders over a cycle that are at least in line with those generated by other leaders in their industry sector.

Values demonstrated by the leaders of high-performing companies

The leaders of high-performing enterprises will manifest clear and marked values in several key domains:

1. They will define the satisfaction of customer needs and sustaining a strong competitive position in their industry as their central purposes.
2. They will invest in product/service development, innovation, efficiency and staff at a level that will maintain competitive advantage.
3. They will also use their own commitment to the quality, usefulness and value of the products or services to generate dedication and a sense of purpose in others in the organization.
4. The top managers of high-performing companies will demonstrate very high commitment to ensuring that they hand over a vital and successful enterprise to their successors. They will take action to 'groom' the next generation of managers, and regard this as a high priority.
5. The first commitment of top managers will be to the organizations that they lead. They will make sure that this commitment is demonstrated by:
   - acting to reinforce the culture, and ensuring that the organization stays open to learning, is sensitive to events in the external environment and is adaptive;
   - setting standards and 'modelling' desirable behaviours through their own actions inside the organization;
   - spending sufficient time on internal leadership and communication to make sure that they are personally demonstrating commitment and are open to signals about internal morale.
6. After this, they will also make sure that key external stakeholders' needs are attended to and met.

WHAT DO THE TOP MANAGERS OF HIGH-PERFORMING COMPANIES ACTUALLY DO?

In this world there are sins of omission and sins of commission. When one observes what top managers do, both kinds of sin are evident.

So, let us start with those things that top managers who aspire to lead robustly high-performing companies will *avoid doing*:

- They will not take huge risks with the future of the enterprise, no matter how appealing it may appear to do so. Most big disasters originate from the corporate office, the 'management factories' referred to earlier in the book.

  The typical 'sins' that originate from the top of organizations include:
  - Making large acquisitions, especially serial acquisitions, without sufficient awareness or thought as to whether the wider organization can cope with them.
  - Inventing strategies that are divorced from the reality of the current business and organization, and trying to cascade them down the organization.
  - Deciding on sudden, drastic 'campaigns' driven top-down from the corporate office. Such campaigns are often aimed at achieving significant cost reductions, and frequently involve external consultants using dreadful techniques such as 'activity value analysis'. The damage that these kinds of blitzes have on trust and commitment is incalculable, and usually invisible to the initiators. As an alternative, share the problems with people, tell them what has to be done and why, and then let them decide on how the changes will be achieved. If they need help, offer it to them. That is called involvement and empowerment.
- They will not fall into the trap of believing that they are the 'sun' around which the whole business revolves. Lord Acton's awful warnings about the corrupting effects of power are at least as apposite for top managers as they are for politicians – in fact more so, as most senior managers can, if they wish, cut themselves off from any sense of accountability to a wider internal constituency and employ a small army of advisers to promote a shiny external image. These behaviours are distressingly common. Eventually such 'Sun Kings' will be found out, but think of the damage they cause along the way!

  There is a great deal of evidence to demonstrate that the leaders of robustly high-performing companies regard themselves as the stewards of the well-being of the enterprise and as people who have serious roles to perform, along with all the other valuable people that make up the organization. This perspective does not allow much room for huge egos, lavish displays of personal power and status or gargantuan pay packets!
- Joseph Fuller wrote an article in the *Harvard Business Review* (2001) entitled 'A letter to the chief executive'. Among other excellent pieces of advice, Fuller exhorted CEOs to avoid letting the key agendas and priorities for the business be dominated by the needs of external agencies, in particular the financial markets.

  He emphasized that the most important things were for leaders to understand what it took for their organizations to satisfy customers' needs and succeed in the competitive race. Allowing the pressures that come from investment institutions to distort and confuse these central objectives would, Fuller averred, cause great damage to the enterprise's long-term prospects.

Having dispensed with the don'ts, let us examine some things that top managers in high-performing companies *will seek to do*:

- They will seek to grow their business from the 'inside' out. This means that leaders of high-performing companies act as a first priority to create a very strong platform for competitiveness and growth by attending to the processes, people and organization that create customer offerings. Allied to this, they will also aim to create a strong and distinctive internal culture, but one that actively values learning and curiosity about the external world. Then, when it becomes really necessary to take 'external' routes such as mergers, acquisitions or partnerships to sustain growth, the business and organizational platforms will be sufficiently strong to assimilate acquisitions or work alongside strong partners without becoming distorted by the relationship.

- They will ensure that they are strongly 'bonded' with the organization that they lead.

  John Kotter, in his previously mentioned book *The General Managers* (1982), describes such bonding well. It means that 'good' leaders will ensure that they know and are known by a wide cross section of the organization's staff as real people. This means networking and, often, travelling extensively. It also means using every medium and opportunity to transmit and reinforce the key messages about values, priorities and direction, as well as listening extensively. And it means doing these things consistently, for all time, because they come from the heart as well as the brain and not because the communications department feels that they are occasionally needed.

  The contrast is stark: 'good' managers know their businesses intimately, are in touch with the detail, 'craft' strategies from a strongly involved position, and have strong commitments to the business and its people. Such bonding is not founded on soft sentiment in high-performing organizations. It is hard work and it is done for hard as well as soft reasons. But in the end, if leaders have to do unpleasant things, it should be that the organization knows that they had to be done for good reasons. Out of such bonding comes the mutual trust that binds people in high-performing enterprises.

WHAT ABOUT 'ACTIVE' STRATEGIES?

What, then, about the 'active' routes that many in the financial markets and press will expect from virile, successful leaders? What about M&A activity, what about portfolio changes, what about 'corporate transformation' and quantum reductions in costs?

It is quite clear that high-performing organizations and their leaders do not automatically shun any of these stratagems. But they keep them in their proper context. For example, a 'good' top management would not indulge in acquisitions unless it knew precisely the strategic reasons for making them and was certain that its organization was strong enough to enable acquisitions to be well assimilated.

Yet again, cost reduction is likely to be managed as a continuous and progressive activity backed by appropriate capital investment and staff development, not by sudden top-down slashing of costs and heads. Most of the behaviours beloved of the press and markets are appropriate only in situations of dire crisis, and the thing about strong, high-performing, well-led companies is that they encounter crises infrequently, unless these are brought about by external agencies.

CREATING VIRTUOUS CYCLES

Many readers will have experience of cycles of interrelated actions and events that may have good or negative eventual outcomes. For example, we referred to one such cycle in a previous chapter with regard to acquisitions. Acquisitive predators like the old Hanson Trust bought companies that had underexploited their assets and stripped them out. Top-line performance showed rapid improvement, but, in the longer term, lack of investment caused the performance of the acquisitions to decline. This effect was masked by further and increasingly large acquisitions, which maintained the profit line, until the music stopped and there were no acquisitions available that were large enough to keep the profits advancing. At this point the illusion of a virtuous cycle of advancing size and profits became revealed as a vicious cycle of underinvestment and declining profitability. When the edifice collapsed, it did so rapidly, surprising only the unwary.

Virtuous cycles are the opposite. We described a 'model' cycle earlier in this chapter. The elements were:

- rigorous focus on the central purposes of the enterprise, starting with the satisfaction of the needs of customers;
- creating the capacity to achieve and sustain competitive advantage through product development, innovation, efficient use of capital assets and creating a better organization;
- satisfying and balancing the needs for internal investment and providing satisfactory returns to shareholders.

The central themes are: 1) focus on the customer market; 2) sufficient and effective investment; and 3) giving balanced attention to the needs of all key stakeholders. If they wished, readers could create their own virtuous cycles from the model. The overall model is likely to be similar for all larger organizations, but the elements will differ from business to business.

So, that's it. We have tracked down and described most of the component elements that can be pieced together and practised in a contingent and sensible manner by any large organization. It all seems to make good business and human sense. Could anyone disagree? Well, let us see.

There has recently been much welcome debate in the investment industry about corporate governance, and the Centre for Tomorrow's Company has launched an extensive study of investment principles and behaviour in early 2003. But some of the more enlightened actors on the UK investment stage have already devoted serious thought to the behaviours that they would like to see from the companies in which they invest. Before we close this chapter, it is important to examine the views of a central influence on company behaviour and performance.

A VIEW ON 'GOOD' MANAGEMENT BEHAVIOUR FROM THE INVESTMENT INDUSTRY

In October 2000, Hermes Pensions Management, one of the larger UK pensions investors, produced a statement of principles designed to make clear its views on what it expects from companies when investing. It accompanied the principles by stating clearly some fundamental convictions that drove Hermes' thinking:

1. It is 'axiomatic' that the primary goal of a UK listed company is to be run in the long-term interests of its shareholders… Central to this goal is the need to create a financial surplus.
2. That financial surplus is achieved by having a competitive advantage.
3. That companies should behave ethically.

Also behind these principles is some recognition of the fact that all is not necessarily well in the world of 'shareholders'. Hermes states, somewhat uneasily, under the heading 'Capital market behaviour', that 'Some participants in the market seek to bet on performance over a short time period. This should not distract company managers from their long-term goals.' It then nods briefly to acknowledge the fact that it is not actually a real shareholder: '(Throughout this document reference to Hermes as the shareholder is in recognition of Hermes as the agent for the owners)'.

The 10 Hermes principles

1. Companies should seek an honest, open dialogue with shareholders. They should clearly communicate the plans they are pursuing and the likely financial and wider consequences of those plans. Ideally, goals, plans and progress should be discussed in the annual report and accounts.
2. Companies should have appropriate measures and systems in place to ensure that they know which activities and competencies contribute most to maximizing shareholder value.
3. Companies should ensure all investment plans have been honestly and critically tested in terms of their ability to deliver long-term shareholder value.
4. Companies should allocate capital for investment by seeking fully and creatively to explore opportunities for growth within their core businesses rather than seeking unrelated diversification. This is particularly true when considering acquisitive growth.
5. Companies should have performance evaluation and incentive systems designed cost-effectively to incentivize managers to deliver long-term shareholder value.
6. Companies should have an efficient capital structure that will minimize the long-term cost of capital.
7. Companies should have and should continue to develop coherent strategies for each business unit. These should ideally be expressed in terms of market prospects and of the competitive advantage the business has in terms of exploring these prospects. The company should understand the factors that drive market growth, and the particular strengths that underpin its competitive position.
8. Companies should be able to explain why they are the 'best parent' of the businesses they run. Where they are not the best parent they should be developing plans to resolve the issue.
9. Companies should manage effectively relationships with their employees, suppliers and customers and with others who have a legitimate interest in the company's activities. Companies should behave ethically and have regard for the environment and society as a whole.
10. Companies should support voluntary and statutory measures that minimize the externalization of costs to the detriment of society at large.

The Hermes principles are a welcome contribution to the 'pot' of thinking about investment and company behaviour. But they expose one massive difference between all the evidence and research about high performance in the industrial economy, and the central axiom that is held by the financial markets and many others in political and financial circles. Companies that perform at a superior and sustained level do not regard their primary goal as to be run in the interests of their shareholders. *They regard their primary goal as being to serve the needs of their customers.*

So, where has the 'axiom' about the primacy of shareholder needs come from? It seems to us a little like a supporting actor suddenly declaring unilaterally that he is the star, and that the rest of the cast should run around serving his every need (and whim, given the behaviour of some investment institutions!). Perhaps the roots of this piece of conceit lie in the age-old belief of the ruling class that money, land and property are more important than people? Or maybe the awesome truth that designing, producing, marketing and selling products and services that meet customers' needs is infinitely more important than counting and speculating on the financial results of these real core activities of industry is just too much for the financial establishment to stomach?

Charles Handy, in his excellent *Harvard Business Review* article 'What's a business for?' (2002) concludes:

> Now (unlike 200 years ago) that the value of a company resides largely in its intellectual property, in its brands and patents and in the skills and experience of its workforce, it seems unreal to treat these things as the property of financiers, to be disposed of as they wish. This may still be the law, but it hardly seems like justice. Surely, those who carry this intellectual property within them, who contribute their time and talents rather than their money, should have some rights, some say in the future of 'their' company.

Handy goes on to say, 'Corporate law in both Britain and America is out of date. It no longer fits the reality of business in the knowledge economy. Perhaps it didn't even fit business in the industrial era.'

Maybe it is time to politely but firmly lead the providers of capital to their proper role as a vital supporter of industrial enterprise, not the centre of the industrial universe. Power should be passed to those who create valuable goods and services for customers and thus resources for reinvestment and rewarding investors.

Part IV

The three Propositions

Introduction to Part IV

So far, we have tried to give a detailed and descriptive outline of the relationships that have developed between the UK financial markets and the large companies whose shares are quoted in the markets. We have also touched on the effects of these relationships on the beliefs, behaviour and actions of those who lead our largest companies and on the enterprises that they lead.

We have examined research about what management behaviours seem to produce positive longer-term performance and contrasted this with an extensive review of what behaviour and actions might cause underperformance and failure.

We have also tried, through the medium of a case study, to indicate that certain kinds of beliefs, behaviour and actions can produce spectacular results for quite long periods, at the same time creating the underlying conditions for eventual and often spectacular decline.

We have stated a belief that these corrosive processes that will eventually cause system breakdown in enterprises are of little interest to the markets, the press or, all too often, to top managers, who are increasingly judged on their short-term and visible actions and not their longer-term management skills.

We have now reached a crucial point where we will try to draw the threads of our story together in a manner that will give you, the reader, an opportunity to hear our case and draw your own conclusions about the current arrangements for financing large enterprises. You can decide whether these are fine as they are, need minor adjustments or need significant reform.

What we *can* state, with a very high level of confidence, is that nearly everybody believes that the current system needs *some* reforms. A series of dramatic company failures have awoken investors, regulators and the public alike to the potential for catastrophic failure inherent in the system as it stands. At first glance the apparent fraud at Enron, WorldCom and Tyco may seem distinct from the acquisition-driven value destruction in Marconi, Vivendi and Invensys, but are they symptoms of the same disease? Are they all consequences of the creation of 'star' corporate leaders whose interests lie not with the long-term future of the organizations they lead but with the need to keep favour with the financial markets in order to benefit themselves?

In the United Kingdom, as in the United States, fraud and dramatic company failure are but the tip of the iceberg. Many would argue that other effects and outcomes of the current financial market arrangements are more serious. These effects might include misleading accounting, mis-selling of financial services products, exploiting smaller investors, excessive rewards for mediocre performance and undermining the security, efforts and livelihoods of those who are not 'inside' the system of relationships between markets and managers. Some would contend that the 'system', as it works currently in the United Kingdom, is a key causal factor behind underinvestment, low productivity and long-term underperformance by many UK-financed companies.

The mechanisms that we will adopt to put our case and encourage you to consider your own position will be to present three 'Propositions' and then to make a case for acceptance of each one, somewhat in the manner a barrister might in a court of law.

THE THREE PROPOSITIONS

The three 'Propositions' emerged from the process of interviewing and research that we conducted before formulating the final plan for the book. We did not make them up first and then look for evidence to prove them, rather the other way round. We considered our own experience, thought about the perspectives and issues that arose through our interviews and discussions, and began to formulate a series of hypotheses that eventually gelled into the three 'Propositions' that underpin the next chapters.

We ask you to judge whether the case made through the Propositions is valid. Thus, readers, if you care to, you can act as a kind of jury and make up your minds as to what you agree and disagree with, and what you think about the significance of the points we are making. We are dealing with very complex matters and it may be that you find it impossible to reach hard and fast conclusions on every issue. If so, you may wish to consider whether the case made is, on balance, more or less convincing. In this way we hope to stimulate constructive thought and debate about matters that are of importance to us all.

Part IV consists of three chapters, each one revolving around a distinct Proposition.

9

Managers and markets

THE PROPOSITION

That the financial markets are the dominant influence affecting the appointments, careers, rewards and tenure of the top management of large quoted companies.

That the players in the financial markets have become more aggressive and domineering since 'Big Bang' and the dominance of the London market by large and ambitious foreign-owned investment banks. Whereas once top management saw their interests as being distinct from those of investors, a much more involved and symbiotic relationship has developed between them in recent years.

Most contemporary top managers understand that great benefits can accrue from pleasing the markets. To do this they employ a wide range of stratagems, from aligning their behaviour and actions to those the markets seem to want, through creating and selling carefully crafted 'stories', to, at the extremes, manipulation of information and outright deceit. Thus top managers and the main players in the financial markets have tended more and more to become part of a 'system' of connected and symbiotic interests. This system, while informal, is coherent and well understood by insiders, and can create huge opportunities for rewarding the players.

The system of interrelationships between managers and the many players in and around the financial markets is, because of its informality and complexity, almost impossible to regulate. It therefore essentially serves only the interests of insiders, and is in no way accountable to other potential stakeholders or the wider society.

This first Proposition was formulated after we completed the interview programme for this book. It represents our considered views, supported by many (but not all) of the people we interviewed. Our task in this chapter is to convince you, the reader, that the Proposition is substantially valid. To do this, we will consider:

- how top managers, in particular CEOs, are appointed and removed (as getting and losing a top job represent two of the most significant experiences in any ambitious manager's career);
- what the financial markets regard as good performance, and therefore what managers have to do to perform well in the eyes of the markets;
- how the system of interactions between managers and the markets works, and what mechanisms link the vital interests of managers and the markets;
- how the players in management and in the markets derive their rewards.

You are perfectly entitled to ask, 'Where is the evidence?' We have drawn on a myriad of sources to assemble 'evidence' to back the Propositions. Starting with our own experience and observations while engaged in management and transactions at the top of two large UK listed multinational companies, we then carried out research specifically to support this book. This has entailed:

- discussions and interviews with over 60 people, all of whom have had lengthy experience of the fields covered;
- group discussions to consider our tentative findings;
- examining surveys and studies carried out by such institutions as Cranfield Business School and the Judge Institute at Cambridge University;
- reading books such as Tony Golding's *The City* (2001), Philip Augar's *The Death of Gentlemanly Capitalism* (2001), Frank Partnoy's *F.I.A.S.C.O.* (1998) and *Infectious Greed* (2003), George Soros's '*The Crisis of Global Capitalism* (1998), Adair Turner's *Just Capital: The liberal economy* (2001), Robert G Hagstrom's *The Essential Buffett* (2001), plus research-based books such as Donaldson and Lorsch's *Decision Making at the Top* (1983) and Collins and Porras's *Built to Last* (1995), and many others to provide background information and insights;
- tracking most of the quality papers' financial and management pages generally for decades and intensively for three years;
- avidly reading quality magazines such as the *Harvard Business Review*, *McKinsey Quarterly*, *The Economist* and, not least, the remarkably well-informed pages of *Private Eye* magazine.

Thus, we feel the research has been reasonably thorough.

The fascination of this book's subject matter arises because a very large part of the relationship between management and the markets lies well outside the public domain. As in many other spheres of public life in the United Kingdom and elsewhere, what happens in the shadows behind the scenes is at least as important as that which is played out in public.

We are both privileged to have worked close to top managers in a variety of large companies and to have been privy to what really goes on, as opposed to what is presented to the world. We are also grateful to many of those with whom we spoke for anecdotes, stories and personal experiences that we cannot attribute, but that carry the ring of truth and accord with our own personal experience.

HOW CEOS ARE APPOINTED AND REMOVED

Appointment

The life of a top manager has, by all accounts, become vastly more pressured in the past two decades. Studies of executive lifestyles, surveys of managers' views and our interviews confirmed this view. Furthermore, at a more circumstantial level our own experience, which stretches back to less pressurized times, strongly reinforces the view that the life of a contemporary top manager is beset by more public pressures than in former days.

The 'headhunters' whom we interviewed all confirmed that most top managers are acutely aware of the pressures not only to perform, but also to demonstrate by actions and words that they are 'high performers'. Managers believe that their time in the sun is likely to be relatively short. It is therefore prudent to accumulate wealth quickly and perhaps to get out of the heat at a relatively early age, before they burn out or the world turns against them.

What are the sources of pressure and influence on contemporary top managers?

Obtaining, keeping or losing a top job is arguably the most important fact of life for many individuals. The role that attracts the most attention and also the most pressure is that of Chief Executive Officer. This role is normally separate from that of Chairperson, except in cases where the Chairperson's role is executive. So, for the purposes of making our case, we will concentrate mainly on CEOs. However, other characters such as Finance Directors, Chairpersons and Senior Non-executive Directors or Deputy Chairperson will appear from time to time and are part of the same symbiotic system.

At face value, the decisions surrounding the appointment of a new CEO are not all that complex. The first and key decision will be whether the new appointee should come from inside or outside the organization. Available evidence from research studies seems to indicate that except where exceptional circumstances prevail, internal appointees ought to have a far better chance of success than external ones. After all, they will know the business and will understand the complexities of the organization, the people and the politics. So, let us start by examining the dynamics behind an internal appointment.

Internal appointments

The key decision-takers in a CEO appointment are the chairperson and some key non-executive directors. Additionally, the appointment of a director needs to be ratified by a vote of the 'shareholders', which, as we have seen, in practice mainly means investment institutions. As non-executive directors are universally regarded as being accountable primarily, if not solely, to the shareholders, they are inevitably going to be acutely aware of the likely market reactions to a particular appointment.

It is very unlikely that any internal candidate will get a look-in if he or she is not already well known to the chairperson and influential non-executive directors. They will most likely have seen the candidates during presentations to board meetings and other formal corporate occasions. They will probably have discussed the candidates' strengths and weaknesses with the outgoing CEO and other relevant individuals at board appointment committee meetings.

So, at the least, they will probably feel that the candidate 'presents well' and that they like the 'cut of his/her jib'.

In the back of their minds will be such questions as 'How will the appointment go down with the person's new colleagues?' or 'Do we feel that he/she is "right" for the job?' (As most influential non-executive directors are already members of the 'great and good', readers may care to consider what a typical group of non-executive directors may mean by 'right'.)

The next crucial question is 'What will the external world think of an internal appointment/appointee?' This is likely to be most easy to answer if the candidate already has an established external profile with investors, other influential figures in the financial community, and the financial press. In very exceptional circumstances, such as an appointment to CEO of a defence contracting company, reputation with the customer (government) may be crucial. Generally, however, it is clear that the approval of financial markets and press is the determining factor.

This means that the easiest route to CEO is via the role of Finance Director, as finance directors of large companies will already have a known profile in the markets and press. Finance directors are the main communicators with the analysts, stand shoulder to shoulder with the CEO at crucial presentations to investors and journalists, and are seen by a financial audience as possessing the vital skill of 'knowing the numbers'. In addition, a study by the Judge Institute (Barker, 1999) supports our own findings that finance directors are more likely than senior managers from other disciplines to align their views with those of the financial markets. Thus it is that a disproportionate number of finance directors (in relation to the total talent pool of directors from operations, marketing or other functions) are appointed to the CEO positions in large companies.

Any internal appointment is likely to be preceded by a 'grooming' period. Grooming will often entail taking a non-executive director role in another public company. The candidate may also be coached in the vital skills of making presentations, and quite often a senior PR or investor relations consultant will give input on appearance and how to 'come across'. It will also help an internal candidate's chances considerably if he or she has a patron, usually a senior member of the 'great and good' with an excellent reputation in the markets. It is also common before making an internal (or external) appointment to take 'soundings' from prominent and knowledgeable figures in the financial markets.

In response to concerns that internal candidates may not offer the company access to 'the best', sometimes the company will commission an executive search company to compare available external talent with the internal candidates. At face value, this practice may appear to be prudent and smacking of thoroughness. At a deeper level, however, it is quite bizarre, entailing as it does, a comparison of people who ought to be well known with people whose real characters are only understood at a very superficial level, ie that of past reputation and an executive search consultant's say-so. (Incidentally, long experience tells us that the abilities of executive search consultants to understand candidates at anything more than a rather surface level vary vastly!)

From a purely management point of view, internal candidates, properly developed, stand a far better chance of being successful in most circumstances. They know the company and their real capabilities can be more accurately predicted. However, there are a number of forces ranged against the appointment of internal candidates, unless they have already been exposed to the external world through a track record as, say, Finance Director. It is extensively reported that analysts and investment institutions prefer to see appointments of people whom they know. And whatever they may say, executive search consultants make the big money from finding external candidates at 30 per cent plus of starting remuneration rather than by advising on comparisons between internal and external candidates.

Internal appointments are not always possible or desirable. For example, where the company is very poor at developing and grooming top managers, or where the business or environment is changing very rapidly and experience of the changing environment is lacking internally, or when the company is facing a crisis of some sort, making an external appointment clearly the best route to take.

External appointments

From an outside perspective there is a definite bias towards external appointments. The appointment of an external candidate to the top position in a large public company usually entails an elaborate process of search, vetting, taking of 'soundings' and references, much of which is veiled in elaborate secrecy. The likelihood of an external (as opposed to internal) appointment is increased by a number of forces.

First, we found a well-developed belief in the financial markets and, more obviously, among the executive search community that top managers should not remain in post for too long. The most commonly expressed belief is that five years in a CEO post is about right, otherwise the incumbent is at risk of becoming 'stale' or running out of fresh ideas. Therefore, the story goes, it is better to bring fresh blood into a company from time to time in order to keep change rolling. This view prevails despite the bulk of evidence, already considered in earlier chapters, showing that good internal management development and prior experience of the business and organization are a far better recipe for long-term success.

A second factor, which we have already referred to, is the notion of the top manager as 'star'. The financial markets and press have a marked tendency to characterize an enterprise as comprising one person, and attach huge significance to that person's influence, even though it is known that sustainable change in a large business entails a complex and long-term process involving many people.

Thus for 'stars', timing is crucial. It is obviously best to take up a position at a time when matters are turning up, or are so low that 'the only way is up', because a new CEO will have a maximum of two years to demonstrate significant improvement as a result of his or her efforts.

The alternative – which, as we have seen, tempts many – is to 'go active' and change the portfolio, slash costs or sell the business. We found that many informed people believed that the markets will accord hero status more willingly to people who follow this route.

Given the conviction of the markets and press that individuals are the crucial factor behind corporate success, it is an easy step to the commonly heard argument that 'We must have the "best of the best" and it is therefore absolutely essential to pay top dollar to attract such people, wherever they may be.' (As an aside, one of Britain's largest companies, searching for a new CEO, announced that it needed a 'heavyweight' to pull it out of the mess created by the departing 'heavyweight'. Just a thought, but maybe a different kind of candidate would do less damage, and come cheaper!)

A typical process of recruitment for an external candidate will start with the selection of an executive search consultant. This may be supplemented quietly in the background by the chairperson taking 'soundings' among non-executive colleagues and other contacts in his or her networks.

The number of search consultants who can be trusted to conduct an international search for a top manager is limited. In London the number amounts to seven or eight search companies. As each is constrained not to poach people from companies that have been clients in the past two years, companies may be forced to use more than one for a top appointment.

The search consultant will prepare a company, job and person profile and begin the search process, using existing databases and researchers to tap their networks looking for other people's ideas on suitable candidates or target companies. Any senior manager worth his or her salt will have received many such calls from a search consultant or researcher, inviting help to find suitable candidates. This obviously gives the person contacted a chance, if they wish, to advance his or her own cause!

Typically, after two months or so the search consultant will have assembled a long-list of candidates, plus feedback on the attractiveness of the company, role and package. Frequently, but not invariably, the package may be felt to be a little on the low side, and, as this will directly affect the search consultant's fee, this is not something that the consultant will automatically argue against. As the arrival of a high-priced newcomer may be felt to prove that existing insiders are out of line with the market rate, the degree of internal resistance may also be quite low!

Next, the shortlist will be compiled and the process of interviews and discussions will begin. In the case of a CEO appointment, the chairperson and certain non-executive directors will be crucially involved, guided possibly by an HR director, but more commonly by the search consultants. Soon the initial shortlist may dissipate as candidates drop off the list. It is normal for a shortlist of five or so to be whittled down to one or two strong candidates.

At this point, confidential 'soundings' can begin. These will usually consist of a fairly comprehensive series of reference discussions with those who have known the candidate in the past.

Alongside this comes the most important part. The absolutely key question 'What will the City think?' has to be answered. This is the crunch point in the process of appointing an external candidate to the top job in a large quoted company. If there is more than the slightest hint of hesitation from influential figures in the investment community, the chances of an individual's being appointed decrease markedly. Search consultants, including our interviewees, tell stories of strong candidates being dropped because of investor hesitancy. One contended that one negative vote from the financial markets would override five positive references from all other quarters.

Senior executives we spoke to were overwhelmingly convinced that support in the market, or the lack of it, could crucially affect their chances of obtaining top jobs. Top managers speak of a reluctance to create negative impressions in the financial markets as being a major factor preventing challenge to the amazingly high levels of investment banking fees. The comprehensive Cranfield survey of FTSE 350 CEOs (Harrington and Steele, 1999) confirms a solid conviction that the views of the 'shareholders' are the most important factor affecting job-getting and tenure. Our interviewees were solidly of the view that the overriding influence on their success and careers was the judgement of the investment community. Most described, often in very colourful terms, the sense of being constantly scrutinized, even dissected, by the financial markets, particularly analysts, investors and the press. One said, 'If the City complain to your chairman, you had might as well take up birdwatching.' Another, as we have seen, described the City–press nexus as like 'a poisonous swarm of insects'. Yet others described the influence of senior analysts and fund managers: 'If Y [a senior industry analyst] says we should get rid of a particular business, we will most likely get rid of it.'

Some described the elaborate processes involved in keeping the investment community sweet. These involve devising elaborate stories calculated to keep sentiment positive, or at least create a climate of expectations that can be exceeded. A senior secretary who had spent many years observing several top manager bosses handling the markets described the process as being 'an elaborate boy's game, having nothing to do with the practicalities of running the company'.

So, how do the processes of taking soundings from the markets about individuals work?

First, nearly every company in the FTSE 100 has at least one non-executive director who has current or past 'City' connections, often cemented by social ties. Second, many chairmen and senior non-executive directors have extensive contacts in the financial markets. Third, senior figures in the markets, particularly house stockbrokers, can take soundings or advise chairpersons on the best people to talk to. Thus another senior secretary described her boss, a chairman, as taking advice from brokers on the best list of investment managers to consult before he made a top appointment, and then spending several days telephoning and seeing them. The 'soundings' are typically of the 'What do you think reactions might be if we appointed X?' or 'I would welcome your ideas on Y' variety. Negative responses to these soundings from investors will be taken very seriously indeed.

If all goes well, however, we reach the end of the process. The final package can be assembled, legal advisers may meet, representing company and individual, and a final contract will be agreed. Last, the appointee needs to be ratified as a director by the next annual general meeting, but this is a formality.

Performing in the eyes of the City

Now that our CEO has been appointed, the next dimension in the success of the new incumbent will be related to how his or her performance is rated.

Assessing these ratings is a very complex matter. Although finite, quantifiable factors, such as the financial performance and growth of the enterprise, are one element, there are also rather more qualitative factors. These include perceptual judgements about the context in which the individual is working and how difficult it is, and yet more intangible factors, such as 'style', confidence and even 'luck'.

If we start by considering who the critical judges of a CEO's performance might be, we can probably reach the kernel of the matter quite rapidly. CEOs are appointed and can be dismissed by a majority of their colleague directors. In effect, this means by the chairperson and non-executive directors. Executive director colleagues may be consulted, but rarely in practice have a deciding influence.

Most executive directors are likely to be direct subordinates of the CEO. They can have some influence if they disagree strongly with the CEO, but generally will exercise this influence indirectly through influencing the perceptions of one of the non-executive directors or the chairperson.

Sir Robert Horton was reported to have been forced out of BP because his colleagues rebelled. In another case in the authors' direct experience, a CEO was forced to resign partly because of unanimous and strong opposition by his colleagues to his preferred strategy for the company. A sensible CEO will therefore ensure that he or she has sufficient support from colleagues to avoid a crisis of this sort!

Occasionally, customers may have a strong influence over the success of a CEO, but this tends to be the exception rather than the rule.

Pressure groups can make life uncomfortable for companies and their CEOs, as the case of the Brent Spar oil rig taught Shell. The position of the CEO can also be threatened by environmental or human disasters involving the company, as in the case of Gerald Corbett of Railtrack.

However, these instances are relatively rare, and in normal circumstances the opinions of employees, customers, suppliers and even government count for little in the minds of chairmen and non-executive directors, who may not even be aware of these 'peripheral' opinions.

So, whose feedback will make a chairperson sit up and take notice? On this matter, there is absolute unanimity: it is the financial markets and the financial press. The view of the markets is expressed through one key proxy: the medium-term share price as compared to that of relevant comparator companies, usually those from the same or analogous sectors.

So, in making judgements about the performance and pay of a CEO, the members of the board appointments and compensation committee will take into account impressions of the deportment, style and skills of the CEO. They will also use their wisdom, experience and skills to make judgements about the difficulties facing the enterprise and reach qualitative judgements about the performance of the CEO relative to the complexity and difficulty of the task in hand. Chairpersons may also go out of their way quietly to brief investors about special or mitigating factors affecting the performance of the company and, with it, the CEO. But in the final resort, if sufficient investment institutions, supported by a chorus of analysts and journalists, are convinced that it is time for a change of CEO and communicate this to the chairperson (or, failing that, the deputy chairperson), the CEO really does not stand much chance of survival.

There are exceptions. Sir Philip Watts, chairman of Shell, has been the butt of much unfavourable comment from investment institutions, who seem to believe that he does not care sufficiently about their needs and feelings. If Sir Philip were the executive chairman of a purely FTSE quoted company, it could be speculated that despite a comparatively good long-term performance by his organization, he would be even more worried than he actually professes to be. Luckily for him, Shell has a complex shareholding structure that includes an influential Dutch element. It was commented in one broadsheet that the fuss being made about him by City fund managers and analysts would probably enhance his standing with Dutch shareholders and his Dutch board colleagues, such was their contempt for the antics of these worthies!

If, as seems to be the universal belief, maintaining a strong share price is the proxy benchmark for a CEO's performance, what can he or she do to ensure that it remains strong? Tony Golding's (2001) summary accords very closely with the views of our interviewees and those of respondents to the Cranfield CEOs survey (Harrington and Steele, 1999):

Produce good numbers

'Good' generally means improving, but in some cases, where it is known that a CEO faces a difficult task, may mean predictable, as 'promised'. As has been seen in recent times, there is much opportunity for presenting 'numbers' creatively. More qualitatively, a CEO who is impressively numerate will usually receive a much better rating than one who has other strengths.

Have a good strategy

'Strategy', in market-speak, usually means 'what the enterprise intends to do to grow'. Extra approval ratings are obtained if the 'strategy' contains a strong commitment to make acquisitions.

Produce a 'good' story

Strongly related to the previous point is the mode of presentation of the 'story', be it strategic or otherwise. Golding (2001) puts it succinctly: 'Stories in boxes are best.' Fund managers are very busy people, with many companies to track, and much appreciate it if they can have two or three bullet points to help them categorize and remember particular companies.

In a previous chapter we have seen one experienced CEO's presentation mode, which he characterized as 'one headline and three bullet points'. Another example comes from the 2001 annual report of Iceland Foods. The company's recovery plan is presented succinctly as:

Year 1: 'Stabilize.'
Year 2: 'Platform for growth.'
Year 3: 'Launch.'
Year 4: 'New territory.'

Deliver

Fund managers abhor uncertainty and unpredictability, and are also wary of enterprises involved in highly complex or uncertain industries. Therefore, at face value, 'delivery' quite reasonably means 'do what you said you would, whatever that takes'.

In reality, the world of competitive business isn't quite like that. Competitive markets are complex, and any organization pursuing a long-term strategy is almost bound to experience some uncertainties or unexpected setbacks. (Incidentally, unexpected good happenings are treated with much suspicion by investors.) Therefore, the well-regarded CEO will 'deliver', year on year, no matter what the long-term effects of this process may be.

One of our interviewees put the consequences of this pressure succinctly: 'The markets will happily buy a story of long-term investment for future performance, provided that targets over several years are very accurately spelled out. The moment there is any divergence from the "delivery promise", they will remove their support. Therefore the pressure is to appear to be on track, even if this means abandoning or modifying investment plans, inappropriately cutting programmes or costs, or whatever it takes to keep the headline numbers apparently on track.

'Companies that follow an organic growth strategy will also be supported while growth remains high and totally predictable. But if, for one or two years, there is a divergence from the "promise", there is a strong temptation to go "active" and make acquisitions as a short cut to growth, no matter how inappropriate this may be.'

It goes without saying that investor approval for companies also attaches to individual managers. Some people therefore attract a following in the financial markets. They will be people who 'deliver' and, as one astute and strongly supported CEO put it, 'show that they are totally dedicated to pleasing investors, whatever it takes'. 'But', continued our interviewee, 'even the best story can go "pear-shaped", so it is best to make your pile while you can, because they are a fickle lot.'

The net result of the 'good managers deliver' pressure is frequently long-term damage to companies. But another effect has been the growth of a culture and whole industry devoted to massaging investors' expectations, promoting 'star' managers, modifying strategies to make them as absolutely predictable and safe as possible, and 'managing' financial information.

Be seen to be doing things

Right through the financial markets, the firm view is that strong leaders are people who do things that are 'decisive', and visible to external observers. Obviously this includes a strong commitment to M&A activity, which we have seen is the most beneficial and lucrative activity for investment bankers, who tend to be the big earners for integrated investment institutions. As Golding (2001) says, 'In the clamour to attract institutional attention worthy but inactive companies tend to get overlooked.' He goes on to say, 'A company that does not engage in significant corporate activity or similarly bold moves risks being labelled by the City as "boring" – even if it is a consistent grower.'

Also included in 'doing things' will be visible hyper-responsiveness to events. Strong approval is likely to be forthcoming for any organization that responds to the slightest difficulty by cutting costs very publicly, preferably in large tranches.

Look good

Informed observers such as stockbrokers, experienced search consultants and many top managers are quite clear that the 'style' of a manager in presenting to the external world and investors, and the press in particular, will strongly enhance his or her chances. We have seen already that Lord Browne of BP is (was?) strongly rated in this regard relative to Sir Philip Watts of Shell, apparently regardless of the companies' relative performance.

Several of our management respondents reported that 'looking good' can place a certain strain on the patience of CEOs, who have to appear polite and appreciative even if they privately believe that the advice or demands placed on them by investors are misplaced. As one CEO put it, 'What do you say to a 29-year-old fund manager who, during a presentation that included a detailed section on the company's cash-flow difficulties, suddenly interrupted and said, "I suppose this means that you are carefully scrutinizing every invoice"?' He went on, 'I just smiled politely. I just couldn't be bothered to tell him that we had some 200 subsidiaries in 35 countries!'

Resignation and removal

John Weston, the CEO of BAE Systems, resigned from his position after a relatively short period in the role. It was not clear to outsiders why Weston had really gone, and the company did little to enlighten questioners. In the absence of a clear explanation as to the reasons why, there was press speculation that his 'style' did not seem to suit what was needed. One broadsheet speculated that it was probable that Mr Weston was too much of a 'process' manager, who had done an excellent job in integrating BAE with the ex-Marconi defence systems businesses but was not high-profile enough in his style to impress investors and probably too tough in his negotiations with the Ministry of Defence.

So, how and why do CEOs get involuntarily terminated?

We have already intimated that the instruments of execution, so to speak, are likely to be the chairperson and non-executive directors. Incidentally, the tenure of these worthies tends to be much longer than that of CEOs. Some chairpersons have outlasted a number of chief executives. The resignation of Sir Roger Hurn as chairman of Marconi might herald a new era, although given the massive scale of the Marconi disaster it is hard to see why anybody in a position of authority should have survived.

In theory, shareholders have the final right to vote for the removal of a director of a company, and small shareholders have often (almost invariably unsuccessfully) tried to pass votes of no confidence in particular directors or occasionally whole boards. The fact is that the investment institutions have the clout in this matter and they usually prefer to work in the shadows rather than in the open.

So let us examine how the financial markets can actually go about exercising their muscle.

Earlier we related the tale of the top fund manager who visited a senior non-executive director and 'regretted' the fact that the CEO was obviously ill and had 'lost the plot'. The fund manager did not demand the removal of the manager concerned, but left our informant in no doubt of what was wanted. Thus when the CEO resigned, the objective was achieved while maintaining 'deniability'.

This kind of juicy story is rather uncommon, however. The more usual process leading to removal is likely to start with a few rather negative remarks attributed by the press to nameless investors or analysts. As time moves on, the stories are likely to take a little more shape, with reasons being quoted for investors' unhappiness and potential remedial actions outlined. The previously mentioned mounting chorus of negative comment about Sir Geoff Mulcahy, the ex-CEO of Kingfisher plc, is a good example of this.

At this stage, investor relations advisers' or internal public affairs managers' antennae will be furiously waving, assessing the weight and reported causes of the dissatisfaction. Quite often the house stockbrokers will also begin to give their feedback and opinions. Should dissatisfaction continue and become serious, it is probable that a number of institutional managers will come together and communicate directly with the chairperson. By this point, matters will have become really serious.

If the chairperson seems unwilling to act, or is, in the view of the institutional managers, unjustifiably supporting the CEO, the case will be taken to the senior non-executive director, if one exists. By this point, the share price and the relative value of the company will have begun to plunge, often to the point of making the company a vulnerable target for a predator. So, it becomes a case of 'go or be acquired'. By this stage also, the press will be constantly briefed by investors and analysts, and the amount of speculation and 'noise' will be vast. In these circumstances it is virtually impossible for any gathering of non-executive directors, many of whom have their own reputations to protect, to hold out and support the unfortunate CEO.

The reasons for such a train of events will almost always have a basis in dissatisfaction by investors about performance. But the 'performance' in question will be seen almost entirely from the angle of the fund manager and analysts. This means that the company has not met its implied 'promises' and is unresponsive to demands that 'something be done'. If investors are seriously disappointed, 'something' almost invariably means corporate activity, which can range through acquisitions to restore growth, disposals of businesses experiencing difficulty, corporate restructuring, or, as often happens, the sale, takeover or merger of the whole entity. Generally, investors will regard the latter as a desirable outcome, as there is usually a tasty premium for them when a company in which they hold shares is acquired.

The most unpopular route for managers to follow is that of managing their way out of difficulty. A 'process' solution such as this is generally likely to be viewed with grave suspicion. But in addition, the actions and sentiments of investment institutions and other City actors will themselves have exacerbated the looming crisis and narrowed the options available for dealing with it.

There is a chance that we may have given the impression that the CEO is a helpless pawn in someone else's game. It is true that there are distinct risks involved for the holders of the role in large public companies, but, as we hope we have demonstrated, there are many stratagems that managers can employ to influence their fates, and the astute and successful ones will employ the whole gamut. And the fact is, a CEO who is regarded as being a success by the markets can, if he or she plays his or her cards right and enjoys an element of luck, end up very rich.

So, the relationships between top managers and the financial markets are not all one-way trade. Managers can and do act very vigorously to influence the markets, just as the markets will seek to influence managers. For the fact is, both need the other to prosper.

HOW THE SYSTEM OF SYMBIOTIC RELATIONSHIPS WORKS

The central players are top managers and the 'active' investment institutions. At the heart of their relationship is the drive for institutions to realize above-average returns from the portfolio of investments that they hold at any time.

This translates into a need for top managers to keep the share price of their company as high as possible. Beating the average means high rewards and reputation for fund managers. In the same way, a high relative share price means success and high rewards for managers.

Flows of information

We have already seen that the 'wiring' that connects top managers and investment institutions is complex and extensive, extending through a series of formal presentations, analyst briefings (as a group or one on one) and meetings with investment bankers who will be eager to promote the latest 'strategic thinking' (usually with a deal or piece of financial engineering attached). Information flows back to managers through brokers or analysts, who act as conduits for messages to top management about 'moves' they should consider, or about investors' views on management. The formal and informal flows of information and opinion between managers and the various market players are considerable. Some CEOs estimate that relating to the press and markets takes up half their time, and for finance directors, particularly ambitious ones anxious to make a name for themselves, it can amount to a lot more.

Pleasing the institutions

These are the mechanics of the system, but what about the motivation? We have already considered the motivation of managers, to get and keep the job, and the importance of pleasing the investment institutions in doing so.

Institutional fund managers are under immense pressure to perform against the previously discussed indexes. Consistent out-performers become 'stars' in their own right. (An example is Patrick Evershed, who managed the Rathbone Special Situations Fund. Such a 'star' was he that when he moved to New Star, Rathbones gave investors in the fund the option to follow him.) Underperformers, even those who underperform for a relatively short time, tend to find themselves looking for new funds to manage.

The problem with performing against an index means that rather than looking at the fundamentals of an investment (ie the underlying company), fund managers need instead to be looking at the share price. They need to guess not only how the price will move in the future but also how other fund managers will think it is going to move in the future. This pursuit of relative, rather than actual, performance is felt by many (including George Soros in his book *The Crisis of Global Capitalism* (1998)) to be a source of instability in the financial markets.

In our case it leads to a disconnection between the fund manager and the corporate reality underlying the shares the fund manager is buying and selling. It results in approval of behaviour that will improve the share price in the short term (as we have seen, deals, transactions and 'heroism'), and so reinforces the disconnection between the corporate manager and his or her business.

Derivatives

This disconnection between the aims of investment managers and the underlying corporate reality can be exacerbated by the fund manager's use of 'derivatives' to manage risk in his or her portfolio. The complex nature of derivatives is outside the scope of this book, but it is worth briefly considering their range.

Some can be relatively simple. For example, many companies use interest swaps (an agreement to exchange fixed for floating interest, or vice versa, for a period of time) or currency swaps (an agreement to exchange an amount of one currency for an amount of another at a specified date in the future). Options, purchased for a fee, give the right but not the obligation to make the exchanges described. At the opposite end of the spectrum, more sophisticated derivatives include complex repackaging of instruments with the aim of changing the appearance of their true nature. Some of these have been used by investment institutions to conceal 'gambles' on risks prohibited by their rules. In between these two extremes are a whole array of instruments and financial engineering packages available to fine-tune exposure to risk, increasing it or decreasing it according to the users' preference.

Any portfolio of shares will be exposed to risks arising from the underlying investments. These investments (companies to you and me) are exposed to both normal trading risks and, particularly as companies become increasingly international and more leveraged, financial risks arising from movements in currencies and interest rates. Companies hedge some of this risk for themselves using derivatives, and fund managers might take further hedging action. For example, a sterling-denominated UK-based fund investing in multinational corporations might use derivatives to hedge against movements between sterling and the US dollar.

One story brilliantly illustrates the effects of this disconnection between investors and the corporate reality represented by their investments. During the 1990s there was hot debate about whether companies should hedge against their exposure to foreign currency movements, particularly against 'translational' risk. (Translational risk is the risk that, say, the consolidated profit and loss account and balance sheet of a UK multinational company will be adversely affected by movements in the reporting currencies of its subsidiaries.) A lot of 'market-wise' experts held that it was unnecessary for companies to hedge against this risk as investment institutions were able to take a view on the exposure and, if they were uncomfortable, could hedge it away for themselves.

John Grout, the then Director of Tax and Treasury for Cadbury Schweppes, spoke eloquently at a conference organized by the Association of Corporate Treasurers. It was important, he argued, for companies to be free to take what hedging action management considered necessary. Sometimes it could mean the difference between business as usual and corporate disaster. For example, erosion of balance sheet values could put the company in breach of its borrowing covenants. Corporate management had to reserve the right to manage such situations.

Some of the questions from his audience made their contempt of such a stance very clear. Presumably, in the minds of these questioners, management should choose corporate annihilation rather than upset the currency hedging stance of their institutional investors!

So, the demands of investors can be quite irrational. However, for the period that managers do manage to keep the shareholders' approval (or at least, keep them concerned that they may depart), they can do very well out of it.

REWARD: 'I'LL SCRATCH YOUR BACK IF…'

Finally, we come to the important matter of how the players in the markets and top management generate the very high levels of reward they undoubtedly receive.

In some years, top bankers, analysts, brokers and fund managers can count their annual bonuses in multiple millions of pounds. When the employing banks are profitable, the bonuses flow. How do banks earn profits? One of the largest sources is the fees earned for corporate finance advice, usually in the form of 'success fees' for supporting transactions. Another is from fees earned by selling derivatives – the more complicated, the higher the fee. So, the incentive is towards action, irrespective of whether or not the deal is good for the company in the long term. No wonder these influential individuals prefer 'active' corporate executives!

Now the market has turned down and jobs are threatened. All the more reason to chase the deals! All the more reason to favour active executives!

As for management, we have seen an explosion in top executive rewards over the past 20 years. It was only 20 years ago that one of the authors was charged by the chairman of Thorn EMI with designing the first executive share option scheme for that company. 'At last', said the chairman, who had been smarting somewhat at the comparison between his compensation and that of the company's US-based music executives, 'we will have a chance to accumulate some wealth for our efforts.' He was anxious to get on with the process, as his retirement loomed! He probably could not have envisaged what would happen over the following 20 years:

- Base pay (annual salary) has soared at a rate that is many times that of pay increases of employees in general.
- Annual cash bonuses have also soared to the point that the median annual bonus ceiling is now 60 per cent of salary. (Of course, not everybody earns that amount, but many, many people do their best, by all available means, to do so.)

The rates of increase in basic salary and bonus pay may be felt by some to be dramatic, but do not account for the massive boom in top executive wealth. The big pay-off has come from a major move from the mid-1980s to align the basis for top executive wealth with the interests of 'the shareholders'. The outcome has been the deliberate creation by management of a truly symbiotic relationship with the financial markets.

The move has been cloaked by persuasive rhetoric. At first it was deemed appropriate that top managers should think and act like 'shareholders', because the interests of the company that they led and those of its 'owners' were inevitably the same. Later, this became dressed up in more intellectual clothes, under the guise of 'shareholder value' and 'value-based management' techniques.

All this caused the explosion of share and, in particular, share option-related bonus and incentive plans. A share option plan grants the manager a quantity of the company's shares at 'today's' value. The executive will be able to buy the shares at specified times in the future, and may then keep or sell them. The greater the share price at the end of the period, the more profit the executive makes. It is usual for options to vest on change of ownership of the company.

For example, a quick scan of the smaller print in the annual report reveals that Stuart Rose, CEO of Arcadia, was granted options over 6,470,589 shares at 51 pence when he joined the company. Alain Levy, CEO of EMI, received a similarly large grant of options when he joined that company. Mr Rose has been particularly lucky. Twenty-five months after he joined it, the company has been sold, grossing him an estimated £26 million.

These are the high-profile examples, but now share-related reward plans are the norm for all top executives. Here is how top executives of FTSE 100 companies were remunerated in 2000–01, according to the survey by the compensation consultants Monks Partnership:

- The median base salary for CEOs in 2001 was £540,000.
- The median base pay increase for CEOs between 2000 and 2001 was 14.5 per cent.
- The median total annual cash payment (base pay plus annual bonus) for CEOs in 2001 was £1,037,000.

Some may think that these levels of pay are quite good, but annual pay is in reality only the base for determining the value of other forms of reward – in particular, share option grants. Once upon a time, the limit on the grant of options was four times annual pay. This limit was changed to a ceiling on the amount that could be granted annually, and now option holdings to the tune of 7 to 10 times annual remuneration are not uncommon. This move was approved by investment industry bodies such as the Association of British Insurers.

At the end of 2001 the pattern of remuneration plans for top executives in FTSE 100 companies was as follows:

- 35 per cent had base salary + annual bonus + long term incentive plan + share options;
- 33 per cent of companies had base salary + deferred annual bonus ('deferred' often means that the company doubles the amount that is held back) + long-term incentive plan + share options;
- 10 per cent had base pay + deferred annual bonus + share options;
- 11 per cent had base pay + annual bonus + share options.

As can be seen, share-related reward is therefore almost universal. The effect of this is to make the company's share price the crucial element that will determine success and reward. It is the share price that top managers will (metaphorically) kill for, using all means at their disposal. And as we have seen, investors approve of 'active' managers who, in addition to whatever they may do inside their organizations, are inclined to make 'moves', including M&A and other forms of corporate activism. That is what keeps the excitement up and the share price moving. And in the last resort, 'value' can be created for some investors by selling parts of the company, or inducing the acquisition or sale of the whole entity.

At the extremes, some companies have attempted to create reward opportunities for simply making 'moves', rather than creating value. In the end, as mentioned previously, even investment institutions drew the line at the immediate award of £10 million to Sir Chris Gent of Vodafone for simply making the acquisition of Mannesmann, regardless of whether or not it created value. And investors are rebelling against payments for failure. However, for a manager who continues to 'deliver' in the eyes of investors, the cash will continue to flow.

And so it is that the final gossamer thread that binds the interests of managers and markets has been woven. The markets require constant, and preferably above-average, growth, achieved year on year. Investors believe that 'active' methods are the best means of achieving such growth, and are hugely rewarded if companies indulge in M&A and other active methods. If the results of excessive activism are that the enterprise falters and fails, the shares can be sold – or better, the company will be sold or taken over, thus creating a significant premium for its investors to place elsewhere. Managers, helped by their advisers and their non-executive colleagues (often executives in other companies), have devised reward schemes that create huge bonus opportunities for ramping up the share price and behaving in other ways that will please the markets.

The factors that are most likely to influence the behaviour of any ambitious or career-conscious top executive are:

- getting and retaining the job;
- rewards when in the job;
- maintaining personal value in the job market.

The one essential requirement faced by a contemporary top manager who wishes to survive and prosper is to communicate with, and please, the markets. This is not to say that many top managers do not expend considerable time and effort in communicating with employees, sponsoring employee development, organization-building, fostering innovation and product development or charitable activities. They will do all or some of these things, but the fact is, in a large, publicly owned UK company, *they are optional, not mandatory.* (It is, however, regarded as essential that candidates for honours should perform some 'good' works of a charitable, social or industry-related variety outside the company.) As we shall see in Chapter 10, this fact has had a marked influence on the values and actions of top managers.

We hope that we have demonstrated convincingly that the overwhelming balance of the evidence is that the financial markets are by far the most powerful influences over management and manifestly influence their thinking and behaviour. We have also sought to demonstrate that top managers have not been passive pawns, but have created reward mechanisms that bring them close to the markets, and in addition now spend huge amounts of effort and money in an effort to influence the markets in their favour. We hope by now that you will agree with us that the bulk of evidence supports the Proposition behind this chapter.

10

Organizational and behavioural impacts of management–market relationships

THE PROPOSITION

The development of increasingly close and symbiotic relationships between top managers and the financial markets represents a fundamental shift in the influence of, and balance of power between, the stakeholders in industry and the economy. One effect of this changing balance of power is that stakeholders, apart from those in the management–market 'system', are becoming increasingly disenfranchised, with little influence over what happens to their interests. However, this fact is often disguised by a fog of myths and downright propaganda. Equally important, the closer relationships between top managers and the financial markets have impacted significantly on the values, behaviour and actions of the managers.

The consequences of these shifts in behaviour are now becoming quite marked and are having a profound effect on the skills and practice of managers and therefore on the organizations that they lead. We are beginning to experience the effects of a marked and enlarging deficit in leadership and organizational skills among top managers.

In Chapter 9 we made a clear case for the proposition that the markets now are the most important influence on the success and rewards of top managers, and that managers have responded by aligning their behaviour with what the markets value. If this is, as we believe, truly the case, there will be observable tendencies for managers to act out their values in their actions. Over time, certain kinds of skills and competences will be emphasized and others will become less evident. Moreover, as leaders have an important effect on their organizations, the effects will, over time, become noticeable in many of the United Kingdom's large companies.

In this chapter we seek out signs that top managers are indeed behaving in ways that are most likely to serve their interests, as one would expect them to, and that this is having marked consequences. We will present our case in the same way as in the previous chapter and at the end invite you, the reader, to think about the issues involved and what you believe.

TOP MANAGERS DESERT THE 'TROOPS'

Once upon a time, there was a strong tendency for top managers to be quite strongly bonded with their organizations by the time that they reached the ranks of top leadership. Large organizations took succession planning very seriously. Recourse to the external job market represented some kind of failure.

This meant that by the time aspirants reached the top, they had spent a long apprenticeship in the company, knew quite a lot about the organization and people, and understood the business in some depth. It may be argued that many of these managers believed that to be a top manager was to be in a state of grace, not just another job. They were insular, inward-looking and, in many cases, rather amateur. However, this was an unfortunate legacy of history rather than a direct consequence of internal succession.

Learning, curiosity and an external interest are a function of an individual's predilections and the nature of management development. It is just as possible to inculcate a desire to know what is going on in the wider world from inside an organization as from outside. In the best companies, an appreciation of external factors was actively encouraged, and management development included mixing with peers from other companies and investigating other management practices. Therefore there tended to be progression from past to future and from middle to top management.

Readers will remember Donaldson and Lorsch's study of top managers in the late 1970s (1983). Managers at that time highly valued the health and strength of their enterprise and, above all, believed that their most important duty was to hand the company on to the next generation in robust condition. In the main, they had also been with their companies for a large part of their careers and regarded the choice and grooming of internal successors as being a prime duty.

All this confirmed a very strong bonding of top managers with their organizations. The bonds were material, but they were strongly emotional too. These managers seem to have loved their companies and valued the health and strength of the enterprise, seeing it as their route to external respect by investors, competitors and society.

If we cut to the United Kingdom today, there are still some companies that strongly emphasize internal development and the bonds between their leaders and the wider organization. BP, Shell, Unilever, Cadbury, Wm Morrison and Tesco are possibly examples of this desirable tendency. But there is no doubt that in the vast majority of large publicly owned UK companies, the linkages between top management generally and the organizations that they lead have significantly weakened, and that top managers have become more detached, both financially and psychologically.

What are the manifestations of this state of affairs?

First, we have seen the strong pressures on managers to dance to the music of the financial markets. We have also seen how the big rewards come from 'shareholder' related performance. Thus the short- to medium-term share price is the prime determinant of reward. We have also seen that the markets have a predilection towards activism, rather than business- and organization-building. As a result:

- The differentials between top management rewards and those of the wider workforce have widened dramatically. In FTSE 100 companies the highest-paid director now, on average, earns more than 68 times that of the average (not the lowest-paid) employee. This differential is far greater than that in most developed countries, apart from the United States. Trust in top managers may be further undermined when employees, many of whom have suffered from a serious deterioration in their pension prospects, realize what many of them are still salting away for their retirements.

  Under the heading 'Fat cats purr on', the Business Focus section of the *Observer* of 18 May 2003 describes the continued burgeoning of top executive pension entitlements. Samples include pensions payable at retirement of £930,000 for Jean-Pierre Garnier of GSK, £860,000 for Lord Browne of BP, £480,000 for Sir Philip Watts of Shell and £530,000 for Sir Chris Gent of Vodafone. Travis Perkins, the building merchant, is quoted as being among companies that have closed their final salary plans for employees, while maintaining it for directors.

  Once again, let us emphasize that top managers tend to be rewarded for creating a high share price, not necessarily a good company. If the top executive drives up the share price and ends by selling or breaking up the company, this can be at least as good an outcome for him or her as making the company stronger and stronger.
- The United Kingdom's top managers are among the most 'active' in the world when it comes to M&A, selling and buying assets, financial engineering and responding to events by active means. It is also a source of pride to some that UK companies have responded rapidly to events by restructurings and lay-offs. But while change and efficiency have to be at the top of managers' agendas, such behaviour does not smack of any great respect for or closeness with the organization. And despite all this, the productivity of UK-owned companies generally languishes far behind that of major competitor countries, as we shall see later.

  As a clue, we can note that high productivity seems to come from attention to operating detail and sound and high internal investment.
- Top managers report that they now spend a very large part of their time, perhaps most of their time, on matters external to the organizations that they lead. It is not possible to account for this exactly, but the top managers that we interviewed and worked around would estimate that 40 per cent of their time is spent on matters connected with the financial markets and 'shareholders'. As one experienced consultant put it, 'Top management now have an increasingly external relations role. This means that they spend less and less time on directing and managing their companies. Unfortunately, they have not handed over the responsibility and authority to do this to the next layer down. Therefore, we are seeing a leadership and continuity "gap" opening up in many organizations.'

- The tenure of top managers, in particular CEOs, has dramatically reduced in the past 20 years. Twenty years ago, the norm was for top managers to spend the bulk of their careers with one company, and, if they moved, to do so in the early part of their careers. Now, more and more top appointments are being made from outside companies. As a result, we are seeing a trend that makes it extremely difficult for leaders to develop anything like a close bond with their organizations.

  In September 2002 our analysis of companies in the FTSE 100 showed the following:
  - Just under two-thirds of finance directors had been appointed from outside their companies.
  - Approximately one-third of CEOs had been appointed from outside their companies.
  - Approximately one-half of chairmen had been appointed from outside.
  - About one-half of all CEOs, chairmen and finance directors had been employed by their companies for seven years or less.

  Short tenure inevitably encourages 'activism', or doing things 'to' rather than 'through' the organization.

The net impact of all of these factors has been to draw top managers more and more away from their organizations, in terms both of time spent and of psychological attachment. As one contemporary chairman put it, 'It doesn't do to identify too much with the organization, you may need to do something nasty to it next week.'

ACTIVISM RULES – OK?

We outlined some of the effects of 'activism' earlier in the book. For the purposes of this chapter, we will examine some of the organizational effects of 'serial activism'.

In the early 1980s, Grand Metropolitan, then one of Britain's largest companies and very well regarded in the financial markets, developed a kind of corporate credo. This was quite simple, and went, 'We are a restless company.' Restlessness was manifested by constant change in the shape and make-up of the business portfolio, a stream of acquisitions and disposals, and frequent changes in organization and management.

Some found the company stimulating and even exciting to work for, and looked back fondly (after they had left!) on the experience of working for 'Grand Met'. In the end, however, the constant and disruptive change process began to take its toll, performance began to languish, investor confidence in management began to wane and 'Grand Met' eventually focused on the international drinks industry and merged with Guinness. The new company, Diageo plc, concentrated on developing an excellent organization and is now a world leader in the drinks industry.

Now consider Ross Johnson, the CEO of RJR Nabisco, as he is described by Bryan Burroughs and John Helyar in their gripping book *Barbarians at the Gate* (1990). Johnson is energized by excitement and action. He is obsessively inclined to change the organization and constantly shuffle the business portfolio. When the company's share price remained obstinately low, he called in investment bankers to consider means to revive it. Johnson became obsessed by what he regarded as undervaluation of the company's shares, although his fellow directors were unworried by a share price that reflected the market's concerns about tobacco companies. The authors go on to say, 'But Johnson couldn't leave well enough alone. The old urges to action were returning, and the stock price was their latest manifestation… By late spring, the word was all over Wall Street that Ross Johnson was ripe to do a deal.'

Another top manager who is known to us, having led his company through a spectacular turnaround, found life distinctly flat after the dust had settled. He could not bear to stand back and let others have their heads. He became first bored and then morose. Very quickly he began to hark back to the 'old days'. Small problems were blown up into major dramas, memos were dictated proposing major portfolio changes, bankers with 'ideas' were solicited, new hurdles were invented halfway through planning periods, and investment programmes were stopped and started according to the whims of the leader. Businesses were bought and businesses were sold, without much noticeable logic driving the transactions. From time to time, people would be summoned to amuse the boss because he was 'bored'. Favourites among his subordinates rose and fell. In short, a person who was a priceless asset when there was a real crisis became a major liability when it had been weathered.

When looking at the behaviour of many top managers in British companies it is possible to draw close parallels between corporate activism and crisis management. We have already seen that the tenure of top managers has reduced and that many top management appointments are made from outside organizations. British companies are at, or near to, the top of the international league when it comes to M&A activity. We have also observed that British management, with the strong approval of the financial markets, are much more 'responsive' than their European counterparts when it comes to lay-offs and cost reductions. Organizations have been subjected to extensive de-layering and slimming down, to the point that many major functions have been stopped or outsourced. In all this there seems to be a tendency to take positive ideas to excessive lengths.

So, short-tenure managers in a hurry, with a critical audience to please in the City, have created circumstances in a significant number of companies analogous to a state of permanent crisis. Not a few are struggling with the effects of multi-layered and sometimes serial bouts of M&A or restructuring activity.

From time to time, business writers have sought to celebrate such behaviours through catchphrases like 'thriving on chaos' and 'creative destruction'. But as we shall see later, while many people in organizations will welcome constructive change, they first like a degree of predictability in the fundamentals of their environment.

Included in the fundamentals are knowing and being committed to particular businesses, having the opportunity to build solid relationships with colleagues and direct bosses, working in a compatible culture and knowing that top management are on the same side. Being led by people who owe their allegiance to external agencies, who come and go frequently and are liable to initiate major changes in organization or business portfolio at the drop of a hat will tend to keep an organization in a debilitating state of anxiety.

There is a double bind in this behaviour. Excessive or inappropriate management activism will create a climate of artificial crisis in organizations.

Persisting with such behaviours for too long is likely to foment a real crisis. Thus we have seen examples of relatively stable companies that have been driven to major crises by excessive activism. Marconi, Invensys, Lucas, Hanson Trust, Bunzl, Plessey, Sears, Tomkins, Powergen and Redland are good examples of this tendency. A number of other companies are experiencing difficulties that may deepen as managements seek to cope with the effects of past activism. The list is probably quite long, and includes Boots, Vodafone, GSK and Scottish Power.

However, this is not the way it is seen from the market's perspective. As one senior management consultant put it, 'Crises are meat and drink to the markets. They create rich seams of fees for transactions, financial restructurings and selling and buying of companies and shares. The "dream" is to help a company make big acquisitions, dispose of past acquisitions and then defend the remains of the company against a predator – or represent the predator, of course!'

All this has increased the rate of company break-up and failure, as we shall see in Chapter 11.

MYTHS, DISTORTIONS, SWINDLES AND PROPAGANDA

In the three years that it has taken to research this book, we have been assiduous readers of the financial press and company statements. In addition, we have had many years as active participants in 'deals' and the whole game of making sure 'the story' is right for the markets or the press. Such experience can lead to cynicism about the values of industry and of the motives of many of those who work in it. But instead of letting dull cynicism take over, we felt that it would be more interesting to examine a number of the practices, myths and 'truths that dare not speak their names' that surround the inner circles of top management and the financial markets.

Any such analysis has to start with the burgeoning field of financial 'tricks' and other practices that have grown up over the years.

The financial regulators in the United Kingdom and the United States labour mightily to swat scams and misleading practices as they arise, as do government finance ministries. However, behind closed doors brilliant brains are employed to think out the next 'structure': ever more technical and complex ways of dressing up facts and 'truth'.

Many of the cleverest and most creative players in this game are employed in the financial markets. Enron's managers didn't dream up ways of disguising the state of their balance sheet all by themselves! They received ideas and practical help from their banking and legal advisers and strategy consultants.

Acquisition accounting has provided great scope for creativity. Despite the closure of some of the more glaring loopholes, there is still great scope for hiding the real performance impact of acquisitions. 'Restructuring' costs can be accrued at the time of acquisition, burying expenses that might otherwise have deflated profits.

On top of this we have seen the high-profile emergence of income recognition as yet a third way of misleading the users of accounts. Optimistic recognition of future earnings and definitions of 'sales' that beggared belief were a feature of dot.com companies. More worryingly, they are emerging in more traditional companies as the spotlight turns on to reported numbers.

All this is helped by the 'move on and don't look back' mentality of the markets and, increasingly, managers. Smart operators can make fortunes destroying companies, and, provided that they get their timing right, do it in series by moving on to the next thing before the consequences of their actions manifest themselves. Readers can create their own interest by compiling lists of people who would be the kiss of death to follow into a job!

Ascending from the murky depths of 'creative' accounting, we can feast on a plethora of myths, commonly accepted 'truths' and sheer propaganda designed to serve the interests of particular groups rather than the common interest. Here are some popular myths and examples of propaganda:

Myth 1

'Shareholders' will, if they are encouraged, control rampant executive pay increases and generally foster better corporate governance.

This mantra is repeated time and time again by government ministers, the press and many commentators.

Let us pick the myth apart. First, who or what do the proponents of this vague hope mean by 'shareholders'? Do they mean investment professionals? Do they mean the associations that represent some of the investment fund managers, such as the Association of British Insurers (ABI)? Do they mean the millions of pension fund members, unit trust investors, holders of insurance policies, on whose behalf the investment professionals purport to work? Do they mean private investors? What do they mean?

What we can state with absolute certainty is that giving 'shareholders' the task of managing corporate governance on behalf of 'society' as a whole has not yet showed the faintest sign of working. Institutions have had very little impact on executive remuneration and, as one of our City lawyer interviewees put it, 'Corporate governance beats few indices.'

When private shareholders have tried to act to stem executive excesses, they have with a few exceptions been overridden by investment institutions' proxy votes. Associations such as the ABI, which do take governance seriously, complain that institutional investors seldom support them when it comes to the crunch.

And even if institutional investors were to espouse governance, which ought to be about top management behaviour and its effects on the long-term interests of enterprises and their multiple stakeholders, what would they do? As one senior broker told us, unless you want to get rid of him or her, you really do have to support the CEO. There is little scope for direct impact on individual issues.

A faint sign of encouragement has been the vote in May 2003 against the 'golden parachute' termination agreement for Jean-Pierre Garnier, the CEO of GlaxoSmithKline, the pharmaceutical giant. Mr Garnier, who is based in Philadelphia, obviously believes that he merits US-style compensation, and this led GSK's remuneration committee to push the boat out too far in proposing a package amounting to a reported £22 million in the event of his employment being terminated by the company. Investors, shareholders and trade unions combined to vote against this staggering proposal, and although the vote is indicative and not binding, it has, with some justification, been hailed as an unprecedented event. This small step, however, indicates the long, long haul that is in prospect, as 'shareholder activism' has focused only on the issue of so-called rewards for failure. The issue of differentials remains so far completely untouched.

One irony during 2002 was the threatened series of strikes by trade union members to protest about the removal of final salary pension schemes. Perhaps we have witnessed the beginnings of a real shareholders' revolt, orchestrated by the trades unions! And from the United States we read that two powerful pension funds are preparing to target big companies over directors' pay, a reaction to the wave of corporate scandals. It will be interesting to see how this runs.

A sub-set of the 'shareholders will fix our problems and let us off the hook' argument is the predictable assertion that non-executive directors should, on behalf of shareholders, take a much more active role in scrutinizing the strategies and behaviour of managers. The much watered down Higgs proposals are an example of how difficult it is to 'get the turkeys to vote for Christmas', to quote a well-known CEO!

Again, we have seen the reality of the non-executive role and the kinds of people who typically occupy non-executive positions. It will take a massive revolution to make any real difference and there is no evidence that the 'great and good' are ever likely to be ready for radical change and real accountability.

We are left with the feeling that the current 'tinkerings' that are likely to be proposed to improve governance will still leave the field clear to those who benefit most by things as they are. It seems rather like making footballers, with huge bonuses at stake, responsible for refereeing the match!

Myth 2

'Deals are good news.'

The thrust of much publicity put about by the markets and big consultancies is that deals, in particular large-scale M&A activity, are the most effective and often the only way to foster efficiency, growth and change in industry. But as it begins to sink slowly into the wider consciousness that business is not just about big deals, which have a tendency to lead to disaster and value destruction, so is the 'story' about mergers and acquisitions changing. The line that has most contemporary currency is that most (but 'most' is not precisely specified) mergers and acquisitions can be made to work successfully, provided that some extra ingredient is added to the 'mix'. The missing ingredient will vary according to what the proponent is selling, but may be better analysis planning and preparation, better human resource management, or enhanced customer profiling. 'Use our insights and support, and your mergers will create better value' is the story. Needless to say, this approach is assiduously pushed by large consultancies, many of which have set up specialist M&A practices to support clients.

A second line, which is also commonly used by investment bankers, is that somehow a high level of M&A activity is good for industry, helping necessary consolidation of maturing industries and bringing greater efficiency and a streamlining of costs all round. An extension of this argument is that it is the industry leaders that will lead the way, and laggards in the M&A race will end up as victims or hopeless losers.

We will not deny that there is a grain of truth in both sets of propositions: better planning and preparation undoubtedly might have mitigated some of the great M&A disasters of our time, and, once in a blue moon, a genuine opportunity will arise for the right candidate to lead the restructuring of an industry or market by merging with a competitor. But the real truth, unspoken by the financial markets, is that most M&A activity creates huge revenues for investment bankers and some consultants, and reputations and wealth for some managers, but erodes the value of many pension funds, investments and savings, and indirectly blights the lives of millions of people who put their faith in the financial markets to provide them with a secure future. So, the unpalatable truth is that most M&A activity should never be allowed to happen, if the yardstick is that it should create beneficial outcomes for the bulk of people and for society more generally. Much greater value would be created if top managers stuck to skilfully managing their companies so as to make them really good and resorted to M&A as an adjunct to their main agenda.

An article by Larry Selden and Geoffrey Colvin in the *Harvard Business Review* (2003) puts the facts in a hard, clear light:

> Deal volume during the historic M&A wave of 1995 to 2000 totalled more than \$12 trillion. By an extremely conservative estimate, these deals annihilated at least \$1 trillion of share-owner wealth. For perspective, consider that the whole dot.com bubble probably cost investors \$1 trillion at most. *That's right: Stupid takeovers did more damage than all the dot.coms combined* [our italics]. The situation is remarkable when you think about it. Many of the failed mergers are done by the world's biggest, most successful companies, advised by highly educated investment bankers who do this for a living.

Exactly, and what a 'living' they can make by destroying value.

Of course, it is highly unlikely that those who want to be left to pursue other routes to long-term success are going to be left to do so by financial markets that are so completely dependent for their livelihoods on 'activity'. If it caught on, employment and rewards in the financial markets would be decimated. So far, we have not seen any signs of players in the markets being willing to sacrifice their well-being for the good of the common man (or woman)!

Myth 3

Free, self-regulated markets are the most efficient instruments for creating wealth.

The assumption that underlies much that happens in the financial markets seems to be based on the idea that competition in a perfect market will in the long run be best for society as a whole. Thus regulation and interference in markets and executive behaviour are likely to produce great distortions and inefficiency. Remember the quotation in Chapter 1 from the ex-chairman of Coca-Cola, invoking the spectre of the Soviet Union when trying to justify adherence to the pure doctrine of maximizing shareholder value?

We are not alone in our suspicion that the pure market ideologists may have got it slightly wrong. George Soros, in *The Crisis of Global Capitalism* (1998), contends that rather than behaving like a pendulum always seeking to return to equilibrium, markets have tended to act like a 'wrecking ball, knocking over one economy after another'. Soros contends that markets are inherently unstable, so imposing market discipline means imposing instability.

We hope that readers will have observed what has happened in the relatively free and booming markets of the past decade or so. Let us discount criminality as being the undesirable tip of the iceberg. We contend that an accurate maxim that applies to the behaviour of 'free', generally self-regulating markets is *'The first priority of "players" in ineffectively regulated markets is to arrange matters to serve their own interests.'*

Arguably, we are seeing the strategies and actions of many British quoted companies distorted to serve the interests of a relatively small number of 'players' in management and the markets. We are learning that ineffective regulation of the actions of players in the US markets has spawned gross acts of corruption and fraud, as well as much unfettered self-serving greed. In the United Kingdom we are prone to congratulating ourselves on the fact that 'dot.com bubbles, Enron/Tyco/WorldCom could not happen here'. Almost certainly we are looking in the wrong direction, when under our noses and quite legally, managers and markets are creating a swathe of destruction across whole sectors of British industry.

Perhaps the last word should be left to John Maynard Keynes, as quoted in the *Guardian* of 22 July 2002:

> Finally, the deregulation of financial markets has made capitalism less stable. As the American Keynesian Paul Davidson has argued, markets are now more liquid, but that is not the same as being more effective. Keynes was adamant that capital markets were there to provide investment for entrepreneurs, not gambling chips. 'Speculators may do no harm as bubbles on a steady stream of enterprise,' he said. 'But the position is serious when enterprise becomes the bubble on a whirlpool of speculation. When the capital development of a country becomes the by-product of the activities of a casino, the job is likely to be ill done.'

We would argue that the fields of corporate governance and investor behaviour need a radical new look based on a clear view of what is good for the interests of the wider economy and society and not the woolly-minded peripheral tinkering that seems to be our best response so far.

Myth 4

We need the 'best of the best' to lead our company.

This is the 'story' we hear. Readers will have heard it many times, even in the pages of this book:

- High-profile leadership figures are the factor that will make the difference between corporate success and failure.
- These people are a very scarce and incredibly valuable resource, and will inevitably command very high rewards.
- If top managers are not paid in line with the upper part of the market range, they will leave, causing devastation in their wake.
- In short, to twist the words of the cosmetics advertisement, 'Because they're worth it.'

As we've said elsewhere, there are points in some organizations' histories, such as serious corporate crises or major turning points, when they may need the attentions of a very high-profile, charismatic and usually externally appointed leader. But all serious research shows that the factor that differentiates the really good long-term performers from other companies is the strength, skills, creativity and adaptability that are contained in the wider organization.

In fact, most of the time, high-profile, high-ego 'heroes' can be a positive liability. Much better is a leadership group who understand the organization and business and can bring out the best in a large number of people. Such people normally will come from inside, and the bulk of their work will be detailed attention to a myriad of internal and industry matters, all of which will be invisible to distant observers in the press and markets. As such people are also unlikely to be impressed by calls for unnecessary corporate activism, and as they are also likely to be internal appointees, they are not going to be much appreciated by search consultants, bankers or many investment fund managers.

As we have previously seen, one effect of the cult of the hero has been massive hikes in top executive rewards. All attempts to justify the differentials that have developed between top executives and the wider workforce start with the argument that 'We need the best, and the market for talent is so international that we must seek them internationally.' This basic theme has spawned many offspring, the commonest being that a regular turnover of top managers is necessary to preserve 'creativity, freshness and objectivity'. For these three virtues it is just as easy to read 'propensity to do deals, lack of attachment to a stable strategy, and psychological distance from the business and the people'.

Attachment to a consistent strategy and closeness to the organization is likely to become interpreted as a craving for 'empire', one of the worst words in the demonology of the financial press and markets. It is a depressing fact that the financial markets and most of those who report on business do not seem to understand that a complex, extensive and large-scale business needs a complex and well-developed organization to support it. It therefore goes without saying that changing the performance of the underlying business is likely to entail harnessing the efforts of many, many people and persuading them to adapt or modify their priorities, behaviour and skills. Only when these things are done by lots of people working together will improvement stick. This takes time, persistence and patience.

Of course, it is possible to take quite a different approach and to rely on presentation and crude surgery applied to the business or organization. Suitably 'spun', such an approach can be presented as decisive leadership and the results of cutting and selling as permanent, as can making acquisitions. And it is this 'quick fix' stuff that receives the greatest approbation from markets and press.

So, finally, here is a not untypical journalistic effort from the *Sunday Times* of 30 December 2001. The article nominates the writer's views of the business 'heroes and villains' of 2001. Under the heading 'Stuart Rose, Chief Executive, Arcadia', the article proclaims:

> They say the harder you work the luckier you get. Well, Stuart Rose appears to have being putting in overtime. Shareholders in Arcadia, the fashion retailer that owns Top Man and Burton, have every reason to be grateful to Rose, the one-man rescue team parachuted in to replace John Hoerner. In the past year, he has presided over a 221% rise in Arcadia's share price, returned the company to profit and 'sold' under-performing brands in a quasi-management buyout. Rose's image as the man with the Midas touch was cemented by the news that the company is in talks about a possible takeover from its 20% Icelandic shareholder, Baugur.

To complete the story, Arcadia was not acquired by Baugur in 2001, but was acquired in September 2002 by Philip Green, who owns Bhs. For Mr Rose the story had a happy ending, as he is reported to have received some £26 million for his time with Arcadia.

The point of this story is not in any way to denigrate Mr Rose, who has acknowledged that Mr Hoerner, his predecessor, together with several thousand other employees, have contributed to the company's good performance, not just a 'one-man rescue team'. What the story does illustrate is the prevalent habit, touched on earlier, in the press and financial markets alike to assume that single, heroic individuals can do everything. It also exposes a lack of real understanding, depth and research on the part of the journalist.

Myth 5

'British success stems from the financial markets.'

Perhaps the greatest example of the effects of misleading information and publicity is the rather vague notion that the success of the British economy in recent years is in any way connected with the behaviour of British top management and the financial markets.

Success can be attributed to many factors, including a favourable tax regime, lack of heavy bureaucracy, intelligent flexible workforces and proximity to European markets. But as we shall see in Chapter 11, it has very little to do with the performance, efficiency, investment levels or competitiveness of larger British quoted companies, whose performance (with a few notable exceptions) in world markets and in comparison with the growing number of foreign-owned companies (including most large players in the London financial market) in the United Kingdom has been lamentable.

NEGLECT OF THE ARTS OF LEADERSHIP, REAL BUSINESS INVOLVEMENT AND ORGANIZATION-BUILDING

Past generations of British top managers have been justifiably criticized for being amateur, parochial, narrowly based in their skills and heavily prone to 'classism'. Undermined by the collapse of protected markets in the Empire, out of touch with the evolving demands of customers and under increasing pressure from militant trade unions (a consequence of past employee exploitation), they led their companies in a retreat from and subsequently a rout in international competitive markets.

Huge swathes of British companies fell in the years following the Second World War, unable to compete in their traditional markets and unable to adapt to new market requirements. Later, Margaret Thatcher's monetarist policies, which could have been a tonic to a healthy industrial base, were applied with a suddenness that killed off another swathe of British companies.

This failure of management was not so marked in other countries, where, in different ways, the practice and development of professional skills and intensive training in management led to a professional class of industrial leaders. In the United Kingdom, for a very long time the most prevalent form of professional training led to accountancy qualifications. Then, as the 1970s passed into history, things began to change. A new generation of professionals began to appear in the financial markets. Business schools popped up in increasing numbers, providing a supply of MBA graduates together with courses for managers up to quite senior levels.

So, have there been really significant changes in the skills and behaviour of the new generation of British top managers?

Under the heading 'Business schools fail to develop leadership', on 14 May 2002, the *Financial Times* reported that despite the rapid expansion of management education in the past 20 years, the main leadership skills are 'in short supply from the top to the bottom of organizations'. The report calls for practical skills and work experience to be incorporated into management courses and be available to all undergraduates whatever their chosen subject at university. The MBA – the flagship of the business school sector – 'has succeeded as a qualification but has not necessarily developed future leaders,' says the report, 'Managers and leaders: raising the game'. David Norburn, director of Imperial College Management School, commented, 'A lot of the schools have copied American, especially East Coast, business degrees which place too much emphasis on formulation and not enough on implementation.' To put this more simply, many business schools teach people sophisticated strategic and financial analysis, but not how to really understand business, lead or manage.

Consider these factors:

1. The vast majority of graduates from most prestigious business schools gravitate to financial services and big consulting companies.
2. Those who do arrive eventually in industrial companies tend to follow a functional route to the top and mostly miss out on experience of junior and middle management jobs, where people develop management skills.
3. Those who act as judge and jury over managements are investment fund managers, analysts, stockbrokers and the financial services industries generally. Their training tends to be in accountancy or banking, or through an MBA.
4. All these people are likely to have a predilection towards financial and strategic analysis. Few of them will have even rudimentary experience of management, and they are unlikely to be enlightened by the management of their own organizations.
5. Therefore, there is a strong tendency for management to be rated according to their grasp of 'the numbers' and their analytical skills. These skills are not central to a manager's ability to lead and manage.

All this would seem to indicate that it is very unlikely that 'leadership skills' will be much valued by the people who really matter. To test this theory, we scanned a number of brokers' reports to try to understand the kinds of intellectual constructs that lay behind them. Here are our conclusions:

What the analysts understand

In addition to a sound understanding of the histories of particular companies and of the dynamics of industries, analysts' reports focus on:

- business economics – competition and market theory, trade cycles, dynamics of economies;

- industry economics – competition and behaviour of competitors, industry cycles, product life cycles;
- strategic analysis – company competitive strategies, market analysis and segmentation, SWOT analysis, company strategic strengths and weaknesses;
- company history, mainly described in terms of financial performance and trends;
- 'organization' – organization structure and the public personalities and behaviour of a few top actors;
- accounting and financial analysis – profit and loss, cash, balance sheets, tax, returns and key ratios, forecasting.

All the reports were particularly strong on financial analysis, and all had a considerable amount of narrative and opinion about the company, presumably derived from talking to management, the press and colleagues in the financial markets. The reports displayed impressive theoretical knowledge.

Many of the managers whom we interviewed reported (some with approval) that the financial markets rate two skills above all: an ability to handle numbers and financial concepts ('hard' facts and data, believed by many to be superior to 'soft' information and intuition), and the ability to present convincingly. Some said that surface confidence and the ability to 'ad lib' with fluency and conviction also count highly.

But Henry Mintzberg, in his excellent book *The Rise and Fall of Strategic Planning* (1994), disagrees that the 'hard' data used by the markets are a real indicator of business reality:

> The message in planning literature has been that such [quantified] data are not only substitutes for the softer, more qualitative data, but they are, in fact, superior to them. For data to be 'hard' means that they can be documented unambiguously, which usually means that they have already been quantified. *That way, planners and managers [and analysts] can sit in their offices and be informed. No need to go out and meet the troops, or the customers, to find out how products get bought or the wars get fought or what connects those strategies to that stock price, all that just wastes valuable time* [our italics].

Mintzberg goes on to nominate four major reasons why hard data alone are a very weak basis for understanding a business:

1. Hard data are limited in scope, lacking in richness and often failing to encompass important non-economic and non-quantitative factors. *Hard data may describe some aspects of business performance, but completely fail to explain the reasons behind it.*
2. Much hard information is far too aggregated for effective use in strategy-making (or understanding and predicting performance). At the level of an investment manager or analyst, the information used might be described as showing large forests, but giving no clues as to the type or health of the trees, or any understanding of what is going on among those trees!
3. Much 'hard' information arrives too late to be of any use in strategy-making (or business analysis). Time is required for trends and events and performance to be recorded as 'facts', more time for these facts to be aggregated into reports, even more time if these reports are to be presented on a predetermined schedule. Thus the information that feeds finance directors

and, much later, the financial markets not only is lacking in richness and understanding, but is too general to be of much use and too late to be currently valid. (Remember the stockbroker who claimed that the markets knew 'everything' about business?)

4. Finally, a surprising amount of 'hard' information is unreliable. Quantitative measures are only surrogates for reality. As Mintzberg says, 'Anybody who has ever produced a quantitative measure – whether a reject count in a factory as a surrogate for product quality, a publication count in a university as a surrogate for research performance, or estimates of costs and benefits in a capital budgeting exercise – knows how much distortion is possible, intentional as well as unintentional.' In the matter of reporting financial information between companies and financial markets, these distortions have frequently been proven to be huge. So, as a final straw, the 'facts and numbers' so beloved of many finance directors, investors and analysts can be grossly inaccurate.

What highly skilled managers actually do

Contrast these skills and use of surrogates for real understanding with those highlighted by the already mentioned John P Kotter of the Harvard Business School, and Henry Mintzberg.

Kotter conducted one of the surprisingly rare in-depth studies of what senior managers actually do, in a study published in his book *The General Managers* (1982). Having studied the working lives of well-rated general managers over a long period, he concluded that these managers:

- set long-run goals and priorities;
- allocated resources between often conflicting priorities for the medium term;
- were concerned with the efficient use of resources in the short run.

In addition to setting goals, allocating resources and deploying money and people efficiently, the managers also handled a plethora of relationships inside and outside the organization, some with people they could direct and some with people they could only influence indirectly. Kotter reported that one of the key demands was the need to make discriminating judgements about how to manage many kinds of different relationships to get the best results. Apart from the fact that numbers and financial analysis did not make an appearance in the results of his study, Kotter's results up to this point seem rather prosaic.

The real interest came when he started to analyse how these excellent managers actually went about doing their jobs and spent their time. He discovered that they had developed a very strong but quite personal understanding of what was important in their businesses and what the directional priorities were. They communicated these understandings in the form of 'agendas' for the business, containing messages about what was important to these top managers and what were the priorities for the organization.

Each one of the managers studied had very extensive networks of contacts at many levels inside the business. They used these networks both to communicate and to receive. Their working days consisted of myriads of short conversations, often very terse and conducted in a kind of shorthand, because they knew many people very well.

Very little of their time was spent in long formal meetings. They used every opportunity possible to pick up and follow through on issues that were important to them.

Kotter says that these high performers were much less formally structured in their behaviour and in how they spent their time than he would have expected. He also found that each of them had a constantly evolving picture in their head about people, relationships, goals, priorities, progress and problems, and that these 'pictures' bore little resemblance to formal business plans: they were much more dynamic, complex and personal.

What Kotter has described is a glimpse of the 'art' of managing. As opposed to the science, the hard data dimension, the art comprises having complex mental images of a business and using a vast number of different relationships to nudge, persuade, pressure and charm people to direct their efforts in the desired directions.

Kotter's findings are strongly reinforced by Henry Mintzberg (1999). Describing his observations derived from 'shadowing' a CEO, he says, 'John Cleghorn's style of management is unusual for someone in his position: he is very involved in the operational details of the bank... All senior executives, Cleghorn included, are expected to spend at least 25 percent of their time with customers and front line employees.' Earlier in the article, Mintzberg explains:

> He sold the corporate jet – he says he was uncomfortable with it – as well as the chauffeured limousines.
>
> During the day he spent time visiting front-line staff in two branch offices and met with institutional investors, as well as regional managers...
>
> In his meetings with employees, Cleghorn aimed to gather information, but also to send signals about the organization, whether by encouraging long-term employees, congratulating people about their presentations, infusing his energy into the organization, or constantly describing the values he finds important.
>
> Rarely did he exercise the CEO's prerogative of control on this particular day. Rather his role was to encourage and enable, with regard to the individual (motivating and coaching), the unit (team building), and the organization at large (culture building).

Both Kotter and Mintzberg describe a style that is a universe away from that of the high-profile heroes so beloved of press and markets. Excellence in the art of managing is likely to derive from a deep understanding of and 'feel' for a particular business and a particular organization. Those who practise it will have spent long enough in the organization to have developed extensive trusting relationships with many people at many levels, and will be able to use these relationships and business understandings to identify and rectify problems well before they show up in 'the numbers'. In this regard, hard data do not become irrelevant, but become just one of many ways of checking on the health of the business.

The art of management is invisible to most external observers, and draws little from the formal analytical skills taught in the classrooms of many of our business schools. In fact, one might go further and say that most of these 'hard' skills have become a kind of commodity. It is expected that all senior managers should have a good understanding of commonly used financial and analytical techniques.

Some business education institutions comprehend the need for practical experience as a basis for developing management skills. However, many of the more prestigious ones seem to still regard management as a kind of high-level academic subject.

Sadly, it seems that practitioners of the art of managing are not really appreciated by those who pass judgement on top management. This is not to say that such people do not exist, but they have to develop and publicly display different skills and behaviours.

It is possible that if we continue to give public approval to and reward smooth, numerate dealmakers, increasingly appointed from outside and with decreasing tenure, there is a real danger that the art of building and leading large, complex organizations will diminish still further. The consequences of this deficit are already there for all to see. We are assailed by an increasing number of failures and disasters due to managerial incompetence. The fact that many of these are in the interface between the public and private domains bodes very ill for the current government's rather touching confidence in the ability of the private sector to 'deliver' efficient public services. The fact is that a large number of the largest publicly quoted companies can now be characterized as collections of assets, rather loosely bound by organizational ties and led by numerate, analytically skilled, articulate and temporary leaders, whose rewards are determined by external judgements and who are emotionally distant from the real business of products, customers and the people that they purport to lead.

THE DEVELOPMENT OF A CLOSED, SELF-CONCERNED WORLD

Markets have many common characteristics. They tend to be very communicative mini-societies in which the traders know a lot about what is going on and who is doing what.

Any gathering of people who have broadly similar interests and ways of making a living will begin to differentiate themselves from other groups of people and develop a set of values that are commonly held among them. Financial markets are no different. Historically, many of them were concentrated in particular cities or even particular quarters of particular cities, like Wall Street in New York or Threadneedle Street in London. These days, electronic communications have made this unnecessary, but the availability of instant data on thousands of screens has if anything tightened the ties that link the players together.

International linkages are strengthened by the development of very large organizations employing thousands of people who are likely to hold common values and beliefs, whose training and skills have common roots, and who share similar goals.

So, what are the factors that indicate that the financial markets really do constitute closed working communities?

Such a list might well start with rewards. It has been reported that people who receive very high rewards for a particular activity come to believe that the things they do are very important and valuable. The availability of high rewards for particular forms of behaviour will tend to perpetuate and make it difficult to question them.

Philip Augar, in *The Death of Gentlemanly Capitalism* (2001), says:

> The money paid to brokers [in the London market] is a social and moral disgrace. With the most basic skills, a broker can earn four times as much as a teacher, twice as much as a GP, and about the same as the finance director of a medium-sized quoted plc. Even if the broker lacks flair, but is pushy and determined enough, he or she can earn the same as a leading heart surgeon and more than some chief executives of FTSE companies. All of this seems outrageous, given that the talent required to earn such sums is not particularly rare and the industry is not very profitable in the City.

Augar's analysis of brokers' earnings in 2000 indicates that middle-ranking traders earned £200,000 and their research equivalents £300,000. When traders reached senior positions, they could earn between £500,000 and £1,500,000. Earnings in research were higher, at between £1,000,000 and £2,000,000.

He quotes even higher figures for investment bankers. In 1996, directors' emoluments in Morgan Grenfell & Co spanned the following ranges:

- 30 directors earned between £500,000 and £1,000,000;
- 16 directors earned between £1,000,000 and £1,500,000;
- 8 directors earned between £1,500,000 and £2,000,000;
- 15 directors earned between £2,000,000 and £4,500,000.

Reward in the financial markets is internally determined. There is no reference to outside bodies that might be able to have a moderating influence, or feed in challenging perspectives. Therefore, several things seem to have happened.

First, as Augar has pointed out, a lot of people whose roles and skills strike external observers as not being very special seem to be hugely rewarded. The skills deployed by brokers, investment bankers and analysts would not seem to stand in the same league as those required from a good senior manager, a senior medical consultant or a top semiconductor designer.

Ah, say some, but what about the value created by good operators in the financial markets? Well, once again there is some evidence of a self-determining system at work. Take investment bankers' fees, for instance.

Rule 3 of the City Code on Takeovers and Mergers stipulates that in the event of a takeover bid, 'the Board of the offeree must obtain independent competent advice on any offer and the substance of such advice must be made known to its shareholders'. Important shareholder protection, no doubt, but it also ensures that members of the 'market' get a good crack at the fees incurred in deals.

So, why do corporate managers not simply refuse to pay such fees? Maybe part of the answer lies in the symbiotic relationships that have developed between managers and the markets. To put it more plainly, many managers have psychologically joined forces with the markets and become immune to feedback from their own organizations and other stakeholders.

Remember that many managers believe they need the goodwill of the markets to be employable in a senior job. Certainly, some Redland managers believed that attempts to screw fees down would be 'career limiting'. In addition, most senior managers have an acute understanding that their own high rewards require at least the passive acquiescence of investment institutions, and some investment institutions are owned by banks!

Martin Dixon, in the *Financial Times* of 6 January 2001, writes:

> [T]he sums involved [in investment bankers' fees] border on the obscene. For example, Blue Circle last year spent some £27 million on advisers – roughly 10% of annual pre-tax profits, a not untypical figure – as it successfully defended itself against Lafarge. Nor are fees obviously related to an adviser's input to a bid… so how can bankers get away with it? Two reasons. Their oligopolistic powers and their clients' fear.

Dixon reports that Sir Fred Holliday tried to start a debate on the issue through the *Times* letters column, but received no support from fellow top managers. One theory behind this 'fear factor' is the anxiety that 'difficult' executives may find their companies stranded without an adviser and on the wrong end of a hostile bid.

To move the focus from clients to customers, surely those in the financial services industry must deserve top dollar for the value they create for customers? Well, not entirely. Of all industries, financial services has developed one of the most fearsome reputations for exploiting and ripping off its customers. Scandals abound. Derivatives trading divisions have aggressively mis-sold instruments to companies, pension funds, states and local authorities, to name but a few. The scandals of Orange County in the United States (whose treasurer purchased interest rate derivatives that the banks knew he didn't understand) and Hammersmith and Fulham in the United Kingdom (where the authority avoided huge losses on interest rate derivatives only by claiming in court that the purchase was *ultra vires* and so should be overturned) are just two of many. On the personal side, in the United Kingdom we have seen personal pensions and endowment mortgage mis-selling and the split capital investment trust row. Now we read of concerns in the United States that investment banks allocated dot.com shares to their 'friends'. If any reader remains unconvinced, just read the description by Frank Partnoy in *F.I.A.S.C.O.* (of derivatives traders rejoicing in having 'ripped the face off' yet another client – that is, sold the hapless manager another risky instrument he didn't fully understand, but that made the bank a lot of money).

According to Will Hutton in the *Observer* of 19 May 2002, 'Companies that have ripped off their customers for decades get away scot-free.' And, he might have added, industrial managers seem to believe that it is perfectly legitimate to decouple their rewards from the performance of the companies that they lead.

To summarize the situation, the players in the financial markets reward themselves very richly by comparison with other professional workers and raise the money to do this, at least in part, by extracting huge fees from clients and exploiting their customers. Some of these very people are among the 'shareholders' that the government would like to exercise a moderating influence on executive pay!

Incidentally, many of their customers are the real shareholders in whose interests everybody is supposed to be working. Put this way, there is much reason for suspicion that a self-determining system of interests is at work.

Closed systems are often cut off from the outside by shared systems of belief and patterns of expression and thought that exclude anything uncomfortable, another symptom of groupthink. Bodies of people become capable of persisting with patterns of thought and action that are damaging or irrational, despite strong external evidence. Also, groups of people may develop forms of expression amounting to a local form of political correctness that may deny or twist the truth because it is uncomfortable.

Evidence of such syndromes in the financial markets? Almost certainly. Probable manifestations are the strong tendency towards herd-like behaviours and espousing of fads and crazes. In the short term, rumours can cause quite violent swings in share prices, even if they often seem far-fetched to outsiders. Some rumours are almost certainly started deliberately and some are simply the product of a rather nervous herd mentality. We must all have seen a flock of sheep suddenly seized by a momentary panic!

Again, to quote George Soros in *The Crisis of Global Capitalism*:

> The belief in fundamentals is eroding and trend-following behavior is on the rise. It is fostered by the increasing influence of institutional investors whose performance is measured by relative rather than absolute performance and by the large money center banks that act as market makers in currencies and derivatives. They benefit from increased volatility both as market makers and as providers of hedging mechanisms.

Thus the field of thoughtful investment is left to a few individualists like Warren Buffett.

We have left the worst feature of the financial markets to the last. It seems that they are subject to recurrent patterns of dysfunctional behaviour. The most obvious manifestation of this is related to business cycles. There is a strong tendency for market behaviour to exaggerate the natural, cyclical ups and downs of economic growth. In bull markets, over-optimism rules and both markets and companies behave as though boom conditions will last for ever. Companies indulge in deals and transactions that will need to be undone the moment the market steadies.

Overpayment for acquisitions becomes rife. Value is destroyed by foolish and risky strategies. Greed becomes rampant, great pressure is exerted by investment banks to exploit the good times by excessive growth, and weird theories heralding the end of cyclical downturns are fervently believed.

Once the inevitable pause in growth occurs, the effects are exaggerated as all the mistakes hidden by the boom come home to roost. In these early years of the 21st century we have seen many of these manifestations.

The sad feature of all this is that most people do not seem to learn from past experience and mistakes. This is probably the most profound effect of having a closed 'system' binding together the interests of management and the financial markets. *It is not in the interests of the players in the system to reflect and learn from experience.* There is infinitely more gain to be had from continuing with things as they are.

For example, if, as might seem sensible, companies indulged much less in deal-driven activity and instead concentrated on building strong businesses by organic means, customers, employees and the economy as a whole would almost certainly benefit. For the sake of argument, it would probably be sensible if 50 per cent of the acquisitions of the past decade had never been made. They destroyed value and caused much human uncertainty and distress. There is much to be learnt by considering the available research and tailoring acquisition strategies as a result.

However, this is not going to provide the huge fees and excitement created by deals. So, managers and their City supporters continue to take predictable and excessive risks, driven not by learning and wisdom, but by wild hope, sensation-seeking and greed.

ALIENATION AND EXPLOITATION OF EMPLOYEES AND CUSTOMERS

The biggest survey in the United Kingdom is the Workplace Employment Relations Survey (Department of Trade and Industry, 1998), and it is from this massive affair that we will draw most of our data.

First, though, to popular perceptions. Here are some: 'The British… together with Hungarians and Italians have the least satisfied workers in Europe… Britain, as it has done since the first tracking trends survey was published five years ago, has maintained its place at the bottom of the ratings.' The *Guardian*, not to be outdone, claimed that, 'Downsizing from the last recession left fewer people doing more work. They are working so hard, they are exhausted and they want to get off the treadmill.' These perceptions would tend to indicate that employees in the United Kingdom are groaning under the yoke of oppressive employers who give them little recognition and inadequate rewards, and use them as sweated labour.

Is this true? Not entirely. British employees seem to like working, and objective surveys indicate a preparedness to give a 'good' employer much commitment and support.

But there are some worrying trends. British companies' productivity, in both manufacturing and service sectors, is much less than that of their US, German and French counterparts. *Of particular concern is the apparent fact that the productivity of British owned manufacturing companies is much lower than that of foreign owned companies in Britain. In addition, it seems that the pay of British employees of foreign-owned companies is some 33 per cent higher than that of their colleagues in British-owned companies.* The main reason for this appears to be a lack of investment in capital equipment and the 'tools' to support people in their work. (Not, incidentally, the yoke of bureaucracy or tax, as such bodies as the CBI would have us believe. French productivity is higher, yet the burden of bureaucracy is at least as great in France, while France and all other European countries, many with higher productivity, are in a totally different 'tax misery' league, according to Andrew Frazer (1999).)

British employees work far longer hours than most of their European counterparts, but a little less than Americans. In July 2003 a survey by the recruitment company Reed revealed that only two people in five took their full holiday entitlement, owing to stress and felt pressures of work. Such behaviour would be regarded as madness in productive continental Europe. There is circumstantial evidence that stress and insecurity are growing. Such authorities as Professor Cary Cooper of UMIST firmly believe that this is the case.

Worst of all, we are now seeing a raft of long-term trouble in the form of a substantial degradation of future pension rights and underfunded pension schemes. This is one of the great paradoxes of our time. In a world that is apparently dedicated to the creation of value for shareholders, it appears that many large companies cannot afford to maintain final salary pension schemes.

Members of pension plans still make up a large proportion of 'real' shareholders. So, what price 'shareholder value'?

The sudden rush to close final salary pension schemes, to the enormous long-term detriment of employees' well-being, seems very short-sighted and likely to cause damage to the relationships between companies and their employees. We are now seeing a resurgence of employee militancy that has not been manifest for many years. Why did not more employers seek other ways of limiting long-term exposure than the 'nuclear' option of closing them completely?

It is worth considering what all this says about the apparent fundamental driving force behind it all, the creation of 'shareholder value'. Shareholders, we might remind ourselves, include pension fund members, investors in mortgages, endowment policies, insurance plans and, not least, the holders of personal pensions. These are the customers of the financial services industry.

The *Observer*, on 15 September 2002, asserted that pressure on pension funds is coming from investment funds as well as top managers. Both are concerned that the costs of funding pension plans will reduce returns for the next few years. This was before even greater falls in share prices devastated fund values. The article claimed that:

> Earlier this year key shareholders approached Unilever, the consumer goods giant and demanded that it shut down its final salary scheme. There seems to have been no good reason for this other than shaving employer contributions from Unilever's balance sheet. The Anglo-Dutch company's fund is worth £4.2 billion and there is no shortfall.

Unilever's chairman, Niall Fitzgerald, is said to have told institutions to 'bugger off'. The company refused to confirm whether it was in effect ambushed, but meetings certainly took place with key shareholders. Unilever publicly confirmed its commitment to the scheme. It might just have helped that Unilever has a complex Anglo-Dutch shareholding structure, which makes the company less susceptible than some to pressures from the London market.

We would ask what the whole game of 'shareholder value' creation is about and what the financial markets and companies are there for, if it is not to support and enhance the interests of 'real' shareholders and employees.

To move on to other issues, it is manifestly the case that job security has decreased over the past 20 years or so. Many more people are working part-time or on temporary contracts. According to the Workplace Employment Relations Survey (Department of Trade and Industry, 1998), in 1990 76 per cent of employees felt secure in their employment. By 1998 the proportion had decreased to 40 per cent, and there is evidence that this ratio has decreased still further since then.

However, there is some very good news. British employees actually like working! And, what is more, they want to feel loyal to their companies. Many of them feel that they share the values of their organizations and quite a few feel proud of the company for which they work.

So, the picture of miserable, stressed and dissatisfied employees is an exaggeration. British employees, taken as a whole, fall somewhere in the middle of a European work satisfaction league, somewhat ahead of French and German employees. It does seem that there is a considerable reservoir of commitment, pride and sense of responsibility to be harnessed by employers who are willing to engage with and demonstrate commitment to staff. Two of the highest-performing car plants in the world in terms of quality and productivity are located in Britain. Both plants are obviously modern and have heavy capital investment to support high productivity.

As we shall see in the next chapter, British subsidiaries of foreign companies invest much more than most of their native counterparts. It also appears that many foreign-owned companies are better managed and enjoy much higher productivity and quality than the generality of British-owned counterparts.

The achievement of consistent quality and high productivity requires a number of rather obvious conditions. First is a high level of attention to detail and a long-term application to improvement and learning. It is well known that long-term dedication will enable plants to improve performance. The process is simply one of eliminating errors and finding myriads of small ways to improve the production process. Second is a dedicated and well-led workforce, with which managers share common cause and are not separated from by artificial barriers of class, status or reward. Third is a high degree of professionalism related to the 'technology' of the business, with as much responsibility as possible for the professional work being devolved to the lowest level possible. This means, of course, a high level of investment in employee development, to levels not historically known in the United Kingdom.

These conditions are not impossible to achieve; other countries manage it, but they do need high levels of support from top management if they are to become permanently embedded in the working culture of British companies. This in turn means a marked shift in behaviour from corporate activism to longer-term attention to the art of managing. And this is just not going to happen if managers continue to be heavily influenced by the prevailing breed of investor.

The opportunity is undoubtedly there to grow another generation of strong, well-founded British-owned companies if the conditions are created to encourage it. There is a high-quality, skilled and potentially world-class workforce that could enable it to happen with skilled leadership and support.

At the beginning of this chapter we set out our second Proposition: that the increasingly symbiotic relationships between managers and markets are manifestly affecting the behaviour and skills of top managers in many British companies. Further, we contended that the interests of shareholders, employees and other stakeholders are suffering from the actions of the market–management 'system', and that is having demonstrably detrimental effects on the performance and prospects of many large British quoted enterprises. Readers, we submit that we have made a strong case for the Proposition.

11

Industrial, economic and social consequences of management–market relationships

THE PROPOSITION

The developing relationship between managers and the financial markets is having corrosive long-term effects on the performance and competitiveness of many larger UK quoted companies, and more generally on levels of innovation and enterprise. These effects are noticeable in the industrial and regional balance of the UK economy, in the relative dominance of the financial services sector, in the lack of innovation by many UK companies and in the rates of company decline and failure.

International manifestations are the failure of UK companies to compete in many modern industries, especially physics-based ones. But there are also noticeable effects in the United Kingdom, where an ever-increasing number of foreign-owned companies perform better and invest at consistently higher levels than their indigenous counterparts. This makes the health of the UK economy increasingly dependent on inward investment and more and more on the acquisition of UK companies by foreign competitors. So far, levels of external investment have been very high, and foreign-owned companies now account for some 50 per cent of the United Kingdom's gross exports. But it is also the case that strategic and key investment decisions affecting large parts of industry, commerce and the financial sector are being made without any UK influence.

The culture, tax, regulatory and education systems, location and general 'business-friendliness' of the United Kingdom make it a country with high potential to attain a sustainably high level of economic performance. However, the financial markets, as they are currently configured, do not enhance this potential and are now causing more harm than good to the economy and society. In particular, they do not generally encourage people and enterprises to innovate and invest for long-term competitiveness.

The 'system' represented by the relationships between industry and the financial markets needs far greater reform than is currently being contemplated.

In the previous two chapters, we have sought to establish:

1. that there are strong formal and informal linkages of mutual interest between top managers and the financial markets;
2. that through these powerful linkages, the financial markets are manifestly affecting the behaviour of top managers and, through them, having mainly negative effects on the enterprises that they lead.

In this chapter we have set ourselves the tasks of examining the tangible consequences for UK industry and commerce of the 'system' that we have previously described. We will trace and track the effects of a complex web of interactions, behaviours and values on the performance of large UK companies and on the economy as a whole. As the chapter progresses, we shall lay our case and our evidence before the jury of you, the readers, and ask you, as before, to reach your own judgements.

Before we start, it is appropriate to put a few stakes in the ground.

First, the UK economy is in reasonably good shape. The 1980s shakeout means that it is not lumbered with a millstone of obsolete 'Industrial Revolution' industries. Furthermore, contemporary governments seem to be willing to maintain a policy framework that is reasonably consistent, unlike the 'left–right' and 'stop–go' lurches that so disastrously marked the first 40 or so years after the Second World War.

It is reasonable to claim that there is still a wellspring of inventiveness and creativity in the United Kingdom equal to that anywhere in the world. And we are not just speaking of a few eccentric individuals (though they need to be treasured!). As an example, the performance of the new industrial complex that has sprung up around Cambridge bodes well for enterprise, if it is given proper infrastructure support.

The UK workforce, contrary to some views, is well motivated, generally hard-working and responsive to high-quality leadership. Just look at the performance of various Japanese-owned enterprises with predominantly British workforces!

Last, but not least, the United Kingdom is a country that has a long history of foreign trading. At official level, unlike France, it is relatively undefensive about foreign influence and open to welcoming inward flows of money and skills.

Thus we are looking at a prospect that holds much promise and potential.

So, what are the 'buts'? These relate to the relative performance of large UK companies and the apparent unwillingness of the financial community to invest in innovation and enterprise. Of huge concern is the performance of UK enterprises in high-innovation, high-science and highly knowledge-based industries, the sorts that need very heavy and consistent investment in R&D and capital. We will show that much of the growth and innovation in the United Kingdom has happened outside the arena occupied by large companies, and that the relative performance of the investment community in funding smaller enterprises isn't so hot either.

In no small measure, we will be describing an old and well-known British syndrome, that of 'lions led by donkeys'.

We would contend that the fact that large UK companies are no longer leaders in many industrial sectors that they once dominated is due to four main influences:

- The rise of foreign competitors that sometimes enjoy special advantages, such as government support, but frequently are just better than their UK counterparts. For example, it was not just bad luck or unfortunate accident that killed the UK-owned motorcycle, car and truck industries; it was the fact that the Japanese/Germans/Italians/Americans made far better and more attractive products much more efficiently and marketed them better.
- The incompetence and lack of professionalism of industrial leaders and the whole culture of elitism and class.
- The actions and policies of many governments of both political persuasions.
- The behaviour and expectations of the suppliers of capital.

In general, we contend, the 'donkeys' have been politicians, financiers and industrial leaders. The 'lions', as always, are the engineers, scientists and inventors and the average men and women who, by all reports, work far harder and longer (but not more productively) than their continental European counterparts.

As a starting point, let your imagination take over for a few paragraphs. Let us imagine two large towns in a far-away country. One, Reichsburg, is reasonably wealthy. The sources of its wealth have been the long-established university and a large science and technology institute. The environment and ambience of the place have made it very attractive to a variety of knowledge-based industries. Thus there is a solid base of relatively well-educated and wealthy citizens.

The town council has been very concerned to support citizens with less privileged backgrounds to gain vocational qualifications and participate in the knowledge economy. It has thus spent liberally on vocational and educational facilities, which, although very expensive in the short term, are a good long-term investment. This heavy investment has meant that there has been continuous friction with the regional treasury, as the council has been unwilling to pay large taxes to be spent or wasted elsewhere. Thus many in central government are waiting for an opportunity to teach these over-independent town councillors a lesson.

The council has also supported a rich variety of artistic and community activities. There are very good theatres, galleries and cinemas, and many clubs and social activities based around the rich social and artistic hubs. Community life is lively and active.

As might be expected, crime levels are relatively low, but there are a few 'hot spots' surrounding poorer and more deprived areas. The council has taken an innovative approach to crime prevention, focusing on education, vocational training and community service for offenders, rather than simple retribution. As a result, the police force is well integrated with most parts of the community and crime levels have been dropping.

Let us now visualize another town some 50 kilometres from Reichsburg. Its name is Schwerstadt. In days past, it was a great manufacturing centre, but for several decades the once-great companies that brought wealth to the town have been suffering as a result of foreign competition. Consequently, the rate of unemployment has been increasing and many areas of the town are becoming poor and rather deprived.

The council has been rather slow to respond to what has been a progressive decline, rather than a collapse, of the local economy. Several initiatives have been started, including support for local landlords to take properties in the declining areas and rent them to poorer people and refugees. As the town became poorer, the council felt the need to tailor expenditure to income and it has cut back on many local services, especially 'non-essential' services, such as the community college and adult education.

The money saved has gone into a rigorous programme of policing. The local police chief, with strong council support, pursues a vigorous 'zero tolerance' approach. The local prisons and detention centres are now reaching capacity. Despite this, crime and disorder are increasing. Some wealthier and more mobile citizens are leaving to go to Reichsburg.

The case of the two towns has come to the notice of an ever-vigilant regional finance ministry, which is by far the most powerful arm of government. This ministry intervenes very strongly in local affairs when the regional coffers might be affected or when it wants to outguess the locals (which is normally the case!). According to the senior officials of the finance ministry, Reichsburg is dangerously independent and even showing signs of overconfidence in its dealings with officials. Schwerstadt presents a different kind of problem. Its evident decline bodes ill for the regional exchequer. While there is a degree of respect for the obviously hardline and controlling nature of the Schwerstadt councillors, it does not seem that this is going to regenerate the local economy.

Then someone in the finance ministry has a bright idea. These two towns are synergistic! Just imagine the results of putting them together! The richer town would provide employment and education for the deprived and unemployed of the other, as well as surplus cash that could be deployed to support the poorer town. On the other side, the council and people of the richer town could have much to learn and gain from the tough-minded and efficient way in which crime and expenditure are controlled by its more disadvantaged neighbour. To cut a long story short, the two towns are merged, with a strong push, approval and support from the finance ministry, which becomes ever more convinced that the synergies to be gained will save a lot of money, and that it will not have to waste increasing amounts of precious funds on supporting the poorer community.

At the local level, things are not so simple. After a fairly lengthy power struggle, the tough-minded councillors of Schwerstadt gain the upper hand, expel their more 'liberal' colleagues and start to impose their will and values on the combined entity. After one year, they declare the merger of the two communities to be 'successfully completed'. The finance ministry, from a great distance, feels that its intervention has been vindicated, and anyhow it is now very preoccupied with similar problems elsewhere. It starts progressively to cut back financial support and investment.

Three years later it becomes apparent that all is not well with the merged communities. Serious riots and civil disturbances have broken out, and the council is asking for more and more money from the government to 'halt rapid decline' in the state of the local economy and communities. It also appears that there has been a massive efflux of modern industries and educated citizens.

The ministry decides that it must act again. This is just not working. Best cut the losses and split the two towns up again. Maybe an even better idea would be to split them into many pieces and encourage every town within a 150-kilometre radius to take a piece!

Why have we occupied your time with this apparently irrelevant story? Because, if we use our imaginations a little, variations of this are what has happened to a significantly large number of FTSE companies over the past 30 years. Readers may have picked up a number of themes underlying our story:

- constant merging and de-merging;
- putting together dissimilar entities in order to realize 'synergy';
- lack of sensitivity to organizations as human and social entities;
- top managements that pursue power and impose their will, regardless of the human effects or long-term consequences;
- cost-cutting;
- underinvestment;
- imposition of very tight central controls, and rigorous policing of them;
- expulsion of those who question the central diktats;
- sudden changes of strategy;
- strong preference for control over innovation;
- distant investors who have much power but little understanding.

In other words, many of the themes that have emerged through researching and writing this book. We will look for signs of these effects on UK companies and the economy more generally, starting with the effects on larger companies.

THE EFFECTS ON LARGER COMPANIES

The place to do this is the FTSE 100. These are the United Kingdom's largest companies. Here are some facts:

1. The relative sizes of the largest companies in terms of market value have increased vastly compared with the rest. Some statistics on this phenomenon are given in Chapter 1. Here are some more. The ratio of the size of the top five companies to that of the bottom five increased from 12.5 in 1994 to a huge 46 in 2002. By March 2003 the ratio had moved to 62 times.

   A cause for concern may be that of the top five companies in 2002, four were the result of mega-mergers. In the case of at least three of them it is far too early to know whether the merger logic has worked, but there are worrying signs that it may not have in at least two cases (Vodafone and GSK).

2. The smaller players in the FTSE 100 have become relatively smaller over time. Their size in terms of market capitalization has remained relatively constant from 1994, despite inflation and the rapid growth of the biggest companies.

   Thus in terms of market capitalization, UK industry is being increasingly dominated by a few giants, the products of mergers, with a growing 'tail' of smaller companies. Some will undoubtedly argue that all this is due to globalization, and that we ought at least to celebrate the fact that the United Kingdom can boast a few retail banks and pharmaceutical and oil companies in the world size league. This ignores the fact that once upon a time, many UK companies were in the world league in engineering, electronics and the physics-based industries, and some, like Rolls-Royce, still are, but receive little investor support.

The dramatic changes in the relative size of the largest and smallest companies are a consequence of the behaviour of investors and managers, as well as of such forces as globalization. The changes say a lot about what investors want, which is growth through transactions, which eventually leads to a high incidence of long-term company decline and failure. The shape of the FTSE 100 is beginning to show this.

In another dimension, the same trend will increase the volatility of the investment markets. Big companies will attract a large slice of available cash; smaller ones below the FTSE 250 mark less. The fortunes of a relatively small number of huge companies will dominate the whole market. Huge companies that are the result of mega-mergers are likely to be more unstable and unwieldy to manage than those that have been carefully 'built', thus increasing the tendency towards volatility and instability in the financial markets.

3. Chapter 1 touched on the instability of large UK companies. Remember that in 2001, only five of the original FTSE 30 companies of 1935 remained in the top ranks. By 2002, only two – GKN (precariously) and ICI (perilously) – remain in the FTSE 100. Even more dramatic is the fact that only 26 per cent of the top 115 companies of 1987 remain in broadly the same shape and in the top echelon. The remaining 74 per cent have merged, been taken over, de-merged, been 'demoted' or gone private.

   This is a very high rate of change, some of which may have been for very good reasons. But a large slice of the change has come from unintended 'events' such as the takeover of Redland by Lafarge or the collapse of Marconi. The rate of 'churn' of assets in the stock market is highly unlikely to have done anything positive for the underlying performance of many, many potentially good companies.

   Next, let us look at what has happened to the mix and balance of industries represented in the FTSE 100. In mid-2002 the FTSE 100 contained:

- no companies in the information technology hardware, engineering and machinery, electrical engineering, and industrial manufacturing sectors;
- one company each in electronics, automobile components (none in auto manufacturing), software and computer services and metals manufacturing;
- two companies in aerospace and defence;
- three companies in pharmaceuticals;
- two companies in chemicals.

The largest company in the aerospace and defence sector, BAE Systems, was, in early 2003, in dire trouble. The ingredients of the company's travails are a toxic mixture indeed. It would appear that BAE is experiencing big cost overruns on major Ministry of Defence contracts (some inherited from the merger with GEC's defence interests) and has been trying to renegotiate the relevant contracts with the ministry. These attempts were possibly a cause of the demise of ex-CEO John Weston, mentioned previously.

The ministry responded by briefing vigorously against the company. Geoff Hoon, the Defence Secretary, described the company as 'not British', an allusion to the fact that BAE is now more than 50 per cent owned by non-British investors. This is a rich irony, as it was the government that removed the proviso that BAE should have majority British shareholding!

All these travails have been badly received by investors, who have sold out in droves, thus reducing the share price drastically. BAE is now in such trouble with the markets that further rumours abound that it will have to find a merger partner. Given the absence of any UK alternative, this will presumably be foreign, possibly Boeing of the United States.

Talk about being destroyed by friendly fire! Anthony Hilton, in the London *Evening Standard* of 20 January 2003, headed his report on the matter, 'Disaster'. He says, of the possible Boeing merger, 'It might be tempting to think Britain would get more US defence work and gain from technology transfer, but it is hard to believe that anything gained would compensate for the loss of control of one of the last world-scale truly important British manufacturers.' Where else but the United Kingdom could such nonsenses happen, where government, financial markets and less than totally competent managers conspire together to destroy great companies?

About 10 per cent of large British companies are in the physics- and chemistry-based industries. This represents a marked change over time and compares with over 50 per cent in Japan, France and Germany and some 30 per cent in the United States. It contrasts with:

- 29 companies in the utility, services and retailing sectors;
- 6 companies in the media and photography;
- 6 companies in drinks and food manufacturing;
- 19 companies in the banking and financial services sectors (but none in investment banking and broking);
- 6 companies in mining, oil and gas.

Many people will shrug their shoulders and mutter, 'So what?' We would counter, 'Has it been deliberate strategy for large UK companies not to be represented in some of the largest, most dynamic international and modern knowledge-based industries?' and 'Has it been a carefully thought out ploy to shape the British economy in a way that all other developed countries haven't thought of?' While a media- and services-based economy might seem to be 'modern', so are economies based on electronic engineering, motor vehicle and motorcycle manufacturing, telecommunications, and computer hardware and software engineering. So, incidentally, are sectors based on international investment banking. Why are there no big UK players in this sector?

UK quoted companies are, however, internationally strong in pharmaceuticals, oil, mining, tobacco and telecommunications services (although it remains to be seen whether Vodafone, the UK leader in this field, is a 'stayer').

The physics- and chemistry-based industries have some common characteristics. They all need above-average levels of long-term research and capital expenditure. They are all very dependent on developing and retaining a committed cadre of very highly qualified, well-paid management and staff. They all need a long-term orientation and consistent attention to complex development programmes that take many years to produce fruits. And they usually need large and complex organizations to support them. Even at this early stage in the chapter, we would contend that there is very strong evidence that the current 'mindset' of the financial markets and top management is not oriented towards supporting companies with such profiles.

Companies that need consistent long-term investment and management are also rather sensitive to being shaken up, pulled apart, put back together and hacked about. For these reasons, the degree of corporate mayhem that has characterized the FTSE 100 in the past 20 years is unlikely to be supportive to physics- and chemistry-based companies. Thus it is sensible, as some commentators have pointed out, to be very cautious about giving unqualified support to the notion that the results of mega-mergers, such as GSK, are going to produce all the wonderful results in terms of enhanced R&D that their top managers claimed at the time of the merger. There is probably rather more reason to be sanguine about the outcomes of the merger of BP and Amoco, creating Britain's largest company, as BP had focused strongly on building a very strong internal culture and organization well before the merger.

INWARD INVESTMENT

Let us move on from a field where UK management and investors have had very mixed fortunes, to one of great success: inward investment. According to Invest UK, a government-supported agency responsible for fostering foreign investment in UK industry (Invest UK Web site, July 2002), in 1996 the United Kingdom attracted:

- 23 per cent of European external direct investment;
- 44 per cent of Japanese external direct investment;
- 38 per cent of US external direct investment;
- 50 per cent of Canadian external direct investment.

In 1998 this amounted to £80 billion, second only to the much bigger US market, which attracted £201 billion.

The levels of inward investment increased from 10.5 per cent of UK GDP in 1978 to 25 per cent in 1998. Inward investment in manufacturing industries increased from 18.5 per cent of manufacturing gross value added in 1978 to 38.5 per cent of gross value added in 1998.

The biggest sectors for inward investment in 1998 were telecommunications equipment, pharmaceuticals, computers and computer software, investment banking and financial services, and multimedia. It is interesting to note that in three of these five sectors, large British companies appear to have given up the ghost and withdrawn from the sector. Later, Marconi did enter the communications and telecommunications manufacturing fields, but in such a transactional manner that the company virtually destroyed itself.

By 1996, foreign-owned companies accounted for:

- 19 per cent of all employment in manufacturing;
- 34 per cent of all capital expenditure in manufacturing;
- 28 per cent of all manufacturing output.

Even more startling is the fact that according to a *Financial Times* survey, 40 per cent of the United Kingdom's top exporting companies are foreign owned and 50 per cent (yes, fifty per cent!) of the United Kingdom's gross exports come from foreign-owned companies.

All this must be seen as unalloyed good news. And the good times continued into 2002. Despite the euro, Britain still heads the European inward investment league. But is there a catch? Well, not exactly a catch, but a gross indictment of UK management and investment practices.

Foreign-owned manufacturing companies in Britain:

- created 24 per cent greater gross value added per head than their British counterparts;
- paid wages that were 33 per cent higher than their British counterparts;
- had 133 per cent higher net capital expenditure than their British counterparts (figures from the National Institute for Economic and Social Research (NIESR)).

Some underlying factors need a little more examination. For example, it might be said that the researchers who provided Invest UK with its data were comparing all UK manufacturers with larger and more professional foreign companies. There is some truth in this. UK companies operating in the United States had higher capital investment than the US average and somewhat higher productivity, but by no means near the margin by which US-owned companies outperformed indigenous companies in the United Kingdom.

Professor Richard Harris of the University of Portsmouth conducted research to find out whether the foreign-owned manufacturing plants in the United Kingdom performed better because they were already better when acquired by foreign companies. Using comparable samples of UK- and foreign-owned plants, he discovered that the 1,800 plants acquired by foreign-owned companies between the late 1980s and mid-1990s were indeed already more productive than plants that were not acquired.

Even then, though, the performance of the foreign-acquired plants was further enhanced. The foreign-managed plants raised gross output per employee and real wage rates significantly. They did this by significantly raising the investment per employee, by between 32 per cent and 55 per cent. And the foreign owners did not raise performance by simply laying people off. In fact, the likelihood of employees losing their jobs was far higher in UK-owned plants.

One or two last paragraphs on the subjects of investment and R&D, as it is so important. Between 1989 and 1999, R&D expenditure by foreign-owned manufacturing companies in Britain increased by 100 per cent. Over the same period, the R&D expenditure by British manufacturing companies *decreased* by 14.2 per cent. Table 11.1 is informative. It shows the productivity and the investment to output ratios of foreign-owned companies compared to those of their UK counterparts in various sectors.

As a last point, inward investment has grown most rapidly in the knowledge-intensive sectors of chemicals, transport equipment and motor vehicles, and electronics for business (source, NIESR).

If the foreign companies can do it in the United Kingdom, why can't the UK-led and -funded companies? It seems a shocking indictment of the 'system' that controls the availability of capital and how that capital is deployed.

Table 11.1 Productivity and investment to output ratios (UK companies = 100)

	Productivity	**Investment : output ratio**
Chemicals	110.8	103.7
Metals manufacturing	140.0	132.2
Electrical engineering	134.0	153.0
Motor vehicles	142.5	177.3
Instrument engineering	124.2	119.1
Transport equipment	104.2	188.5

Further research conducted by the National Institute for Social and Economic Research reveals some more subtle, but worrying, facts:

- US companies produce more physics- and chemistry-based manufactured products and conduct more R&D in Germany than they do in the United Kingdom. The reason for this is that German R&D and technical 'agglomerations' (clusters of facilities, know-how and skills on the ground) are much denser than in the United Kingdom.
- What makes the United Kingdom attractive in the first place is relatively cheap labour and flexible employment practices.

Do we want our country to be an attractive location for inward investment because it is cheap and people can be fired easily, or because the infrastructure supports R&D-intensive knowledge-based industries?

There are already signs in early 2003 that some Far Eastern companies are beginning to pull out from UK-based assembly plants. Lucky Goldstar, the Korean electronics company, is closing its television and computer screens assembly plant in Newport, Wales, with the loss of 900 jobs. Jeremy Warner, in the *Independent* of 24 May 2003, comments:

> Britain can never succeed economically as a home for screwdriver plants for overseas companies. There are too many much more attractive places for such capital to go [presumably with vastly lower labour costs]. In the end, it would seem that only investment in high knowledge and skill-based industries will bring sustainable, well paid employment.

Of course, the picture is not really all that black in the United Kingdom. There are pockets of superb research and technical skills. Consider Microsoft's investment in R&D in Cambridge and the country's superb infrastructure for designing and making racing cars. It is just that the United Kingdom would do even better if indigenous companies and their representative bodies such as the Confederation of British Industry (CBI) and Institute of Directors would support the high-skill, high-investment case, as opposed to their current 'low-regulation, flexible employment' line.

In case you are not persuaded, consider the findings of research by the Department of Trade and Industry, in conjunction, it is interesting to note, with the CBI, Engineering Employers' Association and other worthy bodies (Department of Trade and Industry, 2001 (Dr M Tubbs)). This shows that profitability for international manufacturing sectors rises with investment in the future (R&D plus capital expenditure, as a percentage of sales), as does value added per employee. For the broad engineering sector, total shareholder return over 10 years is generally higher for those companies having higher R&D plus capital expenditure intensity.

However, a survey into R&D during 2001 showed that only 13 of the top 300 companies worldwide are UK owned, and this select number includes Invensys (most of which is being sold in 2003) and Marconi, the future R&D capacity of which must be extremely threatened. This 13 (or 11) compares with 135 US companies, 68 Japanese, 24 French and 21 German.

OK, some will say, all this stuff is about manufacturing and 'old economy' enterprise. What about the future? What about knowledge-based enterprises, what about services? Surely the Conservatives in the 1980s had it right when they implied that manufacturing didn't matter?

Our reply is that a balanced economy with a fair share of science-, physics- and chemistry-based enterprise is likely to be healthier than a totally service-dominated one. A lot of service-based employment is relatively unskilled and low paid. For example, one of the most rapidly growing sources of employment in recent years has been call centres in deprived economic areas, where labour is relatively cheap. This growth is likely to be a rather temporary phenomenon. In September 2002 the Prudential insurance company announced that it was moving a major call centre to India, where labour is even cheaper. It has been followed in early 2003 by BT. Readers might watch for others to follow.

The same applies to computer programming. Hamish McRae, reporting in the *Independent on Sunday* of 14 September 2003, wrote: 'Indian computer programmers have the reputation not only for being cheaper than their western counterparts, but for being better too. The trend there can only grow. This will become something big. And that, of course, would be wonderful for India. For us? Well, we had better think of something else to do.' As we have already tried low-cost, unregulated labour markets, it seems as though it had better be something different.

It is likely that solid clusters of advanced knowledge, skill and R&D will attract more sustainable employment. And it is to foreign companies, drawing their investment support from outside the United Kingdom, that we must look for the future.

To return now to services and the financial sector, surely the United Kingdom leads the way here? Well, certainly not when it comes to efficiency and productivity. Read this quotation from an article in *The Times* of 1 May 2002:

> Why are we so inefficient? The NIESR confirms that a great part of the gap in manufacturing is because of investment levels. The rate of capital intensity per hour worked in French factories is almost double that of the UK. That ties in with conventional wisdom about Britain's satanic mills.
>
> But what about services and the City, where Britain leads the way? Well, it does not. In financial intermediation and business services we are hugely inefficient with the French a quarter more productive in business services and the Germans a third more productive in financial intermediation.
>
> The awful truth is out. Behind the Portland stone and towering steel of the City lies a raggle-taggle army of half-educated, under-resourced bureaucrats pushing paper. At last, we know the reason for the huge commissions and charges imposed by insurers and fund managers. It pays for over-manning and instead of fussing about working hours, the CBI should set its sights on eradicating bad management.

And, we would add, systematic underinvestment.

So, it is not the fault of the lions! There really is strong objective evidence that British employees, supported by strong investment and managed well by foreign owners, can put in world-class performances.

If the fault does not lie with the lions, then what about the donkeys? Perhaps the current government is beginning to get its thinking, if not its implementation, straight by encouraging capital expenditure, productivity, and vocational and higher education. There is no doubt that past governments have barked up the wrong tree: the Conservatives with their 'cheap and flexible' labour policies, and Labour with nationalization. We need flexibility, but not cheap and easy-to-fire labour, as the sole unique selling proposition.

So, we come back to many UK business leaders and the system that provides capital and encourages it to be squandered on deals rather than systematic long-term investment, and award them the supreme 'donkey' appellation!

FOREIGN OWNERSHIP

Very large swathes of UK industry and commerce have been acquired by companies that have their top management and strategic decision-taking located outside the United Kingdom. And although many foreign companies conduct a portion of their research, development and innovation in the United Kingdom, it is still the case that the ownership of the intellectual capital resides with the foreign company. In addition, most foreign large companies have the main locus of R&D and investment decision taking in their home countries.

Two examples may bring the issues involved to life.

Powergen is one of the biggest electricity generators in the United Kingdom. Following privatization, there was a political embargo on UK-owned utilities consolidating the industry. How could they be allowed to consolidate, when the politicians had broken it up to foster 'competition'? This embargo had two effects. First, it caused British utilities to go looking for routes to growth outside the United Kingdom. Remember, no growth, no investor support. Second, it made UK utilities a prime target for foreign acquisition, especially as many of them destroyed vast amounts of value on overpriced acquisitions into foreign markets that they only dimly understood, and were consequently cheap buys.

Powergen moved confidently into the US market and completely ruined its balance sheet. Some time later, Powergen was bid for by Eon, a German utility giant, which had not been constrained from growing in its home market and had thus created a very strong home base from which to make foreign acquisitions.

As the acquisition was not really a contested affair, there were high hopes in the minds of some Powergen top executives that Eon might leave them with some strategic functions for UK/US development, under the banner of 'Eon Atlantic'. After all, they reasoned, Powergen managers had learnt a lot from the US acquisition and this could be useful to the parent in Germany.

This was tentatively proposed to headquarters in Germany, which had not at that time received regulatory approval and therefore remained silent on the subject. The Powergen top managers continued to remain hopeful that they would be more than division managers in a massive international enterprise. However, it progressively became apparent that Eon had no intention of delegating major strategic functions to a UK subsidiary, and hopes were dashed.

While we are on the topic of power utilities, the *Financial Times* of April 2002 reported:

> The independence of the remaining British-owned regional electricity supply companies, Scottish Power and Scottish & Southern, is under threat amid a wave of takeovers and mergers. The two companies are the only survivors of the 14 autonomous regional supply companies floated when the industry was privatised in the early 1990's.The most likely predators are Electricité de France (with a protected home market), Eon and TXU of the US – none of which have obtained the critical mass, in terms of the numbers of UK customers, they would like.

The article goes on to argue that both Scottish companies are likely targets, but also that they could merge, thus creating a UK supplier with real critical mass. Alas, the article concludes, Scottish Power, the larger potential partner, is under a considerable shadow with investors, following massive value destruction as the result of an active acquisition strategy, and hardly in a position to do the needful.

The history of UK utilities is a prime example of what happens when politicians and industrial managers come together. It was almost certainly not the intention of the politicians who dreamt up the particular form of privatization of the utilities that they would end up foreign owned. Nor presumably did they intend that the power generators would close the UK mining industry over a weekend, as nearly happened when they simultaneously decided to end their contracts. A public outcry stopped this, and the industry has been closed more slowly, which at least gave a little time for people and communities to prepare.

We are left with the feeling that these matters are better thought through and managed in at least some other countries. Ford Motor Company of the United States has been a major manufacturer in the United Kingdom for decades. When it decided to close vehicle production at Dagenham and move it to Germany, the effects on the local economy were serious. However, Ford intends to massively increase its production of engines on a site in the Dagenham area. The London *Evening Standard* of 20 March 2002 reports:

> But... Ford also recognised that simply upgrading its own production facilities and contributing to the construction of a supplier park would not be enough. To attract the more highly skilled workers it and its suppliers need, Ford realised it had to play its part in helping to improve not just the appearance of the plant and its surroundings, but also the quality of life of the people living nearby. It also has to keep retraining staff so that they can adapt as engine technology evolves. To achieve these objectives, it decided to play a part in the urban regeneration efforts going on around its engine plant as well as rebuild its facility to produce just diesels.

(Any big UK-owned companies producing diesel engines? We couldn't find them. Pity, engine design and manufacture is a modern, advanced industry.)

The article continues:

> This helps explain why, on top of the millions it is investing in the plant, the company is putting up a third of the £33 million needed for the creation of a Centre for Engineering and Manufacturing Excellence at Dagenham. The government and the London Development Agency are chipping in the rest. For this venture, the Ford name has already proved to be a magnet. Loughborough and Warwick Universities and the Cardiff Business School's Lean Enterprise Research Centre are partners in CEME. So too are tech titan Microsoft and the world's top maker of internet routers, Cisco Systems.

Assuming all this goes ahead, it is a splendid example of how a manufacturing venture can attract research, knowledge, cellular development of associated and 'spin-off' industries and the raising of the skills and value of a whole community. We are sure that there are examples of British-owned manufacturing companies doing the same, probably in the pharmaceuticals industry. But we couldn't find many. Names like IBM, Microsoft and Pfizer come much more easily to mind. Most UK-owned job creation seems to have been in leisure, retail and call centres. These developments, while very welcome, do not create the clusters of knowledge-based, highly paid skills that obviously attract foreign companies. It is almost certain that the massive productivity gap that separates the United Kingdom from other advanced economies will not be narrowed without many more examples of the Ford initiative.

There is no sign that most UK top managers, their investors or industry representative bodies are really prepared to do anything serious about it. As we have seen earlier in the book, their minds are likely to be on other, more immediate matters.

Thus the productivity gap in the United Kingdom between foreign-owned and British-owned manufacturers remains static. Let us say that again. The gap in productivity between UK- and foreign-owned manufacturers has not diminished over many years (Office for National Statistics, 2002). This seems to mean that British managers are not even capable of learning from the good practice on their doorsteps, and leave the cutting edge of productivity to the foreign companies such as Ford, IBM, Microsoft, Nissan and Honda – employing British workforces!

Another side effect of the propensity of UK companies to invest in mergers and acquisitions rather than business development has been to concentrate economic development in the south-east of England. The David Hume Institute, in its research on mergers and acquisitions, found that the headquarters functions of UK acquirers were almost always in the South-East, which has resulted in a progressive shift of power and decision-taking to that region.

Another contributory factor has been the decline of UK manufacturing, especially in physics- and chemistry-based industries. Many of these industries were concentrated in regions outside the South-East, leaving the bringing of skilled work in the North, the West and Scotland more and more to foreign companies. The regions continue their relative decline, as foreign investment is not yet happening at a sufficient rate to compensate for indigenous withdrawal.

To complete a rather dismal picture, science-, physics-, chemistry- and biology-based industries are major supporters of research in universities. As the base of R&D moves from the United Kingdom, it is incumbent on UK universities to find support from foreign companies, or, as has been done so brilliantly in Cambridge, to become industrial powerhouses themselves, spawning new small companies without much help from big UK companies or big investors.

'COCK-UPS', DISASTERS AND MANAGERIAL INCOMPETENCE

The British love a really good 'cock-up', especially one perpetrated by top bosses and politicians. They provide a wonderful opportunity for cheerful grumbling, head-shaking and plenty of good old 'I told you so'.

One of the authors has cheerfully supported a 'professional' football team that has not climbed out of obscurity, recurrent crisis and frequent incompetence in over 50 years! The real pleasure of watching this team play is the gloomy delight experienced by veteran spectators when players fall over the ball, pass to opponents and forget which goal they are supposed to be attacking. The spectators shout; they chant for the sacking of the manager and the board. But, just as in industry, managers are frequently sacked but the board sails serenely and incompetently on! It is just as well that the British are so cheerful about incompetence, because we appear to have much of it among our managers, politicians and financiers.

There now follows a list of apparently disparate events, occurrences, companies and other kinds of organization. Regard this as a quiz. What are the three vital missing ingredients that link all of the following?

- outsourcing maintenance in Railtrack;
- the West Coast main line;
- De Lorean cars;
- pensions mis-selling;
- Marconi;
- Enron;
- Tyco;
- the sudden death of the British mining industry;
- Boots;
- Thorn EMI;
- C&W;
- conversion of Nimrod aircraft to an early warning configuration;
- updating of Nimrod SAR aircraft;
- BT;
- Marks & Spencer;
- ICI;
- public–private partnerships;
- railway maintenance;
- the National Air Traffic Control System;
- Consignia;
- endowment insurance policies;
- digital TV and football;
- Invensys;
- the new Wembley Stadium;
- the demise of the British motor vehicle and motorcycle industries;
- Williams Holdings;
- Slater Walker;
- military tanks that seize up in desert conditions;
- Californian power supply;
- Vivendi;
- Scottish Power;
- the overall performance and cost of the railway system;
- the death of UK investment banking;
- London Underground;
- traffic congestion in the United Kingdom;

- British & Commonwealth;
- national examination boards;
- Redland;
- training of army attack helicopter pilots;
- the performance of the electricity utility 24–7 after the gales of late 2002;
- and, possibly to come, Vodafone, GSK, BAE Systems, etc.

So, have you got it? What is missing is:

- simple, basic attention to the fundamentals of managing and administering well;
- strategic intelligence that links an understanding of the environment and the 'business' with a practical appraisal of what is possible and an acute sense of what the organization can do;
- a steady, long-term approach to investment.

All the examples got into trouble of one sort or another, at one time or another, because they neglected, forgot or were ignorant of the fundamentals of strategic and operational management. One or two, especially the US examples, have the added spice of being connected with impropriety or fraud. In all the cases mentioned, a company or project failed, did not achieve its stated objectives, destroyed large amounts of value or let customers down, or 'the law of unintended outcomes' came into play.

Of particular concern in the United Kingdom is the fact that the interface between government and private industry is a place where failures have become almost commonplace. It would seem that both private and public sectors need to 'up their game' when it comes to the basics of strategic and operational management.

Incidentally, we have thrown in a few foreign examples just to prove that these forms of incompetence happen elsewhere as well. Vivendi is an excellent example of an enterprise getting well beyond itself, led by a reportedly egocentric character, and falling precipitately from grace when the acquisition music stopped.

One journalist who has been writing on the topic of managerial incompetence with a refreshing consistency is Simon Caulkin of the *Observer*. In one article he quotes the final report of the Council for Excellence in Management and Leadership (2002). To paraphrase the report, it said that practical management and leadership skills are in short supply from top to bottom of organizations – and that the educational system, including business schools, are doing little to engender those skills.

What Caulkin does not mention in this article, but has touched on in others, is what the blockages to progress in upping basic management skills are. He mentions an educational system that places excessive emphasis on theory and purely intellectual, as opposed to practical and social, skills, and he is right to do this.

He also touches on a totally poisonous tendency, very strongly exhibited in the United Kingdom by politicians, top managers and the financial community alike, to expect (and promise) 'quick fixes', rapid action, decisive, high and stretching targets without any explanation of how they will be attained. This compression of timescales, allied to a complete ignorance of the human and organizational complexities of managing processes of improvement, is behind many of the failures that we have mentioned above.

Politicians and the financial markets *need* quick results, decisive action, stretching targets and rapid delivery. It is not in their interests as things stand to question the way they and the press, so much more powerful in the United Kingdom than in most countries, generally reinforce the tendency to foreshorten, oversimplify and personalize everything. The general public are therefore brainwashed into expecting miracles and expect to have heads on plates when these do not materialize quickly.

Shareholders and pension fund trustees want very high performance, above the average, as an 'average'. Investors in the markets press managers to ever-higher returns and punish those who fail to deliver to their expectations year in, year out. And managers, mindful of their careers and wealth, seek to impress by doing whatever is necessary to please, even if the delivery is unsustainable. Of course, many will take short cuts to superior performance in the knowledge that fame and fortune are short-term phenomena, and they may not be there when the consequences become apparent.

None of the above encourages the development of deep skills of systematic leadership and execution. It should by now be clear that this will not be achieved when there is a whole system, including managers, investors, bankers, brokers, politicians and business schools, that has nothing to gain and a hell of a lot to lose by changing matters. At best there may be lip service or 'Yes, but' responses, but unless there are much more fundamental changes to the incentives and sanctions that will pull and push change, Mr Caulkin will be writing about the same topics in 10 years and reporting nothing but the fact that we have slipped still further.

HUMAN AND SOCIAL EFFECTS

What, then, of the effects of the management–markets nexus for employees at large, the 'lions' upon whom the future of industry depends?

Observers of voting trends speak of a great deal of cynicism and the distrust of an ever-wider grouping of people and institutions in public life. Banks, the financial services industry, journalists and politicians are regarded with a mixture of distrust and suspicion by the general public. Such scepticism may be healthy, for the fact is that it is absolutely and objectively right. Members of each of the above have been caught out indulging in deception, cheating, incompetence, fraud or misleading 'spin'.

So, what of the 'fat cats' in management and the City? It would be surprising if, given the publicity of the past years, but especially more recently, the public regard for our subjects in top management and the financial markets was any better than for the other objects of suspicion.

What kinds of effects do the behaviours of top managers and, through them, the markets have on employees and 'the public'? Here are some.

Distorted rewards and huge differentials

We have already seen that the total cash earnings of CEOs of the biggest companies are on average more than 68 times those of the ordinary employee.

Remember that top compensation packages contain the following:

- Annual salary plus annual bonus – in the range of £700,000 to more than £2,000,000.
- Long-term bonus plan, which can pay out up to 100 per cent of base salary.
- Share options with an initial value in the range of 4–10 times base pay.
- Contributions to a pension plan. In the case of FTSE 100 CEOs we are speaking of funds of several million pounds to fund pensions amounting to two-thirds of final pay. (The company's contribution to the pension of Lord Browne of BP was £2.4 million in 2001; the value accrued to pay his pension on retirement of £860,000 was reported to be £12.8 million – *Observer* Business section, 18 May 2003.)
- Sundry perks ranging from the standard car and chauffeur to the much more exotic, in the form of travel and accommodation, health, and entertainment, much of which is difficult to access publicly.

For the enlightenment of employees who may have been made redundant or lost a job for other reasons, things are not all that bad either if a top executive should unfortunately happen to lose his or her job. In 2001, seven directors of FTSE companies received more than £1,000,000 as 'golden goodbyes'. The star turn was Ken Berry, the ex-CEO of EMI, whose terminal package amounted to £6,076,200.

For the average employee, all of this is from another planet, and something altogether beyond their influence. They have to make do with a weekly or monthly wage or salary and rapidly diminishing pension entitlements.

We are not going to enter the lists shouting how 'unfair' all of this is, but we would comment that such differentials do tend to cause a huge psychological gap to develop between the top and the bulk of employees. Perhaps top managements ought to be encouraged to explain to their colleagues – the employees whom they lead – the exact details of the pay and perks they receive, and account for what they have done to merit them.

Increasingly 'absent' bosses

We have seen how top managers have to spend much time transacting and communicating with the financial markets and working with advisers who will help them to get their message across. We have also seen what happens when a CEO, in this case Sir Philip Watts, the chairman of Shell, is felt to be taking investors too lightly. We have seen that many managers can find themselves taking the knife to their own businesses or organizations in order to satisfy investors that they are being decisive.

We have seen that top executives' wealth is increasingly tied to the financial markets measures of corporate performance, and less and less to any more qualitative assessment of how well they lead their organizations. Only very occasionally might today's top managers feel that they are accountable in any real way to the people whom they are supposed to lead. Perhaps this tendency will cause top managers to be more often surprised by the behaviour and reactions of staff, as was Rod Eddington, CEO of British Airways, when the airline was nearly brought down by a walkout of check-in staff at Heathrow Airport.

All this is tending in many cases to distance top managers from the organizations they lead, without, incidentally, any noticeable increase in empowerment of middle managers to fill the leadership vacuum left by their superiors. The trend seems to be shaping the psychology and skill sets of top managers. Perforce, they need to focus on numbers and analytical presentation rather than the basic human skills of leading people. Thus it is the case, both in our experience and according to the Council for Excellence in Management, that many very successful top executives do not have the human management skills that we, the authors, might have expected from a junior supervisor. (The Council is too polite to put it that way!) As John Seddon of Vanguard Consulting so eloquently put it, 'Most [top] managers sit in management "factories" insulated from the real work of the organization and only dealing with abstract data. Leadership is about getting back in touch with the work.' Quite so, but right now this is unlikely to generate millions of pounds in pay, so why should managers bother?

Employee stress and insecurity

UK workers put in more time, less productively, with less time off, than most of their continental European counterparts. They are supported by less capital equipment. At the same time, they generally enjoy less job security than in days gone by. Now, many are finding that their retirement benefits are being reduced by top managers under great pressure from investors to produce uniformly high returns to maintain 'shareholder value'. It is reported by survey after survey that all this is at last beginning to take its toll on a generally tolerant and hardworking workforce. Militancy is again on the increase, family life is said to be suffering and stress is increasing. And now the risks of providing retirement benefits are being passed from companies to individuals. This does not seem to be a very positive set of circumstances, combining as it does, in many British-owned companies at least, underinvestment, declining benefits and overwork. It is hard to keep the word 'exploitation' at bay.

TO SUM UP...

Readers, we have laid out our case before you. We contend that the symbiotic relationships that have developed in recent years between top managers and the financial markets are now causing active damage to the underlying performance and long-term prospects of UK-owned companies, especially those in industries that require consistent strategies and investment.

The 'system' that we have described presses very hard indeed for high performance and frequently appears, on the surface, to achieve it. But too often such 'performance' is achieved at the cost of sustainable, long-term success and the blatant exploitation of employees and customers. In other words, the interests of vital stakeholders are being ignored by a closed 'system' that seeks to reward insiders at the expense of wider society.

This is not a sustainable position. Something must break, and we hope that we have demonstrated that serious cracks are beginning to appear. In fact, it is almost axiomatic that every large UK company will be destroyed or seriously weakened by the financial markets in their current shape, if one allows a sufficiently long time span.

The markets will punish companies that have destroyed value by being too active. They will brief and act against managements whom they regard as under-active and therefore 'boring', encouraging them to take what is often inappropriate action. Companies that set very high performance targets and slip from their growth trajectory will be severely downgraded, as will companies that miss assumed 'promises' to the markets.

In fact, such is the hyperactive, fickle and inconsistent behaviour of investors, always looking for some 'action' or an angle that will give them short-term advantage, that the only companies that are likely to be relatively safe from the predations of investors are those that are protected by multinational ownership, like Unilever and Shell – or, of course, the foreign companies that are progressively buying British industry. With the weakening of the indigenous industrial base is likely to come an increasingly 'skewed' economy, overly dependent on consumer spending and financial and leisure services, with recurring and worsening balance of payments problems, such as the one we are beginning to perceive in 2003.

Last, but by no means least, this progressive loss of competitiveness and international positions in industries driven by innovation, technology and advanced knowledge could have serious long-term political effects. It is these industries that support superior wealth creation and a developed economy.

Underlying the debate about the nature of the United Kingdom's relationships with Europe on the one hand and the United States on the other, is the notion that the United Kingdom could act with a degree of independence and become a vital bridge between these two great sources of power. The loss of the only real source of economic independence – a powerful, indigenous industrial and commercial base, capable of leading the world in important and growing industries – such as is currently happening, can only constrain the United Kingdom's scope to make independently minded political decisions. If current trends continue, there will be two choices only: close alignment with the European Union or close alignment with the United States, because the United Kingdom will have become highly dependent on them for national wealth creation. Re-establishing a stronger economic base has to be a key item in the debates about national identity and the United Kingdom's role in the world.

So there you have the three Propositions. Financial markets are the dominant influence on management tenure, so managers have adjusted their behaviour to please the markets. Increasingly symbiotic relationships have developed, which have served to disenfranchise other stakeholders (including the real risk-takers). Furthermore, these relationships and the resultant behaviours are having corrosive long-term effects on the performance and competitiveness of UK quoted companies.

If we have convinced you, you must agree that the outlook for larger UK-owned enterprises, especially those in the more intelligent, knowledge-driven and technology-driven sectors of the economy, is pretty bleak unless some radical interventions are made to bring the destructive behaviour to a halt and create a more supportive environment for innovation and sustainable performance.

Interlude: 'time out' for reflection

About two-thirds of the way through writing this book, we decided to check out some of our conclusions with a group of people who had been very helpful during the research, so we invited them to lunch. The experience in the group was quite mixed: participants included a business school professor, a non-executive director of a large public company, a strategy consultant, a senior executive search consultant, an investor relations director, a finance director, and a business psychologist who specializes in assessing top managers and benchmarking large companies' managements against their competitors. As people left at the end of the lunch, we were left with very mixed feelings ranging from excitement to apprehension. The time had come to pause and reflect about where our researches and writing had taken us.

Our first reflection was that this book and its conclusions will not be popular in several quarters. It could be taken as critical of their values and actions by:

- many 'players' in the financial markets who earn a very substantial living out of the way matters are currently arranged;
- the top management 'great and good': non-executive directors who might feel that we are accusing them of supporting the general status quo and sometimes being asleep on the bridge;
- some current CEOs and other top managers who could feel that we are criticizing the fruits of their labours and their substantial rewards;
- many business academics, who might feel that we are indirectly accusing them of misleading their pupils into believing that numbers and analysis are somehow what management is about;
- business journalists, some of whom might come away with the impression that we see their work as superficial and sensation-seeking.

There is no doubt that a book of this nature is going to attract criticism, and we therefore took the feedback very seriously and would like to share some key questions asked by our guests.

First, the general feeling of the group was that the central precepts of the book were sufficiently valid to make a valuable contribution to the debate about the roots of some of the problems in UK and Anglo-Saxon capitalism. However, there was much debate among the group. In the end, they decided that they could give us the most help by rehearsing some of the questions and criticisms that we might encounter from a management and City audience. Here are some of the points and questions that our lunch guests raised:

1. Free capital markets may have their flaws, but they are by far the most effective mechanisms for ensuring that investment resources are distributed to the strongest enterprises, and promote efficiency. Mild comments about the need to regulate markets would be greeted from some quarters by cries of 'bureaucratic interference'. One of our colleagues advanced the argument that if markets do cause distortions and some destruction, this is a small price to pay for a generally very efficient system, and anyhow, they would always self-adjust in time without interference.
2. Another school might advance the view that the current arrangements are one step on the road towards the discovery of an all-embracing set of metrics. When discovered, these would finally connect the interests and needs of all stakeholders and link the short term with the long term. In other words, while the notion that 'maximizing shareholder value is perfectly in the interest of all stakeholders' seems not to have worked out as planned, it simply means that we have not yet found the right metrics for measuring value creation.
3. We would be strongly challenged to justify our assumed criticism that all is not well with the current arrangements in management and the markets. The challenge would take the form of demands for us to prove:
   - That the current state of things is not a thousand times better than the 'old days' when the reins of power rested in the hands of bureaucratic and often incompetent managers, and shareholders did not get a look in.
   - That we are not simply witnessing one of many cycles in which power swings from one stakeholder interest to another. In time, will our preoccupation with top managers and markets not be superseded by a new set of problem dynamics?
4. Another argument would be that we are quite wrong to single out the UK financial markets and British top managers because:
   - the world is completely global, and global capitalism is far more powerful than the interests of one small economy; or
   - every country has its particular problems, and those in the United Kingdom are either the same as everybody else's or quite different and not as bad as those of Germany, France, etc.

   The suggestion that we should rewrite the book as a fully fledged international comparison was rapidly squashed by the authors as interesting but too time-consuming, given the publisher's deadlines!
5. Interestingly, nobody present seemed to think that we were paranoid, or fantasizing about the relationships between managers and markets. Nor

did anybody seem to believe that these relationships are unimportant in shaping behaviour. There were, however, some votes for the proposition that any attempts to modify the effects of the relationships could do more harm than good, and support for the view that governmental or quasi-governmental regulation or interference is liable to be bureaucratic, crass and ineffectual.

6. Last, but not least, our friends and colleagues warned us against appearing to be purely negative, indulging in orgies of 'Ain't it all bleedin' awful' without making practical suggestions about how to make matters better. They also counselled that we should remain quite clear in our focus and not attempt to aim at too many targets at once.

Stimulated by the discussion and challenge, we reviewed where we are 'coming from' with regard to some of the fundamental points made by our friends. We have picked out two main points:

- about markets and regulation;
- about the notion that 'what comes around, goes around' and there is nothing much that can be done about cycles of change in the relationships between the stakeholders in the economy.

MARKETS

We, like our friends, believe strongly in the efficacy of markets and the competition for resources and capital to fund industry and commerce. Effective markets tend to be information rich and usually can function more intelligently in allocating resources and responding to needs than governments and bureaucrats. We know this. Look at the Soviet Union and what happened to centrally planned economies, including the United Kingdom, in the late 1960s and early 1970s.

However, we also believe that the ideal of perfect markets, in which all the players behave rationally in line with the availability of perfect information, is simply that: an ideal. It ignores the fact that there will never be perfect information and it rather naïvely ignores the fact that human beings can be emotional, greedy and stupid. In particular, it glosses over the fact that the behaviour of human herds can be much more extreme than that of individuals. Furthermore, although markets may be good at reflecting individual choice, some very necessary things are beyond the scope of individual choice. By this we mean the 'common' and 'non-monetary' needs such as an efficient public transport system and a clean environment. We therefore believe that markets must be regulated by a strong framework of law and enforced rules, as well as self-restraint by the market animators, if they are to function and not descend to mob rule, the survival of the most dishonest, and rampant corruption and greed.

Fantasy? Not really. Look what has happened in a relatively well-regulated market in the United States over the past few years. We believe that the champions of liberty and free markets in the United States will now take vigorous regulatory action to rectify loopholes and imperfections and bring 'villains' to book. In the United Kingdom, however, where the scandals appear to be not fraud but, rather, rampant destruction of value and companies, nothing very much is happening.

Regulation has several valuable roles to play, according to Philip Augar (2001). He contends that 'the chosen system of regulation [in the 1980s] was often criticised for being too cumbersome, but few realised that the regime was not rigorous enough. One of the few was Sir John Nott.' Nott wrote, 'In my view, the City was unwise to promote the concept of self regulation. The Bank of England was even more unwise to promote it. When the next bear market comes along there are going to be firms going bust. Politically, no one is going to distinguish between bankruptcy and fraud.' This was written in the late 1980s. It has not needed a bear market since then to bring about a great deal of corporate failure, and we have probably not yet seen the worst!

Augar concludes:

> The model for the legal authority that Nott had in mind was the SEC in New York. It was adequately staffed, had wide reaching powers and compelled brokers to follow high professional standards of control. In turn, this instilled a degree of professionalism into the management which the laissez-faire system of self-regulation followed in London failed to encourage.

In the light of subsequent events, even the SEC was not strong enough. Watch for the next US moves to strengthen the constraints on unfettered market forces.

Below the levels of law and statutory regulations, there are rules and codes that can provide guidance to market insiders and outsiders alike as to what conduct is regarded as acceptable. And beyond all this, governments and regulatory bodies can provide a range of incentives and checks that will 'nudge' the behaviour and actions of players in the market in the right directions. We will attempt to suggest a range of such actions in the final chapter.

Maybe a metaphor might be helpful. We see the capital market mechanism as being rather like a complex, highly tuned and powerful engine. If properly harnessed, controlled and directed, it can produce fantastic performances from the vehicle that it is powering. However, if it is allowed to get out of control it can cause huge damage, eventually oscillating violently and destroying the vehicle itself.

We believe that very significant and permanent modifications are needed to the whole system that is centred around the financial markets and the enterprises that they fund. We know that bringing about change will be extraordinarily difficult and that every form of conceivable obstacle will be put in the way of effective action. The ultimate threat, and one that would certainly cause timid UK governments to shrink away from action, is that of removing operations from the London market to another place, where players will have less interference in doing whatever they like. Therefore, it is likely that international action will also be necessary.

The consequences of not acting will, we believe, be much worse than the threats of possible retribution. The markets in their current form and the managers that they dominate are consuming and destroying the indigenous industrial base and the skills and enterprise culture that supports it. This process is, we believe, not simply a temporary manifestation of boom times, but a long-term corrosive process. To make matters worse, sufficient powerful people in both management and the markets benefit so richly from the way things are currently set up that they and their supporters are not going to relinquish their privileges without vigorous resistance.

So, we reaffirm our belief in the market mechanism as by far the best devised for funding investment in private-sector competitive enterprises. But such a belief should not be naïve or carried to ridiculous purist extremes. There is not one 'perfect' model for a market. There are many variations on a market economy, ranging from Sweden to the United States. The United Kingdom's version is different in many ways from either of those.

Markets are vulnerable to being distorted by many factors, not the least of which is the self-interest and greed of those who animate them. We want markets that are healthy and constructive contributors to the economic and civil societies that surround them. To return to our metaphor, we want the engine to provide the smoothest possible power and performance, not shake the vehicle to bits.

'WHAT GOES ROUND COMES ROUND': CYCLES OF CHANGE

The second point is that the dysfunctional manifestations of the management–markets relationship simply represent a phase in a cycle that is much more virtuous than those preceding it. To crudely paraphrase the argument, 'It may not be perfect now, but by God, it's a damned sight better than what went before. So don't mess with the current arrangements. You could make things worse.'

There is, we think, some power in this argument. But it is not, in our view, valid to move on and claim that the current cycle is a result of mysterious forces beyond the power of humankind to understand or influence. The overall arrangements in the current international capital markets have arisen from a great deal of human intervention and learning following the Great Depression, when markets went mad and for a time governments made matters infinitely worse. It may be worth placing our deliberations into some kind of historical context, however.

We have experienced within living memory at least three different 'cycles' in the distribution and use of power between the various stakeholders in UK industry and commerce. The United Kingdom has, to the detriment of industrial performance, probably seen more than most developed Western economies.

The early 20th century

From the early part of the 20th century until the Second World War, the United Kingdom was still experiencing the dying glow of empire. Markets were relatively captive, and 'British was best'.

Inside industry the scenario was like the British class system writ large. Managers wielded great power, and that power was only weakly tempered by shareholders and occasionally by labour militancy. Where the system worked well, it brought about consistency of leadership and dedication to companies. Unfortunately, in many cases the 'system' bred a narrow-minded complacency that ignored or discounted the progress that was being made in the rest of the developed world.

From 1945 to the 1980s

The post-war period up to the early 1980s saw a radical shift in power from the managerial class to the state. For quite significant periods from the 1940s to the 1970s, many previously private enterprises were nationalized. From time to time, attempts were made to make industry conform to a kind of bureaucratic model. Think of the various pay freezes for the higher paid, and government attempts to impose 'planning agreements' on large companies.

Along with attempts to introduce central planning and direction to the economy, the power of large industry and craft-based trade unions burgeoned, to the point that union leaders could bring down governments.

The Thatcher revolution

The reaction to the excesses of 'statism' was marked and radical. Driven forward by Margaret Thatcher and given intellectual octane by Sir Keith Joseph and many academic monetarists and free-marketeers, the trappings of state and public enterprise were demolished with vigour and speed. The era of self-regulated, 'free' markets was ushered in and regulation and all forms of 'bureaucratic' constraint were derided.

It was in this relatively recent period that the fervent belief emerged in the efficacy of 'market forces' as the panacea for all maladies. In relation to the functioning and regulation of the financial markets, this is still where we in the United Kingdom are, to a rather greater extent than even the United States, where regulation of the markets has been rather tighter.

The 'Third Way'

For a short time, a different philosophy emerged timidly into the limelight, only to disappear apparently without trace at the first signs of opposition. We speak, of course, of the so-called Third Way, the brainchild of Tony Blair, Bill Clinton and various academics and journalists.

The point of this outbreak of amateur economic and political history is to:

- Point out that each of the phases or cycles that we have mentioned whatever its virtues, has been enormously destructive of the indigenous industrial and commercial base. Companies and whole industries failed because their products and services were simply not competitive on an international stage. Further failures and decay occurred as a result of inefficiency, high costs and poor quality. And then the sudden, wrenching plunge into a free market, 'weak to the wall' phase, certainly caused many industries and enterprises to do just that, go to the wall, without any real chance to anticipate or prepare for radical change.
- Raise a flag for market forces and to opine that the system that we have now does not need to be swept away and be replaced by a radical antidote. Almost uniquely among developed Western economies, the United Kingdom has experienced radical swings and shifts in industrial strategy and been lumbered with a powerful class system that should have no place in the world of work. The fact that we have a relatively healthy economy is in large measure due to the influx of foreign capital and know-how, and the inherent excellence of British staff. This is very good, but is not the final answer. What we should now do is devote all our attentions to *making the current arrangements work better*.

To our minds, this means – to paraphrase one of our lunchtime contributors – finding better ways of creating sustainable value in a 'customer-, organization- and people-friendly manner'. As our friend said, this will, among other things, mean developing more effective metrics to measure long-term performance and prevent short-termism. However, unlike our friend, we do not believe that simply finding the magic value metrics will cause much change.

There are three main angles of attack to making real, sustainable improvements:

1. The first dimension to work on is Time. We must cause all constituents to lengthen their timescales dramatically. Then it can also be recognized that all businesses, no matter how well managed, will have good periods and weaker periods. Lengthening timescales will cause observers and investors to recognize good performance or underperformance as a process and not a series of isolated events.
2. Linked to Time, we must educate players and commentators alike to recognize the reality of Sequence and Process. If we had our way, it would be made a serious offence to:
   - ascribe the achievement of complex, long-term tasks to one man or woman;
   - lionize individuals and not teams or organizations;
   - demand instant solutions to complex tasks or processes, or superficially attractive 'short cuts' to achieving sustainable performance or change;
   - demand high performance without understanding or taking responsibility for specifying how that performance will be achieved;
   - be unable to describe, in detail, the differences between building a strong, sustainable enterprise, and 'empire-building'.
3. Then we need to recognize that enterprise, innovation, high quality and sustainable performance need consistent investment and intelligent *nurturance,* and not impatience, stop–start spending, endless new and disconnected 'initiatives', and frequent pulling of the plant up by the roots to see how it is doing.

If, by sensible and determined incentives and appropriate intervention, we can shift the current system of speculation in industry and move it significantly towards the Buffett or Keynesian models of investment, the future could be very bright. But there is much to be done, and, as we have seen, many obstacles and resistances to overcome.

12

So, where *do* we go from here?

We have seen how the share price/City popularity focus of management can, and does, destroy both shareholder value and the health of the underlying enterprises. We have seen the dramatic, damaging consequences through our case study of Redland plc. We have seen how good investment practices and good management practice can benefit all interests.

Unfortunately, 'good' examples are the exception rather than the rule in investment management by City institutions, whose preference for management by transaction means that few industrialists are allowed the time for more enterprise-sustaining strategies. In fact, we will go further. We believe that the dynamics of the relationships between top management and the financial markets has reached the point of such malign momentum that great damage has already been done to that sector of the economy sustained by larger companies. If the current situation does not change, even greater damage will be inevitable. We further believe that the interests and actions of the key players involved are no longer aligned to the wider interests of the other stakeholders in industry and commerce, or society more broadly.

We are convinced that the market players and management are deeply involved in serving their own interests and are not really susceptible to outside influences. Thus we are faced with a situation where many top managers are richly rewarded for being in thrall to the markets, and the major players in the markets are able to rake off enormous rewards at the expense of the other stakeholders in the economy.

All this is strongly supported by many elements in the popular financial press, acting as cheerleaders for frantic activism perpetrated by charismatic heroes who can rapidly turn into villains, and a highly animated and somewhat vengeful horde inaccurately known as 'shareholders'.

The central purpose of the financial markets – to channel the wealth of millions in order to sustain a long-term value-creating industrial economy – has been to a great extent hijacked by the selfish interests of an insulated, self-serving system. To cap it all, the financial services industry has been a sink of malpractice on both sides of the Atlantic, its worst excesses being reserved for its hapless customers. As a senior investment banker put it, 'At the heart of your book lie two issues: leadership and morality. Once upon a time, business leaders felt a strong sense of responsibility towards the companies and people that they led and investors and bankers developed strong and lasting relationships with managers, getting to know them and their businesses well. In the 1980s and 1990s, moral behaviour has been overtaken by financial interest, and relationships have been replaced by transactional associations.'

This system has proved extremely resistant to regulation or change. Successions of UK governments have shied away from taking a strong reforming lead, preferring to hand the responsibility to others, such as 'shareholders', or by commissioning committees to report on narrowly focused single issues.

In short, the 'system' is presently beyond the control of any forces representing the interests of 'society'.

Although this system is by no means confined to the United Kingdom, the United Kingdom is more vulnerable than most other developed economies, as the power and size of the financial markets compared to the industrial sector is far greater. In the United States, France and Germany, for example, not only is the relative size of the industrial economies compared to the financial markets far greater, but also the proportion of equity financing is far less than that in Britain.

There is a real paradox at the centre of the problem that we face. It should be the case, as many commentators have pointed out, that the London financial market is a jewel in the national economic crown. Instead, the situation might be more accurately characterized as that of a powerful animal which, if properly harnessed and directed, could pull the carriage of industry fast and tirelessly, but which has become malign, has broken out of its traces and is smashing the carriage and trampling its occupants. Surrounding the scene of destruction is an excited crowd waiting to carry off the more valuable parts of the carriage and pick the corpses of the occupants clean. And further off are the spectators of Fourth Estate, reporting the whole affair as some kind of exciting game.

So, where *do* we go from here?

It is tempting to take a broad and lofty perspective and propose grandiose strategies for sweeping change that will have no chance of leaving the hangar, still less fly. So, to keep the debate on track, we will put a few stakes in the ground.

STAKES IN THE GROUND

1. We go right back to the start of this book: we said in the Introduction that the main goal of society should be to strive to ensure the greatest well-being of its members as a whole. Industry and commerce sit at the core of any society's wealth, and are vital to its well-being. It is therefore appropriate for a society to take an interest in the complex matter of the distribution of wealth and what should be done about abuses.
2. We have a strong belief in capitalism as the central theme of economic management. Free competition and market forces are the best way of ensuring that companies function efficiently and consumers have choice.

However, is it manifestly clear that allowing market forces to determine all outcomes has severe limitations. In some circumstances other arrangements need to be made.

3. The stock market can provide by far the most effective way of allocating capital between competing enterprises. However, at present the basis of making investment decisions is at odds with the needs of many potentially successful enterprises.

   It is also, more often than not, at odds with the attainment of long-term sustainable returns. On the assumption that the larger the number of stocks held, the less should be the risks, and the more stocks traded, the greater the returns, it should be the case that widely diversified, very active managers will outperform the market by the biggest margins. In fact, the opposite is the case. An analysis of 3,000 of the most active US funds, holding on average shares in more than 250 companies, showed that over a 10-year period, only 63 beat the market. Over the same time frame, 808 out of 3,000 funds holding on average 15 stocks beat the market.
4. We have demonstrated that thoughtful management, closely aligned to the underlying business, is most likely to perform well in the long run.
5. The current management–market system does not encourage or support the development of long-term sustainable industry and commerce. We therefore need to modify it to make it worthwhile for the key players to make long-term, business-sustaining decisions and to avoid a short-term, knee-jerk, transaction-driven approach. Transactions have to be a weapon in the armoury, but undertaken only when they are demonstrably the best route for the long-term viability of the enterprise.

   The key players whose interests need to be influenced are the *fund managers*, who exercise power as a proxy for the real, risk-taking investors, and *top management*, who make the key business decisions.
6. Self-regulation alone will not achieve the desired long-term outcomes. It has already resulted in behaviour that destroys value in the short term and businesses in the long term. Improving the system will require a mixture of incentives, legislation, regulation and codes of practice – all supported by a tax system that rewards desirable behaviour.

ADJUSTING THE BALANCE

So, now that we have set out our stall, what needs to be done to swing the balance of interest back in favour of nurturing and supporting enterprises and, in the long term, sustainable economic benefit?

This is a large, complex and intimidating question. Whatever solutions are proposed will undoubtedly be challenged, both by those with vested interests in resisting change and by those who would rather see different outcomes.

It is always best when starting out on any change programme to have some idea of where you are headed. We have the following underlying aims:

1. to create a more balanced economy, with equal attention being paid both to the development of enterprises requiring consistently high investment in advanced knowledge and technology, innovation and creativity, and to service and leisure-based industries;

2. to encourage higher performance and productivity on the part of indigenously owned enterprises, and higher investment in the processes, systems and capital equipment required to support the development of superior value creation;
3. to develop over time management and investment cultures that interact and collaborate to nurture and sustain high-performing enterprises;
4. to foster the development of an ample supply of top managers with deep business and organization-building skills, and a high-knowledge/high-skill, highly rewarded workforce, up to the standards of the most advanced economies.

There is no one solution that will suit all interests, and probably no perfect solution that will achieve all the desired outcomes. So, rather than seeking a rigid answer, let's just consider what the world might look like if our society could marshal the will to declare the success of the industrial economy to be more important than narrow vested interests.

We have already indicated that the key behaviour changes need to come from institutional investors and management. We will now consider each in turn.

A NEW ENVIRONMENT FOR INVESTMENT

We looked at the various investment types in a previous chapter. However, let's remind ourselves briefly of the main investment practices, remembering that we are concerned in the main with equity investors, a slender slice of the overall financial markets.

Active investment management

Active investment managers seek to generate returns greater than those on a specified index – for example, for UK companies, the All Share, the Smaller Companies or the UK Growth indices. They spread risk by holding a wide portfolio of shares and theoretically generate superior performance by buying stocks predicted to gain short- to medium-term value.

Generally speaking, active managers' ability to study companies in depth is restricted because of their portfolio spread, and it is true to say that as a breed they have little sense of responsibility towards the companies whose shares they buy and sell. What matters to them is near-term share price movements. If a share is felt to be low relative to its short-term prospects, buy. When it appreciates in value, sell.

We have already seen that, despite all this activity, actual index outperformance is low. In the United States, fewer than 10 per cent outperformed the index in 1999.

Index-tracking investment

Index-tracking investment has increased in popularity over the past decade or so. Index trackers simply invest in a range of shares designed to profile the shape of the whole stock market or whatever comprises their chosen index. The performance of an index tracker fund should closely follow the performance of the underlying index. Index tracker funds have no loyalty or real responsibility whatsoever for the companies in the market; they simply invest in a range of shares that simulate the target index.

They do, however, increase market volatility. For example, if a large company gets larger by a merger and increases its size relative to the market, index tracker funds will sell shares in other companies to 'make up their weight' in the shares of the big company. Thus the shares of other companies may be quite actively traded, regardless of their underlying performance or prospects.

As we have said previously, equity investors comprise only a small slice of the market. The bulk of activity is carried on by traders in options and warrants, forwards and futures, currencies and interest rates, packages and repackages of the myriad of instruments available. However, we confine our interest to equity investors as these are the most influential when it comes to management behaviour.

In fact, all the above investment activity could be categorized as speculation on market movements, rather than investment in the future of enterprises.

In contrast, we have also seen another kind of investor, less publicized than the others, characterized by Warren Buffett, who, with his partner Charlie Munger, has outperformed most other investors in a most spectacular fashion ever since 1965. In the 35 years to 2000 these two and their company, Berkshire Hathaway, have outperformed the US S&P 500 index in 31 of those years!

Remember Buffett's 'rules'? He spends a lot of time understanding his investments, both financially and managerially. He concentrates his investments on outstanding companies run by strong management. He thinks long term: 5 to 10 years is an average horizon. He limits the number of companies he invests in. He is not thrown by volatility.

Speculating on why there are not more investors of this kind, Robert G Hagstrom in his book *The Essential Buffett* (2001) postulates that the reasons are complex and multifold. Among them is the fact that the vast majority of institutional investors are deeply wedded to a totally different philosophy, supported by the portfolio theory (spread risk to reduce risk) and a copious underpinning of other theories and analytical 'tricks'. Furthermore, the pressure to perform relative to each other tends to push them towards replicating behaviour rather than breakaway originality.

So, what objectives should we have for investors?

Objectives for changes in investor behaviour

1. To encourage investors' commitment to supporting the long-term success of the enterprises in which they invest their clients' money, as this not only will be the best way of protecting and increasing their wealth and that of their clients, but is also the most economically and socially responsible behaviour.
2. To shift support from the 'do it to' macho manager towards leaders committed to long-term competitive behaviour through operational excellence rather than short-term transactions.
3. To foster the education of the ultimate shareholders in the range of investment strategies that they could support, and the consequences for enterprises and the wider economy of various investment strategies and behaviours.
4. To stimulate more informed discussion and wider knowledge of the 'arrangements' that support industry and enterprise, so that 'society' can exercise more influence over the behaviours of the markets and management.

We would not seek to outlaw or prevent current investment practice. In a free economy, investors, market-makers and speculators should be free to behave, within reason, as their inclination dictates. However, given our social and industrial objectives, there is no reason why the more damaging practices should be carried out in the same favourable environment as the more nurturing ones.

Our new environment for investment would therefore seek to positively encourage investors to accept a degree of responsibility for the success of the companies in which they invest. Given the demonstrably massive effects that institutional investors have on companies, and especially bigger companies, there is a very strong case to be made for the fact that power should not be exercised without responsibility.

GLOBALIZATION AND REGULATION

Many will argue that the capital markets are global, so change can take place only within a global context. We would say yes and no. It is true that capital markets are global and that money is able to move freely between developed and relatively deregulated economies. However, capital markets continue to be regulated by and large on a national basis. There are very few truly international arrangements. The International Monetary Fund, the World Bank and the Bank for International Settlements (BIS) arrangements to ensure adequate capitalization of banks are the ones that spring easily to mind.

In any case, we would argue that the ability of the authorities to come together to achieve the changes needed on a global scale is next to zero. Just witness the time already spent on just two projects requiring cross-national co-operation: the attempt to update the BIS rules and the efforts to negotiate a European takeover code! And these two are relatively straightforward. Furthermore, if someone as influential as George Soros cannot persuade the international community that it is time to change (as he attempted to specifically during the Russian debt crisis and subsequently through books, as described in *The Crisis of Global Capitalism* (Soros, 1998)), then what hope do we have? So we will concentrate on what we could possibly do in the United Kingdom.

The argument that capital will simply flee from a 'non-competitive' (ie more restrictively regulated) economy holds true only to a certain extent. There are investment restrictions on the way that funds can use their money – some regulatory, others voluntary – as part of the fund's stated exposure profile. The markets are not wholly 'perfect'.

Then there is the drive for deregulation, the argument that regulation is bad in itself and our overall target should be to minimize governmental interference and let the markets get on with the serious business of making money. Here we will turn to Adair Turner, who reflected in *Just Capital: The liberal economy* (2001) that deregulation has become a dogma rather than a tool with which to achieve desired ends. He went on later in the book to suggest that governments need to focus on the difficult things where we cannot rely on the motivation of private profit to achieve desirable ends. It would appear that, from the evidence we have discussed earlier in this chapter, the current behaviour of financial markets is far from that required to achieve our aims as outlined at the start of the chapter.

In any case, all these arguments miss one vital point. If investors can be persuaded to behave in ways that encourage genuinely good industrial and commercial management, encourage the growth of truly strong businesses, and discourage the knee-jerk and the transactional, then surely businesses will be able to attract investment because of their fundamental performance and underlying virtues.

The final argument against our proposals hinges on governmental willingness to sponsor change. Here, we must confess, we are less confident. So far no government has dared to put a toe into the waters of investment choices (as opposed to governance codes and fee caps), and there would be outraged protest if any were to consider doing so. Yet governments happily opine on equally important issues such as the National Curriculum, the minutiae of tax legislation and employer behaviour in a whole range of issues from workplace temperature to recruitment practices. So why should something so fundamental as the future health of UK industry be a no-go area?

So, let's think about what might need changing, and how it might happen.

ENCOURAGING RESPONSIBLE INVESTMENT

Clear, objective and publicly available research is essential to define the elements of investment practice that encourage long-term business development, promote good management and challenge incompetence and inertia. The current investigations into investment strategies by Tomorrow's Company could possibly be a starting point. What is essential is that the objectives of the research be clearly defined, and the work be carried out by truly objective individuals. All too often such 'studies' are headed by market insiders with little incentive to propose departures from current practice or original thought. The timescale should also be short, within reason. This can be an iterative process; we don't have to get it all right first time!

As a result of the research, certain elements of 'responsible investing' could then be defined. Investment practices could then be categorized as 'responsible' or 'speculative', with 'responsible' qualifying for certain advantages not otherwise available. Pre-empting any research, but keeping in mind the Buffett tenets, we suggest that the elements of 'responsible' investing could include the following:

- Shareholdings taken with a view to investing for the long term. In any fund, some sales would obviously be necessary from time to time, but in principle the portfolio would be stable. It might be possible to determine a level of, say, 80 per cent of investments held for more than, say, two years.

  Focus investing should take place of portfolio diversification. We fully appreciate that given the size of many investment funds, an overall restriction on the number of investments is impractical. However, we are trying to find a level that allows the investment manager to properly understand the economic fundamentals of the businesses' underlying current and potential performance. The size of an investment fund's portfolio could be limited to, say, 15 investments per experienced investment manager.

  Furthermore, we appreciate that it will not be possible, even with focus investing, for all funds to outperform the market. Pure mathematics renders it impossible, which is why the current 'beat the index' mentality can lead to violent distortions in perceptions of value. However, if responsible investment genuinely results in healthier companies, all investors will benefit in the medium term.

- The funds could issue, and adhere to, a code of principles on responsible investing, possibly including statements on:
  - investors' beliefs about the characteristics of well-run companies;
  - how the fund managers will act to support companies' prospects of long-term success;
  - how the fund managers will communicate with companies and the media.

Underlying these principles should be the basic acceptance that responsible investors have a dual duty to serve the needs of their clients and to sustain the success of the companies in which they invest. They will seek to reconcile and optimize the needs of both in the belief that this will serve the best long-term interests of the real shareholders and companies.

The medium-term aim should be that the bulk of funds invested by institutions on behalf of clients should be in 'responsible investment' funds. We therefore need to create real advantages and incentives for these funds. These could include:

- Tax advantages for the profits and dividends earned by the funds. More favourable tax rates could apply to these income streams. Speculative investment, no matter what its purpose, should be taxed at full rates. If we were really committed to the principles, this could include removal of exempt status from pension funds where the investments were not 'responsible'.

  Again, some people we have talked to hold that the government would not seek to create a tax environment that favours one type of investment over another. We have dealt with this to some extent already, and further believe that if objective research is able to demonstrate the desirability of industry-supporting behaviour, the tax system is one appropriate mechanism to use. Furthermore, the practice of favouring 'long-term capital gains' has precedence within many tax regimes.
- Voting rights at annual and extraordinary meetings of shareholders could be restricted to 'responsible investors'; speculative investors would not have the right to vote. 'Responsible investors' should likewise have precedence when accepting or rejecting takeover bids.

  We appreciate that this proposal runs contrary to the enshrined doctrine that owners of a company must have the right of approval or veto on fundamental issues. However, most real owners are disenfranchised by virtue of investing via funds, and some of their representatives have proved unworthy to exercise this valuable right. In future, the right could be earned through 'responsible investing'.

  In order to make this workable, investors would have to declare at the point of share purchase whether they were 'responsible' or 'speculative'. Dishonest declarations would carry heavy financial penalties. The share register would include this information so that the registrar would know who to send voting forms to. Obviously, in the case of 'show of hands' voting other verification processes would be required.
- 'Responsible' investors could be given special rights of access to companies' management and information. For example, company

investment 'panels' could be set up, with rights of privileged access to planning and reporting processes. The Financial Services Authority (FSA) would need to police funds to ensure that those claiming the privileges and benefits genuinely complied with the 'responsible' criteria. The aim of this is simply to encourage closer, more nurturing behaviour from investors, and to give companies the benefits of developing relationships with supportive shareholders.

A 'sustainable enterprises' market

The attractions to investors of companies whose fundamental qualities surpass that of the average ought to be that they can expect superior returns over a long time period, compared with 'run of the mill' enterprises. When it is also the case that such companies are likely to have good values and practices in relation to business ethics, environmental care and social policies, investors can enjoy the double glow of pocketing superior returns safe in the knowledge that they are also doing good.

There are already distinctive innovations in socially and environmentally responsible investment, through, for example, the 'FTSE4Good' Index, and, most interestingly, the Dow Jones Sustainability Indexes. The Sustainability Indexes require companies to submit themselves to a rigorous examination of their policies and practices in three main dimensions: economic, environmental and social. The examination is through a comprehensive questionnaire with 86 categories of question, covering topics ranging from corporate governance to organizational learning. In addition to filling in the questionnaire, the company has to undergo an interview process, and the whole system is backed by rigorous research.

The 'FTSE4Good' indices are a little simpler, and focus on 'good' industries, excluding such activities as arms manufacture, tobacco and the like. Then, having excluded certain industrial activities, the indices focus on good practice in the fields of environmental impact, social policy, stakeholder relations and human rights.

We feel that these developments represent an enormous leap forward and point the way for further developments. The massive Dow Jones questionnaire and the copious research data thus generated must give investors all they need to know to make informed judgements, mustn't they?

Well, not entirely, in our view. First, it is not clear that being 'good' in all the categories included in the Sustainability Indices necessarily leads to superior performance. Second, there is a serious risk that the existing indices will lead to an outbreak of 'box-ticking', in which the form and public relations aspects of being 'good' come to outweigh the substance. Excessive formalism and filling returns can get in the way of real active commitment.

We believe that there is still much scope for developing the practice of investment and the clarity and transparency of offerings to the final shareholder. We would like to see a new movement spearheaded by a new index, possibly supported by specific investment funds, with these objectives:

- to offer the real shareholders an opportunity to invest in companies that serve their markets superbly, are well run to produce excellent current and long-term performance, and have good social and environmental practices;

- to communicate clearly and directly with potential shareholders in the form of pension fund trustees and members, private pension and insurance holders and private investors, so that they can make decisions about investment independently of investment institutions;
- to act as a force for positive change in encouraging (initially) UK-owned companies to focus on becoming excellent;
- to advance the quality of investment management through seeking new ways of understanding how to identify and assess the potential of companies through their management practices and the quality of organization and leadership.

A 'performance with integrity' index

We would like to see the development of a new offering to investors, broadly along the lines of the two indices that we mentioned above. We would add an additional purpose: that of identifying and encouraging companies that aim for excellent performance by following the strategies that the research evidence shows pays off in the long term. Companies eligible for inclusion would have to satisfy the requirements of good governance and good economic, environmental, social and employment practice. Readers interested in understanding what this might entail could do no better than to access the somewhat awesome Dow Jones Sustainability Index questionnaire, available on the Dow Jones Web site.

But we would want to go further, and proceed somewhat differently. We would want to see into the target enterprises' brains, we would want to get a feel for their emotional lives, for it is these dimensions that will distinguish good companies that are adept at filling in questionnaires from really excellent enterprises.

We would want to ask about and obtain insights into whether top management are fully committed to the company and its people, through equitably sharing the rewards of success and the pains of failure with them. We would want to know if they are capable of understanding their environment, of 'looking over the hill' and pointing to what will be important in the future. We would like to know if they can release creativity and energy and by their actions evoke loyalty and commitment from others.

We would like to know if many people love the company, what it produces and what it stands for. We would also dearly like to know a lot about the abilities of leaders and key staff, and how these abilities match up to the challenges facing the company and compare with those of competitors. Last, we would like to know something of the next generation of corporate leaders: their backgrounds, their abilities, and how they are being prepared to meet the challenges of leadership. We would want to know about all these factors, because they are the unique ingredients that make the difference between ordinary and excellent performance.

The answers to these and many other questions ought to be (but are currently generally not) known to companies' non-executive directors and are at least to a degree accessible to investors with the time and skill to amass what investor Benjamin Graham described as the essential 'scuttlebutt' about a company. Some may describe such subjective information as trivial beside real, 'hard' numbers. We would disagree. It is what, in the medium term, drives the numbers.

So, to put the same issues in slightly more analytical form, we would return to what the research data indicate are the fundamentals of well-run companies. The companies that would be eligible for inclusion in our 'performance with integrity' index would have some very distinctive characteristics:

1. They would define their central purposes as satisfying the needs of their customers and sustaining a strong competitive position in their customer markets.
2. They would be managed from the 'inside' out, in the sense that the prime commitments of top management are to the people and organizations that they lead. Transactional means of developing the company, such as acquisitions, will be adjuncts to the prime concerns of creating a high-performing organizational platform to carry the business.
3. Top management would be highly concerned to hand on a successful and vital enterprise to their successors and would invest much time and energy on grooming and developing future mangers and leaders.
4. They would have strong and distinctive value systems that generate widely held commitment to the purposes of the organization and provide challenge to innovate, perform, learn and adapt.
5. Above all, they would be regarded by all connected with them as human societies with customer-serving, economic and social purposes – not collections of tradeable assets.

As means of rating and judging the fundamental quality of companies develop and improve, they should be added to the repertoire of the market. For example, some specialist consulting companies in the United Kingdom and the United States are developing means of helping companies to assess and 'benchmark' the quality and capabilities of their management cadres against those of competitors and international norms. And, of course, effective means of assessing the attributes and abilities of current and future leaders are already available and increasingly widely used by the best companies. In time, such innovations could be very useful to responsible investors in helping them make crucial judgements about the quality and values of the leaders of the companies in which they invest.

New investment markets can be test beds for the proposition that future innovations in investment are now much more likely to come from psychology and the social sciences than from the currently dominant domains of 'hard' economic and financial analysis.

Initially, the 'performance with integrity' index could be drawn from the companies traded on the London Stock Exchange, with privately owned and soon-to-be-listed companies perhaps being included at a later date.

New and innovative markets, like the one we have outlined, could be eligible for research grants and for research work aimed at enhancing the general understanding of what makes for very high and durable performance.

Last, but not least, the success of such an index would depend on the development of a new breed of investment professional who would have actual experience of managing and working inside real companies and a 'feel' for that which makes enterprises excellent, derived from practice. The contrast with the formula and numbers-driven tendencies that prevail among the current generation of investment professionals would be considerable: the 'new' investor would be skilled at using 'soft' and intuitive information, based more on feel and experience. In order to do this, they would need to get closer to the enterprises in which they invest – hence our interest in the thoughts of Karl Sternberg of Deutsche Asset Management about getting closer to companies. However, the task of developing investors with the appropriate skills, experience and attitudes would be massive, needing a veritable revolution to bring about positive change.

In this new environment for investment, with financial and information benefits for responsible investors and the 'performance with integrity' index, a lot of the unhealthy pressure for short-term and knee-jerk management action would be removed. So what about our second critical category of players, the top managers?

REWARDING POSITIVE MANAGEMENT BEHAVIOUR

Again, let us remember briefly the situation that has developed over the past couple of decades. Managers today are sharply aware of the moods and pressures of the markets, are concerned to (at least) avoid displeasing investors and have constructed reward structures for themselves that are justified severally by 'creating value', needing to be internationally competitive and recognizing of 'star' qualities.

There has been, and continues to be, a marked reduction in the length of tenure of top executive managers, both in specific jobs and in companies. There has also been a marked increase, over the period we have covered, in 'active' and transactional behaviour, which has placed large UK companies at or close to the top of the international league for M&A activity. Managers are rated by their most important audience according to their presentation, analytical and numeracy skills, and, understandably, most have sought to hone such skills, giving rise to a whole industry to support them in doing so.

Is this universally true of all top managers in the United Kingdom? Obviously not. There are still a significant number of business leaders with a rounded balance of analytical and emotional skills, with a deep understanding of their business and high-level organization-building and people leadership skills. There are even some who are brave enough to resist pressures for seeking 'active' routes to growth where they are not appropriate and who also resist abusing the organizations that they lead in the name of cost reduction for its own sake. But this band has diminished over the years and is set to diminish further unless the dynamics of the relationships between managers and markets are changed drastically.

So, what would we like to see changing in the behaviours of top managers? We would like to see less naked greed and a progressive lessening of the obscene differentials that have been created between the pay of top managers and the workforce in general. We would like to see many fewer high-ego 'CEO superstars' and much more concentration on building strong teams and strong organizations.

In short, we would like to encourage the development of a new breed of top managers who feel deeply responsible for the health of the enterprises that they lead, who have top-class business-building abilities and the highest quality of leadership and people development skills. We would naturally also like our managers to be well equipped with a full armoury of analytical skills enabling them to understand finance, markets and competition, because such skills should by now be a commodity and not a mark of distinction. And last, we would like to see a convergence of interest between business-building managers and long-term, focus investors.

Good managers demonstrate a high degree of concern for the vital interests of their organizations and value the basics of what the enterprise stands for. They are visibly bonded with the organizations and people that they lead and they are likely to stay long enough to have an impact that 'sticks'. Our first concerns, therefore, are to restore the integrity of the relationships between top managers as a class and their organizations, and to place management in a proper perspective. To put it as simply as possible, we would like to encourage a few particular aspects of top management behaviour, with the aims of achieving the following:

Changing managers' values

1. To place the building of durable, competitive and high-performing enterprises at the centre of top managers' concerns.
2. To encourage top managers to identify strongly with the interests of the companies that they lead. To make the long-term health and success of the company their most important objective.
3. To cause top managers to act in ways that balance the needs and interests of the stakeholders in the enterprise and to seek as far as is possible to satisfy all stakeholder needs. Where this is not possible, to regard the success and survival of the company as being their first priority.
4. To encourage the development of leadership and business-building skills as being the mark of the best managers.

How could this be achieved? By aiming for a positive convergence between changes in investor and management behaviours.

Our proposals to change investor behaviour and priorities will have a real and positive impact on managers' behaviour. As institutional investors begin to focus more on long-term business-building than on price-movement speculation, the pressure on managers will change focus too. When investors begin to value long-term nurturance, the fly-by-night chief executive who doesn't stay around long enough to learn from his or her own mistakes is likely to become less fashionable. Tenures will lengthen; focus will return to the underlying business and away from day-to-day share price movements.

We also need to consider more direct influences to impact on managers' behaviour. In this we need to consider both executive and non-executive directors, collectively and separately.

All directors

Under the present Companies Act the responsibilities of directors are not clearly defined. Proposals for a new Companies Act do include clarification of directors' responsibilities, and we believe this to be essential.

The directors of companies should be held responsible and accountable for serving the interests of the company, and should be able to demonstrate that they have taken balanced account of the interests of key stakeholders – in particular, employees and shareholders – in their deliberations, decisions and actions. They should not have a 'default' position with regard to stakeholders' interests, especially that of giving priority to the interests of 'shareholders' (mainly investment institutions). These provisions would need to be included in the Companies Act.

In addition, directors should be required to provide a publicly available evaluation of the benefits and risks to the long-term interests of shareholders, employees and the community when proposing or supporting large acquisitions, significant changes in the business portfolio, or the sale of parts or the whole of the enterprise. At present, under the Listing Rules only the shareholders have a right to information and to vote on large proposed transactions, and even this information is somewhat limited. Employees should have the same rights of access to information as investors and shareholders (although not perhaps the right to vote!).

Non-executive directors

Non-executive directors have been demonstrably ineffective in many dimensions, frequently failing to stop their executive colleagues from acting in ways that have seriously damaged companies and the interests of many stakeholders. They have patently failed to stop abuses of power when determining rewards.

Most non-executive directors are highly dependent on the management for their understanding of the company, and mainly rely on financial information prepared by the management. Generally, they are not very accountable for their stewardship.

Lord Young of Graffham recently queried whether in their current mode, non-executive directors are worth retaining. We believe that the governance and direction of large and complex companies needs two strong and separate forms of director: the executive and the 'overseeing'. However, the current system requires significant overhaul rather than the ineffectual 'fiddling' that attempts by government and the industrial 'great and good' have so far produced.

The most recent review of boards and non-executive directors was the Higgs Report, commissioned, as is usual, by the government. The Higgs Report contains, in our view, nuggets of useful opinion and guidance, such as the observation that the current crop of non-executive directors is drawn from a very narrow base, and that the same individual should not be chairperson of two major companies. There is much broad comment about job descriptions, assessment of competences and appraisal of individuals. The report also recommends that full-time executive directors of major companies should not hold more than one non-executive position. It also enshrines the position of the independent, senior non-executive director.

However, in essence the Higgs Report is another in the seemingly endless procession of small, incremental changes that go just far enough to enable some to claim them to be 'steps' on the road to real progress and change. Higgs starts from the stated view that governance arrangements in the United Kingdom are fundamentally sound, but could benefit from incremental changes. This is exactly what would be expected from asking the industrial/financial establishment to inspect itself and come up with some ideas for change. But the furore that the Higgs Report has raised in some quarters might lead the innocent observer to think that it was prepared by the Socialist Workers League!

It is our belief that the current 'arrangements' are outdated, ineffective and damaging to industry. In particular, the importance of industrial stakeholders other than 'shareholders' is understated and their rights virtually unrecognized. As Charles Handy has said, this line of thinking derives from the 18th century and hardly acknowledges the knowledge economy. The 'arrangements' need much more fundamental change, still within an effective market system, than establishment insiders will ever volunteer.

We would propose the following changes:

Changes for non-executive directors

1. Non-executives as a body should possess a range of experience and skills to enable them to contribute on all key facets of strategy and management. This means that they should possess or have access to industry knowledge and the range of disciplines required to understand a modern business. In particular, the non-executive body should not have a bias towards any one skill, but have appropriate general management and technical, finance, marketing and people / organization experience.

   To promote this scope of skills, each company should develop a policy about board diversity. This policy should form part of the annual reporting to shareholders, together with details about how the board constitution and, particularly, new appointees fit with the stated aims.
2. Non-executive directors should spend sufficient time on the affairs of the company to be able to demonstrate, individually and collectively, that they have a sufficient first-hand depth of knowledge of the company's operations and activities to be able to make informed judgements about the plans and actions of management.

   It is highly unlikely that a non-executive director would be able to meet these requirements in less than 50 full days per year. This may at first glance seem excessive, but, as we saw in an earlier chapter, the 2003 Independent Remuneration Solutions survey (conducted in association with 3i) showed that at present a non-executive director of a company with turnover of over £1 billion will spend on average 26 days with the company. This includes three days for 'plant visits and other non-formal occasions'. We have already accepted that current practices do not allow for the development of sufficient depth of understanding. More time, well used, could rectify this, allowing non-executive directors to perform their duties far more effectively.
3. Whether full-time executive directors of other companies should continue to hold non-executive positions needs serious thought. The arguments in favour are:
   - That they bring broad experience to the board. This may be true in some cases but both authors, having held senior positions in public limited companies, can testify that such lofty attainment serves to narrow as much as broaden your viewpoint.
   - That non-executive positions are good training grounds for up-and-coming executives from other companies. Surely directing our leading companies is too important to be used as 'training'?

   On the flip side, it is doubtful whether a full-time executive of another company would be in a position to dedicate the 50 days per annum to the job that we are suggesting.

Maybe the outcome of the debate would be 'use sparingly', which would lead to a widening of the 'pool' of talent from which non-executive directors are drawn. One argument frequently raised against widening the pool is that other people won't understand the issues or will be intimidated. That, frankly, is arrogant nonsense.

Furthermore, we really need to see a reduction in plural directorships and a change in the incestuous relationships between non-executive and executive directors in such matters as remuneration.

4. Three major changes should be made in the way companies report to stakeholders. First, non-executive directors should become the main medium through which the company reports to shareholders. If this were so, then non-executive directors, especially the chairperson, would be the first line of accountability to investors and shareholders, with executive directors taking second place in this dialogue with the investment institutions and analysts. Investor relations staff and consultants would report to the non-executive directors.

   The relationships would have to be worked out with care. It would still be important for the investors to know the executive management in order to properly judge some of the issues discussed in the previous section. However, any arrangement would ideally keep the focus of the chief executive and the executive team on *managing the business, not the share price*.

   We also know this proposal will be met with outrage, given some of the reactions to the Higgs suggestion that a senior non-executive director should speak with institutional investors on occasions. Our proposal may also seem rather draconian, but could be the best way of achieving several vital objectives, in particular:
   - making sure that non-executive directors are well acquainted with the company's affairs;
   - focusing the executive clearly on their overriding duty of managing the company;
   - dissipating the tendency to create executive 'superstars'.

   Second, directors should report against something like a 'balanced scorecard' of factors. These could include comments on financial and marketing/competitive strategies, the strength and development of management and staff, with key employment and development philosophies and actions; plus an assessment by the directors of the main risks and opportunities facing the company.

   Third, this report should also contain a plain-language description of the directors' compensation, with an exact description of the relationships between performance and pay for each executive director and other managers of equivalent pay. The same reports would be made available to both external and internal audiences. A clear and precise description of the fully costed pay, shares, pension and benefits packages of directors, together with a clear description of increases and the reasons for increases, should also be presented to representatives of employees by non-executive directors and circulated to the wider employee population.

5. Non-executive directors' remuneration also needs to be considered. Remuneration in cash, not shares, and at a high day-rate for their work, would enable individuals to earn a respectable living by doing the job well.

6. A non-executive director's rigorous and thorough qualification should be developed. Training should be tailored to the non-executive role, and be to the standard of a senior advanced management programme such as those offered by major international business schools, plus practical investigative and project work. At the end of the programme, examination and interview would assess suitability for the role.

   Although such a qualification would not be mandatory for board appointment, the chairperson should be required to explain any new appointment of an individual not holding the qualification.

Executive directors (including shadow directors)

Executive directors should be strongly encouraged to devote their attentions to leading the enterprise, and that entails a primary focus on the business and its customers, employees, industry bodies and the communities affected by the company.

We have already noted that a change in investor focus will result in a diminution of some of the more damaging excesses of current managerial activity. The decoupling of executive directors from routine dialogue with institutions would also facilitate the change, allowing a move away from transactional 'stars' to business-growers. A closer focus on and involvement with the business would also tend to lengthen tenure.

However, there is still the issue of remuneration to contend with. Current remuneration practice is negative in two aspects:

- the vast differentials between chief executives' pay and that of other employees;
- the preponderance of share-based incentives, leading to an investor-oriented focus and transactional behaviour.

One of our respondents, a top compensation consultant, shared a private belief that the time has come for a 'back to basics' movement on top executive remuneration. We heartily agree. A fundamental rethink of both the design and the reporting of executive remuneration arrangements is long overdue:

1. The full cost of all aspects of directors' and top managers' remuneration and benefits should be accounted for and disclosed in a clear format through the accounts. These costs should include the full range of benefits and special facilities made available to directors and top managers. Included in this should be company-supported travel and accommodation, such as apartments, leased hotel facilities and corporate transport used for work or leisure purposes, and the controversial matter of accounting for the value of share options, another matter on which emotion is raging.

   This is vital, as shareholders and employees should have the right to see the real cost to the company of top executives' employment practices and how the company's money is being spent.
2. Senior pay should have two components: first, pay for doing the job; and second, an element of discretionary long-term reward for performance achieved. Base pay should account for at least half of total cash compensation.

The discretionary element should be based on performance over long time frames, as the taking of short-term expedients has been demonstrated as damaging. By 'long-term' we mean the same timescales as those that appeal to responsible 'focus' investors – that is, at least five years.

3. Top managers' compensation should be substantially divorced from the share price of the company and other investor-oriented considerations. As we have said, it is axiomatic that the primary duty of managers should be to the company and all its key stakeholders.

   A very tight limit should be re-imposed on the award of share-related compensation, and the time perspective should be very long term. In particular, the practice of allowing vesting of share-related grants on change of control of the company should be banned.

   Share awards should be limited and should be made subject to a service qualification of at least three years. The award of share-based 'golden hellos' should be prohibited. Any inducements to join a company should be in fully disclosed cash. Cash-based rewards tend to be simpler to administer, easier to account for, and more transparent – all desirable characteristics of remuneration packages.
4. Directors and other employees should be free to purchase their companies' shares at full price, should they be willing to take the same risks as ordinary shareholders.
5. Over time, there should be an aim to reduce the grossly inflated differentials that have grown between the rewards of top managers and the wider workforce. There is absolutely no justification for the current differences. In the long run, top managers are just as dependent on the performance of the people whom they lead as the wider workforce are on their leaders.

   Furthermore, one of the most fundamental responsibilities of any business leader is to develop others in the organization fully equipped to take over at the top. If this is done, there will be healthy competition for the top jobs and the price tag will fall. One suspects that the current batch of 'star' executives are ignoring this vital responsibility and failing to develop managerial successors.

   The basic fact is, that all employees of modern companies should be vital contributors to performance and success, and having such dramatic differences between the pay of top managers and others simply emphasizes the unhealthy separation of the top managers from the wider organization.
6. Top management is a pressurized and sometimes risky occupation. It is, in our view, right that those who take on such roles should enjoy a degree of security. Therefore, it is reasonable that top managers should have contracts that entitle them to one year's notice or a cash sum in lieu of one year's base pay. No further enhancements or embellishments should be allowed.

THE OTHER MARKET PLAYERS

The scandals of the late 1990s and after have disclosed a system of interests in the markets on both sides of the Atlantic that has escaped the control of regulators and lawmakers. In the United States the law enforcers are taking a hard line with some of the transgressors. A number of investment banks have faced heavy fines, with the ongoing possibility of class actions that could cost even more. In

London the FSA has recently fined Credit Suisse First Boston £4 million for 'systematically lying to financial and tax regulators', to quote Nick Cohen in the *Observer* of 22 December 2002. The contrast in the level of sanctions is stark. The vision of the CEO of Tyco standing handcuffed in a New York court, accused of misappropriating his company's assets, has probably also had a salutary effect!

The recent scandals have revealed a positively incestuous state of affairs behind the sumptuous exteriors of the large integrated investment banks. At the centre of much of the trouble lie four factors:

1. That investment bankers, brokers and analysts have created a position where they can reward themselves at a level that to any rational lay observer is beyond belief.
2. That the goose that creates the golden eggs for all is investment banking support for corporate deals and financial transactions.
3. That 'activism', as characterized by deals, is in the interests of all who work in the larger, integrated international banks. So, bankers want as many deals as possible.
4. That investment banks therefore pressurize management to embark upon and complete deals that are not in the long-term interest of the company. Surely developments such as H P Bulmer's costly 'strategic' move into the United States could only originate in the fertile mind of an investment banker?

The only big-time losers in this lucrative system of relationships are anyone outside the system, and that means most of us.

Regulatory threats, fines and adverse publicity are already having an impact on the structure of these integrated investment banks. Many are looking hard at internal relationships and future structure. This is good, but will not of itself relieve the overwhelming pressure on management to 'do deals' rather than manage.

Key to real reform is our 'new investment environment'. As 'responsible' investors recognize the importance of wider aspects of management, the whole atmosphere surrounding transactions should change. They will be viewed as one of a series of strategic options, rather than the default position for the chief executive to prove his or her worth.

Voting on transactions

The Listing Rules provide shareholders with the right to vote on any proposed transaction that will significantly impact the proposing company. A series of formulaic tests effectively give this right on any transaction equal to 25 per cent or more of the company's size or value.

However, this right is rarely exercised to prevent transactions. Institutions tend to support incumbent management's proposals. One broker commented that, 'To vote against a proposal would be a fundamental signal of lack of trust in the chief executive.' On the other side, we have personally witnessed the way in which egos get invested in 'getting the deal through shareholders' and the frenzied discussions with investment bankers on 'the best way to present the story' and 'what we need to do to get them to swallow it'. There is indeed the feeling that a refusal by shareholders is a rejection of the chief executive him- or herself.

But why does it have to be this way? What on earth is wrong with an honest discussion of pros and cons, open debate with the owners' representatives and employees of the company? OK, so this does happen to some extent, but not to anything like the extent that will be claimed, and not in the context of informed debate rather than well-groomed presentations.

Again, this is something of a natural result of the situation where hard-pressed fund managers have little time to properly understand the proposals. In these circumstances it is understandable that they support the incumbent management unless there is a really pressing reason not to. However, if funds had fewer investments, and were invested for the long term, a far more mature approach would be to have an honest, informed debate with fund managers. And if those fund managers were to decide that an expensive acquisition is not the way they would like to see the company taken forward, then a mature business-focused chief executive would not throw his or her toys out of the pram!

Accountability for transactions

The following further actions may help substantially to put deal-making in its proper economic perspective:

1. The separation of investment banking, analysis and broking should be moved forward. In order to be credible, any organization publishing investment advice to investors and shareholders should be able to demonstrate that it they had freedom from influence by investment bankers. The definition of independence would include ownership and any form of reward that might come from supporting the interests of bankers, but would not include independently commissioned and paid for consulting work.
2. It would be worthwhile making the investment bankers' fees contingent upon value created by the deals they support. The fees charged for deals should be made public and a substantial portion withheld for at least three years, and released only if stated value creation targets are achieved.

   Investment bankers will argue that it is the task of management to deliver value from an acquisition. This is true, and we would not wish to dilute managements' responsibilities. However, when promoting deals, the investment banks will often produce research on market prospects and the 'benefits of a dominant position'. The contingent fees could be dependent upon bank-generated forecasts bearing some relation to the real outcome, to discourage deals being promoted on the back of gung-ho optimistic estimates. After all, we have seen that banks initiate more than half the transactions, and we have also seen the immense pressure they put on chief executives and boards.
3. In place of the usual league tables of numbers of transactions or transaction value produced by the investment banks, tables of value created or destroyed by transactions advised on would be interesting. Perhaps these could become an industry norm!
4. When seeking consent for a transaction from shareholders, companies could be required to account for the results of all previous deal activity over a 10-year period. It could be helpful, too, if they were also required to give

details of their processes for evaluating the outcomes of transactions and the role of the audit committee in evaluating the outcomes of deals. This information would be made available not only to shareholders, but also to employees and the general public. In addition, information showing exactly how value will be created and on the likely effects on employee interests would help to consolidate the picture.

This information should be published well in advance of any recommendations to shareholders, should be freely available to shareholders and the public at large, and be subject to the same quality standards as all other Listing Rules disclosures.

Management will no doubt object to some of these proposals, possibly claiming that they entail additional 'bureaucracy' and workload. Surely responsible managers are already monitoring the effect of their investment, and learning from the good and the bad? And in a new, open investment environment, such things would surely be basic good practice!

WHAT ABOUT THE REAL SHAREHOLDERS?

So far we have concentrated on measures to affect the behaviour of the key players: investment institutions, management and banks. But what about the real investors: those who take the real economic risks? We have already defined this population in previous chapters as including members of private and defined contribution pension schemes, companies providing defined benefit schemes, savers and investors in endowments, unit trusts and other forms of investment fund, and private shareholders.

A cursory glance at most of the advertising material will show that despite the warnings demanded by regulation, most of the copy is designed to talk up return prospects, emphasizing massive historical profits over and above the building society alternative. On top of that, the bulk of investment advice to the public focuses on fund manager performance against indices and compared to other managers as opposed to thoughtful consideration of underlying business performance. So once again we have a dislocation between the decision as to where to place investment and the theoretical beneficiaries: businesses.

Informing the public

We need to focus on education. We need to get real information to the people taking key decisions.

The financial understanding of the average member of public (including non-financially trained professionals) is woefully inadequate. It is amazing that, given the repeated financial scandals, so little official focus has been on educating the population to understand the concepts and responsibilities of whole-life financial management. In fact, we go in the opposite direction. Pensions are complicated. Investments are made complicated by jargon, illusion and the terms and conditions of the funds.

There is an urgent need to provide better information. People need to be encouraged to learn about financial management so that the population is equipped to take self-responsibility and to view investment as a means of creating long-term wealth for the country rather than for individuals to try to get rich quick.

For a start, the trustees of pension funds should be compulsorily trained in the basic principles of investment, including the impact and likely performance of various investment styles, before they are allowed to take their places on trustee boards. It is ironic that many employee trustees have behaved in ways that have caused them and their colleagues in other companies to lose their jobs!

A further solution must be to make more information, produced and communicated in a useful and digestible form, available to all those who have a professional or personal concern about what the financial markets and managers are doing to their interests. There are already several bodies that conduct research and make the results of their efforts available, either to subscribers or to the general public, so this is not a ground-breaking proposal.

Some strategic information goals would be:

- To provide the public at large with properly researched information on the workings of the industrial / financial system and to cast light on the actions of the financial markets and managements. To highlight what works and what does not, from the standpoint of industry, the general interests of society, and the range of their personal objectives.
- To provide all who have an interest or need with appropriate advice and guidance on the industrial and financial system. To enable organizations, institutions and individuals to make sensible choices about their financial affairs and to use the services available to them in an informed manner. To provide impartial information on the products and services provided to the public, and advice on how to challenge the system.

It is important to remove control of this information provision from the financial services industry to ensure objectivity. Readers may like to consider the following suggestions:

1. We have already discussed the need for some research into the impact of different investment practices. This should be an ongoing process. There is a strong case for setting up a *research institute*, possibly funded by a levy on the financial services industry. The institute could be sponsored by a serious academic institution, such as the London School of Economics or the Judge Institute at Cambridge University. Its research would be dedicated to industrial investment and the performance of enterprises in the private and public sectors. There would be a focus on the impacts of different investment and management strategies and practices on economic performance, together with internationally comparative studies. The institute would also have a limited teaching capacity.
2. In addition, a publicly funded *advisory body* could be set up, with the twin objectives of determining priorities for research according to public need, and translating the research outcomes for public communication. It would also sponsor training and education for the pension fund trustees, local financial advisers, trade union officials and the public at large.
3. Local advice and information provision could be built upon existing bodies such as credit unions and the Citizens' Advice Bureaux.

The whole system could be supported by fully accessible Web sites and Internet facilities. The main focus of local information and advice should be managing pensions and savings provisions. These are going to be the main financial concerns of the citizenry for the rest of this century.

4. The trade unions have, through the Trades Union Congress (TUC), been active and vociferous about the withdrawal by companies from final-salary pension schemes.

   Unions have a legitimate concern about the provision of benefits to their members and to employees more generally. The TUC also has an excellent 'pool' of experience on the subject of pensions, and should be encouraged, with financial support if necessary, to make a contribution to the institute and the other bodies that we have proposed. Given the dearth of organized pressure coming from other quarters, it is possible that the unions could be a major representative body for the real shareholders!

Having discussed this idea with a number of people who have professional experience in the provision of scarce or sensitive information to the public, we believe that an active, investigative, objective body, making its findings available to the public in an accessible manner, would richly repay the investment made in it and be far more useful than more regulation. The scourge of those who profit from private 'arrangements' is good, readily accessible information.

WHO WILL DO WHAT IS NEEDED?

We have a horror of excessive bureaucracy. Therefore, we have quite deliberately held off from recommending solutions that require extensive regulation from public bodies, preferring those that focus mainly on information and incentives. But inevitably, achieving significant change in a status quo that so richly rewards a few and so comprehensively excludes the vast majority will entail some degree of force and impetus from outside the 'system'. Remember, there is a place for regulation intended to mitigate the unhealthy impact of a free market.

The history of the financial markets and management shows that self-regulation just doesn't work. What does work is a judicious mix of legislation, the threat of legislation and action by responsible industry bodies. The trouble is, representative bodies in the financial markets tend not to act of their own volition until matters have reached crisis point, and the same seems to apply to management bodies. Why should the Confederation of British Industry own up to the fact that many of its members are woefully deficient in the skills required for effective leadership and others are disgracefully overpaid for the damage that they do?

The bottom line is that not very much will happen without some action from government. So, we have tried to make it relatively easy for our politicians to act. We are not asking for radical change, just a number of connected initiatives that will, we hope, start the long process of change in the behaviours of managers and investors.

In broad terms, here is what our political leaders could be expected to do:

1. To stimulate the development of more responsible investing, the new regulatory environment differentiating between 'responsible' and 'speculative'

investment would need to be incorporated, presumably into the Financial Services Act. In addition, tax incentives, privileged access and enhanced voting rights for long-term investors need to be introduced. These would require minor legislation and changes in tax provisions.

2. In regard to the duties of directors, a clear statement of responsibilities should be incorporated into the Companies Act. The requirement for disclosure of training for non-executive directors and time spend with the company could be incorporated into the Listing Rules.

   The provision of appropriate training for non-executive directors may also require government funding.
3. In regard to the remuneration of executives and the reporting requirements on directors about pay and other matters, changes in the law and Listing Rules would be required. It is high time that government intervened anyhow to begin to curb the disgraceful differentials that have developed between top executive pay and that of the wider workforce. This national outrage will not cure itself.
4. The Listing Rules would also need to be amended to incorporate the requirement for investment bankers and companies to provide much more information on the outcomes of deals and the disclosure and contingent nature of fees.
5. In regard to the establishment of an institute and associated educational and information bodies, government funding would be necessary. However, the amounts are very small by comparison to the damage being caused to companies, individuals and the economy in general. Also, there is a history of the government providing funding for the provision of research and information in such areas as race and homelessness. Our field of investigation is equally important to the well-being of society.
6. The role of the FSA should be reviewed to add a stronger investigative and communications role in regard to reviewing good and bad practice in the fields of investment, investment banking and such fields as pension investment.
7. As for the rest, there is plenty of scope for industry and other representative bodies to help curb the excesses of the activities that they represent. But the catalyst must be government.

A little sensible reflection will show that provided the dynamics of the systems of privilege and interlocking interests are properly understood, a remarkably small amount of non-bureaucratic intervention, coupled to the provision of much more open information, could have transforming effects.

So, that's it, really. We know that many will not like these proposals, but think of it this way. What we have done is to suggest ways of:

- encouraging top managers to take the long-term success of the businesses seriously by following strategies that research shows work best;
- giving preference to investors who are willing to take a long-term and knowledgeable approach to serving their clients and to supporting the companies in which they invest;
- reducing the rewards available for behaviour and actions that are likely to damage the interests of the majority of stakeholders in industry;

- providing the public at large with useful information by which to judge the actions of those who have the most influence on their economic well-being.

What can possibly be wrong with that?

CHANGING THE SYSTEM

Much of what we have included in this chapter may appear prescriptive. This is because we have tried to pull together a way in which our overall objectives could be met. We are aware that others may have different ideas, and we hope that this book may stimulate them to air them. However, one thing we are very clear about is that continued attempts at tinkering and applying sticking plasters will not even start to lead to the changes so desperately needed.

The central message of all this is that we need to be looking at the whole system, not just parts of the system. That is why our possible solutions may appear radical or even impractical when weighed against the priorities of the system that we are suggesting is in need of change. If we do no more than stimulate informed and considered debate along the lines of system change, we may have at least contributed to the health of British industry and commerce.

FINAL THOUGHTS

Some final thoughts before we finish. One concept has been remarkably absent throughout this review of the behaviour of the leaders of industry and their key influencers, the investors. The concept of integrity, of doing what is right because it's right, has hardly raised its head.

Tyco became a byword for corporate excess, but a new management team has been appointed. Jack Krol was named the group's lead director in September 2002. He analyses the old situation as arising from new companies with 'no value and culture system' built in. He also describes a very different situation at Du Pont, his former company. 'Everyone at Du Pont knew where the ethical line was drawn. If they even saw the line, they were already too close; if they crossed the line they had to seek employment elsewhere.'

Integrity, for us, takes many forms. First, as we have already said, it means adhering to clear and generally acceptable ethical norms – in other words, doing what is right because it is right, without needing special rewards or inducements to do so.

But we believe that the concept of integrity in business goes further. For companies, it must mean concentrating with commitment on doing what the enterprise was set up for in serving customers and paying due attention to the needs of its stakeholders. There is no room within this concept of integrity for creative accounting, trading the company as a set of disposable assets, despoiling the environment, regarding employees as dispensable costs or rewarding top managers at exorbitant levels by comparison with their colleagues. Readers will remember the 'Credo' of Johnson & Johnson.

Equally, there is as much if not more opportunity for the investment industry to clean up its act. Apart from the myriad examples of short-changing, confusing, misleading and downright deceiving its customers, the banking and financial services industries seem to have moved further and further from their basic and useful functions. Rather than serving their customers' financial needs in a responsible and transparent manner and channelling investors' funds into effective industrial enterprise, they have enthusiastically taken part in the creation of a complex froth of financial devices and instruments. Over the past few decades these have created a situation in which many customers have no idea of where their funds are really going, and auditors and regulators are struggling to catch up with ever more complex financial manipulation.

At its basic and most useful level, investment in industry is about funding good companies for long-term profit and taking an intelligent interest in the strategies and effectiveness of the enterprises invested in. We need a strong movement back in this direction, as the current system is out of control.

Isn't it time that we, the real risk-takers in industry, through our own savings, pension funds, investments and membership of society, demanded that a clear line be drawn in the fields of investment and management? Furthermore, should we not demand that our 'leaders' stay well inside those lines, in terms of value-destructive behaviour and personal reward?

It is absolutely inevitable that the 'arrangements' for funding and managing industry and commerce will be significantly reformed. Why? Because, in the end, employees will not stand for being exploited, the populace at large will not stand for seeing small groups of people obscenely rewarded for damaging businesses, and the customers of the financial services industry will not stand for being periodically ripped off.

A knowledge-based economy cannot be sustained by the current 'arrangements'. If the United Kingdom is to retain an indigenously owned and managed modern economy, big changes will have to be made. Already, great damage has been caused and this will progressively get worse. (Note that some of the last advanced engineering companies, like Rolls-Royce, have recently dropped out of the FTSE 100, leaving a big hole where physics-based industry should be.)

It would be nice to think that the industrial/financial establishments would have the foresight to make the necessary changes on a voluntary basis. But we think that is unlikely. For example, the furore that has greeted the rather sensible and modest Higgs proposals for changes in corporate governance has a nice historic ring to it. The reported 'outrage' of many of the industrial great and good could be likened to the reactions of believers in absolute monarchy on first hearing of democracy!

In our view, boards should be organized to serve the interests of all the key stakeholders in a publicly quoted company. In that sense, legitimate and effective industrial leaders must treat their roles as being primarily there to serve the interests of all stakeholders, and that means adding customers and employees firmly to the current list of one: shareholders.

If one stands back and takes an objective and commonsense perspective on boards and directors, it is verging on outrageous that a relatively small and mainly self-perpetuating group of directors should be allowed for one moment to:

- arrange how they will organize their own affairs with little regard to the people they lead;
- set their own levels of reward, with scant external interference;

- pick their own acquaintances and fellows as co-directors;
- seek to maintain the support of an often unreasonable investor community for their own ends, no matter what the consequences may be for the enterprises that they lead.

It is as though directors and investors are playing a game of their own in a world divorced from the life of the rest of us. One day the game will have to change. Or maybe the way to keep it going for longer is to delay the full impact of the knowledge economy by exiting industries that need a full working populace of highly educated, highly qualified people, who are unlikely to tolerate being abused and exploited by those in power. Maybe an industrial economy mainly made up of retailing, catering, distribution, leisure and 'general services' businesses, employing large numbers of staff whose efforts can be leveraged by a few dominant and controlling leaders, might enable those leaders to continue with the way things are. Maybe that is the way the FTSE 100 is heading, leaving the clever stuff to foreign and smaller companies!

Well, we did say at the start of this chapter that our proposals would be a dream of what the world might look like if any government really had the courage to declare industry more important than the vested interests of a privileged few and take a strong, reforming lead.

Let us leave the final words with Lord Eustace Percy. In 1944 he said:

> Here is the most urgent challenge to political invention ever offered to statesman or jurist. The human association which in fact produces and distributes wealth, the association of workmen, managers, technicians, and directors, is not an association recognized by law.
>
> The association which the law does recognize – the association of shareholders, creditors and directors – is incapable of production or distribution and is not expected by the law to perform these functions.
>
> *We have to give law to the real association and to withdraw meaningless privileges from the imaginary one* [our italics]. (quoted in Handy, 2002)

End thought: why is the 'system' so hard to change?

Winston Churchill once said that democracy was a flawed, inefficient and generally imperfect system of government. The trouble was, he ruminated, all other systems were worse. Best to stick with democracy.

We have heard the same arguments advanced to support the status quo in regard to the financial markets and management. The most commonly voiced case is that while there may be flaws in the current arrangements, the previous ones, dominated by unaccountable top managers, were even worse. Furthermore, argue the apologists, just think of the horrors that excessive regulatory bureaucracy would bring in its wake. Best leave things as they are. It is worth tolerating a few glitches and flaws because the benefits bestowed by the current system are so large.

But if we just pause for a moment and think about it, what kind of system are we contemplating? The current system that has grown around the financing and direction of companies:

- disempowers the vast majority of the working population, handing almost absolute discretion to do as they wish to a small group of top managers and those who strongly influence them from the financial markets;
- enriches the same small group of players at levels that grossly exceed the average rewards of the rest of the working population, for performing work that, when objectively analysed, is no more responsible or skilled than that of other professionals and often causes more damage than good;
- frequently disadvantages and sometimes swindles the very people in whose interests the system is supposed to act: the employees of companies, together with pension fund members, small investors and other customers of the financial services industry;

- often damages or destroys the companies that participants in the 'system' invest in and lead.

This system hardly represents 'that which is for the best, in this best of all possible worlds', to slightly misquote Voltaire. It is difficult to argue that a system that bestows huge benefits on a tiny minority and damages the interests of the huge majority of participants in the process is simply the 'least worst' alternative and not a suitable subject for extensive change. Such changes could be easily implemented without undermining the fundamentals of competitive markets for capital and industrial investment.

Yet the system remains intact, despite much adverse publicity and, occasionally, threatening noises from politicians on both sides of the Atlantic when excesses create public outcry. There is no real evidence that either the Bush or the Blair administration has the faintest intent of seriously intervening in the system; and it is hard to see other forces, which are essentially inside the system, doing more than minor tinkering.

Why is a system that is damaging the interests of so many not a prime subject for major reform? We think that the reasons are not hard to understand.

First, the system is controlled by networks of people who have a massive interest in keeping things broadly as they are and who possess enormous powers of influence and patronage.

Second, the system is based on informal understandings between interested parties and is essentially invisible or obscure to outsiders. It is therefore possible to deflect and diffuse the efforts of potential reformers or even to deny that a 'system' exists at all.

Third, the current capital market arrangements, especially those in the United States and the United Kingdom, are backed by a very strong ideology: to wit, that free market capitalism is best and has demonstrated its virtue by comprehensively defeating its arch-rival, communism.

Fourth, there is an additional dimension in Britain that derives from history. Britain – or, more accurately, England – has historically had a ruling class that managed to retain power and avoid radical change over many centuries by deploying a range of stratagems, shadows of which can still be seen today.

So, what makes the current system so resistant to change, especially externally imposed change?

BLOCKING CHANGE

Threats to withdraw from London

The banking and financial services industries are international and control the use and movements of vast amounts of capital. From a UK perspective, the London financial market is a crucial and increasingly important element in the economy, especially as other sectors, such as technology and manufacturing, decline. But ownership of the key players in the London markets resides almost exclusively with very large foreign banks. This makes the United Kingdom, and UK governments, extremely vulnerable to threats to move capital and operations out of London to other locations.

Interestingly, the same syndrome can be noticed in companies and top managers. Increasingly, companies that the British government displeases, such as GlaxoSmithKline, or companies whose top executive remuneration policies are criticized, such as Vodafone, have taken to issuing threats to relocate their corporate offices to more congenial places, usually the United States.

It is probably true to say that UK governments have come to a point where their perceived ability to directly influence the actions of the financial markets is limited. While this must not let national governments 'off the hook' in taking action that will benefit their own economies and people, it means that effective action has to be national and, where possible, multinational – for example, through the European Union and other intergovernmental bodies.

Multi-faceted nature of the 'system'

The 'system' that we have described in the book is multi-faceted and complex. It is therefore unlikely that any one agency, other than governments, or bodies such as the European Commission, will be able to develop strategies and a range of interrelated interventions that will influence the whole 'system' and each of its component parts. This is also why there is a need for more independent research and investigation into the inner workings and salient impacts of the market–management nexus. Without comprehensive and insightful understanding of the whole system and how it works, it is nearly impossible to design strategies that will make it more responsive to the wider interests of society.

Deep-rooted ideological opposition to change

In the many discussions and interviews that we conducted while researching this book, we occasionally encountered reactions that surprised us by their vehemence. These reactions most commonly came from people who had strong connections with the financial markets, and took the form of very strong assertions that any attempts from the outside to regulate or modify the current free market arrangements would be disastrous (and that people who dare propose reform are dangerous fools or left-wing radicals!).

As we became sensitized to these reactions, we began to perceive patterns of behaviour from many different sources. These included some of our interviewees, a number of ex-colleagues (especially Americans), some disciples of 'Thatcherism' and such publications as *Forbes Magazine*. Thus it occurred to us that there is a very strong body of ideology that backs the notion that free market capitalism is best. An ideology might be defined as a set of strong beliefs that has become accepted as representing the fundamental truth. Sometimes ideologies become rather complex and connected with fundamental views about the nature of the world.

In the case of one group of US ex-colleagues with whom one of us had a mutually bruising encounter, the complex of beliefs seemed to be as follows:

1. Free market capitalism is the basis of the American way of life.
2. The American way of life is the best and most successful in the world.
3. America is blessed by God.

Therefore, by association, free market capitalism is God's favoured way.

Seen in this light, the US version of capitalism was believed to be absolutely right. Furthermore, any perceived attack on it was treated as an attack on the United States, and possibly God as well! Thus, arguing, quite reasonably it seemed, that capitalism was OK, but there were many forms, some of them quite different from the US model and from which Americans might learn, was greeted with a surprisingly hostile response!

There are many people who have accepted that the current arrangements in the financial markets are as good as it can get. There are many more who seem to believe, as did one of our stockbroker interviewees, that the markets are the repositories of most of the knowledge and wisdom that exists about business. To believers, to argue that the current system is simply a stage on a road to effective capitalism and needs serious and fundamental reform is tantamount to heresy.

Even worse, there are many powerful people who enjoy huge riches as a result of the current arrangements. Thus reformers are faced by a truly difficult task in tackling a set of arrangements that are rooted in a powerful ideology *and* that also benefit many rich and powerful people.

Undermining of critics of the 'system'

Any influential 'establishment', when faced with a threat to its power, has a large number of well-tried stratagems to hand that can be used to deflect, diffuse or diminish the actions of those who might threaten its privileges. In addition to the full range of propaganda tools, which, in the case of large companies and the financial markets, is backed by a whole industry of special interest, lobbying and PR firepower, there are a number of well-tried but more subtle means of undermining potential critics. Two of them are 'recruitment' and tactical concessions.

Recruitment

One of the most potent stratagems that has been used by privileged establishments for centuries is 'recruitment' of potentially powerful or threatening outsiders. The management–markets nexus has been noticeably active in using this approach.

In the United Kingdom and the United States, politicians from most parties have been comprehensively 'recruited' through the medium of political subscriptions. This has been conclusively proven for both Conservative and Labour administrations in the United Kingdom, and in the United States the Bush administration is believed to be significantly supported by large corporations, especially those in the energy industries.

But more subtly, the prospect of lucrative advisory and director positions, either during a political career or after it has finished, has been obviously attractive to many senior politicians. For example, John Major, since resigning as leader of the Conservative Party, is estimated to earn over £1 million a year from a range of advisory and director appointments and speaking engagements. Likewise, Lord Wakeham, a former UK Energy Minister, collected many directorships after – in some cases, shortly after – he had retired from politics, including a directorship of Enron. Those who adopt a highly critical approach are obviously less likely to get the call. Senior politicians of both main parties have fallen over themselves to make it clear that they are business-friendly, which probably explains the highly tentative approach taken to limiting the excesses of management and the markets.

'Recruitment' can be even more subtle than the granting or promise of current or future rewards. The granting of 'insider' status can be a remarkably powerful mechanism. Such status can be regarded as having bestowed upon the majority of non-executive directors of large companies and also on many (but not all) senior journalists. For non-executive directors, in addition to reward for remarkably little effort, there is the subtle distinction of belonging to a restricted and privileged network that grants status, information and contacts, and of course the prospect of future preferment. For journalists, the prospect of being an 'insider', privy to juicy titbits of gossip and a conduit for 'leaks' and briefing, can be very seductive, if not essential.

Feinting and tactical concessions

If it becomes clear that the forces advocating change are irresistible, there are still many stratagems left to establishments. Nearly all of them entail making limited concessions, playing up their significance, while working very hard behind the scenes to retain as much influence over future change as possible.

A favourite mechanism for achieving this is self-regulation, which is a usual response to the threat of legislation. In the United Kingdom it is usual to appoint a committee or commission of inquiry with a remit to report in months or years, stuffed with 'safe' members usually drawn from the very system that is being investigated. In the past, it has not been unknown for the findings of such bodies to be carefully edited or restricted in their circulation, further diminishing the possibility of serious change.

Thus a stream of ineffectual attempts to bring real change can often be presented as a 'process', with each non-change being represented as a 'step' towards a really significant final result. It is not too unkind to describe the plethora of investigations into corporate governance in the United Kingdom in this way.

The English dimension

England has experienced a revolution only once, and that was short-lived. Since the time of Cromwell's Commonwealth, the English upper classes have, until very recently, maintained a dominant position in the political, economic and social lives of the nation. That they have been able to do so is remarkable in a world that witnessed the overthrow of the old social order by revolution in almost every developed country. The means employed by the monarchy, the aristocracy and upper classes have generally been the processes of recruitment and tactical concessions.

Over several centuries, economically powerful people have been 'recruited' into the upper classes and have responded by adopting the manners and behaviour of the social establishment, to the extent that their grandchildren became fully absorbed members. In the same way, the aristocracy managed to keep itself fresh and not inbred by 'recruiting' wives from outside the established system.

Thus the established orders in England, and hence the United Kingdom, became remarkably skilled at controlling change and diffusing forces that might have been seriously damaging to their interests. Added to the strategic wiles of the establishment have been the traditions of informal networking and secrecy as a means of keeping undesirable intruders into the power game at bay.

Thus today's financial and managerial establishments are the inheritors of a long tradition that valued property and money more than people and has had deep experience of keeping real change at bay through a combination of recruitment and tactical withdrawal. Supporting them are civil service and political establishments that have traditionally been deeply suspicious of letting 'the people' have too much information or power. Even politicians who seemed to espouse real change in the power balance of the managerial and investment systems, such as those in the current government, became curiously secretive and tentative about change once in power. Thus the United Kingdom has been endowed with a system that is extremely resistant to consciously planned and executed strategic change.

But there is one last twist in the English dimension: the concept of gentlemanly behaviour. Bence-Jones and Montgomery-Massingberd, in their book *The British Aristocracy* (1979), variously define the status of gentleman as being central to the identity of the English upper class. These authors found that the definition of a gentleman is, like the British Constitution, marked out as much by precedent and behaviour as by formal rules. But central to the idea of 'gentleman' is loyalty to one's class, reliability and predictability. A gentleman is likely to be polite and discreet and not to boast about his gentlemanly status. Even to speak of oneself, or of someone else, as a gentleman seems to be rather ungentlemanly. What is absolutely clear is that gentlemen are unlikely to cherish thoughts of radical or revolutionary change, will be loyal to others of their kind and will be discreet in their public behaviour. A gentleman is highly unlikely to 'rat' on his own kind or to push for social or economic change that may disadvantage his fellows. In short, gentlemen are likely to be rather conservative and suspicious of change coming from outside the social and economic system to which they belong.

Thus we come to the last element of a total system that has been, and will remain, remarkably resistant to deliberate, planned change. If a perceived threat to the 'established' interest should appear, this is a likely sequence of defensive actions:

1. Ignore the potential threat; pretend that it doesn't exist.
2. Acknowledge the potential threat, but belittle it as being trivial.
3. Take it seriously: attempt by all means to counter the threatening party's case.
4. Attack the personal credibility or legitimacy of the threatening party.
5. Attempt to 'recruit' or seduce the threatening party.
6. Portray the disastrous consequences of change in the most lurid terms that it is possible to get away with. *Private Eye* magazine used to describe such parody defences as 'Huge Snakes Will Roam the Countryside'!
7. Stage a tactical withdrawal: give a little ground, try to maintain privileges, while making a big fuss about how much has been given up.
8. Threaten to leave the country, taking your money and/or invaluable expertise with you.
9. Actually leave the country: go to a place where you will be able to enjoy your privileges in peace.

References

Adams, S (1996) *The Dilbert Principle*, Harper Business, London
Augar, P (2001) *The Death of Gentlemanly Capitalism*, Penguin Books, London
Barker, R (1999) *Accounting and Business Research*, Judge Institute, Cambridge
Bébéar, C (2003) *Ils vont tuer le capitalisme*, Editions Plon, Paris
Bence-Jones, M and Montgomery-Massingberd, H (1979) *The British Aristocracy*, Constable, London
Burroughs, B and Helyar, J (1990) *Barbarians at the Gate: The fall of RJR Nabisco*, Harper, New York
Collins, J and Porras, J (1995) *Built to Last*, Random House, London
Council for Excellence in Management (2002) *Managers and Leaders: Raising Our Game*, chaired by Sir Anthony Cleaver, May
Department of Trade and Industry (DTI) (1998) *National Survey of Employment Relations* (Workplace Employment Relations Survey), The Stationery Office, London
DTI (2000, 2001) Surveys of relative capital expenditure and R&D investment levels, DTI F&I Unit, London
Donaldson, G and Lorsch, J (1983) *Decision Making at the Top*, Basic Books, New York
Frazer, A (1999) *Tax Misery Index*, Invest in Britain Bureau
Fuller, J (2001) Letter to a CEO, *Harvard Business Review*, October, pp 94–105
Golding, T (2001) *The City*, Financial Times / Prentice Hall, London
Hagstrom, R (2001) *The Essential Buffett*, John Wiley, New York
Handy, C (2002) What's a business for?, *Harvard Business Review*, December, pp 49–55
Harrington, V and Steele, M (1999) *The Life and Times of the CEO*, Cranfield University
Hobsbawm, E (1998) *On History*, Abacus Books, London
Institute of Public Policy Research (IPPR) (1990) *Takeovers and Short-termism in the UK*, IPPR, London
Janus, I (1982) *Groupthink*, Houghton Mifflin, Boston
Kennedy, A (2000) *The End of Shareholder Value*, Orion Business Books, London
Khurana, R (2002) The curse of the superstar CEO, *Harvard Business Review*, September, pp 60–66
Kotter, J (1982) *The General Managers*, The Free Press, New York
KPMG (1999) *Unlocking Shareholder Value: The keys to success in M&A*, KPMG, London

McKinsey Quarterly (2000) Mastering revenue growth in M&A, *McKinsey Quarterly*, Summer

Mintzberg, H (1994) *The Rise and Fall of Strategic Planning*, The Free Press, New York

Mintzberg, H (1999) Managing quietly, *Leader to Leader Institute Quarterly*, Spring

Monks Partnership (2001) *Board Pay and Incentive Practice*, Monks Partnership, Saffron Walden

Murphy, S (2002) *KPMG Perspectives*, March

Office for National Statistics (2002) Productivity of UK companies relative to foreign-owned companies, in *Economic Trends*, Stationery Office, London

Partnoy, F (1998) *F.I.A.S.C.O.: The Inside Story of a Wall Street Trader*, Profile Books, London

Partnoy, F (2003) *Infectious Greed: How deceit and risk corrupted the financial markets*, Times Books, London

Peacock & Bannock (1988) *Corporate Takeovers and the Public Interest*, David Hume Institute

Rankine, D (2001) *Why Acquisitions Fail: Practical advice for making acquisitions succeed*, Financial Times / Pearson Education, London

Selden, L and Colvin, G (2003) M&A needn't be a loser's game, *Harvard Business Review*, June, pp 70–79

Smith, T (1996) *Accounting for Growth*, Century Business Books, London

Soros, G (1998) *The Crisis of Global Capitalism*, Little, Brown

Thompson, E P (ed) (1970) *Warwick University Ltd*, Penguin Educational Specials, London

Turner, A (2001) *Just Capital: The liberal economy*, Macmillan, London

Wiersema, M (2002) Holes at the top: why CEO firings backfire, *Harvard Business Review*, December, pp 70–77

Index